Use these handy Zagat bookmarks to mark your favorites and the places you'd like to try. Plus, we've included re-useable blank bookmarks for you to write on (and wipe off). Browsing through your Zagat guide has never been easier!

Must Try
Must Try
Must Try
Must Try
Love it!
Love it!
Love it!
Like it!
Like it!
Top Pick
Top Pick

ZAGAT®

Europe's Top Restaurants 2008

Including 1,568 Restaurants in 27 Cities
From the Diner's Point of View

EDITOR
Catherine Bigwood

Published and distributed by
Zagat Survey, LLC
4 Columbus Circle
New York, NY 10019
T: 212.977.6000
E: eurotops@zagat.com
www.zagat.com

ACKNOWLEDGMENTS

We thank Pepa Aymami, Bibiana Behrendt, Jelena Bergdahl, Tom de Bruijn, Sholto Douglas-Home, Claudia Eilers, Maria Pilar Gallas, Barbara Goerlich, Agnes Goyvaerts, Katrin Gygax, Alfredo Hervías y Mendizábal, Beau Higgins, Florian Holzer, Aina Keller, Susan Kessler, Claire Klinkert, Lynn Levine, Alexander Lobrano, Cecilia Lundgren, Lucy Mallows, Toni Massanés, Bernd Matthies, Mimi Murphy, Vânia Nogueira, David Noguera, Ariane van Notten, Anna Olsson, Stepan Ondrusek, Svend Rasmussen, Joanna Sanecka, George Semler, Oxana Soleil-Degtiar, Eugenia Stavropoulou, Karol Stein, Jan Ghane Tabrizi, Gail Mangold Vine and Enzo Vizzari, as well as the following members of our staff: Rachel McConlogue and Kelly Stewart (assistant editors), Sean Beachell, Maryanne Bertollo, Sandy Cheng, Reni Chin, Larry Cohn, Deirdre Donovan, Caitlin Eichelberger, Alison Flick, Jeff Freier, Shelley Gallagher, Caroline Hatchett, Roy Jacob, Natalie Lebert, Mike Liao, Christina Livadiotis, Dave Makulec, Chris Miragliotta, Andre Pilette, Becky Ruthenburg, Troy Segal, Carla Spartos, Kilolo Strobert, Liz Borod Wright, Sharon Yates and Kyle Zolner.

The reviews published in this guide are based on public opinion surveys, with numerical ratings reflecting the average scores given by all survey participants who voted on each establishment and text based on direct quotes from, or fair paraphrasings of, participants' comments. Phone numbers, addresses and other factual information were correct to the best of our knowledge when published in this guide; any subsequent changes may not be reflected.

ISBN-13: 978-1-57006-902-4
ISBN-10: 1-57006-902-6
Printed in the
United States of America

Contents

About This Survey

This **2008 Europe's Top Restaurants Survey** is an update reflecting significant developments as reported by our editors since our last Survey was published. It covers 1,568 of the continent's best restaurants, including 180 important additions. We've also indicated new addresses, phone numbers, chef changes and other major alterations.

WHO PARTICIPATED: Input from 14,828 avid diners forms the basis for the ratings and reviews in this guide (their comments are shown in quotation marks within the reviews). Collectively they bring roughly 2.9 million annual meals worth of experience to this Survey. We sincerely thank each of these participants - this book is really "theirs."

HELPFUL LISTS: To help guide you to Europe's top meals, we have prepared a number of lists. See Top Food (pages 7-8) and Most Popular (pages 9-10). We've also provided handy indexes and, with the aim of saving you time, have tried to be concise.

OUR TEAM: We especially thank our editor, Catherine Bigwood, a former editor at *Food & Wine, Women's Wear Daily, W* and *Harper's Bazaar.* This is the seventh edition of this guide that she has produced. Thanks also to all our participating authorities abroad.

ABOUT ZAGAT: This marks our 29th year reporting on the shared experiences of consumers like you. What started in 1979 as a hobby involving 200 of our friends has come a long way. Today we have over 300,000 surveyors and now cover dining, entertaining, golf, hotels, movies, music, nightlife, resorts, shopping, spas, theater and tourist attractions worldwide.

SHARE YOUR OPINION: We invite you to join any of our upcoming surveys - just register at **zagat.com,** where you can rate and review establishments year-round. Each participant will receive a free copy of the resulting guide when published.

AVAILABILITY: Zagat guides are available in all major bookstores, by subscription at **zagat.com** and for use on a wide range of Web-enabled mobile devices via **Zagat To Go** or **zagat.mobi.** Either of the latter two products will allow you to contact any restaurant by phone with one click.

FEEDBACK: There is always room for improvement, thus we invite your comments and suggestions about any aspect of our performance. Is there something more you would like us to include in our guides? We really need your input! Just contact us at **eurotops@zagat.com.**

New York, NY
November 9, 2007

Nina and Tim

Nina and Tim Zagat

What's New

Our *2008 Europe's Top Restaurants* Survey celebrates the dual delights of dining and travel. Despite general economic challenges, more strenuous flight restrictions for airline passengers and the fact that 61% of surveyors say they are paying more per meal this year than last, a whopping 91% of them report that they're eating out the same amount as or more than they did last year.

PASSPORT TO PRIME DINING: We geared this guide to the upscale traveler, soliciting restaurant recommendations from professional food critics in 27 major European cities. To ensure a global perspective, we then asked both savvy locals and experienced trekkers to rate and review these establishments. Since busy diners demand convenience, we restricted our coverage to venues no more than an approximate 20-minute cab ride from a city's center. Restaurants receiving too few votes are listed with contact information as "Other Noteworthy Places."

CALLING ALL CUISINES: Receiving 34% of the vote, Italian reigns as our surveyors' favorite cuisine, followed by French and Mediterranean fare, with 24% and 15%, respectively. But, ever-increasingly, dozens of other ethnic cooking styles are being showcased in high-end restaurants. In fact, there are 101 different cuisines featured in this guide.

BUT MAKE THEM GREEN: Whatever the accent on the cuisine, our surveyors would like to see healthier cooking coming out of those global kitchens - in fact, 65% want trans fats abolished from restaurants. They are even willing to up the ante if there is environmentally conscious consideration of ingredients, as evidenced by 59% of reviewers responding that they are willing to pay more for sustainably raised or procured produce.

TIP TALK: Forty percent of our surveyors rated Italy as the country with the continent's friendliest service, with that of Spain and Ireland earning second and third places, respectively. But no matter how warm a staff may be, when it comes to rewarding them, most of our surveyors prefer the independent American approach to tipping rather than the continental custom of having it automatically included in the bill.

BUTT OUT: Seventy-three percent of surveyors say smoking should be extinguished in restaurants, and European governments are helping clear the air by imposing smoking bans, which began in Ireland and have swept across France, Italy, the Netherlands, Spain, Sweden and, most recently, the U.K.

WE'RE LISTENING: Your opinions are what make our guides the best in the business, so we hope you'll continue to keep us posted on all your fine- and not-so-fine-dining experiences.

New York, NY
November 9, 2007

Catherine Bigwood

Ratings & Symbols

	Name	Symbols	Cuisine	FOOD	DECOR	SERVICE	COST
Area, Address & Contact*	Tim & Nina's	◐	*British*	▽ 23	5	9	I

Area, Address & Contact*: **Covent Garden** | Exeter St., WC2 (Covent Garden) | (44-20) 7123 4567 | www.zagat.com

Review, surveyor comments in quotes: Open seven days a week, 24 hours a day (some say that's "168 hours too many"), this "chaotic" Covent Garden dive serving "cheap, no-nonsense" fish 'n' chips is "ideal" for a "quick grease fix"; no one's impressed by the "tired, tatty decor" or "patchy service", but judging from its "perpetual queues", the "no-frills" food and prices are "spot-on."

Ratings **Food, Decor** and **Service** are rated on the Zagat scale of 0 to 30.

0 - 9 poor to fair

10 - 15 fair to good

16 - 19 good to very good

20 - 25 very good to excellent

26 - 30 extraordinary to perfection

▽ low response | less reliable

Cost is estimated by the following symbols:

I Inexpensive

M Moderate

E Expensive

VE Very Expensive

A restaurant review listed without ratings is either a **newcomer** or survey **write-in.**

Symbols

◐ serves after 11:30 PM

Ⓢ closed on Sunday

Ⓜ closed on Monday

(no-card symbol) no credit cards accepted

* From outside Europe, dial the international code (e.g. 011 from the U.S.), then the listed number.

Top Food

Ratings are to the left of names. Lists exclude places with low votes.

AMSTERDAM

28 Ron Blaauw
27 Yamazato
Van Vlaanderen
La Rive
26 Bordewijk

ATHENS

29 Spondi
26 48
Varoulko
24 Sale e Pepe
Pil Poul et Jérôme Serres

BARCELONA

28 Passadis del Pep
Drolma
Àbac
27 Gaig
Alkimia

BERLIN

26 VAU
24 Lorenz Adlon
Maxwell
23 Alt Luxemburg
Die Quadriga*

BRUSSELS

28 Comme Chez Soi
Bruneau
27 La Truffe Noire
Sea Grill
26 La Maison du Cygne

BUDAPEST

28 Baraka
Vadrózsa
27 Páva
25 Lou-Lou
Kacsa

COPENHAGEN

27 Era Ora
Restaurationen
26 Søllerød Kro
Kong Hans Kælder
25 Krogs Fiskerestaurant

DUBLIN

27 Thornton's
Patrick Guilbaud
26 Seasons
25 L'Ecrivain
One Pico

FLORENCE

27 Enoteca Pinchiorri
La Giostra
26 Alle Murate
Fuor d'Acqua
Cibrèo

FRANKFURT

25 Gargantua
Osteria Enoteca
24 Rest. Français
23 Aubergine
Sushimoto

GENEVA

29 Dom./Châteauvieux
26 Auberge du Lion d'Or
25 Patara
24 La Vendée
Chez Jacky

HAMBURG

25 Haerlin
23 Jacobs
Landhaus Scherrer
Le Canard Nouveau
Doc Cheng's

ISTANBUL

26 Borsa
25 Körfez
Develi
Seasons
Tugra

LISBON

27 Varanda
Rist. Hotel Cipriani
Sua Excelência
24 Gambrinus
Casa da Comida

LONDON

28 Chez Bruce
G. Ramsay/68 Royal
Hunan
Square, The
Pétrus

* Indicates a tie with restaurant above

27 La Trompette

Pied à Terre

La Trompette

Le Gavroche

River Café

Nobu London

MADRID

28 Santceloni

27 Zalacaín

Goizeko

26 Príncipe de Viana

Combarro

MILAN

29 Il Luogo/Aimo e Nadia

28 Sadler

27 Rist. Cracco

25 Da Giacomo

Boeucc

MOSCOW

25 Mario

24 Palazzo Ducale

23 Café Pushkin

Cantinetta Antinori

22 Vogue Café

MUNICH

27 Tantris

25 Vue Maximilian

Schuhbeck's

Boettner's

24 Königshof

PARIS

28 Taillevent

Pierre Gagnaire

Alain Ducasse

Le Cinq

Guy Savoy

27 Le Grand Véfour

Hiramatsu

L'Ambroisie

Le Bristol

L'Astrance

PRAGUE

26 Allegro

25 Aquarius

David

V Zátiší

Essensia

ROME

26 Vivendo

La Pergola

Alberto Ciarla

La Rosetta*

Agata e Romeo

Mirabelle

Sora Lella*

25 Al Vero Girarrosto Toscano

Quinzi e Gabrieli

Antico Arco

L'Altro Mastai*

STOCKHOLM

28 Paul & Norbert

Wedholms Fisk

27 F12

26 Lux Stockholm

Ulriksdals Wärdshus

VENICE

27 Vini da Gigio

26 Da Ivo

Osteria Da Fiore

Corte Sconta

25 Fortuny

VIENNA

28 Steirereck

26 Imperial

25 Coburg

24 Demel

Walter Bauer

WARSAW

25 Rest. Polska Tradycja

Dom Polski

23 U Kucharzy

Parmizzano's

22 Malinowa

ZURICH

27 Petermann's

26 Rest. Français

Lindenhofkeller

24 Ginger

Casa Aurelio

Most Popular

AMSTERDAM

1. D'Vijff Vlieghen
2. Dylan, The
3. La Rive
4. Christophe'
5. De Kas

ATHENS

1. Spondi
2. Daphne's
3. GB Corner*
4. 48
5. Milos Athens*

BARCELONA

1. 7 Portes
2. Botafumeiro
3. Barceloneta
4. La Dama
5. Ca l'Isidre
6. Los Caracoles*

BERLIN

1. VAU
2. Borchardt
3. Lorenz Adlon
4. Margaux
5. Bacco/Bocca

BRUSSELS

1. Comme Chez Soi
2. Aux Armes/Bruxelles
3. Belga Queen
4. La Maison du Cygne
5. L'Ecailler/Palais Royal
6. L'Ogenblik*
7. Sea Grill*

BUDAPEST

1. Gundel
2. Páva
3. Kacsa
4. Café Kör
5. Centrál Kávéház
6. Spoon Café*

COPENHAGEN

1. Krogs Fiskerestaurant
2. Café Ketchup
3. Era Ora
4. Le Sommelier
5. Café Victor

DUBLIN

1. Patrick Guilbaud
2. Shanahan's
3. Seasons
4. Tea Room
5. Eden

FLORENCE

1. Enoteca Pinchiorri
2. Cibrèo
3. Il Latini
4. Villa San Michele
5. Cantinetta Antinori

FRANKFURT

1. Apfelwein Wagner
2. Holbein's
3. Edelweiss
4. Gargantua*
5. Aubergine
6. Opéra

GENEVA

1. Auberge du Lion d'Or
2. Le Relais/l'Entrecôte*
3. Brass. Lipp
4. Dom./Châteauvieux
5. Les Armures

HAMBURG

1. Jacobs
2. Doc Cheng's
3. Haerlin
4. Rive
5. Cox
6. Landhaus Scherrer
7. Windows*

ISTANBUL

1. Seasons
2. Tugra
3. Laledan
4. Körfez
5. Ulus 29
6. Develi

LISBON

1. Gambrinus
2. Bica do Sapato
3. Alcântara Café
4. Varanda
5. A Travessa

LONDON

1. Nobu London
2. G. Ramsay/68 Royal
3. J. Sheekey
4. G. Ramsay/Claridge's
5. Le Gavroche

6. Zuma
7. Square, The
8. Zafferano
9. Pétrus
10. Amaya
11. Yauatcha
12. Tamarind

MADRID

1. Botín
2. Zalacaín
3. Viridiana
4. Balzac
5. La Trainera*

MILAN

1. Bice
2. Rist. Cracco
3. Armani/Nobu
4. Tratt. Bagutta
5. Il Teatro

MOSCOW

1. Café Pushkin
2. Galereya
3. Shinok
4. Scandinavia
5. Cantinetta Antinori

MUNICH

1. Tantris
2. Dallmayr
3. Königshof
4. Käfer-Schänke
5. Chinesischen Turm

PARIS

1. Taillevent
2. L'Atelier/J. Robuchon
3. La Tour d'Argent
4. Guy Savoy
5. Le Cinq
6. Le Grand Véfour
7. Alain Ducasse
8. Pierre Gagnaire
9. L'Arpège
10. L'Ami Louis
11. Lasserre
12. Les Ambassadeurs

PRAGUE

1. Kampa Park
2. Allegro
3. Bellevue
4. Pravda
5. U Modré Kachnicky

ROME

1. La Pergola
2. Imàgo
3. Harry's Bar
4. La Terrazza
5. Dal Bolognese
6. La Rosetta
7. Agata e Romeo
8. Piperno
9. Nino
10. Al Moro
11. 'Gusto
12. Vecchia Roma*

STOCKHOLM

1. Operakällaren
2. F12
3. Wedholms Fisk
4. Berns Asian
5. Sturehof*

VENICE

1. Harry's Bar
2. Fortuny
3. Osteria Da Fiore
4. La Terrazza
5. Al Covo

VIENNA

1. Demel
2. Steirereck
3. Imperial
4. Korso bei der Oper
5. Drei Husaren

WARSAW

1. Rest. Polska Tradycja
2. Belvedere
3. Blue Cactus
4. Dom Polski*
5. Malinowa
6. Oriental, The*

ZURICH

1. Kronenhalle
2. Petermann's
3. Widder
4. Brasserie Lipp
5. Rest. Français

RESTAURANT DIRECTORY

FOOD | DECOR | SERVICE | COST

Amsterdam

TOP FOOD RANKING

	Restaurant	Cuisine
28	Ron Blaauw	French/International
27	Yamazato	Japanese
	Van Vlaanderen	French/Mediterranean
	La Rive	French/Mediterranean
26	Bordewijk	French/Mediterranean
	Christophe'	French
	Blauw aan de Wal	French/Mediterranean
	Visaandeschelde	International/Seafood
25	Excelsior	French/Mediterranean
24	Chez Georges	French
	Vermeer	French/International
	De Silveren Spiegel	Dutch
	Dylan, The	French/North African
	Beddington's	French/Asian
23	Tempo Doeloe	Indonesian
	De Kas	Dutch/Mediterranean
	Blue Pepper	Indonesian
	Sichuan Food	Chinese
22	Tomo Sushi	Japanese/Sushi
	Ciel Bleu	New French
	Gala	Catalan
	French Café	French
21	Marius	French/Mediterranean
	Zina	African/Mediterranean
	Dynasty	Pan-Asian
	Envy	International/Med.
	D'Vijff Vlieghen	Dutch
	Pulitzers	International
	Pont 13	French
	Janvier	French
20	Le Garage	French/International
	Brasserie van Baerle	French Brasserie
19	Bice	Italian
	Silex	French
	FLO Amsterdam	French
18	Herengracht	International

Beddington's S M *French/Asian* 24 | 18 | 18 | E

Frederiksplein | Utrechtsedwarsstraat 141 | (31-20) 620-7393 | fax 620-0190 | www.beddington.nl

"Long live Jean!" exclaim fans of this "nice place" in the Frederiksplein area that's "run by female chef" Jean Beddington, who is always cooking up a "hot menu" of "excellent", "inventive" French-Asian fare; still, some find the "small", "sober" space with "only a few tables" somewhat "cold" and suggest the "informal (but correct) service" "could use some work", saying the "restaurant just misses being really superior."

	FOOD	DECOR	SERVICE	COST

Bice [S] *Italian* 19 | 18 | 19 | E

Leidseplein | NH Amsterdam Centre Hotel | Stadhouderskade 7-9 | (31-20) 589-8870 | fax 412-2931 | www.bice.nl

Those who've come to "expect quality" from its "worldwide" family of restaurants predict you won't be disappointed by this "very good" outpost in a "great location" within the NH Amsterdam Centre Hotel in the Leidseplein area thanks to "reliable Italian fare" that's some of "the best in the city" and "well worth the cost"; "waiters with personality" who contribute to the "overall atmosphere" are other reasons most aver they "would go again" - even if a few find the experience "inconsistent."

Blauw aan de Wal [S] [M] *French/Mediterranean* 26 | 22 | 23 | E

Centrum | Oudezijds Achterburgwal 99 | (31-20) 330-2257 | fax 330-2006

"Hidden away" at the end of "a small alley" in the Centrum, this "smallish", "serene spot" with its own "private dining terrace" offers a "great respite from the Red Light District" "just around the corner"; its "cozy, peaceful setting" is home to "sweet", "enthusiastic" staffers who "are happy to explain in great detail" their "terrific" French-Med "fare made from the best ingredients" and accompanied by a "well-selected", "solid wine list"; no wonder so many consider it an "absolutely wonderful", "special place."

Blue Pepper *Indonesian* 23 | 20 | 22 | M

Centrum | Nassaukade 366 | (31-20) 489-7039 | www.restaurantbluepepper.com

If you "want something other than" "the standard rijsttafel", "go straight to this top-notch" Centrum "treat" where a "creative" "nouveau Indonesian" kitchen delivers "dazzling", "delicious dishes" that are "full of flavor" and definitely "out of the ordinary"; the "friendly, accommodating staff" provides equally "sizzling service" and will happily "inform you about the details of the menu", but insiders insist that "the tasting menu is a must."

Bordewijk [M] *French/Mediterranean* 26 | 18 | 23 | E

Jordaan | Noordermarkt 7 | (31-20) 624-3899 | www.bordewijk.nl

The "chef visits" "your table" and "takes your order" at this "terrific place" "in a charming Jordaan location", a "favorite" of many for its "incredible" French-Med "haute cuisine", "comprehensive wine list" and "fantastic" service; still, some sigh it's "too bad" the "noisy room" "doesn't do justice to the rest of the experience", adding that "the restaurant is less inviting" to tourists since the staff is not as welcoming "if you are not a native."

Brasserie van Baerle *French* 20 | 19 | 18 | M

Oud-Zuid | Van Baerlestraat 158 | (31-20) 679-1532 | fax 671-7196 | www.brasserievanbaerle.nl

A "delicious variety" of "very traditional, very rich French" brasserie fare served by an "efficient" staff has earned this "friendly" venue "a long-standing reputation"; located in the "classy old neighborhood" of Oud-Zuid, it's "especially great for lunch when visiting" "the museums and concert hall nearby", and if the space strikes you as too "stark", avail yourself of its "lovely garden", which offers "wonderful outdoor dining" "in the summer."

	FOOD	DECOR	SERVICE	COST
Chez Georges *French*	24	21	23	E

Jordaan | Herenstraat 3 | (31-20) 626-3332 | fax 638-7838

"It's always full" at this tiny Jordaan French in the nicest part of Amsterdam, because the "beautifully classic" cuisine is "superb", particularly the "fine" five-course tasting menu, which is a "great value"; a "staff that takes such pride in what it serves" and a "charming", "cozy" and "civilized" interior are other pluses.

	FOOD	DECOR	SERVICE	COST
Christophe' *French*	26	22	24	VE

Jordaan | Leliegracht 46 | (31-20) 625-0807 | fax 638-9132 | www.restaurantchristophe.nl

"Brilliantly inventive" and "beautifully presented" "dishes that combine upscale French cuisine" with "Mediterranean ingredients" and "African influences" "delight the eye and palate" at this "perfectly located" "canal-side" Jordaan "jewel" manned by an "eager-to-please staff"; those who think the "atmosphere is rather dull" quip that the "lovely" interior is "as quiet and peaceful as the floral arrangements, and about as lively", but most report "a special night out"; N.B. post-Survey, Jean-Christophe Royer turned over the chef-ownership reins to his long-standing protégé, Jean-Joël Bonsens.

	FOOD	DECOR	SERVICE	COST
Ciel Bleu *French*	22	21	21	E

Pijp | Hotel Okura | Ferdinand Bolstraat 333, 23rd fl. | (31-20) 678-7450 | fax 678-7788 | www.okura.nl

"Go on a clear night" to this "peaceful" establishment on the 23rd floor of the Hotel Okura in the Pijp to enjoy "marvelous views" (perhaps the "best in the city") along with "exquisite", "original and delicate" New French dishes that are delivered by a "helpful staff"; all agree that the "food is up to the level of the location", though some feel "the boring decor needs an upgrade" – still, it's "definitely a place for a repeat visit."

	FOOD	DECOR	SERVICE	COST
De Kas *Dutch/Mediterranean*	23	26	21	E

Oost | Frankendael Park | Kamerlingh Onneslaan 3 | (31-20) 462-4562 | fax 462-4563 | www.restaurantdekas.nl

Set in an "impressively large" and "beautiful greenhouse" "situated in the Park" Frankendael in Oost, "this sparkling glass temple to food" takes its "sensitivity and passion for local", mostly "organic ingredients" "to a whole new level", creating "a daily prix fixe menu" of "stellar" Dutch-Mediterranean fare "based upon the day's harvest"; whether seated in "the stunning dining room" or on the "lovely terrace", expect an "absolutely enchanting" experience as you "inhale the heady fragrances" of "fresh vegetables and herbs" growing all around you.

	FOOD	DECOR	SERVICE	COST
De Silveren Spiegel *Dutch*	24	22	22	VE

Centrum | Kattengat 4-6 | (31-20) 624-6589 | fax 620-3867 | www.desilverenspiegel.com

This "beautiful little historic" Centrum treat "tucked away" "near Centraal Station" may be so "old" (circa 1614) that it "looks as though it's falling over", but its kitchen actually "impresses" with an "interesting" array of "well-executed dishes" that are some "of the best" examples of "nouvelle Dutch" cuisine; the "quaint" setting with "lead-glass windows and candles" is an "old-world delight" whose "warm", "intimate atmosphere" is abetted by "gracious service" from a "staff with exceptional knowledge of" the "great wine list."

D'Vijff Vlieghen *Dutch* 21 | 23 | 20 | E

Centrum | Spuistraat 294-302 | (31-20) 530-4060 | fax 623-6404 | www.thefiveflies.com

"Small rooms connected by narrow winding corridors" spanning "five charming old houses" in the Centrum are the "marvelous setting" of this "Amsterdam institution" that's "still going strong", serving up a "great variety" of "flavorful" Dutch dishes that are more "contemporary" than you'd expect; still, some say it's "living on its reputation" and complain that it's "chronically overfilled" with "tons of tourists" and "complacent", "slow" servers - so "be prepared" for a "long (though memorable) evening"; P.S. "the name means 'The Five Flies.'"

Dylan, The ☒ *French/African* 24 | 26 | 23 | VE

Jordaan | Dylan Hotel | Keizersgracht 384 | (31-20) 530-2010 | fax 530-2030 | www.dylanamsterdam.com

Though the "name has changed", this "don't-miss place" "within the hip, tasteful" Dylan Hotel in the Jordaan remains "trendy", in part because its "sleek, cool interior" continues to "wow" the city's "handsome people", but also because the kitchen creates "beautifully presented" French-Northern African cuisine; in fact, it's so "tremendous across the board" most overlook that the "stuck-up staffers" still "take themselves too seriously.

Dynasty *Pan-Asian* 21 | 17 | 19 | E

Centrum | Reguliersdwarsstraat 30 | (31-20) 626-8400 | fax 622-3038

Supporters of this "consistent" Centrum spot have "no complaints" about its "large menu" of "excellent" Pan-Asian fare including "Chinese, Vietnamese and Thai cooking", its "friendly service" or its "pleasant surroundings" (with a "lovely" terrace); foes, though, find "nothing exciting about the food" or "tired, worn-out decor"; N.B. closed Tuesdays.

Envy *International/Mediterranean* 21 | 23 | 18 | E

Centrum | Prinsengracht 381 | (31-20) 344-6407 | www.envy.nl

Whether you'll envy the experience at this "hip and trendy" International-Med in Centrum is a matter of debate: foodies sniff you'll get the kind of "customary fare that goes along with a lounge scene and loud music" (in other words "a lot of whoosh that doesn't quite wash"), but scensters swear there's "creative, fresh" tapas-style cuisine to be enjoyed in an "amazing" setting with moody spot lighting and "great people-watching."

Excelsior *French/Mediterranean* 25 | 24 | 25 | VE

Centrum | Hotel de L'Europe | Nieuwe Doelenstraat 2-8 | (31-20) 531-1705 | fax 531-1778 | www.leurope.nl

"Fine dining in Amsterdam" is found at this "luxurious" venue "within the Hotel de L'Europe", a "beautiful" Centrum establishment "with old European charm", where chef Jean-Jacques Menanteau creates "delicious" "traditional French-Med dishes" that are "worth the splurge"; fans feel the "excellent service" and "elegant" interior "recall the graciousness of times past", but even "bored" sorts who say the "stuffy decor" "could use an upgrade" are "simply delighted" by the "lovely" terrace with its "romantic view" of the Amstel River.

	FOOD	DECOR	SERVICE	COST

NEW FLO Amsterdam ◐ *French*

FOOD	DECOR	SERVICE	COST
19	19	18	E

Leidseplein | Groupe FLO | Amstelstraat 9 | (31-20) 890-4757 | fax 890-4750 | www.floamsterdam.com

For an "Amster-dam good time", hedonists head to this new offshoot of the classic Parisian brasserie chain for "the freshest platters of piled-high chilled seafood" and a traditional red-velvet banquette and brass rail setting; the "drinks may flow more easily than the service", but the "convenient location" near the famous Rembrandtplein draws an upscale business crowd.

French Café, The [$] [M] *French*

FOOD	DECOR	SERVICE	COST
22	19	20	E

Pijp | Gerard Doustraat 98 | (31-20) 470-0301 | fax 670-5702 | www.thefrenchcafe.nl

The straightforward name sums up this French cafe in Pijp, where patrons are "pleased" with "delicious" classic dishes served in a "chilled-out atmosphere"; the intimate interior includes an open kitchen and in summer a handful of tables spill outside.

NEW Gala [M] *Catalan*

FOOD	DECOR	SERVICE	COST
22	20	20	E

Leidseplein | Reguliersdwarsstraat 38 | (31-20) 623-6303 | www.restaurantgala.com

This "hip" and "trendy" new "place to be seen" in the Leidseplein area offers a narrow, sexy and stylish setting with a moodily lit bar that makes for a "romantic evening"; influenced by contemporary Catalan cooking, the kitchen turns out "excellent Spanish tapas" that are indeed a gala "celebration of good eating."

Herengracht *International*

FOOD	DECOR	SERVICE	COST
18	20	17	M

Leidseplein | Herengracht 435 | (31-20) 616-2482 | fax 775-0299 | www.deherengracht.nl

"With lots of space to lounge", this "hip place" in the Leidseplein area is an "informal neighborhood spot" "catering to a somewhat arty" clientele that clamors for its "swell" International food, including "reasonably priced appetizers and entrees"; still, some say "the service is not that great" and claim that the crowds of patrons sometimes cause the room to get "stuffy" and "noisy."

Janvier [M] *French*

FOOD	DECOR	SERVICE	COST
21	19	18	E

Leidseplein | Amstelveld 12 | (31-20) 626-1199 | fax 626-6059

"For local color", head for the terrace of this lovely old former church "in a great location" on Amstelveld square overlooking a canal and order a glass of wine and just "relax"; for those more interested in eats than aesthetics, the spot bills itself as a *proeflokaal*, a place where you can please your taste buds, so there's "well-prepared" French fare served by a "welcoming" staff.

La Rive *French/Mediterranean*

FOOD	DECOR	SERVICE	COST
27	26	26	VE

Oost | InterContinental Amstel | Professor Tulpplein 1 | (31-20) 520-3264 | fax 520-3266 | www.restaurantlarive.nl

"You know you've a-Rived when you" visit "this breathtaking waterfront restaurant" "right on the river" "in the city's premier hotel", the "elegant" InterContinental Amstel in Oost, where the "fabulous views" are actually trumped by the "phenomenal", "magical" French-Med creations of "master chef Edwin Kats"; furthermore, "you'd be hard-pressed to find a grander dining room" or more "wonderful" staff to "wait on you hand and foot", so it's no surprise "sated" surveyors swear the experience produces "ecstasy"; P.S. "in summer, dine waterside" on the "beautiful terrace."

Le Garage *French/International* 20 | 21 | 20 | E

Oud-Zuid | Ruysdaelstraat 54-56 | (31-20) 679-7176 | fax 662-2249 | www.restaurantlegarage.nl

"Bring sunglasses to shield yourself from the high-gloss crowd" at this "buzzy, convivial", "cool place" "in the Museum Quarter" in Oud-Zuid, an "evergreen" favorite that's "always" "packed" with Amsterdam "VIPs" trying to get "a glimpse of" its "famous owner", "Dutch TV celebrity Joop Braakhekke", while downing "innovative" French-International fare served by an "excellent staff"; the "Paris Hilton-beautiful-people atmosphere" is "too much of a scene" for some, but "rockin'" sorts insist it's "the best show in town."

Marius [S] [M] *French/Mediterranean* 21 | 19 | 20 | E

Westerpark | Barentszstraat 243 | (31-20) 422-7880

Supporters say "thumbs-up" about this "cozy" spot in Westerpark, whose Chez Panisse-trained chef produces market-driven menus and "delightful" French-Med cooking; an open kitchen and crockery displays make for a relaxed, homey feel.

NEW **Pont 13** *French* 21 | 21 | 21 | E

Westerpark | Stavangerweg 891 | (31-20) 770-2722 | www.pont13.nl

Set inside a sprawling former 1927 ferry with industrial decor and an outdoor deck is this newcomer with a view of the IJ River, near Strand West, which is a "bit far from the inner city"; still, its "hip" vibe and "surprisingly good" hearty French dishes, many of them grilled, make it a "very neat place to try."

Pulitzers *International* 21 | 22 | 22 | E

Jordaan | Hotel Pulitzer | Keizersgracht 234 | (31-20) 523-5282 | fax 627-6753 | www.pulitzers.nl

Art aficionados aver that this "beautiful restaurant" in the "fantastic" Hotel Pulitzer, "made up of [25] historic canal houses" in the Jordaan, is "worth [a visit] just to view" its "unique" collection of "great paintings", a highlight of the "lovely decor"; surveyors are split, though, on its other "qualities" - while fans report being "pleasantly surprised" by its "delicious, fresh" International cuisine and "accommodating service", foes feel the "barely memorable" dining experience "should be better given" the "special" setting.

Ron Blaauw [S] [M] *French/International* 28 | 21 | 24 | VE

Ouderkerk aan de Amstel | Kerkstraat 56 | (31-20) 496-1943 | fax 497-5701 | www.ronblaauw.nl

Expect "a real feast" at this "wonderful" winner, rated No. 1 for Food in Amsterdam, that "can be counted on" for "consistently high-quality" French-International cuisine offered in "surprising" multi-course menus of "gorgeous, creative tapaslike dishes that go on and on"; servers who ensure "you're really pampered" and "great" decor also make it "worth" "the journey" to an "out-of-the-way" location in Ouderkerk aan de Amstel; P.S. "on a hot summer evening, head for a seat on the terrace."

Sichuan Food *Chinese* 23 | 16 | 18 | M

Centrum | Reguliersdwarsstraat 35 | (31-20) 626-9327 | fax 627-7281

"Extraordinary Peking duck" and "great oysters from the wok" are the stars of the show at this "classic" Chinese in the Centrum that fans call a "wonderful place" for its "high-quality" cuisine, including "some dishes that are actually authentic"; still, heat-seekers say there's "not much spice" in the Westernized fare, while others insist that "service can be slow when it's busy" and the "outdated decor" is "slightly gaudy."

Silex Ⓢ Ⓜ *French* 19 | 19 | 18 | E

Pijp | Daniël Stalpertstraat 93 | (31-20) 620-5959 | fax 620-8901 | www.restaurantsilex.nl

An "elegant" space with dark brown walls and leather seating is the "stylish" backdrop for French food, including a "great early-evening fixed-price menu"; just note that since "service can be slow you should savor every morsel"; a post-Survey move from the Centrum to this address in Pijp may outdate the above Decor score.

Tempo Doeloe *Indonesian* 23 | 15 | 19 | M

Rembrandtplein | Utrechtsestraat 75 | (31-20) 625-6718 | fax 639-2342 | www.tempodoeloerestaurant.nl

"Fantastic fare" "keeps patrons coming back" to this "classic Indonesian rijsttafel restaurant", a "moderately priced" and "always crowded" "Amsterdam favorite" "on a beautiful block" in the Rembrandtplein area, where the "attentive owner" and his "friendly", "patient servers will explain the entire menu" ("let them guide you"); some "critics claim the decor", "stuffy atmosphere" and "tight quarters" "take away from the experience", "but real foodies would travel far for cooking this authentic"; P.S. "ring the bell and the door opens."

Tomo Sushi *Japanese* 22 | 16 | 20 | M

Centrum | Reguliersdwarsstraat 131 | (31-20) 528-5208 | fax 528-5207

"Don't tell too many people" plead patrons panicked that this "small" Japanese place "hidden away" "near the Rembrandtplein" "will become overcrowded" with customers clamoring for its "excellent sushi" "cut well and served imaginatively" ("awesome" yakitori too); other pluses include "good", "friendly service", "hip decor" with a "clean", "modern design" and relatively "low prices" that make it "a good value."

Van Vlaanderen Ⓢ Ⓜ *French/Mediterranean* 27 | 20 | 24 | E

Leidseplein | Weteringschans 175 | (31-20) 622-8292

"An antidote to overly trendy places" is this "lovely, low-key" spot in the Leidseplein area featuring "fantastic" French-Mediterranean fare that "always pleasantly surprises"; perhaps the "informal", "quite-small" interior "with not much space between the tables" doesn't fully do justice to "the caliber of cuisine", but it's nevertheless "a quiet" refuge from "the heart of the action", and the "nice", "capable waiters do their utmost to make your dinner a success."

Vermeer Ⓢ *French/International* 24 | 23 | 24 | VE

Centrum | NH Barbizon Palace Hotel | Prins Hendrikkade 59-72 | (31-20) 556-4885 | fax 624-3353 | www.restaurantvermeer.nl

"Outstanding cuisine" is a hallmark of this "top-class" "favorite" in the Centrum's NH Barbizon Palace Hotel, where the French-International "food is amazing" and the "wine list elaborate"; some find "the majorly elegant dining room" "pretty", others "a bit stiff", but all agree the "friendly yet professional staff" provides "impeccable service", leading most to insist that you "couldn't have a more enjoyable evening."

Visaandeschelde *International/Seafood* 26 | 20 | 21 | E

Rivierenbuurt | Scheldeplein 4 | (31-20) 675-1583 | www.visaandeschelde.nl

"Visitors to Holland" in search of "wonderful" International cuisine "with a focus on seafood" should follow the hordes of locals who crowd this "very hip place" that's "a little out of the way" in the Rivierenbuurt; after all, "you come here for really great fish" dishes, which incorporate Japanese, French and Mediterranean influences, and are "nicely served" at "well-situated tables" by a "stellar" staff; P.S. "don't forget the excellent wines."

Yamazato *Japanese* 27 | 19 | 25 | VE

Pijp | Hotel Okura | Ferdinand Bolstraat 333 | (31-20) 678-8351 | fax 678-7788 | www.okura.nl

"For real Japanese food, this is the place to be in the Netherlands" say fans of this "absolute treat" in the Pijp's Hotel Okura that serves "fresh", "fabulous presentations" of "some of the best sushi in Europe" along with other "outstanding" offerings, all backed up by an "extensive sake list"; "alas", some say, it's a "shame the decor doesn't quite reach the same level", but "excellent service" from the "trilingual staff" more than compensates - "be prepared" for the bill, though, as it's definitely "costly."

Zina [S] [M] *African/Mediterranean* 21 | 20 | 20 | E

Oud-West | Bosboom Toussaintstraat 70 | (31-20) 489-3707 | www.restaurantzina.com

"Very creative North African-Mediterranean cooking" including "excellent tagines and small plates" makes this relative newcomer in Oud-West "very popular with locals" so "reserve well in advance"; the "stark" but atmospheric setting consists of white walls, pillow-strewn banquettes and lots of flickering tapers and lanterns.

Other Noteworthy Places

Altmann Restaurant & Bar *Asian/International*
Amsteldijk 25 | (31-20) 662-7777 | fax 679-8952 | www.altmann.nl

Caruso *Italian*
Hotel Jolly Carlton | Singel 550 | (31-20) 623-8320 | fax 626-6183 | www.restaurantcaruso.nl

De Compagnon [S] *Burgundy*
Guldehandsteeg 17 | (31-20) 620-4225 | fax 320-8138 | www.decompagnon.nl

Greetje [M] *Dutch/French*
Peperstraat 23-25 | (31-20) 779-7450 | www.restaurantgreetje.nl

Groot Paardenburg [S] *French*
Amstelzijde 55 | (31-20) 496-1210 | fax 496-9109 | www.engelgroep.com

Het Bosch *French/International*
Jollenpad 10 | (31-20) 644-5800 | www.hetbosch.com

Jean-Jean [M] *French/Italian*
Anjeliersdwarsstraat 14 | (31-20) 627-7153 | www.jean-jean.nl

Kaiko [S] *Japanese*
Jekerstraat 114 | (31-20) 662-5641 | fax 676-5466

Lute [S] *French*
De Oude Molen 5 | (31-20) 472-2462 | fax 472-2463 | www.luterestaurant.nl

Mamouche *Moroccan/French*
Quellijnstraat 104 | (31-20) 673-6361 | www.restaurantmamouche.nl

Mansion, The [S] *Chinese*
Hobbemastraat 2 | (31-20) 616-6664 | fax 676-6620 | www.the-mansion.nl

Quartier Sud [S] *French*
Olympiaplein 176 | (31-20) 675-3990 | fax 675-4260 | www.quartiersud.nl

Rosarium [S] *Dutch/International*
Europaboulevard Amstelpark 1 | (31-20) 644-4085 | fax 646-6004 | www.rosarium.net

Segugio [S] *Italian*
Utrechtsestraat 96 | (31-20) 330-1503 | fax 330-1516 | www.segugio.nl

Spring [S] *French/International*
Willemsparkweg 177 | (31-20) 675-4421 | fax 676-9414 | www.restaurantspring.nl

VandeMarkt [S][M] *French/Mediterranean*
Schollenbrugstraat 8-9 | (31-20) 468-6958 | fax 463-0454 | www.vandemarkt.nl

Van Harte *French/Dutch*
Hartenstraat 24 | (31-20) 625-8500 | fax 320-6819 | www.vanharte.com

Voorbij Het Einde [S][M] *French*
Sumatrakade 613 | (31-20) 419-1143 | www.voorbijheteinde.nl

Zaza's [S] *International/Mediterranean*
Daniël Stalpertstraat 103 | (31-20) 673-6333 | fax 676-2220 | www.zazas.nl

FOOD | DECOR | SERVICE | COST

Athens

TOP FOOD RANKING

	Restaurant	Cuisine
29	Spondi	French/Mediterranean
26	48, The Restaurant	Greek
	Varoulko	Mediterranean/Seafood
24	Sale e Pepe	Italian
	Pil Poul et Jérôme Serres	French/Mediterranean
	Thalassinos	Seafood
23	Parea	Greek
	Kiku	Japanese/Sushi
	Vassilenas	Greek
	Daphne's	Greek/International
22	Papadakis	Greek
	Milos Athens	Greek/Seafood
	7 Thalasses	Greek/Seafood
21	GB Corner	Mediterranean
20	Kafeneio	Greek
	Balthazar	Mediterranean
	Boschetto	Mediterranean
	Premiere*	Greek/Mediterranean
19	Mamacas	Greek
18	Orizontes	Mediterranean

Balthazar ◐ *Mediterranean* 20 | 24 | 18 | E

Ampelokipi | Tsoha 27 & Bournazou | (30-210) 641-2300 | fax 641-2310 | www.balthazar.gr

"Dangerously trendy", this Mediterranean in the "hip" Ampelokipi neighborhood is "great in the summer" when diners forgo an "amazing" modern art-filled interior for the century-old mansion's "superb" garden; the fare is "up to par" though "not exquisite", but that doesn't bother the "beautiful" "people-watchers" at the bar.

Boschetto ◐ ☒ *Mediterranean* 20 | 19 | 21 | VE

Kolonaki | Evangelismos Park | Gennadiou St. & Vassilissis Sofias Ave. | (30-210) 721-0893 | fax 722-3598 | www.boschetto.gr

A "favorite of foreigners, businessmen" and affluent Athenians, this sophisticated "old reliable" in Kolonaki combines "good" "Italian-inspired" Mediterranean cuisine with "friendly" service; an elegant glass-conservatory interior looks out onto the National Gallery, while terrace tables in "lovely" Evangelismos Park make it an oasis amid "magnificent" greenery.

Daphne's *Greek/International* 23 | 23 | 21 | E

Plaka | Lysikratous 4 | (30-210) 322-7971 | fax 322-7971 | www.daphnesrestaurant.gr

Set in a restored 19th-century townhouse, this "wonderful" Greek-International in the Plaka is "a find", starting with its "beautiful", en-

* Indicates a tie with restaurant above

closed courtyard and continuing on to its "superb" old-world decor replete with "lovely" Pompeii-esque frescoes painted by the owner; the interior's "warmth and charm" extends to an "attentive staff" and a menu of "traditional" favorites - "by all means, don't miss the rabbit *stifado* (stew)."

48, The Restaurant ◐[S] *Greek* — 26 | 26 | 25 | VE

Ampelokipi | Armatolon & Klefton 48 | (30-210) 641-1082 | fax 645-0662 | www.48therestaurant.com

"Easily the coolest place I've ever been to" assert admirers of this "beautiful", "modern" Ampelokipi Greek featuring dramatic lighting and a "magical" courtyard where patrons literally "dine over the water" via a see-through platform; chef Christoforos Peskias caters to a "hip", "pretty" clientele with pricey, "innovative takes" on traditional fare, while "friendly service" and an extensive French wine list round out the "wonderful experience."

GB Corner ◐ *Mediterranean* — 21 | 22 | 22 | VE

Syntagma | Hotel Grande Bretagne | Syntagma Sq. | (30-210) 333-0000 | fax 322-8034 | www.grandebretagne.gr

Situated in the lobby of the stately Hotel Grande Bretagne, this "bit of old Europe" in a "beautiful space" attracts power-lunchers with its "good", "very expensive" Mediterranean cuisine, "attentive but not intrusive" staff and "excellent wine list, including Greek vintages"; P.S. for a more "serene" experience, romantics recommend the GB Roof Garden upstairs, with its "incredible, magical views of the Acropolis to your left and Parliament to your right."

Kafeneio ◐[S] *Greek* — 20 | 14 | 19 | M

Kolonaki | Loukianou 26 | (30-210) 722-9056

"For a true Kolonaki dining experience", try this trendy but "traditional" "treat" serving "quite original" takes on "affordable" Greek favorites; the simple, nondescript interior boasts "little atmosphere", so a mostly local clientele advises "eat outside" at one of the sidewalk tables that are "great for people-watching" in this "hot" section of Athens.

Kiku ◐[S] *Japanese* — 23 | 16 | 21 | VE

Kolonaki | Dimokritou 12 | (30-210) 364-7033

Considered "the best sushi restaurant in town", this Japanese located on a busy side street in Kolonaki is an "excellent" choice "for a business meal" of "good" raw fish, albeit at "expensive" prices; the minimalist setting - think blond wood and hanging scrolls - strikes some as "boring", but its "nearly authentic" cooked dishes make it a "favorite of Japanese tourists" as well as those "living in Athens."

Mamacas ◐ *Greek* — 19 | 19 | 16 | M

Gazi | Persephone 41 | (30-210) 346-4984 | www.mamacas.gr

'*Mamaca*' is Greek for 'mommy', and this pioneer of the modern, "fashionable" taverna contrasts its contemporary clean lines and whitewashed walls with "great, homestyle", like-mom-used-to-make cooking that's so "traditional" some snipe it "doesn't even pretend to be imaginative"; while critics claim that it's "overrated", it remains a "Gazi favorite" that's "packed" with a hip, late-night crowd and "great for people-watching."

Milos Athens ◐ *Greek/Seafood* 22 | 22 | 23 | VE

Kolonaki | Hilton Athens | Vassilissis Sofias 46 | (30-210) 724-4400 | fax 728-1111 | www.hilton.com

With long-standing restaurants in New York City and Montréal, chef-owner Costas Spiliades came home to open this "starkly modern" Greek seafooder with a "convenient" location in the landmark Hilton Athens; an "elegant" dining room (complete with open kitchen and marble display cases) and outdoor terrace set the stage for "superb" seasonal specialties and grilled fish "so fresh, you'll have to wash the salt spray off of your face" - much as you'll do with your smile once the über-"expensive" check arrives.

Orizontes ◐ *Mediterranean* 18 | 22 | 19 | VE

Kolonaki | Lycabettus Hill | (30-210) 722-7065 | fax 721-0700 | www.kastelorizo.com.gr

There's no other way to get there, so "take the funicular up Lycabettus Hill and get ready" for a "spectacular view" - the name means 'horizons' - overlooking the Acropolis and all of Athens from this "memorable", upmarket Mediterranean; several terraces make summer dining "a treat" for tourists and the city's see-and-be-seen elite, although some say the "good", globally influenced fare doesn't live up to the setting or "justify the cost."

Papadakis ⊠ *Greek* 22 | 19 | 21 | E

Kolonaki | Voukourestiou 47 & Fokilidou | (30-210) 360-8621 | fax 724-3904

On a citrus-tree-lined street in the heart of Kolonaki lies this "popular" Greek import "straight from Paros Island" that specializes in "excellent", "imaginative" fish dishes, along with "ample alternatives for carnivores and vegetarians", all at "fairly reasonable" prices; a "welcoming staff" presides over a small but "beautiful" setting that evokes "a seaside taverna."

NEW Parea ◐ Ⓜ *Greek* 23 | 22 | 22 | E

Kerameikos | Eridanus Hotel | Pireos 78 | (30-210) 520-0630 | fax 522-8800 | www.eridanus.gr

Top toque Lefteris Lazarou of the highly rated Varoulko is producing "excellent food" at this new Hellenic in the basement of the Eridanus Hotel; come summer it moves up to the rooftop terrace to take advantage of views of the Acropolis, the ancient cemetery of Keramikos and Philoppapou Hill; whatever season, it all adds up to "a wonderful evening and great memories" - "everything anyone could ask for the full Greek experience."

NEW Pil Poul et Jérôme Serres ◐ ⊠ *French/Mediterranean* 24 | 25 | 22 | E

Thisio | Apostolou Pavlou 51 & Poulopoulou | (30-210) 342-3665 | fax 210-341-3046 | www.pilpoul.gr

Star chef Jérôme Serres (ex his own namesake spot and Spondi) has just joined forces with this establishment in a beautiful restored mansion in Thisio and the result is "great" "creative" French-Mediterranean cuisine served by an "excellent" staff; the "incredible" setting includes "a dreamlike" terrace with "one of the most magnificent views of the Acropolis."

ATHENS

	FOOD	DECOR	SERVICE	COST

Premiere *Greek/Mediterranean*

FOOD	DECOR	SERVICE	COST
20	19	18	E

Neos Kosmos | Athenaeum InterContinental | Syngrou Ave. 89-93 | (30-210) 920-6981 | fax 920-6500 | www.interconti.com

The Greek-Med food at this venue on the rooftop of the Athenaeum InterContinental is "good", but it's the all-white outdoor terrace and its "amazing", "under-the-stars" view of the Acropolis and Lycabetus Hill that gets the most applause; sculptures and paintings from renowned contemporary collector Dakis Ioanou and an "attractive" clientele stand out against a minimalist backdrop.

Sale e Pepe *Italian*

FOOD	DECOR	SERVICE	COST
24	18	22	E

Kolonaki | Aristippou 34 | (30-210) 723-4102

A "lovely dining experience", this "high-class Italian" "aims to please" with simple, "well-executed" dishes and a "pleasant", antiques-filled setting; "great service" and a chef who "adds a personal touch" draw a chic crowd from surrounding Kolonaki, although most visit this "gem" for "one of the best wine lists in Athens", an "exquisite" selection of over 5,000 bottles.

7 Thalasses *Greek/Seafood*

FOOD	DECOR	SERVICE	COST
22	20	22	E

Kolonaki | Omirou 11 & Vissarionos | (30-210) 362-4825 | fax 362-4825

The name of this Kolonaki establishment means 'seven seas', so the fact that this Greek specializes in "excellent" fish should come as no surprise; the nautically decorated setting "could use an update", but "good value for the money" keeps luring locals back.

Spondi *French/Mediterranean*

FOOD	DECOR	SERVICE	COST
29	24	26	VE

Pangrati | Varnavas Sq. | Pyrronos 5 | (30-210) 752-0658 | fax 756-7021 | www.spondi.gr

At this elegant Pangrati restaurant rated No. 1 for Food in Athens, travelers and the city's well-to-do are "totally blown away" by chef Arnaud Bignon's "excellent", "creative" French-Mediterranean fare that's praised for its "outstanding taste and presentation"; set on three "beautiful" floors with a "spectacular" courtyard and terrace, this pricey 'offering to the gods' (the meaning of its name) rounds out the experience with "wonderfully attentive" service and a "superb wine list", including a "nice selection of Greek" labels.

Thalassinos *Seafood*

FOOD	DECOR	SERVICE	COST
24	17	23	M

Tzitzifies | Irakleous & Lysikratous 32 | (30-210) 940-4518

Seafood lovers from around the city descend on this "Athens treasure", a "quality" Tzitzifies taverna that's a good choice for "exquisite fish" and a "great variety" of other "delicious" dishes; some deem the rustic, tchotchke-filled interior "dull", but moderate prices help this local favorite "stay busy."

Varoulko *Mediterranean/Seafood*

FOOD	DECOR	SERVICE	COST
26	20	23	VE

Kerameikos | Pireos 80 | (30-210) 411-2043 | fax 522-1800 | www.varoulko.gr

This "can't-miss" Med seafooder in historic Karameikos from acclaimed chef-owner Lefteris Lazarou "continues to surprise" a host of regulars who appreciate a "uniquely executed", ever-changing menu that exhibits the wealth of "Poseidon's bounty"; a simple, elegant interior dotted with modern sculpture lets the "fresh" fish shine, although wallet-watchers warn the fin fare also "really bites - once you get the check."

Vassilenas ◐ M *Greek* 23 20 23 M

Piraeus | Aitolikou 72 | (30-210) 461-2457 | fax 411-0015 | www.vassilenas.gr

"One of the best" tavernas in Athens, this stalwart "has modernized its cuisine while maintaining some original" Greek dishes, with an emphasis on fish; moderate prices lead locals to the simple basement space near Piraeus, but in summer the action moves to the flower-bedecked rooftop.

Other Noteworthy Places

Alatsi ◐ $ *Greek*
Vrasida 13 | (30-210) 721-0501 | fax 721-0506

Alekos Metropolitan $ *Italian*
Mitropoleos 74 | (30-210) 331-9650 | fax 331-9651

Baraonda ◐ *Mediterranean*
Tsoha 43-45 | (30-210) 644-4308 | fax 644-1778

Beau Brummel $ *Mediterranean*
Dimitriou 9 & Theodoron | (30-210) 623-6780 | fax 623-6981 | www.beaubrummel.gr

Central *International*
Platia Filikis Etairias 14 | (30-210) 724-5938 | fax 722-9646 | www.central-island.gr

Cibus ◐ *Italian/Mediterranean*
Zappion Garden | Amalias Ave. | (30-210) 336-9363 | fax 325-2952 | www.aeglizappiou.gr

Edodi ◐ $ *International*
Veikou 80 | (30-210) 921-3013 | www.edodi.gr

Filippou ◐ $ *Greek*
Xenokratous 19 & Plutarchou | (30-210) 721-6390

Freud Oriental ◐ $ *Japanese*
Xenokratous 21 | (30-210) 729-9595 | fax 729-9597

Gefsis ◐ *Greek*
Kifisias Ave. 317 | (30-210) 800-1402 | fax 620-2158

Hytra ◐ $ *Greek*
Navarhou Apostoli 7 | (30-210) 331-6767

Kallisti ◐ M *Greek*
Asklipiou 137 | (30-210) 645-3179 | www.kallisti-restaurant.gr

Karavi ◐ *French*
Sofitel Athens Airport | Spata | (30-210) 354-4000 | fax 354-4444 | www.sofitel.com

Katsourbos ◐ *Greek*
Amynta 2 | (30-210) 722-2167 | www.kisland.gr

Kollias ◐ *Seafood*
Stratigou Plastira 3 | (30-210) 462-9620 | www.kollias.gr

Le Grand Balcon ◐ *Mediterranean*
St. George Lycabettus Hotel | Kleomenous 2 | (30-210) 729-0711 | fax 729-0439 | www.sglycabettus.gr

ManiMani *Greek*
Falirou 10 | (30-210) 921-8180

Monastiri *Greek*
Ventiri 5 | (30-210) 723-7700

Ouzadiko *Greek*
Lemos Shopping Ctr. | Karneadou 25-29 | (30-210) 729-5484

Pasaji *Greek*
City Link Mall | Stoa Spyromiliou | (30-210) 322-0714 | fax 322-0714

Piazza Mela *Italian*
Kifisias Ave. 238 | (30-210) 623-6596 | fax 623-6597

Rena Tis Ftelias *Greek*
Ikostis Pembtis Martiou 28 | (30-210) 674-3874

Sea Satin *Mediterranean/Seafood*
Fokilidou 1 | (30-210) 361-9646 | fax 361-9679

Telemachos BBQ Club *Mediterranean/Steak*
Fragopoulou 22 & Botsari | (30-210) 807-6680 | fax 807-4015 |
www.telemachosrestaurant.gr

Vardis *French/Mediterranean*
Hotel Pentelikon | Deligianni 66 | (30-210) 623-0650 | fax 801-9223 |
www.hotelpentelikon.gr

Vlassis *Greek*
Paster 8 | (30-210) 646-3060

Zephyros *Greek/Mediterranean*
Athens Ledra Marriott Hotel | Syngrou Ave. 115 | (30-210) 930-0060 |
fax 935-8603 | www.marriott.com/athgr

Barcelona

TOP FOOD RANKING

	Restaurant	Cuisine
28	Passadis del Pep	Mediterranean/Seafood
	Drolma	Catalan
	Àbac	Catalan
27	Gaig	Catalan
	Alkimia	Catalan
26	Jean Luc Figueras	French/Catalan
	Cinc Sentits	Catalan/Mediterranean
	Hofmann	Mediterranean
25	Caelis	Catalan/French
	Comerç 24	Spanish/International
	Ca l'Isidre	Catalan/Mediterranean
	Lasarte	Basque
	La Dama	Catalan/Mediterranean
	Botafumeiro	Seafood/Galician
24	Els Pescadors	International/Seafood
	Neichel	French/Mediterranean
	Gorría	Basque/Navarraise
	Arola	Catalan
	Espai Sucre	Dessert
	Tapaç 24	Catalan
	Bilbao	Catalan
23	Shunka	Japanese/Sushi
	Colibrí	Mediterranean
	Tapioles 53	Asian/Mediterranean
	Silvestre	Catalan
	Jaume de Provença	Catalan
22	Casa Calvet	Spanish/Mediterranean
	El Racó d'en Freixa*	Catalan
	Can Majó	Spanish/Seafood
	Cuines Santa Caterina	International/Catalan
	Fishhh*	Seafood
	Mondo	Seafood
21	Inòpia	Catalan
	Moo	Catalan
	Manairó	Catalan/Mediterranean
	Evo	Basque
	Garden, The	Asian
	Casa Leopoldo	Mediterranean/Seafood
	Barceloneta	Mediterranean/Seafood
	L'Olivé	Catalan/Mediterranean
	7 Portes	Catalan
20	Vía Veneto	Catalan/International
	El Mirador de la Venta	Spanish
	Negro*	Catalan
	Torre d'Alta Mar*	Mediterranean/Seafood

* Indicates a tie with restaurant above

	Los Caracoles	Spanish
	Tragaluz	Mediterranean/Spanish
19	Can Cortada	Catalan
18	Pòsit Marítim	Mediterranean/Seafood
15	Bestial	Italian

Àbac Ⓢ Ⓜ *Catalan* 28 | - | 26 | VE

Sarrià-Sant Gervasi | Avenida Tibidabo 1357 | (34-93) 319-6600 | fax 319-4519 | www.restaurantabac.com

Foodies and the fashionable flock to this "exciting" modern Catalan for top toque Xavier Pellicer's "original" "cutting-edge" cuisine with an "amazing combination of flavors" and textures, "especially the tasting menu"; the staff works the room with "choreographed gracefulness", leading gastronomic groupies to conclude it's "top-notch in every way"; N.B. post-Survey the restaurant moved from the Born district to this new locale in Sant Gervasi.

Alkimia Ⓢ *Catalan* 27 | 21 | 22 | E

Eixample | Indústria 79 | (34-93) 207-6115

"Currently one of the best restaurants in Barcelona" state supporters of star chef Jordi Vilà's new-wave Catalan in the Eixample, with its "excellent" and "unusual amalgam of explosive flavors"; the "white minimalist" setting evokes a "sense of purity that is carried over into the food", while alchemy symbols on the wall stylishly suggest the restaurant's name.

Arola Ⓜ *Catalan* 24 | 25 | 24 | VE

Port Olímpic | Hotel Arts | Marina 19-21 | (34-93) 483-8090 | fax 221-2018 | www.arola-arts.com

Chef Sergi Arola, a Ferran Adrià disciple who also runs Madrid's groundbreaking La Broche, heads up this "trendy" modern Catalan in the "fantastic" Hotel Arts; a "beautiful"-looking staff serves "creative", "attractive small plates" in a "perfect location" with "wonderful views" of the Olímpic Harbor and the sea.

Barceloneta ◐ *Mediterranean/Seafood* 21 | 18 | 18 | M

Barceloneta | Moll dels Pescadors | L'Escar 22 | (34-93) 221-2111 | fax 221-2111 | www.rte-barceloneta.com

This big, "boisterous", "fairly priced" Med with "top-quality fish" and a "cordial" staff has an "excellent location on the water" in Barceloneta; the "dining room doesn't need a lot of decoration because the view is enough", and in summer "a table on the terrace" is even more ideal.

Bestial ◐ *Italian* 15 | 20 | 16 | E

Port Olímpic | Ramón Trias Fargas 2-4 | (34-93) 224-0407 | fax 224-0649 | www.bestialdeltragaluz.com

"Chic" decor and a "stunning" "beach location" in Port Olímpic with a sea view are the draws at this trendy Italian whose interior sports an amusing "graphic ant motif"; the food is only "average" and service comes with "attitude", but wags wager the experience is a "must for interior designers" and anyone with a "stylish entourage."

Bilbao ◐ Ⓢ *Catalan* 24 | 20 | 20 | E

Gràcia | Perill 33 | (34-93) 458-9624

For years locals have been heading to this bustling, two-tiered Catalan in Gràcia for "wonderful classic cuisine" like fried eggs with black truffles that's backed up by a "fantastic" wine list that stars deep, dark Spanish reds; it draws a "good crowd", which also makes it popular for "people-watching."

Botafumeiro ◐ *Seafood/Galician* 25 18 23 VE

Gràcia | Gran de Gràcia 81 | (34-93) 218-4230 | fax 415-5848 | www.botafumeiro.es

For the "freshest seafood", particularly the "pristine cold shellfish platter", many head to this 31-year-old "emblematic" Galician in Gràcia with a "good" regional wine list, "warm" setting and popular bar; the sprawling, "hustle-bustle" space can be "noisy", and it's "expensive", but that doesn't keep loyal crowds from coming back.

Caelis Ⓢ Ⓜ *Catalan/French* 25 23 26 VE

Eixample | Hotel Palace | Gran Via de les Corts Catalanes 668 | (34-93) 510-1205 | fax 510-1205 | www.caelis.com

The former "grande dame" that was called Diana got a new name and a redo and the result is this handsome contemporary space in the Eixample that's a suitable backdrop for "superior service" and chef Romain Fornell's "excellent" Catalan-French cuisine; it ain't "cheap", but what do you expect, "it's the Palace."

Ca l'Isidre Ⓢ *Catalan/Mediterranean* 25 18 23 VE

El Raval | Les Flors 12 | (34-93) 441-1139 | fax 442-5271 | www.calisidre.com

"Creative but not froufrou" describes the "culinary delights" found at this family-run Catalan-Med in El Raval, where chef Núria Gironés, the daughter of the owner and former noted chef, especially excels at "superb" desserts like the "best chocolate soufflé"; a "most accommodating and helpful staff" presides over a quietly "elegant" room with original art - Picasso, Miró - on the walls; "it's expensive but you leave with the sense that you invested your money very well."

Can Cortada *Catalan* 19 18 15 M

Horta | Avinguda de l'Estatut de Catalunya s/n | (34-93) 427-2315 | fax 427-0294 | www.gruptravi.com

"Very good" "classic" cuisine is served in this Catalan housed in an 11th-century stone tower in Horta, with a "rustic", "country house" interior with vaulted brick walls; service can be "poor" when the vast four-floor space is busy, but moderate prices and a summer garden appeal to many of the businesspeople who frequent the place.

Can Majó Ⓜ *Spanish/Seafood* 22 13 19 M

Barceloneta | Almirall Aixada 23 | (34-93) 221-5818 | fax 221-5455 | www.canmajo.es

If you're looking for a "welcoming place to go on the beach", try this "excellent" Spanish seafood stalwart in Barceloneta; the nautical decor is simple, but the terrace overlooks the Mediterranean, and moderate prices mean it's "very appropriate for families."

Casa Calvet Ⓢ *Spanish/Mediterranean* 22 25 22 E

Eixample | Casp 48 | (34-93) 412-4012 | fax 412-4336 | www.casacalvet.es

Aesthetes assert "this is the first place I go when I'm in Barcelona" about this "beautiful" Antonio Gaudí-designed art nouveau Spanish-Med in the Eixample; a "delicious", "upmarket" menu and "formal service" mean "you'll spend a lot" but you're getting "a lot of quality."

Casa Leopoldo Ⓜ *Mediterranean/Seafood* 21 | 17 | 19 | M

El Raval | Sant Rafael 24 | (34-93) 441-3014 | fax 441-3014 | www.casaleopoldo.com

"It doesn't look like much" but this traditional Mediterranean seafooder in El Raval has been luring finatics with "wonderful" "straightforward" fare since 1929; the neighborhood can be "iffy", but a "homey" vibe and "moderate prices" make for a high comfort level once you get here.

Cinc Sentits ◐Ⓢ *Catalan/Mediterranean* 26 | 22 | 24 | E

Eixample | Aribau 58 | (34-93) 323-9490 | fax 323-9491 | www.cincsentits.com

"Barcelona is the new capital of world dining" and this family-run Catalan-Med in the Eixample showcasing Jordi Artal's "creative but intelligible cuisine" is "one of its heads of state"; surveyors single out the tasting menus paired with "surprising but always exquisite wines" as providing not only "a great meal but a great foodie deal"; "service is a rare blend of refinement and genuine hospitality", and the setting is sleek contemporary chic.

Colibrí Ⓜ *Mediterranean* 23 | - | 21 | E

Eixample | Casanova 212 | (34-93) 443-2306 | fax 442-6127 | www.restaurantcolibri.com

A former chef from the highly regarded Ca l'Isidre runs this Med with "extremely well-prepared" "original" dishes made from "top-quality" seasonal market ingredients; a post-Survey move from the Raval district to this Eixample address makes for much bigger digs.

Comerç 24 ◐ⓈⓂ *Spanish/International* 25 | 23 | 22 | E

El Born | Comerç 24 | (34-93) 319-2102 | fax 319-1074 | www.comerc24.com

"Exciting, unpredictable" and "adventurous" sums up this avant-garde Spanish-International in the Born district run by "dynamic" chef-owner Carles Abellán, a disciple of legendary Ferran Adrià of El Bulli; "inventive", "unforgettable" tapas are "taken to a sexy new level" and served by a "charming staff" in a cooler than cool, colorful minimalist setting, making this a "must-eat-at in Barcelona."

NEW **Cuines Santa Caterina** *International/Catalan* 22 | 21 | 18 | M

Barri Gòtic | Mercat Santa Caterina Avda. Francesc Cambó | (34-93) 268-9918 | www.grupotragaluz.com

The latest venue from the Tragaluz Group is this International-Catalan inside the "snazzy", "beautifully restored" Santa Caterina Market where the "freshest ingredients from nearby vendors" make for "excellent" food and "a wide range of dishes" from soups, salads and pastas to ethnic fare; it can be "noisy" and "service can be slow", but "reasonable prices" help pacify most.

Drolma Ⓢ *Catalan* 28 | 25 | 27 | VE

Eixample | Hotel Majestic | Passatge de Gràcia 68 | (34-93) 496-7710 | fax 445-3893 | www.hotelmajestic.es

Chef Fermí Puig's "outstanding" modern Catalan in the Hotel Majestic features "out-of-this-world", cutting-edge cuisine (glazed baby goat is his signature) and a small but "stylish" setting with views of the Passeig de Gràcia; it's "exceptionally expensive", but that hasn't kept it from becoming a "bastion for Barcelona's rich and powerful."

El Mirador de la Venta Ⓢ *Spanish* 20 17 20 E
Tibidabo | Plaça Doctor Andreu s/n | (34-93) 212-6455 | fax 212-5144 | www.restaurantelaventa.com
"One of the best locations in town", with "wonderful views over the city and shoreline", is found at this Spanish spot in Tibidabo; the staff is "attentive" and the food is "tasty", but it's the terrace here that's tops.

El Racó d'en Freixa Ⓢ Ⓜ *Catalan* 22 18 17 VE
Sarrià-Sant Gervasi | Sant Elies 22 | (34-93) 209-7559 | fax 209-7918 | www.elracodenfreixa.com
Surveyors are split on this long-standing, family-owned modern Catalan in Sarrià-Sant Gervasi: fans of young chef Ramón Freixa, who inherited his position from his father, praise his "imaginative", "beautifully prepared and presented" dishes, the "understated, tasteful setting" and "terrific wine cellar"; the less-enthused find the "very expensive" cuisine "disappointing", the decor "impersonal" and the service "standard."

Els Pescadors ◐ *International/Seafood* 24 19 21 E
Poblenou | Plaça Prim 1 | (34-93) 225-2018 | fax 224-0004 | www.elspescadors.com
This large International stalwart with "great seafood" ("amazing salt-baked fish") and a strong Spanish wine list is "worth the trip to Poblenou" (about a mile down the waterfront north of the Olympic Port); there's a trio of dining rooms to choose from, and in summer terrace tables are a cool alternative.

Espai Sucre Ⓜ *Dessert* 24 20 23 E
Ciutat Vella | Princesa 53 | (34-93) 268-1630 | fax 268-1523 | www.espaisucre.com
"How sweet it is" to come upon this small but daring dessert specialist-cum-pastry school in the Ciutat Vella; be "prepared to have your culinary sensibilities upended" by sampling chef Jordi Butrón's bold tasting menus, and you can even make a spirited match with over 100 wines; N.B. there are a few salty dishes on the menu for those trying to avoid sugar shock.

Evo Ⓢ *Basque* 21 22 20 E
Hospitalet de Llobregat | Hotel Hesperia Tower | Valencia 169 | (34-93) 453-4759 | www.evorestaurante.com
A "top-notch" entry in the Hotel Hesperia Tower from highly lauded "star chef Santi Santamaria" (of Madrid's Santceloni among others) is how admirers assess this Spanish Basque that relies on prime market produce for its "fresh, creative" cuisine; the glass-enclosed roof-dome setting includes "super-cool" decor that resembles a space ship and contributes to the "refreshing experience"; P.S. "don't skip the cheese course."

Fishhh Ⓢ *Seafood* 22 21 20 E
Les Corts | Illa Diagonal | Ave. Diagonal 557 | (34-93) 444-1139
"The only place the seafood is fresher is in the sea" say supporters of this fish house/market "conveniently located" in an all-white minimalist space in a Les Corts shopping center; there's a surprisingly sophisticated selection of champagnes and local *cavas* to complement the briny bites.

Gaig Catalan — 27 | 21 | 24 | VE

Eixample | Cram Hotel | Aragó 214 | (34-93) 429-1017 | fax 429-7002 | www.restaurantgaig.com

Though this family-owned establishment in the Eixample dates back to 1869, its current chef, Carles Gaig, produces "creative" modern Catalan cuisine that's "among the best in Barcelona", with the "emphasis on elegant dishes made with the best ingredients"; an "intimate", "quiet" setting and "superb service" add to the "fine-all-around", "very expensive" experience.

Garden, The Asian — 21 | 21 | 19 | E

Les Corts | Hotel Rey Juan Carlos I | Avinguda Diagonal 661-671 | (34-93) 364-4040 | fax 364-4264 | www.hrjuancarlos.com

Like the name says, whether you are sitting indoors or out at this Asian in Les Corts' Hotel Rey Juan Carlos I, you'll have a view of lush gardens, plus a swimming pool; "good" food and a wine list that's big on winning, robust Riojas and Riberas also grow on the clientele here; N.B. a post-Survey chef change and renovation may outdate the above scores.

Gorría Basque/Navarraise — 24 | 16 | 20 | E

Eixample | Diputació 421 | (34-93) 245-1164 | www.restaurantegorria.com

Long-standing, family-run Basque-Navarraise in the Eixample featuring "classic" dishes like suckling pig and "meat as good as Peter Luger's in Brooklyn"; a timeless "rustic" setting with wood, brick walls and stained glass, an "excellent wine list" and "doable" prices add to the laid-back vibe.

Hofmann Mediterranean — 26 | 19 | 21 | E

La Ribera | Argentería 74-78 | (34-93) 319-5889 | fax 319-5882 | www.hofmann-bcn.com

"They aim high in the kitchen and succeed most of the time" at this restaurant/culinary school in La Ribera run by chef/owner/teacher Mey Hofmann; "fantastic" Mediterranean dishes and "work-of-art" desserts are served in a series of "charming" dining rooms housed in a 19th-century building; N.B. closed Saturday-Sunday.

NEW Inòpia Catalan — 21 | 16 | 19 | M

Eixample | Tamarit 104 | (34-93) 424-5531 | www.barinopia.com

"Tapas with a pedigree" is the take on this new, fairly priced Catalan "delight" in the lower Eixample from Albert Adrià, who is also the pastry chef at his brother Ferran's legendary El Bulli, about 200 miles to the north of Barcelona; the brightly lit space is not much to look at but the small-bites "bar of your dreams" is very busy serving "witty updates of old favorites" to "a hot crowd."

Jaume de Provença Catalan — 23 | 19 | 20 | E

Eixample | Provença 88 | (34-93) 430-0029 | fax 439-2950 | www.jaumeprovenza.com

Considered a pioneer in the modern Catalan cooking movement, chef Jaume Bargués has been producing "excellent, imaginative" cuisine with an International accent for 27 years in this Eixample establishment; loyalists like the "well-mannered staff" and "romantic" room, but others object to dated decor that's "old."

Jean Luc Figueras ⓢ *French/Catalan* 26 | 24 | 28 | VE

Gràcia | Santa Teresa 10 | (34-93) 415-2877 | fax 218-9262

If you feel like French-Catalan while you're in Spain, try Jean Luc Figueras' "top-notch", "inventive" cuisine, which is served in "the refined" and "elegant" setting of legendary couturier "Balenciaga's former studio" in a 19th-century Gràcia palace; "superb service" and a "wonderful wine list" add to a "memorable evening" that's "worth every euro."

La Dama *Catalan/Mediterranean* 25 | 26 | 25 | VE

Eixample | Avinguda Diagonal 423 | (34-93) 202-0686 | fax 200-7299 | www.ladama-restaurant.com

"Absolutely elegant", this "grand, old" dame excels with a "gorgeous", "romantic" art nouveau setting in a 1918 Eixample building; "very good" creative Catalan-Mediterranean food, an exceptional wine list and "immaculate", "not stuffy", service also lead devotees to declare "it's a gem that could hold its own anywhere."

Lasarte ⓢ *Basque* 25 | 23 | 23 | E

Eixample | Hotel Condes de Barcelona | Mallorca 259 | (34-93) 445-3242 | fax 445-3232 | www.restaurantlasarte.com

This modern Spanish Basque "masterpiece" owned by star chef Martín Berasategui and located in the Hotel Condes de Barcelona was one of the city's most anticipated openings; "outstanding food and attention to detail" and a "beautiful" split-level contemporary space make it a "must-stop" hot spot for foodies and fashionistas alike.

L'Olivé ◐ *Catalan/Mediterranean* 21 | 19 | 20 | M

Eixample | Balmes 47 | (34-93) 452-1990 | fax 451-2418 | www.rte-olive.com

"Lively and vibrant" Catalan-Med in the Eixample with "fine food", "professional service" and "pleasant", "pretty" modern decor with touches of green that evoke its namesake ingredient; moderate prices also make it popular for business lunches.

Los Caracoles ◐ *Spanish* 20 | 18 | 17 | M

Barri Gòtic | Escudellers 14 | (34-93) 302-3185 | fax 302-0743

The name of this "cavernous", "rustic" 1835 "landmark" Spanish in Barri Gòtic translates as 'snails' and that's the specialty here along with "wonderful, spit-roasted chicken" and "paella served in skillets the size of flying saucers"; sure, it's "touristy", "campy" and "service is slap-dash", but most maintain it's a "must for first-time" visitors and "reasonable prices."

Manairó ◐ⓢⓜ *Catalan/Mediterranean* 21 | 19 | 20 | E

Eixample | Diputació 424 | (34-93) 231-0057 | www.manairo.com

Chef-owner Jordi Herrera is making waves at his "very creative" Catalan-Med with the experimental "tools and techniques he develops" like cooking steaks on red hot spikes; his small Eixample venue is being dubbed by some "one of the best restaurants in Barcelona."

Mondo ⓜ *Seafood* 22 | 21 | 20 | E

Port Vell | Moll d'Espanya s/n | (34-93) 221-3911 | www.mondobcn.com

"If you've got the money" and "want a great seafood restaurant with a waterfront location", this aerie that's also appropriately adjacent to the Barcelona Aquarium is "the place"; some of the fresh catches of the day come from the fish market a stone's throw away, and the airy, expansive and upscale glass-walled interior, which feels like the deck of a ship, continues the nautical theme.

Moo ⓢ *Catalan* 21 | 25 | 19 | E

Eixample | Hotel Omm | Rosselló 265 | (34-93) 445-4000 | fax 445-4004 | www.hotelomm.es

"Trendy" types head for this "stylish" spot in one of Barcelona's "hippest" hotels in the Eixample, where respected restaurateurs, the Roca brothers, oversee "inventive" modern Catalan dishes, which can be ordered in half-portions; but skeptics say the "cool" setting is better than the "witty" "food that could be improved", since apparently not everyone is sweet on "perfume-inspired desserts" - a little bite of Ralph Lauren Polo Sport Woman, anyone?

Negro ◐ *Catalan* 20 | 21 | 18 | M

Sarrià-Sant Gervasi | Avinguda Diagonal 640 | (34-93) 405-9444 | fax 405-9221 | www.negrodeltragaluz.com

Even after seven years, this "good" creative Catalan in Sarrià-Sant Gervasi from the ever-growing Tragaluz Group is still "fashionable"; a "friendly staff", "great prices" and a DJ add to its appeal.

Neichel ⓢⓜ *French/Mediterranean* 24 | 21 | 22 | VE

Pedralbes | Beltrán i Rózpide 1-5 | (34-93) 203-8408 | fax 205-6369 | www.neichel.es

"Everything is great" enthuse admirers of this 26-year-old French-Med where chef-owner Jean-Louis Neichel's "fantastic food" and a "superb wine list" are served by an "impeccable" staff in a room overlooking a garden in residential Pedralbes; but the less-impressed assess the experience as "old-fashioned" and "very expensive."

Passadis del Pep ⓢ *Mediterranean/Seafood* 28 | 21 | 25 | E

El Born | Plaça de Palau 2 | (34-93) 310-1021 | fax 319-6056 | www.passadis.com

"Don't expect a written menu or a choice" at this "difficult-to-find gem", a Mediterranean seafooder in El Born that's voted No. 1 for Food in the city; the second you sit down, you'll be served sparkling *cava* and an "extravaganza" of "plate after plate" of appetizers that "just keep coming" ("don't forget to say stop"), followed by a main course ("if you can still fit it in") that's "the best fish in the world"; it all adds up to a down-to-earth "awesome experience."

Pòsit Marítim *Mediterranean/Seafood* 18 | 21 | 18 | E

Port Vell | Moll d'Espanya s/n | (34-93) 221-6256 | fax 792-2471 | www.posit.es

"You feel like you're outside of the city, on the ocean, surrounded by boats" at this "good" and "luminous" Med-seafooder in Port Vell's yacht club; "service can be slow", but that doesn't keep the business crowd from booking at lunch or couples from coming at dinner; N.B. a post-Survey redo and ownership change may outdate the above scores.

7 Portes ◐ *Catalan* 21 | 21 | 20 | E

Ciutat Vella | Passeig Isabel II 14 | (34-93) 319-3033 | fax 319-3046 | www.7portes.com

"An old standard that's still going strong", this sprawling 1836 Catalan "institution" and "paella palace" in Port Vell is "one of the oldest continuously operating restaurants in the world"; although "touristy" and "hectic", most maintian "good value for the money" and a "festive" atmosphere that "reeks of old-world charm" "make up for it."

Shunka Ⓜ *Japanese* 23 | 15 | 17 | M

Barri Gòtic | Sagristans 5 | (34-93) 412-4991 | fax 342-4877

The "best Japanese in town" is this small, "reasonably priced" spot with "excellent", "innovative" dishes and specials in the Barri Gòtic; the decor is negligible, but that doesn't seem to bother Spain's superstar chef Ferran Adrià who is said to favor the sushi here.

Silvestre ◐Ⓢ *Catalan* 23 | 20 | 22 | E

Sarrià-Sant Gervasi | Santaló 101 | (34-93) 241-4031

Chef Guillermo Casañé is in the kitchen turning out "excellent", market-driven Catalan cuisine while his English speaking wife, Marta Cabot, is out front at this "friendly" spot with a series of restful dining rooms in Sarrià-Sant Gervasi that's become one of Upper Barcelona's best-loved watering holes.

NEW Tapaç 24 ◐ *Catalan* 24 | 20 | 21 | E

Eixample | Diputació 269 | (34-93) 488-0977 | www.tapac24.com

Supporters say "*olé!*" to star chef Carles Abellán, of the city's highly rated and experimental Comerç 24, and his new Catalan in the Eixample, where "sublimely simple" traditional tapas "full of flavor" like ham croquettes are complemented by an "excellent wine list"; open from 8 AM to midnight, the place draws a continuous crowd that clusters at the bar, tables and small dining terrace.

Tapioles 53 ⓈⓂ *Asian/Mediterranean* 23 | 19 | 22 | M

Poble Sec | Tapioles 53 | (34-93) 329-2238 | www.tapioles53.com

At this semi-secret former umbrella factory in Poble Sec, you must reserve in advance with chef Sarah Stothart whose market-driven, moderately priced Asian-Mediterranean cuisine has enthusiasts exclaiming "excellent", "interesting" and "original"; it's an "intimate", clubby experience as the space only seats 25, and Stothart will be chopping and chatting away with you in her open kitchen.

Torre d'Alta Mar Ⓢ *Mediterranean/Seafood* 20 | 21 | 16 | VE

Barceloneta | Passeig Joan de Borbó 88 | (34-93) 221-0007 | fax 221-0090 | www.torredealtamar.com

"For people who don't have vertigo", this "unique" Mediterranean seafooder 75 meters up in a former cable-car tower in Barceloneta "provides a spectacular view of the city on one side" and "of the ocean on the other"; the food is "sophisticated", the white decor is chic and prices are as elevated as the setting; N.B. thank god it doesn't revolve.

Tragaluz ◐ *Mediterranean/Spanish* 20 | 21 | 18 | E

Eixample | Passatge de la Concepció 5 | (34-93) 487-0196 | fax 487-7083 | www.grupotragaluz.com/tragaluz

"As stylish as Barcelona itself", this "airy, modern" Mediterranean-Spanish in the Eixample district attracts a "hip" crowd along with businessmen and tourists to its tri-level space dominated by a dramatic and "wonderful" sliding skylight; the food is "delicious" and "decently priced" for what it is.

	FOOD	DECOR	SERVICE	COST
Vía Veneto *Catalan/International*	20	19	23	E

Sarrià-Sant Gervasi | Ganduxer 10 | (34-93) 200-7244 | fax 201-6095 | www.viavenetorestaurant.com

"I saw Dali here in the '60s" says one long-standing fan of owner José Monje's Sarrià-Sant Gervasi grande dame; "excellent service", "very good" Catalan-International cuisine and old-world decor still appeal.

Other Noteworthy Places

Àpat *Catalan/Mediterranean*
Aribau 137 | (34-93) 439-6414 | www.apat.es

Boix de la Cerdanya ◐🅂 *Catalan*
Consell de Cent 303 | (34-93) 451-1547 | fax 451-5075 | www.restaurantboix.com

Can Costa *Mediterranean/Seafood*
Passeig Joan de Borbó 70 | (34-93) 221-5903 | fax 221-4262 | www.cancosta.com

Can Ravell *Catalan/Mediterranean*
Aragó 313 | (34-93) 457-5114 | www.ravell.com

Can Solé 🄼 *Mediterranean/Seafood*
Sant Carles 4 | (34-93) 221-5012 | fax 221-5815 | www.restaurantcansole.com

Cardamon ◐🄼 *Catalan/Indian*
Carders 31 | (34-93) 295-5059 | www.cardamon.es

El Bistrot de Sants ◐🅂 *Mediterranean*
Barceló Hotel Sants | Plaça Països Catalans | (34-93) 503-5300 | fax 490-6045 | www.bchoteles.com

El Lobito 🅂🄼 *Mediterranean/Seafood*
Ginebra 9 | (34-93) 319-9164

Florentina 🄼 *Catalan*
Saragossa 122 | (34-93) 211-2695

Galería Gastronómica ◐ *Mediterranean*
Passatge de la Concepció 7 | (34-93) 272-3880 | fax 272-3881 | www.galeriagastronomica.com

Gargantua i Pantagruel ◐ *Catalan*
Còrsega 200 | (34-93) 453-2020 | fax 453-2020

hisop *Catalan*
Passatge Marimon 9 | (34-93) 241-3233 | www.hisop.com

La Balsa *International*
Infanta Isabel 4 | (34-93) 211-5048 | fax 418-4606 | www.labalsarestaurant.com

La Maison du Languedoc Roussillon 🅂 *French*
Pau Claris 77 | (34-93) 301-0498 | fax 301-2552

La Provença *Mediterranean/Provençal*
Provença 242 | (34-93) 323-2367 | fax 451-2389 | www.laprovenza.com

Le Quattro Stagioni 🄼 *Italian/Mediterranean*
Doctor Roux 37 | (34-93) 205-2279 | www.4stagioni.com

L'Oliana ◐ *Catalan/Mediterranean*
Santaló 54 | (34-93) 201-0647 | fax 414-4417 | www.oliana.com

Merendero de la Mari *Mediterranean/Seafood*
Port Vell | Plaça de Pau Vila 1 | (34-93) 221-3141 | fax 221-5502 | www.merenderodelamari.com

Merlot [M] *Spanish/Italian*
Diputació 381 | (34-93) 265-9083

Nonell ◐ *Mediterranean/International*
Plaça Isidre Nonell | (34-93) 301-1378 | www.nonell.es

Paco Meralgo ◐ *Mediterranean/Tapas*
Muntaner 171 | (34-93) 430-9027 | www.pacomeralgo.com

Peixerot [M] *Catalan/Seafood*
Tarragona 177 | (34-93) 425-1803 | fax 426-1063

Petit Paris ◐ *Mediterranean*
Paris 196 | (34-93) 218-2678

Restaurant Coure [S] *Catalan*
Passatge Marimon 20 | (34-93) 200-7532

Rías de Galicia ◐ *Galician/Seafood*
Lleida 7 | (34-93) 424-8152 | fax 426-1307 | www.riasdegalicia.com

Roig Robí *Catalan*
Sèneca 20 | (34-93) 218-9222 | fax 415-7842 | www.roigrobi.com

Saüc Restaurant [S][M] *Mediterranean*
Passatge Lluís Pellicer 12 | (34-93) 321-0189 | www.saucrestaurant.com

Speakeasy ◐[S] *Catalan/Mediterranean*
Aribau 162-166 | (34-93) 217-5080 | www.drymartinibcn.com

Suquet de l'Almirall *Mediterranean*
Passeig Joan Borbó 65 | (34-93) 221-6233 | fax 221-6233

Taktika Berri [S] *Basque*
Valencia 169 | (34-93) 453-4759

Teppan-Yaki [S] *Japanese*
Marina 19-21 | (34-93) 225-2182 | fax 225-2182

Tramonti 1980 ◐ *Italian*
Avinguda Diagonal 501 | (34-93) 410-1535 | fax 405-0443 | www.tramonti1980.com

Tram-Tram [S] *Catalan*
Major de Sarrià 121 | (34-93) 204-8518 | fax 204-6725 | www.tram-tram.com

Vinya Rosa-Magí [S] *Catalan/French*
Avinguda Sarriá 17 | (34-93) 430-0003 | fax 430-0041 | www.vinyarosamagi.com

Windsor [S] *Catalan*
Còrsega 286 | (34-93) 415-8483 | fax 238-6608 | www.restaurantwindsor.com

Yashima [S] *Japanese*
Josep Tarradellas 145 | (34-93) 419-0697

Zure Etxea [S] *Basque*
Jordi Girona 10 | (34-93) 203-8390

FOOD DECOR SERVICE COST

Berlin

TOP FOOD RANKING

	Restaurant	Cuisine
26	VAU	International
24	Lorenz Adlon	French
	Maxwell	French/International
23	Alt Luxemburg	New French/Med.
	Die Quadriga*	New French/Med.
	44	New French/International
	Vox	New French/Asian
	Ana e Bruno	Italian/Mediterranean
22	Hartmanns	German/Mediterranean
	Margaux	French
21	Aigner	Viennese
	Guy	French/Mediterranean
	Balthazar	Mediterranean
	San Nicci	Italian
	Grill Royal	Seafood/Steakhouse
	Altes Zollhaus	German
	Borchardt	French/German
	Bacco/Bocca di Bacco	Tuscan
	Diekmann	German/International
20	MaoThai	Thai
	Paris-Moskau	French Brasserie/Med.
19	Fellini	Italian
16	Paris Bar	French Brasserie
	Lindenlife	German
13	Dachgartenrestaurant	German

Aigner ◐ *Viennese* 21 | 19 | 19 | E

Mitte | Französische Str. 25 | (49-30) 203-751-850 | fax 203-751-859 | www.aigner-gendarmenmarkt.de

"Pretty, fashionable people" flock to this "popular" "place in Mitte", "on the Gendarmenmarkt", where you'll "want to order seconds" of the "excellent Viennese cooking" that's "well-rounded" with German influences – the signature roast "duck is spectacular" – and served by a "friendly, fast" staff; though located within a typical GDR-style 'Plattenbau' (concrete slab building), its "wonderful" 19th-century bistro setting comes from transplanting "beautiful decor" from the former Café Aigner in Vienna.

Altes Zollhaus [S][M] *German* 21 | 17 | 20 | E

Kreuzberg | Carl-Herz-Ufer 30 | (49-30) 692-3300 | fax 692-3566 | www.altes-zollhaus-berlin.de

Located within an "old customs office" in a "picturesque setting beside" the Landwehrkanal in Kreuzberg, this "standby" boasts "rustic" yet "dignified decor" that complements its "appealing", "extensive menu" of "excellent" traditional *Deutsch* dishes, which are served by

* Indicates a tie with restaurant above

an "accommodating" staff; some say it's "a bit touristic", but more maintain it "successfully straddles the line between historical kitsch and authentic old-style German eating"; N.B. its Smugglers Barn space is perfect for parties.

Alt Luxemburg 🅂 *French/Mediterranean* 23 | 21 | 25 | E

Charlottenburg | Windscheidstr. 31 | (49-30) 323-8730 | fax 327-4003 | www.altluxemburg.de

"One expects the old Kaiser to walk in" to this "wonderful place", a "Berlin standard" not far from the Charlottenburg Castle, where the "fast service" provided by Ingrid Wannemacher's "nice" staff always "satisfies", as does her husband Karl's "comprehensive menu" of "delicious" New French-Med cuisine ("no schnitzel here") offered amid "quiet" surroundings; no wonder so many regulars are "happy" to call it a "favorite."

Ana e Bruno 🅂🄼 *Italian/Mediterranean* 23 | 17 | 22 | E

Charlottenburg | Sophie-Charlotten-Str. 101 | (49-30) 325-7110 | fax 322-6895 | www.ana-e-bruno.de

"Made for a lovely, quiet evening", this "cozy" Charlottenburg spot is home to "accommodating chef" Bruno Pellegrini, whose "ambitious" menu offers a taste of "*bella Italia*" via "excellent, inventive" Italian-Mediterranean cuisine at prices that may be "high" but are "appropriate for the quality of the food"; some call the decor "less than striking", but at least "you know you're in good hands" with the "polite staff"; P.S. "be sure to make reservations as tables are limited."

Bacco *Tuscan* 21 | 19 | 19 | E

Charlottenburg | Marburger Str. 5 | (49-30) 211-8687 | fax 211-5230 | www.bacco.de

Bocca di Bacco ◐ *Tuscan*

Mitte | Friedrichstr. 167/168 | (49-30) 2067-2828 | fax 2067-2929 | www.boccadibacco.de

The Mannozzi family oversees this Tuscan pair, the original an old-fashioned trattoria "with history" that's been serving "good, traditional cuisine with no surprises" in Charlottenburg since the late-'60s, and its 'mouth of Bacchus' offshoot in Mitte a more "sophisticated", "upmarket" eatery offering "nouvelle" fare and a "good selection of wines" in a "modern, stylish" setting; both, however, are often "star-studded", and feature "fresh ingredients" and "charming, attentive" staffers, making either one "worth a try."

Balthazar *Mediterranean* 21 | 20 | 20 | E

Wilmersdorf | Kurfürstendamm 160 | (49-30) 8940-8477 | fax 8940-8478 | www.restaurant-balthazar.de

Tucked into a classical Berlin townhouse in Wilmersdorf, at the "less-fashionable end of Kurfürstendamm", is this urbane-looking Mediterranean with Asian accents that offers "enjoyable", "high-class cuisine", a "great wine list" and "warm staff"; moreover, the practical point out there's a bargain 10 euros business lunch and at dinner "you can walk away without emptying your wallet."

Borchardt ◐ *French/German* 21 | 20 | 19 | E

Mitte | Französische Str. 47 | (49-30) 8188-6262 | fax 8188-6249

"Popular" with "politicians, movie stars" and other "celebrity patrons", "this Gendarmenmarkt classic" in Mitte is known for a "wonderful menu" of French-German fare – including "delicious fish" dishes and some of "the best Wiener schnitzel in Berlin" – "hospitably" presented in a "large", "beautiful" "brasserie" setting with "pre-war flair"; still, those with "unfulfilled expectations" posit that "one pays for the stargazing" and "glam" scene, adding that certain "snooty" staffers are "less accommodating when serving Mr. and Ms. Average."

Dachgartenrestaurant *German* 13 | 18 | 14 | E

Mitte | Platz der Republik | (49-30) 226-2990 | fax 2264-9943 | www.feinkost-kaefer.de

With its "fabulous setting atop the restored Reichstag" in Mitte, this "modern" spot overlooking "both historic and new Berlin" is "an absolute must" for first-time visitors; most say there's "nothing special" to report about the "ok" German cuisine or the "conveyor-belt service" from "stressed-out" staffers who "pack the tourists in, get them fed, take a photo and get them out", but "who cares" when there are such "to-die-for views"?; P.S. "you'd better make a reservation" "to bypass the long line."

Diekmann *German/International* 21 | 18 | 21 | M

Charlottenburg | Meinekestr. 7 | (49-30) 883-3321 | fax 8855-3159
Dahlem | Châlet Suisse | Clayallee 99 | (49-30) 832-6362 | fax 8322-1955 ◐
Mitte | Weinhaus Huth | Alte Potsdamer Str. 5 | (49-30) 2529-7524 | fax 2529-7525 ◐
NEW **Mitte** | Hauptbahnhof | Europlatz 1 | (49-30) 209-1929 | fax 2091-1929 ◐
www.j-diekmann.de

Of this "fantastic"quartet serving "German food with a nouveau twist", "the original", a brasserie on the ground floor of a townhouse in a "beautiful Charlottenburg spot", "offers a genteel experience", while the "always-bustling Potsdamer Platz" branch in Mitte provides a "reliable dinner before the Philharmonie"; unlike its French-inflected siblings, the one in Dahlem has a Swiss flavor and the newest locale on Europlatz boasts an oyster bar, but each is "a safe bet" for a "good selection" of "tasty", "well-prepared food" served by "friendly people" in "pleasant" digs.

Die Quadriga ☒ *French/Mediterranean* 23 | 25 | 23 | E

Wilmersdorf | Brandenburger Hof | Eislebener Str. 14 | (49-30) 2140-5650 | fax 2140-5100 | www.brandenburger-hof.com

"A memorable meal" awaits at this "nice hotel dining" venue whose two rooms flank a "beautiful [Japanese] garden" in Wilmersdorf's Brandenburger Hof; chef Bobby Bräuer creates a "varied menu" of "exquisite" New French-Mediterranean cuisine, which is accompanied by an extensive all-German wine list and "incredible service" from a "helpful, charming" staff; sure, it's "somewhat expensive", but it's definitely a "first-class" experience; N.B. there's live jazz on Tuesdays.

Fellini ◐ *Italian* 19 | 20 | 22 | E

Mitte | Hilton Berlin | Mohrenstr. 30 | (49-30) 20230 | fax 2023-4269 | www.hilton.com

"Wonderful service" from "attentive" staffers who "always have a smile on their faces" sets the mood at this Italian "in the basement" of the Hilton Berlin, at the Gendarmenmarkt in Mitte; admirers advise "spoil yourself with something good" from the "delicious" menu and enjoy the "eye-catching decor" of the "beautiful" "cellar vault"; some say there's "nothing spectacular" going on in the kitchen, but more appreciate the "pleasing food" and "surprisingly" "appropriate" prices.

44 *French/International* 23 18 21 VE

Wilmersdorf | Swissôtel | Augsburger Str. 44 | (49-30) 220-102-288 | fax 220-102-222 | www.restaurant44.de

Fans of chef "Tim Raue, one of the *'junge wilde'* (young wilds)", credit him for translating his "good ideas" into "excellent", "inventive" New French-International cooking that "never fails to excite", making "multiple" visits to this "quiet, romantic" venue on the top floor of Wilmersdorf's modern Swissôtel "a joy"; critics, though, claim the menu "tries very hard to be interesting" but "overwhelms the taste buds with competing flavors"; N.B. ask for a table on the small terrace overlooking the famous Kurfürstendamm.

NEW Grill Royal *Seafood/Steak* 21 20 20 E

Mitte | Friedrichstr. 105B | (49-30) 2887 9288 | www.grillroyal.com

This "great" new steakhouse and seafooder in trendy Mitte (the "best location in Berlin") offers "delicious" food and is "often packed" with a chic crowd that doesn't complain about the "expensive" tabs; the spacious wood and marble setting boasts a vintage motor boat, a "spectacular" terrace and a view of the Spree River.

Guy *French/Mediterranean* 21 19 19 E

Mitte | Jägerstr. 59-60 | (49-30) 2094-2600 | fax 2094-2610 | www.guy-restaurant.de

Ensconced "in a courtyard" in Mitte between the Gendarmenmarkt and the Friedrichstrasse shopping area, this French-Med is a "favorite regular stop in town", "satisfying" surveyors with "delicious" fare that's "hard to beat", not to mention "tasteful decor" and "excellent service" from a "well-trained staff"; "it isn't cheap, but the bill isn't irritating" - especially if you "go on someone else's tab"; P.S. though the "dining area is beautiful", "the terrace is an oasis."

NEW Hartmanns *German/Mediterranean* 22 20 19 E

Kreuzberg | Fichtestr. 31 | (49-30) 6120-1003 | fax 6120-1380 | www.hartmanns-restaurant.de

Chef-owner Stefan Hartmann's intimate and "enjoyable" new spot combines German and Mediterranean influences and the result is a "delicious" and "very creative" combination; set in the basement of a classical turn-of-the-century Kreuzberg townhouse, the serene minimalist space gets a kick of color from modern art and strikingly spare floral arrangements.

Lindenlife *German* 16 15 14 M

Mitte | Unter den Linden 54-60 | (49-30) 206-290-333 | fax 206-290-335 | www.lindenlife.de

Located in a parliament office building, this "established" spot in Mitte attracts businessmen, politicians and visitors to its "prominent location" "along the historic Unter den Linden tourist mile" even through the "average" German fare is "not exciting"; while the "environment is pleasant" enough, offering a "view into a TV broadcasting studio", a recent renovation may make those who say it "is not an eye catcher" change their minds.

	FOOD	DECOR	SERVICE	COST
Lorenz Adlon	24	24	22	VE
MaoThai am Fasanenplatz	20	16	20	M
Margaux	22	23	20	VE
Maxwell	24	21	16	E
Paris Bar	16	18	14	E

Lorenz Adlon *French*

Mitte | Hotel Adlon Kempinski | Unter den Linden 77 | (49-30) 22610 | fax 2261-2222 | www.hotel-adlon.de

"Indulge yourself" at this "romantic" "gourmet restaurant" in Mitte's Hotel Adlon Kempinski, "just steps from the Brandenburg Gate"; it features classic French cuisine, a "comprehensive list" of "exquisite wines", a "stylish" setting and "refined staff" that gives one a "feeling of being pampered"; yes, it's "very expensive", but most are prepared "to pay a little more" for such a "luxe" experience - after all, "you have to spoil yourself sometime."

MaoThai am Fasanenplatz *Thai*

Wilmersdorf | Meierottostr. 1 | (49-30) 883-2823 | fax 8867-5658

MaoThai Stammhaus *Thai*

Prenzlauer Berg | Wörther Str. 30 | (49-30) 441-9261 | fax 4434-2090

"Tasty, tempting" Thai fare made from "fresh" ingredients and prepared at "all levels of spiciness" ensure that patrons "eat well" at this Wilmersdorf Siamese set in a "pleasantly" restored townhouse; the "friendly, quick" staffers decked out in "nice costumes" are "accommodating" and "always able to cope with large groups"; N.B. its Stammhaus sibling opened post-Survey.

Margaux *French*

Mitte | Unter den Linden 78 | (49-30) 2265-2611 | fax 2265-2612 | www.margaux-berlin.de

With its "impressive decor", this "fine-dining" venue in Mitte is a "chic", "cosmopolitan" showcase for the "world-class" creations of chef-owner Michael Hoffmann, whose "high-end" "classic French fare" is "prepared with amazing care" (and some avant-garde touches) then offered with "generous pours" from "an extraordinary wine list"; many are also "wowed" by the "excellent staff", though a few feel they "could do better"; P.S. the desserts are "unbelievable."

Maxwell *French/International*

Mitte | Bergstr. 22 | (49-30) 280-7121 | fax 2859-9848 | www.restaurant-maxwell.de

For "some of the coolest dining" around, experience an "enjoyable meal" at this "trendy" spot set in a "former brewery" "tucked away in a courtyard" in Mitte, where an "inventive" French-International menu of "excellent" cuisine (incorporating Asian, Italian and German influences) is offered in a "beautiful high-ceilinged" space with "modern but not chilly furnishings"; sure, "the service could be more efficient", but at least "the friendly staff" "will smile at you - which in Berlin is like striking gold."

Paris Bar *French*

Charlottenburg | Kantstr. 152 | (49-30) 313-8052 | fax 313-2816 | www.parisbar.de

Offering a "great getaway from the Teutonic vibe of Berlin", this "happening" Charlottenburg "landmark" with a "classic French" brasserie feel "has been here forever" and is "always crowded" with fans who "love" "sitting beside" "celebrities and captains of industry" in "homey" digs; still, those who find the "food unremarkable" and the "staff arrogant" insist this "institution" is "now well past its prime", adding "you'll have to dig deep into your pockets" when the bill comes.

Paris-Moskau ⊄ *French/Mediterranean* 20 | 18 | 20 | E

Tiergarten | Alt-Moabit 141 | (49-30) 394-2081 | fax 394-2602 | www.paris-moskau.de

A "special place" to many, this French-Med brasserie in Tiergarten, "near the Reichstag" and "on the old rail tracks" between Paris and Moscow, features a "varied" menu of "imaginative creations" with "great flavor combinations"; the "friendly" staffers "know their jobs extremely well" and the "cozy" setting - a half-timbered tavern dating from 1898 - has "great ambiance", so even if the cash-only experience "could be cheaper", most come away "satisfied."

NEW **San Nicci** ◐ *Italian* 21 | 19 | 21 | E

Mitte | Friedrichstr. 101 | (49-30) 3064-54980 | www.san-nicci.de

"Who knew Italian in Germany translates well?" but that's what supporters say about this Mitte sibling of Berlin's very popular Borchardt that's being touted as the "new place to go" for breakfast, lunch and dinner; it boasts a "great location" a stone's throw from the Admiralspalast theater, and the "cosmopolitan" brasserie setting includes dramatic columns and an expansive courtyard.

VAU ⊠ *International* 26 | 23 | 25 | VE

Mitte | Jägerstr. 54-55 | (49-30) 202-9730 | fax 2029-7311 | www.vau-berlin.de

"You can't miss" this Mitte "must", an "exquisite-in-every-way" "oasis" "next to the famous Gendarmenmarkt" that's rated No. 1 in Berlin for Food; chef and TV personality Kolja Kleeberg's "heavenly menu" of "excellent", "extremely creative" International cuisine, a "quality wine list", "wonderful service" from a "thoughtful, unintrusive" staff and "cool", "crisp, modern" decor add up to a "superb dining experience" that most insist is "worth the splurge", even if your "wallet still hurts" long after (at least the "lunch prices are more reasonable").

Vox ◐ *French/Asian* 23 | 23 | 24 | E

Tiergarten | Grand Hyatt | Marlene-Dietrich-Platz 2 | (49-30) 2553-1234 | fax 2553-1235 | www.berlin.grand.hyatt.com

"Everything is top-notch" at this hotel restaurant overlooking the Potsdamer Platz shopping area in Tiergarten's Grand Hyatt, where the service from the "well-trained staff" is "discreet and attentive", the "unconventional decor" is "posh and stylish" and the "great open kitchen's" "fantastic" food - ranging from "excellent sushi" to "interesting" New French-Asian dishes - "is a pleasure for the palate"; no wonder some foreigners insist they "would fly to Berlin just to have dinner here again."

Other Noteworthy Places

Desbrosses *French*

Ritz-Carlton Berlin | Potsdamer Platz 3 | (49-30) 337-777 | fax 337-775-555 | www.ritzcarlton.com

Edd's ◐ Ⓜ ⊄ *Thai*

Lützowstr. 81 | (49-30) 215-5294 | fax 2300-5794 | www.edds-thairestaurant.de

Enoiteca Il Calice ◐ *Italian*

Walter-Benjamin-Platz 4 | (49-30) 324-2308 | fax 324-9737 | www.enoiteca-il-calice.de

Facil [S] *Eurasian*
Mandala Hotel | Potsdamer Str. 3 | (49-30) 590-051-234 | fax 590-052-222 | www.facil.de

Felix ClubRestaurant [S][M] *Mediterranean*
Adlon Palais | Behrenstr. 72 | (49-30) 206-2860 | fax 206-28611 | www.felixrestaurant.de

First Floor [S][M] *French*
Hotel Palace | Budapester Str. 45 | (49-30) 2502-1020 | fax 2502-1119 | www.firstfloor.palace.de

Fischers Fritz *French/Seafood*
Regent Berlin Hotel | Charlottenstr. 49 | (49-30) 2033-6363 | fax 2033-6119 | www.fischersfritzberlin.com

Grand Restaurant M ◐ *German*
Maritim Hotel | Stauffenbergstr. 26 | (49-30) 2065-1029 | fax 2065-1000 | www.maritim.de

Horváth ◐[M] *German/International*
Paul-Lincke-Ufer 44a | (49-30) 6128-9992 | fax 6128-9595 | www.restaurant-horvath.de

Hugos [S] *French/Mediterranean*
Hotel InterContinental | Budapester Str. 2 | (49-30) 2602-1263 | fax 2602-1239 | www.hugos-restaurant.de

Lochner [M] *German/Mediterranean*
Lützowplatz 5 | (49-30) 2300-5220 | fax 2300-4021 | www.lochner-restaurant.de

Midtown Grill ◐ *American/Steak*
Marriott Hotel | Ebertstr. 3 | (49-30) 220-006-410 | fax 220-001-000 | www.midtown-grill.de

Ming's Garden *Chinese*
Tauentzienstr. 16 | (49-30) 211-8914 | fax 217-7095

Pan Asia ◐ *Pan-Asian*
Rosenthaler Str. 38 | (49-30) 2790-8811 | fax 2790-8812 | www.panasia.de

Quarré *International*
Hotel Adlon Kempinski | Unter den Linden 77 | (49-30) 22610 | fax 2261-2222 | www.hotel-adlon.de

Remake ◐ *Mediterranean/European*
Große Hamburger Str. 32 | (49-30) 2005-4102 | fax 2005-4103 | www.restaurant-remake.de

Rutz ◐[S] *International*
Chausseestr. 8 | (49-30) 2462-8760 | fax 2462-8761 | www.rutz-weinbar.de

Shiro I Shiro *Japanese/European*
Rosa-Luxemburg-Str. 11 | (49-30) 9700-4790 | fax 9700-4795 | www.shiroishiro.com

Vitrum [S][M] *European*
Ritz-Carlton Berlin | Potsdamer Platz 3 | (49-30) 337-777 | fax 337-775-555 | www.ritzcarlton.com

Vivaldi *Mediterranean*
Schlosshotel | Brahmsstr. 10 | (49-30) 895-840 | fax 8958-4800 | www.schlosshotelberlin.com

FOOD | DECOR | SERVICE | COST

Brussels

TOP FOOD RANKING

	Restaurant	Cuisine
28	Comme Chez Soi	Belgian
	Bruneau	Classic French
27	La Truffe Noire	French/Italian
	Sea Grill	International/Seafood
26	La Maison du Cygne	Classic French
25	Chez Marie	Classic French
24	L'Ecailler du Palais Royal	Seafood
	Villa Lorraine*	Belgian/French
	L'Ogenblik	French
	Café des Spores	European
	Bon-Bon	Belgian/French
23	Blue Elephant	Thai
	Le Fourneau	French/Tapas
	La Maison du Boeuf	Classic French
	Scheltema	Classic French/Brasserie
	L'Idiot du Village	Belgian/French
	La Manufacture	French
22	Lola	French/Italian
	La Porte des Indes	Indian
	Friture René	Belgian
21	Le Marmiton	Belgian/French
	Aux Armes de Bruxelles	Belgian
20	La Quincaillerie	French Brasserie
	Bonsoir Clara	French/Mediterranean
19	't Kelderke	Belgian
	Brasseries Georges	Belgian/French
	In 't Spinnekopke	Belgian
18	Belga Queen	Belgian
16	Amadeus	International

Amadeus M *International* | 16 | 22 | 16 | M

Ixelles | Rue Veydt 13 | (32-2) 538-3427 | fax 537-2542

"Mediocre" International food and service "do not quite ruin the experience of eating in one of the most atmospheric restaurants in Ixelles", a converted artist's studio with "candlelight", intimate "alcoves" and a "charming" "old courtyard"; if you're a "romantic" and a wallet-watcher, moderate prices also add appeal.

Aux Armes de Bruxelles M *Belgian* | 21 | 19 | 19 | E

Ilôt Sacré | Rue des Bouchers 13 | (32-2) 511-5550 | fax 514-3381 | www.armesdebruxelles.be

It's "a jewel in the otherwise pedestrian" and tourist-trap-laden Rue des Bouchers say supporters of this Belgian "favorite" since 1921; "few things are better than mussels in Brussels" so the ones here are a "must", along with "wonderful *waterzooi*" from the "wide

* Indicates a tie with restaurant above

classic menu"; it's a "popular", "prototypical brasserie" for "eating like the locals."

Belga Queen ◐ *Belgian* — 18 | 27 | 17 | E

Lower Town | Rue du Fossé aux Loups 32 | (32-2) 217-2187 | fax 229-3179 | www.belgaqueen.be

"Sexy" describes the "fab" setting - an "ornate" "domed", stained-glass ceiling, moody lighting and cool unisex loos - of this Belgian brasserie housed in what was a former belle epoque bank in the Lower Town; gourmands gripe that the "food is nothing to write home about" and say "stick to the seafood platter" and raw bar, but scenesters simply shrug and check out the "beautiful people."

Blue Elephant *Thai* — 23 | 22 | 21 | E

Uccle | Chaussée de Waterloo 1120 | (32-2) 374-4962 | fax 375-4468 | www.blueelephant.com

For 27 years, this Thai in Uccle (with other outposts from London to Dubai) has been leading loyalists on a "wonderful culinary journey" with "fine", "wonderfully spiced" fare; a "beautiful" setting "complete with coconuts and flowers" leads to thoughts of "lush" lands and away from the realities of "Belgian weather."

Bon-Bon Ⓢ Ⓜ *Belgian/French* — 24 | 19 | 19 | E

Uccle | Rue des Carmélites 93 | (32-2) 346-6615 | fax 538-7982 | www.bon-bon.be

Chef Christophe Hardiquest's market-driven "modern and refined" Belgian-French cuisine is improvisational and "excellent" and earns him "rising star" status; located in a quiet residential street in Uccle, his intimate bistro relies on claret-colored walls and gray banquettes for its attractive, unpretentious appeal.

Bonsoir Clara *French/Mediterranean* — 20 | 20 | 17 | E

St-Géry | Rue Antoine Dansaert 22-26 | (32-2) 502-0990 | fax 502-5557 | www.bonsoirclara.be

"Hip" French-Mediterranean set on a cool bohemian shopping street and in a "good location in St-Géry, with all the lively bars and pubs just around the corner"; while the food is not "memorable" it's "well done" and as "colorful" as the multitoned, illuminated art deco glass panels on the walls.

Brasseries Georges ◐ *Belgian/French* — 19 | 16 | 17 | E

Uccle | Avenue Winston Churchill 259 | (32-2) 347-2100 | fax 344-0245 | www.brasseriesgeorges.be

This big, bustling brasserie next to the Bois de la Cambre park in Uccle is a classic lunch destination; "simple" Belgian-French fare with an emphasis on seafood (including 16 varieties of the "best fresh oysters" in season), "reasonable prices" for the quality, 30 wines by the glass and a "friendly" atmosphere make it a "popular" place, so "reserve."

Bruneau *French* — 28 | 25 | 28 | VE

Ganshoren | Avenue Broustin 73-75 | (32-2) 421-7070 | fax 425-9726 | www.bruneau.be

"Exquisite" exclaim admirers of this 31-year-old Classic French in an elegant double townhouse in residential Ganshoren, about a 15-minute taxi ride from the City Center; chef-owner Jean-Pierre Bruneau's "outstanding" cuisine is complemented by equally "excellent service", a "tremendous" wine list, handsome dining rooms and a summer garden terrace; in all, it's a very "costly" but "outstanding" experience.

Café des Spores ◐ 🅂 *European* 24 | 20 | 23 | E

Saint-Gilles | Chaussée D'Alsemberg 103 | (32-2) 534-1303 | www.cafedesspores.be

Fungi fans sprout up at this small, simple European cafe in Saint-Gilles for the namesake spores - namely, "delicious" and "varied fresh mushroom dishes" that are market-driven; oenophiles can also be accommodated since there is "a fine array of wines" to complement the earthy ingredients.

Chez Marie 🅂 🄼 *French* 25 | 21 | 22 | E

Ixelles | Rue Alphonse de Witte 40 | (32-2) 644-3031 | fax 644-2737

A firm favorite with EU professionals, this Classic French in Ixelles features chef Lilian Devaux's "delicious" cuisine, including a great "value" prix fixe lunch at 17 euros; "tiny", "warm" and "cozy" with "low lights", mirrors and candles, it's also "romantic."

Comme Chez Soi 🅂 🄼 *Belgian* 28 | 24 | 27 | VE

Lower Town | Place Rouppe 23 | (32-2) 512-2921 | fax 511-8052 | www.commechezsoi.be

Pierre Wynants and his son-in-law Lionel Rigolet's "sublime" Belgian in the Lower Town is Voted No. 1 for Food in Brussels; a "very attentive but unobtrusive" staff presides over a "fantastic" art nouveau setting with stained-glass flower motifs, although the chef's table in the kitchen is also a coveted spot; it's "extremely expensive", but it's a "gem that's a joy to visit" and "one of the world's great restaurants."

Friture René *Belgian* 22 | 17 | 19 | M

Anderlecht | Place de la Résistance 14 | (32-2) 523-2876

Locals love this unpretentious (a red neon sign marks the spot) but "renowned" 1932 Anderlecht Belgian specializing in some of the "best moules and frites in Brussels"; "come hungry" knowing that the "portions are quite large" and the price is right.

In 't Spinnekopke 🅂 *Belgian* 19 | 18 | 17 | M

St-Géry | Place du Jardin aux Fleurs 1 | (32-2) 511-8695 | fax 513-2497 | www.spinnekopke.be

'In the Little Spider's Head' features over 100 "great" Belgian beers, many of which also turn up in the "tasty", "authentic", moderately priced dishes; set in a former 1762 stagecoach inn in St-Géry, its interior with low ceilings and sloping floors is "cozy" and "charming", making it "a favorite of locals and savvy tourists alike."

La Maison du Boeuf *French* 23 | 18 | 22 | E

Upper Town | Hilton Brussels | Boulevard de Waterloo 38 | (32-2) 504-1334 | fax 504-2111 | www.hilton.com

"When you miss USA prime ribs, this is the place to go" urge enthusiasts of this Classic French with a focus on beef in the Upper Town that's "fantastic for a Hilton"; a "tremendous wine list", "attentive" service and a warm setting with views of palatial gardens make for an "enjoyable experience even if dining alone."

	FOOD	DECOR	SERVICE	COST
La Maison du Cygne	26	27	24	VE
La Manufacture	23	24	20	E
La Porte des Indes	22	21	19	E
La Quincaillerie	20	26	18	E
La Truffe Noire	27	22	25	VE
L'Ecailler du Palais Royal	24	21	22	VE

La Maison du Cygne ☒ *French*

Grand' Place | Rue Charles Buls 2 | (32-2) 511-8244 | fax 514-3148 | www.lamaisonducygne.be

"Beautifully decorated" and in a "stunning location" "overlooking the historic Grand' Place" is this long-standing Classic French in a former 17th-century guildhall; velvet banquettes and paintings by Belgian masters are the "magnificent" backdrop for "excellent" cuisine, "exceptional service" and an "extensive wine list"; given the stratospheric prices, it's ironic that Karl Marx once worked on his Communist Manifesto here.

La Manufacture ☒ *French*

Ste-Catherine | Rue Notre Dame du Sommeil 12-20 | (32-2) 502-2525 | fax 502-2715 | www.manufacture.be

Housed in a "famous old" former handbag factory - hence the name - this "innovative", "delicious" and fashionable French in the up-and-coming Ste-Catherine district is "not expensive if you compare the price with the quality of the meals"; the "great atmosphere" comes from an expansive, dramatic industrial space with leather banquettes, stone tables and a "sexy staff."

La Porte des Indes *Indian*

Ixelles | Avenue Louise 455 | (32-2) 647-8651 | fax 640-3059 | www.blueelephant.com/pi

"The best Indian food in Brussels by far" brag believers in this "expensive" subcontinental in Ixelles, the brainchild of Karl Steppe, a Belgian antiques dealer, who also owns the global Blue Elephant chain; a traditionally clad staff and vibrant red-and-mauve "setting that's unapologetically colonial" - wooden carvings, tropical flowers and potted palms - add to the authentic experience.

La Quincaillerie ☒ *French*

Ixelles | Rue du Page 45 | (32-2) 533-9833 | fax 539-4095 | www.quincaillerie.be

This "unique" two-story Ixelles "setting couldn't be more quaint" - an old former hardware store (which is what its name means) with brass fittings, a "wall full of little drawers" and a giant clock; "good", "hearty" French brasserie fare and a "festive" atmosphere draw couples to its balcony and business folks to its oyster bar.

La Truffe Noire ☒ *French/Italian*

Ixelles | Boulevard de la Cambre 12 | (32-2) 640-4422 | fax 647-9704 | www.truffenoire.com

A "must for truffle lovers", this "excellent" French-Italian in Ixelles features the unearthed fungus from start (with carpaccio) to finish (substituting its sweet chocolate namesake at dessert); "perfect service" and a "sophisticated" room with modern paintings round out the extravagant experience; of course, you'll be digging deep too when it comes time to pay the big bill.

L'Ecailler du Palais Royal ☒ *Seafood*

Grand Sablon | Rue Bodenbroek 18 | (32-2) 512-8751 | fax 511-9950 | www.lecaillerdupalaisroyal.be

Since 1967, not a morsel of meat has passed through the portals of this "top-quality" seafooder featuring "fish, just fish, but the best" of the catch in the Grand Sablon; "excellent service" and a "wonderful" two-story setting (one room with soothing traditional plaid decor, the other a scarlet salon) make it "great for business lunches", but the exuberant bar with "turquoise fish-scale tiles" is "good for single diners too."

NEW Le Fourneau *French/Tapas* 23 | 20 | 21 | E

Ste-Catherine | Place Sainte-Catherine 8 | (32-2) 513-1002

A "must-visit" is what supporters say about this "excellent" new French small-plates specialist whose "sophisticated" "handling of ingredients on a continuously changing menu" "makes it a place to return to whenever the season changes"; you'll "love the location" on medieval Sainte Catherine square, and inside a handful of tables, long bar and open kitchen are set against a spare but stylish black-and-white room punctuated with snappy red lights.

Le Marmiton *Belgian/French* 21 | 19 | 20 | E

Ilôt Sacré | Rue des Bouchers 43A | (32-2) 511-7910 | fax 502-1864 | www.lemarmiton.be

At this long-standing "gem in the Rue des Bouchers", the city's packed restaurant district, the emphasis of the "good quality" classic Belgian-French fare is on fish dishes like bouillabaisse; it's a "favorite" haunt for many because the "unpretentious" but pretty bistro setting - brick walls, brass lamps and a view of the beautiful arcade, Les Galleries Royales St. Hubert - makes for "a cozy night out."

L'Idiot du Village *Belgian/French* 23 | 21 | 21 | E

Marolles | Rue Notre-Seigneur 19 | (32-2) 502-5582

You'd be the idiot if you didn't book way ahead at this popular tiny boîte tucked away in a 17th-century house in Marolles; "inventive" Belgian-French cuisine that "soars with flavor" and a "quirky" "bohemian-chic" atmosphere with "whimsical" flea-market decor attract "Eurocrats wanting to get in touch with their inner hippie."

L'Ogenblik *French* 24 | 18 | 20 | E

Ilôt Sacré | Galerie des Princes 1 | (32-2) 511-6151 | fax 513-4158 | www.ogenblik.be

"What a bistro should be" declare devotees of this French that's in part of the "beautiful" glassed-in Galeries Saint-Hubert, the "oldest shopping arcade in Europe"; there's "delicious food", an "excellent wine list", "attentive service" and a homey setting, so although it's been a "favorite Brussels haunt" since 1969, it still attracts a cosmopolitan crowd.

Lola *French/Italian* 22 | 20 | 19 | E

Grand Sablon | Place du Grand Sablon 33 | (32-2) 514-2460 | fax 514-2653 | www.restolola.be

This French-Italian establishment is in a "great location" for "people-watching" on the "beautiful" Place du Grand Sablon; "tasty" food, "charming" service and "cool" "modern" decor with bright primary colors add to its appeal.

Scheltema *French* 23 | 19 | 19 | E

Ilôt Sacré | Rue des Dominicains 7 | (32-2) 512-2084 | fax 512-4482 | www.scheltema.be

Named after a Dutch poet, this huge, "bustling", bi-level Classic French brasserie in the Ilôt Sacré features "excellent seafood and desserts" and a warm burnished wood setting; "friendly waiters" and an "Old Europe without the stiff upper lip atmosphere" add to the "wonderful experience."

Sea Grill [S] *International/Seafood* 27 23 27 VE

Lower Town | Radisson SAS Royal Hotel | Rue du Fossé aux Loups 47 | (32-2) 217-9225 | fax 227-3127 | www.seagrill.be

"Embedded in the Radisson SAS Royal Hotel" in the Lower Town is this "top-class" International seafooder with "superb" cuisine, "an excellent wine list" and "incomparable service"; still, some carp about the corporate atmosphere and sky-high prices – it's so "expensive" that even "expense accounts will get strained here."

't Kelderke ◐ *Belgian* 19 17 16 M

Grand' Place | Grand' Place 15 | (32-2) 513-7344 | fax 512-3081 | www2.resto.be/kelderke

"If you really want to eat as the Belgians do", this 1921 stalwart right on the Grand' Place is "the place"; generous portions of "traditional dishes", an interesting beer selection, "warm", vaulted-brick-cellar setting and "inexpensive prices for the locale" mean it's always "crowded and difficult to get a table."

Villa Lorraine [S] *Belgian/French* 24 25 25 VE

Uccle | Chaussée de la Hulpe 28 | (32-2) 374-3163 | fax 372-0195 | www.villalorraine.be

Nestled on the fringes of the "beautiful" Bois de la Cambre in Uccle, about a 20-minute taxi ride from the City Center, is this "landmark" "temple of Belgian-French haute cuisine" in a 19th-century villa; a "posh" setting, "fine food", sterling service and a "stellar wine cellar" lead to long, lovely lunches or "romantic evenings", particularly out on the summer garden terrace; N.B. jacket required.

Other Noteworthy Places

Bleu de Toi [S] *Belgian/French*
Rue des Alexiens 73 | (32-2) 502-4371 | fax 502-4371 | www.bleudetoi.be

Bocconi *Italian*
Hotel Amigo | Rue de l'étuve 9 | (32-2) 547-4715 | fax 547-4767 | www.ristorantebocconi.com

Castello Banfi [S] [M] *Italian*
Rue Bodenbroek 12 | (32-2) 512-8794 | fax 512-8794 | www.castellobanfi.be

Ce Soir On Dîne à Marrakech [M] *Moroccan*
Avenue Brugmann 408 | (32-2) 347-7601 | fax 346-6423 | www2.resto.be/cesoirondineamarrakech

Claude Dupont [M] *French*
Avenue Vital Riethuisenlaan 46 | (32-2) 426-0000 | fax 426-6540

De Bijgaarden [S] *French*
Isidoor Van Beverenstraat 20 | (32-2) 466-4485 | fax 463-0811 | www.debijgaarden.be

De La Vigne à l'Assiette [S] [M] *French*
Rue de la Longue Haie 51 | (32-2) 647-6803 | fax 647-6803

de Maurice à Olivier [S] [M] *French*
Chaussée de Roodebeek 246 | (32-2) 771-3398

Jaloa 🅂 *French/Mediterranean*
Place Vieille Halle aux Bles 31 | (32-2) 512-1831 | www.jaloa.com

La Belle Maraîchère *French/Seafood*
Place Sainte-Catherine 11A | (32-2) 512-9759 | fax 513-7691 | www.labellemaraichere.com

La Canne en Ville 🅂 *Belgian/French*
Rue de la Réforme 22 | (32-2) 347-2926 | fax 347-6989 | www.lacanneenville.be

L'Alban Chambon 🅂 *French*
Hôtel Métropole | Place de Brouckère 31 | (32-2) 217-2300 | fax 218-0220 | www.metropolehotel.be

L'Ancienne Poissonnerie 🅂 *Italian*
Rue du Trône 65 | (32-2) 502-7505

Le Chalet de la Forêt 🅂 *French*
Drève de Lorraine 43 | (32-2) 374-5416 | fax 374-3571 | www.lechaletdelaforet.be

Le Fils de Jules Ⓜ *Basque/French*
Rue du Page 35 | (32-2) 534-0057 | www.filsdejules.be

Le Loup-Galant 🅂Ⓜ *French*
Quai aux Barques 4 | (32-2) 219-9998 | fax 219-9998 | www2.resto.be/loupgalant

Le PaSSage 🅂 *French*
Avenue Jean et Pierre Carsoel 13 | (32-2) 374-6694 | www.lepassage.be

L'Epicerie *French*
Le Méridien | Carrefour de l'Europe 3 | (32-2) 548-4716 | fax 548-4080 | www.brussels.lemeridien.com

Les Brigittines 🅂 *Belgian/French*
Place de la Chapelle 5 | (32-2) 512-6891 | fax 512-4130 | www.lesbrigittines.com

Les Salons de l'Atalaïde ◐ *French/Mediterranean*
Chaussée de Charleroi 89 | (32-2) 534-6456 | fax 537-2154 | www.lessalonsatalaide.be

L'Huitrière *Seafood*
Quai aux Briques 20 | (32-2) 512-0866 | fax 512-1281

Notos 🅂Ⓜ *Greek*
Rue de Livourne 154 | (32-2) 513-2959 | www.notos.be

San Daniele 🅂Ⓜ *Italian*
Avenue Charles-Quint 6 | (32-2) 426-7923 | fax 426-9214 | www.san-daniele.be

Senza Nome 🅂 *Italian*
Rue Royale Sainte-Marie 22 | (32-2) 223-1617 | fax 223-1617

Tour D'y Voir 🅂Ⓜ *French*
Place du Grand Sablon 8-9 | (32-2) 511-4043 | fax 511-0078 | www.tourdyvoir.be

Vismet 🅂Ⓜ *Seafood*
Place Sainte-Catherine 23 | (32-2) 218-8545 | fax 218-8546

FOOD | DECOR | SERVICE | COST

Budapest

TOP FOOD RANKING

	Restaurant	Cuisine
28	Baraka	International/Mediterranean
	Vadrózsa	Hungarian/International
27	Páva	Italian
25	Lou-Lou	French Bistro
	Kacsa	Hungarian/International
24	Gundel	Hungarian/International
	Fausto's	Tuscan
23	Café Kör	Hungarian/International
	Rézkakas	Hungarian
	Segal*	International
	Bistro Jardin	Hungarian/International
	Papageno*	International
	Kisbuda Gyöngye	Hungarian/International
21	Cyrano	Hungarian/International
	Kárpátia*	Hungarian
	Chez Daniel	French
20	Alabárdos	Hungarian
	Belcanto	Hungarian/International
	Remiz*	Hungarian/International
	Bagolyvár	Hungarian
	Múzeum	Hungarian/International
	Abszint	French
19	Mokka	International
17	Spoon Café & Lounge	Med./International
	Robinson	Hungarian/Mediterranean
	Centrál Kávéház	Hungarian/International
16	Menza	Hungarian

Abszint *French* 20 | 18 | 16 | M

Andrássy út | Andrássy út 34 | (36-1) 332-4993 | fax 332-4993 | www.abszint.hu

"Truly delicious" and "reasonably priced" Provençal dishes make for "a gourmet experience" at this "fun, lively" French spot "in a hip part of town" overlooking the busy Andrássy út; the "cozy" space, with its "nice light and colors", is "not ostentatious" but does have "lots of atmosphere", and the "courteous" staffers are "always polite", though "they tend to be a bit slow" when it's "full"; P.S. yes, it's a "great" "place for absinthe" too.

Alabárdos ☒ *Hungarian* 20 | 21 | 21 | E

Várnegyed | Országház utca 2 | (36-1) 356-0851 | fax 214-3814 | www.alabardos.hu

The "original decor" of weaponry on display recalls "the age of chivalry" at this "top-flight" Várnegyed spot with a "hospitable" staff and an "excellent menu" that offers both "gourmet and traditional" Hungarian

* Indicates a tie with restaurant above

"favorites"; if some feel tabs are "a bit higher than they should be", at least "big portions" come with the "big prices."

Bagolyvár *Hungarian* 20 | 18 | 20 | M

Városliget | Állatkerti út 2 | (36-1) 468-3110 | fax 363-1917 | www.bagolyvar.com

A "woman's" touch defines this "charming" Városliget "spot adjacent to the Budapest Zoo" that's "entirely staffed by ladies", from the "quick, precise" servers to the female "chefs who do a fine job" with the "wonderful traditional Hungarian cuisine"; a few feel its "restrained" "antique decor" "could be better", but all appreciate its "especially nice garden", and "compared to Gundel", its far pricier sibling next door, "it is indeed a better value."

Baraka *International/Mediterranean* 28 | - | 27 | E

Andrássy út | Andrássy Hotel | Andrássy út 111 | (36-1) 462-2189 | fax 322-9445 | www.andrassyhotel.com

"Truly one of Budapest's great finds", this "outstanding" International-Med ranking No. 1 for Food in the city moved Uptown from Belváros to a glam silver-and-black art deco-style space in the Andrássy Hotel; "running the show" is the "husband-and-wife team" of David and Leora Seboek, whose "regularly changing menu" of "inventive" "world cuisine" is "complemented by" an "expensive wine list" and "excellent service"; P.S. you'll also stand "a good chance of seeing local celebrities."

Belcanto ◐ *Hungarian/International* 20 | 18 | 24 | E

Terézváros | Dalszínház utca 8 | (36-1) 269-2786 | fax 311-9547 | www.belcanto.hu

Set in Terézváros, this "friendly" Hungarian-International is applauded by "music lovers" in part because it's "located near the [State] Opera" House but also because its "informal, relaxed staff" is composed of "smooth", "attentive" waiters who not only provide "impeccable service" "but are great singers too"; folks are further "impressed" with its "endless menu" of "proper food" - perhaps it's "a trifle expensive" and "not gourmet, but it's very good" and there's "plenty of it."

Bistro Jardin *Hungarian/International* 23 | 22 | 21 | E

Belváros | Kempinski Hotel Corvinus | Erzsébet tér 7-8 | (36-1) 429-3777 | fax 429-4777 | www.kempinski-budapest.com

You "can bring the most fastidious of guests" to this "favorite" in the Kempinski Hotel Corvinus in Belváros since you "can always rely on" chef Rudolf van Nunen's "high standards", as evidenced by his "delicious" Hungarian-International fare; the "pleasant atmosphere", "elegant" setting (including a "nice outside" terrace) and "first-class service" further "justify" the "expense"; meals here are accompanied by live jazz on Sundays, which adds to "the grand experience."

Café Kör ⊠⇏ *Hungarian/International* 23 | 18 | 23 | M

Lipótváros | Sas utca 17 | (36-1) 311-0053 | www.cafekor.com

Anyone "looking for delicious food at reasonable prices" - from "intellectuals" to "tourists" to "expats" - should check out this "charming", "classic" "hot spot near St. Stephen's" Basilica in Lipótváros, where a "wide choice" of "excellent" "traditional Hungarian fare" "and International dishes" is offered in "generous portions" by "friendly, upbeat" staffers who make you "feel as if you were surrounded by friends"; P.S. "don't skip dessert", as "you won't believe the variety of cakes and pastries!"

Centrál Kávéház *Hungarian/International* 17 | 19 | 16 | M

Belváros | Károlyi Mihály utca 9 | (36-1) 266-2110 | fax 266-4570 | www.centralkavehaz.hu

There's "always an interesting crowd" at this coffeehouse, "an island of peace and quiet" in bustling Belváros with an "authentic" 19th-century "period feeling" and a "welcoming atmosphere"; true, "there are better choices" for Hungarian-International food, and "service can be a bit perfunctory", but the staffers are "friendly" (save for "one or two grumpy ones") and "they don't rush you", which makes it a "great place to hang out, have strong coffee and chat with friends."

Chez Daniel *French* 21 | 16 | 16 | E

Terézváros | Szív utca 32 | (36-1) 302-4039 | fax 311-6670

"Indulge" in "good-sized portions" of "fine French food" featuring "quite outstanding flavors" at this "pleasant spot" inTerézváros, where regulars know to "ask the chef to choose" for them, ensuring a "memorable meal"; still, some are "stung [by] the price" (especially considering the "nothing-special decor"), while others cite "repeated requests" as evidence that the "service is acceptable but could be better"; P.S. wags wager it's fortunate that "Daniel's dog", who has the run of the restaurant, "is very well behaved."

Cyrano ◐ *Hungarian/International* 21 | 22 | 19 | E

Terézváros | Kristóf tér 6 | (36-1) 266-3096 | fax 266-6818

"Trendy and posh", this "recently remodeled" spot boasts an "elegant" yet "relaxing ambiance" (and an unusual chandelier shaped like an inverted Christmas tree); the "consistently creative" kitchen is "always experimenting" with the "very good" Hungarian-International menu, and the "attentive, polite" staff is "well trained and helpful"; in short, it's "one of the better places for a stylish lunch or dinner off of Váci utca" - especially on the "outside terrace."

Fausto's ⊠ *Tuscan* 24 | 18 | 24 | E

Erzsébetvaros | Székely Mihály utca 2 | (36-1) 877-6210 | www.fausto.hu

"A great evening" of "chic eating" awaits at this "excellent Italian" "in the old Jewish quarter" in Erzsébetvaros, where "top-notch service" from an "attentive" but "not constantly hovering" staff is matched by chef Fausto Di Vora's "outstanding" Tuscan fare; perhaps the food's "expensive", but fans insist there's "value" for the money, saying you'll "pay more for less in many other restaurants - on either side of the river."

Gundel *Hungarian/International* 24 | 26 | 25 | VE

Városliget | Állatkerti út 2 | (36-1) 468-4040 | fax 363-1917 | www.gundel.hu

"Memories are made" at this "venerable" Hungarian "legend" "near Hero's Square", a "palatial", "elaborately decorated", ultra-expensive "salon" with "turn-of-the-century grandeur" and "beautiful views" of Városliget; within its "elegant setting", a "cultured" staff "indulges" "lucky" patrons with "the epitome" of "quality service" and a "delicious menu" of "national and International cuisine"; factor in "marvelous strolling musicians" playing "wonderful" "live gypsy music" and you can expect a "magical evening in a magical city"; N.B. jacket required.

	FOOD	DECOR	SERVICE	COST
Kacsa ● *Hungarian/International*	25	19	23	E

Viziváros | Fö utca 75 | (36-1) 201-9992 | fax 201-9992 | www.kacsavendeglo.hu

Its "name means 'duck'", and "as you'd expect" you'll find "excellent" examples of that fowl's flesh on the "wide-ranging and delicious menu" of "magnificent" Hungarian-International fare at this "stellar" spot in Viziváros, where the "amazing meals" are heightened by "wonderful service" from a "lovely staff"; it's "pricey but not outrageous", and while the "not particularly captivating" "decor could be improved", at least the "atmosphere is romantic", making it "a must when you're in Budapest."

	FOOD	DECOR	SERVICE	COST
Kárpátia *Hungarian*	21	23	19	E

Belváros | Ferenciek tere 7-8 | (36-1) 317-3596 | fax 318-0591 | www.karpatia.hu

"The historic past makes its mark" on the present at this "fairly pricey" venue set in a circa-1877 Belváros building in which there's "not an unadorned inch" in the "over-the-top" yet mostly "tasteful" interior; the "varied" menu of "excellent" cuisine - including a "great Sunday smorgasbord" in winter - is "authentically Hungarian", the service is a "pleasure" (even if a few fault certain "indifferent" staffers) and a "nice gypsy violin ensemble" helps cement its status as a true "taste of Budapest."

	FOOD	DECOR	SERVICE	COST
Kisbuda Gyöngye ☒ *Hungarian/International*	23	19	23	E

Óbuda | Kenyeres utca 34 | (36-1) 368-9246 | fax 368-9227 | www.remiz.hu

A 'pearl' in Óbuda, this "favorite" is peopled by "observant" staffers with "high standards" who serve "exceptionally well-prepared" Hungarian-International fare featuring "all the good flavors of home cooking"; a few find the flea-market ambiance of its "intimate" setting "a little contrived", but most are won over by its old-world atmosphere and live piano, "wondering what else do you need?"

	FOOD	DECOR	SERVICE	COST
Lou-Lou ☒ *French*	25	18	20	E

Belváros | Vigyázó Ferenc utca 4 | (36-1) 312-4505 | fax 472-0595 | www.loulourestaurant.com

"Always a treat", this French bistro in Belváros brings a "modern" approach to its "delicious" fare, while its "excellent" staff provides "quick, attentive service", making for an "overall good dining experience"; as for the setting, perhaps the "tables are too close together for intimate conversation", but "the food is so scrumptious you don't mind the slightly cramped dining room"; N.B. a chic, post-Survey major renovation may outdate the above Decor score.

	FOOD	DECOR	SERVICE	COST
Menza ● *Hungarian*	16	17	16	M

Andrássy út | Liszt Ferenc tér 2 | (36-1) 413-1482 | fax 413-1483 | www.menza.co.hu

While the name of this Andrássy út spot translates to the rather prosaic "cafeteria", that doesn't keep a buzzing "mixed clientele" from "time-traveling to 1970s Hungary" via its "retro decor" and creative take on foods the locals "used to have in the school canteen"; the "not-too-fancy" digs and fare may be too "no-frills" for some, but the "friendly staff" "has a sense of humor", and the "reasonable prices" mean "people of modest means can have a nice meal out in Budapest."

Mokka ◐ *International* 19 | 21 | 20 | E

Belváros | Sas utca 4 | (36-1) 328-0081 | fax 328-0082 | www.mokkarestaurant.hu

This "trendy" spot near "St. Stephen's Basilica, just off a beautiful square" in Belváros, "takes guests on a culinary trip" with "wonderful" "Eastern"-influenced decor and an "eclectic" assortment of "creative" International fare served by a "smiling" staff; some say its "overly ambitious menu" marked by "exotic names and unusual ingredients" "tries too hard", with results ranging "from very good to passable", but most feel "it's worth the extravagant" prices.

Múzeum Ⓢ *Hungarian/International* 20 | 18 | 19 | M

Belváros | Múzeum Körút 12 | (36-1) 267-0375 | fax 338-4221 | www.muzeumkavehaz.hu

"Satisfied" surveyors salute this "classic" venue "quite close to the National Museum" in Belváros for Hungarian-International fare that's "well executed" "in a modern style", resulting in "attractive, delicious" dishes that are lighter yet still "traditional"; those who "fancy a bit of romance" also appreciate the "high standards" of the "courteous staff", as well as the "elegant dining room" whose "atmosphere, heavy with fin de siècle nostalgia", "recalls the old days of Hungary."

Papageno ◐Ⓢ *International* 23 | 19 | 22 | E

Belváros | Semmelweis utca 19 | (36-1) 485-0161

This "smart little" International bistro a "bit off the beaten path" on a quiet Belváros side street offers a "small but well-thought-out menu" and "innovative" cuisine; "wonderful service from a hip proprietor" and a "cozy" but chic atmosphere also make it "perfect for a romantic dinner."

Páva Ⓢ *Italian* 27 | 26 | 25 | VE

Belváros | Four Seasons Gresham Palace | Roosevelt tér 5-6 | (36-1) 268-6000 | fax 268-5000 | www.fourseasons.com/budapest

"First-rate Italian food on the banks of the Danube" is found at this "winner" (whose name means 'Peacock') within the "gorgeous" "art nouveau" Four Seasons Gresham Palace hotel "across from the Chain Bridge"; its "cutting-edge" cuisine is complemented by "a perfect Hungarian wine list", decor of "classical elegance (radiant but not ostentatious)", "lovely views" and "excellent service" from a "considerate" staff; in short, it's "one of the city's best" "for the real connoisseur."

Remiz *Hungarian/International* 20 | 17 | 20 | M

Zugliget | Budakeszi út 5 | (36-1) 394-1896 | fax 200-3843 | www.remiz.hu

A "likable staff" of "well-trained waiters" who are "precise, polite and not pushy" will "patiently" help you choose from the "great range of outstanding dishes on the menu" at this Zugliget Hungarian-International whose "ingenious decor" pays homage to the same-named tram depot next door; regulars report that "the grilled meat dishes are wonderful", but all "the cooking's great" - and "the prices are not sky-high"; P.S. don't miss "the especially beautiful garden area."

Rézkakas ◐ *Hungarian* 23 | 22 | 25 | E

Belváros | Veres Pálné utca 3 | (36-1) 267-0349 | fax 318-0038 | www.rezkakasrestaurant.com

An "excellent attitude toward customers" distinguishes the "professional" staff's "unusually" "top-notch service" at this "truly captivating" Belváros venue, a "lovely", "romantic" wood-paneled dining room where "terrific traditional Hungarian cuisine is complemented by a wonderful musical ensemble" playing "live gypsy music"; for such a "magical" (albeit "somewhat touristy") experience, most say "never mind the cost - what's important is that you enjoy yourself."

Robinson *Hungarian/Mediterranean* 17 17 16 E

Városliget | Városligeti tó | (36-1) 422-0224 | fax 422-0072 | www.robinsonrestaurant.hu

"Individual whims are satisfied" by the "varied" Hungarian-Med menu at this "pleasant" venue named after Daniel Defoe's *Robinson Crusoe* and situated "in a good spot" - its own tiny island; "lightning" staffers provide "fast service", but critics complain that the "not-so-great food" "costs too much, especially considering" the "small portions."

NEW **Segal** ◐ *International* 23 - 22 E

Terézváros | Ó utca 43-49 | (36-1) 354-7888 | www.segal.hu

"Superstar" chef Viktor Segal (ex top-rated Baraka) has opened his own new namesake establishment and the result is "innovative" and "excellent" International cuisine that "advances the Budapest palate to the next level" and is complemented by "attentive service"; N.B. a post-Survey move from Belváros to these new larger digs in Terézváros also comes with a garden.

Spoon Café & Lounge ◐ *Mediterranean/International* 17 22 18 E

Belváros | Vigadó tér 3 Kikötö | (36-1) 411-0934 | fax 411-0946 | www.spooncafe.hu

Set "on a boat" "docked on the Danube" by the Chain Bridge in Belváros, this "stylish" tri-level "floating restaurant" and "fashionable lounge" attracts a "cooler-than-thou crowd" of "trendy and chic" "hipsters" with its "novel concept"; some find "the wide-ranging menu" of Med-International fare to be "not particularly enticing", but most are content to "sit back and enjoy" "the spectacular view of Castle Hill across the river"; P.S. "visiting the restrooms is a must" experience!

Vadrózsa ◐ *Hungarian/International* 28 24 24 E

Rózsadomb | Pentelei Molnár utca 15 | (36-1) 326-5817 | fax 326-5809 | www.vadrozsa.hu

"Come hungry" to this "outstanding" "off-the-beaten-path" Rózsadomb 'Wild Rose' whose "fresh" Hungarian-International fare is "lovingly prepared" "with the finest ingredients" and full of "interesting flavors"; its "classic, elegant" setting (complete with a "charming private garden terrace") is "lovely, romantic and a little magical" thanks in part to "polite" staffers who provide "wonderful old-world service" "and a pianist who plays requests" - so "if you can't live in a mansion", at least "you can dine in one."

Other Noteworthy Places

Arany Kaviár *Russian/Seafood*

Ostrom utca 19 | (36-1) 201-6737 | fax 225-7371 | www.aranykaviar.hu

Arcade Bistro 🅂 *International*

Kiss János altábornagy utca 38 | (36-1) 225-1969 | fax 225-1968 | www.arcadebistro.fw.hu

Arrabona *Hungarian/Mediterranean*
Hilton Budapest WestEnd | Váci utca 1-3 | (36-1) 288-5500 | fax 288-5588 | www.hilton.com

Bock Bistro [S] *Hungarian/Mediterranean*
Corinthia Grand Hotel Royal | Erzsébet körút 43-49 | (36-1) 321-0340 | www.bockbisztro.hu

Brasserie Royale *French*
Corinthia Grand Hotel Royal | Erzsébet körút 43-49 | (36-1) 479-4000 | fax 479-4333 | www.corinthiahotels.com

Café Bouchon [S]≠ *French/Hungarian*
Zichy Jenö utca 33 | (36-1) 353-4094 | fax 354-0728 | www.cafebouchon.hu

Carne di Hall *International*
Bem rakpart 20 | (36-1) 201-8137 | fax 201-0124 | www.carnedihall.com

Chelsea *International*
Art'otel | Bem rakpart 16-19 | (36-1) 487-9487 | fax 487-9488 | www.artotel.hu

Corso *Hungarian/International*
Hotel InterContinental Budapest | Apáczai Csere János utca 12-14 | (36-1) 327-6393 | fax 327-6357 | www.interconti.com

Costes Restobar ◐ *French/Hungarian*
Ráday utca 4 | (36-1) 219-0696 | fax 219-0697 | www.costes.hu

Krizia [S] *Italian*
Mozsár utca 12 | (36-1) 331-8711 | fax 331-8711 | www.ristorantekrizia.hu

La Fontaine [S] *French*
Mérleg utca 10 | (36-1) 317-3715 | www.lafontaine.hu

Le Bourbon *French/Hungarian*
Le Méridien Budapest | Erzsébet tér 9-10 | (36-1) 429-5770 | fax 429-5555 | www.lemeridien.com

Le Jardin de Paris *French*
Fö utca 20 | (36-1) 201-0047 | www.lejardindeparis.hu

Mágnáskert *Hungarian*
Csatárka utca 58 | (36-1) 325-9972

Maligán borétterem [S] *Hungarian*
Lajos utca 38 | (36-1) 240-9010 | fax 240-9010 | www.maligan.hu

Mélyvíz *Italian*
(aka Deep Water)
New York Palace | Erzsébet körút 9-11 | (36-1) 886-6166 | fax 886-6199 | www.newyorkpalace.hu

Nusantara *Indonesian*
Városmajor utca 88 | (36-1) 201-1478 | fax 201-1478 | www.nusantara.hu

Óceán Bár & Grill ◐ *Seafood*
Petöfi tér 3 | (36-1) 266-1826 | www.oceanbargrill.com

Pata Negra *Spanish*
Kálvin tér 8 | (36-1) 215-5616 | www.patanegra.hu

Rivalda Café & Restaurant *International*
Színház utca 5-9 | (36-1) 489-0236 | fax 489-0235 | www.rivalda.net

Salaam Bombay *Indian*
Mérleg utca 6 | (36-1) 411-1252 | fax 411-1253 | www.salaambombay.hu

Trattoria Pomo D'oro ◐ *Tuscan*
Arany János utca 9 | (36-1) 302-6473 | fax 301-0716 | www.pomodorobudapest.com

Udvarház *Hungarian/International*
Hármashatárhegyi út 2 | (36-1) 388-8780 | fax 367-5962 | www.udvarhazetterem.hu

Uhu Villa ☒ *Hungarian*
Uhu Villa | Keselyü utca 1/a | (36-1) 275-1002 | fax 398-0571 | www.uhuvilla.hu

FOOD | DECOR | SERVICE | COST

Copenhagen

TOP FOOD RANKING

	Restaurant	Cuisine
27	Era Ora	Northern Italian
	Restaurationen	Danish/French
26	Søllerød Kro	French
	Kong Hans Kælder	French/International
25	Krogs Fiskerestaurant	French/Seafood
	Alberto K at the Royal	Italian/Scandinavian
24	Pierre André	French
	Paul, The	International
	Koriander	Indian
23	Slotskælderen hos Gitte Kik	Danish
	Kanalen	Provençal
	Le Sommelier	French
22	D'Angleterre	New French
	Den Sorte Ravn*	French
	Leonore Christine	Danish/French
	Fifty Fifty	Asian
21	Kiin Kiin	Thai
	Søren K	New French
	Salt	European
20	Sticks'n'Sushi	Japanese/Sushi
	Umami	Japanese/French
	Custom House	Japanese/Italian/Danish
	Divan 2	Danish/French
19	Sankt Gertruds Kloster	French/International
	Den Tatoverede Enke	Belgian
18	Els	French/Danish
	Nørrebro Bryghus	Scandinavian
17	Nyhavns Færgekro	Danish
	Café Ketchup	International
	Café Victor	French/Danish
16	Grill Bar	International

Alberto K at The Royal *Italian/Scandinavian* 25 | 24 | 23 | E

Vesterbro | Radisson SAS Royal | Hammerichsgade 1, 20th fl. | (45-33) 42-61-61 | fax 42-61-00 | www.alberto-k.dk

Chef Betina Repstock's "superb" Italian-inspired Scandinavian cuisine "melts in your mouth" at this "fantastic location" on the 20th floor of the Radisson SAS Royal in Vesterbro; in addition to "to-die-for views" outside, it's "a treat for the eye" within, as well, thanks to a "so-cool interior" that's overseen by a staff that will "treat you like dignitaries"; the cost is as "high" as the altitude, but most maintain it's "worth the krona."

Café Ketchup *International* 17 | 18 | 15 | E

Indre By | Pilestræde 23 | (45-33) 32-30-30 | fax 32-30-95

* Indicates a tie with restaurant above

(continued)

Café Ketchup

Tivoli | Tivoli Gardens | Vesterbrogade 3 | (45-33) 75-07-55 | fax 75-07-57 www.cafeketchup.dk

"Night after night, young beauties pack" this "large" "place to be seen" "in Tivoli" to "enjoy the view of the gardens" (and each other) "while dining on good food from" a "modern" International menu; foes, though, find factors "going against it", including "pricey" fare that's "nicely presented" "but nothing extraordinary", "dull decor" "lacking intimacy", "lagging service" and too many "tourists"; P.S. insiders assert that "its more sophisticated sibling across town" in Indre By "is better" - plus it's open year-round.

Café Victor *French/Danish* 17 17 14 E

Kongens Nytorv | Ny Østergade 8 | (45-33) 13-36-13 | fax 91-13-40 | www.cafevictor.dk

"Sharpen your elbows to get past" the "pretty people" "packed into" this "classic but hip" Kongens Nytorv "fixture" that's "still hot" with "the well-heeled crowd" that "loves" "to be seen" "on either side" of its divided space - "trying the cafe", with its "limited menu", then "returning another night" to the "restaurant, which has more choices" of "good French" cuisine (at lunch the dishes are Danish); some suggest it's too "snobbish", with "slack service" from a "pretentious staff", but few fault the "fun atmosphere."

NEW **Custom House** *Japanese/Italian/Danish* 20 20 19 E

Nyhavn | Havnegade 44 | (45-33) 31-01-30 | www.customhouse.dk

Surveyors are split over English restaurant guru Sir Terence Conran's venture in a "handsomely converted" Nyhavn customs house building: devotees declare "it's the new 'in' place in Copenhagen", a "sleek, beautiful multirestaurant complex" "right on the waterfront" serving "high-quality" Japanese, Italian and Danish cuisine in separate "amazing" settings; but critics counter the "comfort food at uncomfortable prices" is "not up to the view" of the harbor.

D'Angleterre *French* 22 25 22 VE

Kongens Nytorv | Hotel D'Angleterre | Kongens Nytorv 34 | (45-33) 37-06-45 | fax 12-11-18 | www.remmen.dk

"Passersby must envy diners" at this "don't-miss" destination (formerly known as Wiinblad) in the "charming old-world" Hotel D'Angleterre that's graced with a "spectacular setting overlooking Kongens Nytorv" and a burnished brown-and-gold formal dining room; the kitchen produces "wonderful" New French creations with an Asian accent that are served by a staff that is "attentive without being overbearing."

Den Sorte Ravn *French* 22 20 21 E

Nyhavn | Nyhavn 14 | (45-33) 13-12-33 | fax 13-24-72 | www.sorteravn.dk

Occupying a "great location on the canal", "on the main street of the Nyhavn neighborhood", this "small cellar" spot (whose name means 'The Black Raven') is one of the area's more "high-class" venues, where "delicious" French fare is "pleasantly" served by a "friendly, attentive" staff; some dub the decor "a bit worn", quipping that "the shiny black feathers are molting a bit", but most find the "simple" interior "inviting" - and if it's "expensive", at least the "quality matches the price."

FOOD	DECOR	SERVICE	COST

Den Tatoverede Enke ☒ *Belgian* 19 | 15 | 15 | M

Kongens Nytorv | Baron Boltens Gaard | Gothersgade 8C | (45-33) 91-88-77 | www.dentatoveredeenke.dk

Those with a "negative bias toward Belgian cuisine" may find their opinions "changed" by the "exciting", "unusual" and "fairly priced" dishes produced by this "innovative kitchen" housed in "cozy, cramped" Kongens Nytorv premises; there's a "beer hall below" featuring a "nicely varied selection" of "interesting" brews delivered by "friendly" staffers who "actually know something about" "what they're serving."

Divan 2 *Danish/French* 20 | 18 | 22 | E

Tivoli | Tivoli Gardens | Vesterbrogade 3 | (45-33) 75-07-50 | fax 75-07-30 | www.divan2.dk

When "wandering through Tivoli" Gardens, drop into this "divine" "classic" on the lake, where a "tip-top" staff of "charming" servers proffers an "appealing" (if "too expensive") menu of "delicious", "well-seasoned" Danish-French fare to a largely "tourist" clientele; those who find its "pretty decor" "a bit dated" suggest you take advantage of the "beautiful surroundings" by "nabbing a private gazebo" on the "lovely terrace" "before the tour buses invade!"; N.B. open mid-April through late September and most of November and December.

Els *French/Danish* 18 | 18 | 19 | VE

Nyhavn | Store Strandstræde 3 | (45-33) 14-13-41 | www.restaurant-els.dk

A "friendly" staff will make "you feel welcome" in the "cozy surroundings" of this former 19th-century coffeehouse in Nyhavn, "a Copenhagen institution" where "good, solid" French-Danish cuisine is served amid "historically appropriate decor" featuring six "original" murals depicting women representing the four seasons and the muses of dance and music; still, the "expensive meals fail to excite" some surveyors, who say they're "great for grandma but dull for anyone else."

Era Ora ☒ *Italian* 27 | 21 | 24 | VE

Christianshavn | Overgaden Neden Vandet 33B | (45-32) 54-06-93 | fax 96-02-09 | www.era-ora.dk

For "a meal you'll remember", "you just have to go" to this "always-crowded" Northern Italian along the canal in Christianshavn, whose "authentic" Tuscan and Umbrian fare "bursting with natural flavors" (and "accompanied by delicious wines") earns it the ranking of No. 1 for Food in Copenhagen; "excellent in every way", it's manned by a "warm, extremely efficient" staff providing "impeccable service" "from start to finish" and features a "gorgeous atmosphere to match the gorgeous food"; "bring a really fat wallet", though, as it's "wildly expensive."

NEW **Fifty Fifty** ☒ *Asian* 22 | 20 | 21 | E

Vesterbro | Vesterbrogade 42 | (45-33) 22-47-57 | www.fiftyfiftyfood.dk

There's far more than a 50/50 chance both carnivores and finatics will "love" this "cool" Asian newcomer in Vesterbro since it offers grilled meats and raw fish; "good value and high standards" also have made it a "fast favorite of the hungry 'beautiful people.'"

Grill Bar ☒ *International* 16 | 19 | 17 | E

Kongens Nytorv | Ny Østergade 14 | (45-33) 14-34-54 | fax 14-34-74 | www.grill-bar.dk

Among the "places to see and be seen in Copenhagen" is this International in Kongens Nytorv that features, like the name says, a gigantic grill and an enormous cocktail bar; "the young and those trying to be fabulous" like "living well beyond their means" in its loungey setting, but the less-impressed assert it's "loud", the "food is ordinary" and "service is slow" ("if I hadn't asked for the check a couple of times I'd probably still be sitting there").

Kanalen ☒ *Provençal* 23 | 20 | 22 | E

Christianshavn | Wilders Plads 2 | (45-32) 95-13-30 | fax 95-13-38 | www.restaurant-kanalen.dk

"Good-size portions" of "delicious", "basic French fare" "will make you smile" at this "charming", "upmarket" Provençal in a "superb location" in "beautiful" Christianshavn, providing it with a "lovely canal view"; the "simple" space is "a bit tight", but most find its "intimate atmosphere" "delightfully" "cozy" "and romantic", and the "excellent wine list" is another reason it's considered "a true pleasure."

NEW **Kiin Kiin** ☒ *Thai* 21 | 21 | 20 | E

Nørrebro | Guldbergsgade 21 | (45-35) 35-75-55 | fax 35-75-59 | www.kiin.dk

This "hip" and "ambitious newcomer" "takes Thai to another level" with the chef-owner's "modern and untraditional interpretation of that cuisine"; throw in "spacious seating", futuristic decor interspersed with big golden Buddhas and a "trendy" bohemian neighborhood locale in Nørrebro and no wonder fans feel it "deserves praise."

Kong Hans Kælder ☒ *French/International* 26 | 25 | 24 | VE

Kongens Nytorv | Vingaardsstræde 6 | (45-33) 11-68-68 | fax 32-67-68 | www.konghans.dk

"One of the best culinary experiences" in Copenhagen can be found at "this historic, vaulted-ceiling wine cellar" "situated in King Hans'" 16th-century royal mint (the city's "oldest" building) in the Kongens Nytorv area; "out-of-this-world" French-International cuisine – with an emphasis on "top-notch" fish dishes – is offered in a "lovely" setting with "nicely spaced tables" by a "personable" staff that "looks after you really well"; yes, you'll "pay through the nose", but "you should visit at least once in your lifetime."

Koriander ☒ *Indian* 24 | 23 | 21 | E

Kongens Nytorv | Store Kongensgade 34 | (45-33) 15-03-15 | fax 15-04-15 | www.restaurantkoriander.dk

This trendy, "excellent" Indian that's set in a glittering ultramodern space in Kongens Nytorv takes its name from coriander, a key ingredient in that cuisine, and is complemented by an expansive wine list that leans toward German whites; on the downside, it's "expensive" and service can be "slow."

Krogs Fiskerestaurant ☒ *French/Seafood* 25 | 20 | 22 | VE

Indre By | Gammel Strand 38 | (45-33) 15-89-15 | www.krogs.dk

The "fabulous" "fresh fish" is "fit for a king" at this "old-fashioned", "high-class" French seafooder in Indre By; though the "sublime food" (with "wonderful wine pairings") is certainly "the center of attention", "everything about the place is elegant" - from the "superb service" to the "lovely setting" - which may explain why faithful fans forgive that the fare is "ferociously expensive", the room can be "stuffy" and some staffers are "a bit pretentious."

Leonore Christine *Danish/French* 22 19 22 E

Nyhavn | Nyhavn 9 | (45-33) 13-50-40 | fax 13-50-40 | www.leonore-christine.dk

"Pleasant without being intrusive", the "very competent staff" of this "crowded and popular" Nyhavn spot, "in the sailor part of town", performs a "table ballet" nightly while delivering "gorgeous" plates of "super" Danish-French fare, accompanied by a "good wine selection"; perhaps the interior of its circa-1681 building with low ceilings and crooked floors "feels a bit faded", but a recent redo may have remedied that, and there's "lovely alfresco dining" as an alternative.

Le Sommelier *French* 23 18 23 E

Kongens Nytorv | Bredgade 63-65 | (45-33) 11-45-15 | fax 11-59-79 | www.lesommelier.dk

"As the name indicates", the "fantastic wine list" at "this friendly restaurant" in the Kongens Nytorv area "is in a class of its own", but rest assured that the "excellent French cuisine" is also "outstanding" ("well prepared" and "quite flavorful") - as is the "warm welcome" from the "professional" staff; a few feel the decor of its "large, open" and "very white" interior "could be better", but more are put "at ease" by the "peaceful", "relaxed" and "well-laid-out" space.

Nørrebro Bryghus *Scandinavian* 18 16 16 M

Nørrebro | Ryesgade 3 | (45-35) 30-05-30 | fax 30-05-31 | www.noerrebrobryghus.dk

Expect "a full house" at this "fun" Nørrebro microbrewery that's always hopping with "lots of people" sampling "big portions" of "good", "sensibly priced" Scandinavian fare while quaffing "A-ok fresh brews" from the "fantastic selection" made on the "spacious premises" in "large", "gleaming vats"; some suggest the "young" staffers are "a bit disorganized" and "inexperienced", but others credit them for providing "information about which beer goes with which dish."

Nyhavns Færgekro ◐ *Danish* 17 16 17 E

Nyhavn | Nyhavn 5 | (45-33) 15-15-88 | fax 15-18-68 | www.nyhavnsfaergekro.dk

"Opt for a lunch visit" to "this canal-side restaurant" "on the Nyhavn row" - "although it's a bit touristy", "it's a good place" to sample "fresh" Danish fare including the famous *sildebord* (a "big herring buffet") and a large selection of "great *smørrebrød*" (open-faced sandwiches) accompanied by "flavored schnapps", "aquavit and beer"; some find the "so-so decor" "dull" and the cuisine "slightly uninspiring", saying there are "more advanced Scandinavian choices", but the service is "pleasant" and "the rooms are cozy."

Paul, The ⊠ *International* 24 21 21 VE

Tivoli | Tivoli Gardens | Vesterbrogade 3 | (45-33) 75-07-75 | fax 75-07-76 | www.thepaul.dk

"Small dishes with gigantic flavors" are featured on chef-owner Paul Cunningham's "very expensive" International menu at this "impeccable" venue whose "modern" setting - a light-drenched, white-on-white glass pavilion - is an "enjoyable refuge from the masses in Tivoli Gardens"; "yes, you do pay the usual premium" for the area, but affluent "gourmets" insist it's "worth the money", while clever folks of lesser means advise "this is your pick when somebody else is paying"; N.B. open mid-April-late September and most of November and December.

Pierre André S M *French* 24 | 18 | 23 | E

Indre By | Ny Østergade 21 | (45-33) 16-17-19 | fax 16-17-72 | www.pierreandre.dk

Named for the proprietors' two sons, this "classic French" in Indre By features chef-owner Philippe Houdet's "exciting, well-prepared", "elegant" dishes, which are offered by an "observant" staff overseen by his wife, Sussie; some see a "romantic edge" to the "traditional" decor, while others sigh that it's "not the most exciting in the city", but all agree the "choice of prix fixe menus to fit both mid and high budgets" adds up to "great value for the money."

Restaurationen S M *Danish/French* 27 | 21 | 27 | VE

Indre By | Møntergade 19 | (45-33) 14-94-95 | www.restaurationen.com

"Run by people who truly love good food", this "just amazing" Danish-French in Indre By offers a "well-rounded" five-course prix fixe menu nightly - "no à la carte!" - of "innovative, gorgeous dishes" made from "the best ingredients", accompanied by an "excellent wine" list and "presented by owner Bo Jacobsen" and his wife, Lisbeth, or by their "attentive" staff; a few find "nothing to cheer about" in the "nice-but-nothing-special" decor, but most maintain the overall "experience is absolutely superb."

Salt *European* 21 | 21 | 18 | E

Indre By | Copenhagen Admiral Hotel | Toldbodgade 24-28 | (45-33) 74-14-44 | www.saltrestaurant.dk

Sir Terence Conran's "stylish adaptation of a waterfront warehouse" with "huge timbers" is the "well-designed setting" of this "thoroughly enjoyable" venue in Indre By's Copenhagen Admiral Hotel; the "innovative" menu of "delicious" modern European cuisine is backed up by an "unexpectedly good wine list", but some suggest the "competent" staff "could be warmer"; N.B. the inspiration for the restaurant name comes in part from having each table topped with three kinds of sea salt.

Sankt Gertruds Kloster *French/International* 19 | 22 | 20 | VE

Indre By | Hauser Plads 32 | (45-33) 14-66-30 | fax 93-93-65 | www.sgk.as

"About as romantic as you can get", this "memorable" (if "a bit touristy") venue "set in the reconstructed remains of an old monastery" in Indre By boasts "a wonderful setting" "with lots of candles", "caverns", "small corners" and "uneven flagstone" floors; most surveyors also have "praise" for the "skillful, friendly" staff and "delicious" French-International fare, but even those who claim "the quality is patchy" concede that the "cozy, intimate atmosphere" "overshadows any missteps in service or food."

Slotskælderen hos Gitte Kik S M *Danish* 23 | 21 | 21 | E

Indre By | Fortunstræde 4 | (45-33) 11-15-37

"One of the outstanding purveyors" of "good, old-fashioned Danish open sandwiches" is this lunch-only Indre By "classic" *smørrebrød* specialist dating back to 1910; choose from the likes of herring or tiny shrimp, beer or schnapps and join the crowd of MP's from the nearby parliament building that frequents this popular place.

Søllerød Kro *French* 26 | 24 | 25 | VE

Hellerup | Søllerødvej 35 | (45-45) 80-25-05 | fax 80-22-70 | www.soelleroed-kro.dk

For French "food at its best", a "to-die-for wine list" and "an evening to remember" "this is it" say supporters of this 1677 "charmer" in Hellerup, about a 15 minute cab ride from the city center; housed in an "authentic Danish cottage" surrounded by a garden and pond, it comes with an "impossibly romantic atmosphere" and a very "expensive" price tag.

Søren K *French* 21 | 20 | 18 | E

Indre By | Søren Kierkegaards Plads 1 | (45-33) 47-49-49 | fax 47-49-51 | www.soerenk.dk

"Start your trip off on the right foot" at this "modern" spot (named for famed philosopher Søren Kierkegaard) in Indre By, where the "delicious, light, experimental New French" cuisine is "well prepared" using as little cream and butter as possible and the "incredible building" - a shiny, black-granite extension of the Royal Danish Library - offers "fine minimalist" decor and "amazing" vistas "of the Copenhagen harbor"; nevertheless, some detractors declare that "divine food, clean lines and sexy views don't make up for lackluster service."

Sticks'n'Sushi *Japanese* 20 | 16 | 16 | E

Frederiksberg | gl.Kongevej 120 | (45-33) 29-00-10
Hellerup | Strandvejen 199 | (45-39) 40-15-40 | fax 40-15-48
Indre By | Nansensgade 59 | (45-33) 11-14-07 | fax 11-14-09
Østerbro | Oster Farimagsgade 16 | (45-35) 38-34-63 | fax 38-34-23
Vesterbro | Istedgade 62 | (45-33) 23-73-04 | fax 23-73-05
www.sushi.dk

A pioneer "of sushi and yakitori in Copenhagen", this Indre By Japanese "original" is "still going strong", remaining "an 'in' place" for more than a decade and spawning a slew of siblings, each serving up its trademark brand of "fine, festive", "freshly made" raw-fish creations along with "high-quality sticks" of skewered, grilled chicken in "minimalist" digs; sure, they're on "the expensive end", but "not more so than" some competitors.

TyvenKokkenHansKoneOgHendesElsker - | - | - | VE
French/Danish

Indre By | Magstræde 16 | (45-33) 16-12-92 | www.tyven.dk

When the highly rated Kommandanten lost its space in the Kongens Nytorv area, its chef, Kasper Rune Sørenson, brought his staff and took over ownership of this equally notable and "beautiful restaurant" "in a historic building" in Indre By; the French menu has also acquired a Danish emphasis now, but they've kept the mind-boggling name, which was borrowed from the 1989 film *The Thief, The Cook, His Wife & Her Lover.*

Umami *Japanese/French* 20 | 24 | 20 | E

Kongens Nytorv | Store Kongensgade 59 | (45-33) 38-75-00 | www.restaurantumami.dk

"Copenhagen has always envied the other big cities their high-class Japanese-French cuisine and now it's here" at this "trendy" bar/

restaurant in Kongens Nytorv; there are "exciting" cooked dishes and sushi, as well as an "outstanding wine list" (including 30 served by the glass) and sake selection, so no wonder this "funky, sexy place" is "where the coolest and most beautiful Danes dine."

Other Noteworthy Places

Al-Diwan [M] *Indian*
Vesterbrogade 94 | (45-33) 23-10-45 | fax 23-59-50

Aura Bar & Restaurant [S][M] *Mediterranean*
Rådhusstræde 4 | (45-33) 36-50-60

Bleu *Asian Fusion*
Hotel Skt. Petri | Krystalgade 22 | (45-33) 45-98-20 | fax 45-91-10 | www.sktpetri.dk

Brasserie Mühlhausen *Mediterranean*
Hotel Alexandra | H.C. Andersens Boulevard 8 | (45-33) 74-44-66 | fax 74-44-88 | www.muhlhausen.dk

Café à Porta [S] *Danish/French*
Kongens Nytorv 17 | (45-33) 11-05-00 | fax 11-03-05 | www.cafeaporta.dk

Ensemble [S][M] *French*
Tordenskjoldsgade 11 | (45-33) 11-33-52 | fax 11-33-92 | www.restaurantensemble.dk

Famo *Italian*
Saxograde 3 | (45-33) 23-22-50

Famo 51 [S] *Italian*
Gl. Kongevej 51 | (45-33) 22-22-50
www.osteriafamo.dk

formel B [S] *French/Danish*
Vesterbrogade 182 | (45-33) 25-10-66 | www.formel-b.dk

Fox Kitchen *Scandinavian*
Hotel Fox | Jarmers Plads 3 | (45-33) 38-70-30 | www.foxkitchen.dk

Fregatten Sct. Georg III *French/Danish*
Tivoli | Vesterbrogade 3 | (45-33) 15-92-04 | fax 11-18-61 | www.bojesen.dk/fregatten

Geranium [S][M] *Danish*
Kronprinsessegade 13 | (45-33) 11-13-04 | www.restaurantgeranium.dk

Godt [S][M] *European*
Gothersgade 38 | (45-33) 15-21-22 | www.restaurant-godt.dk

Guldanden *Danish/French*
Sortedam Dossering 103 | (45-35) 42-66-06 | fax 42-66-05 | www.guldanden.dk

Hamlet Nordic Grill [S] *Scandinavian*
Hilton Copenhagen Airport | Ellehammersvej 20 | (45-32) 50-15-01 | fax 52-85-28 | www.hilton.com

Khun Juk Oriental [S] *Thai*
Baron Boltens Gård | Store Kongensgade 9 | (45-33) 32-30-50 | www.khunjuk.dk

Kokkeriet [S][M] *French*
Kronprinsessegade 64 | (45-33) 15-27-77 | www.kokkeriet.dk

Kyoto *Japanese*
Radisson SAS Scandinavia Hotel | Amager Boulevard 70 | (45-33) 96-57-29 | www.copenhagen.radissonsas.com

Lumskebugten [S] *Danish*
Esplanaden 21 | (45-33) 15-60-29 | fax 32-87-18 | www.lumskebugten.dk

Luns [S][M] *International*
Øster Farimagsgade 12 | (45-35) 26-33-35 | www.restaurantluns.dk

MR [S] *Danish/French*
Kultorvet 5 | (45-33) 91-09-49 | www.mr-restaurant.dk

Noma [S] *Scandinavian*
Strandgade 93 | (45-32) 96-32-97 | www.noma.dk

1.th [S][M]≠ *Danish/French*
Herluf Trolles Gade 9 | (45-33) 93-57-70 | fax 93-67-69 | www.1th.dk

Paustian v. Bo Bech [S] *International/Scandinavian*
Kalkbrænderiløbskaj 2 | (45-39) 18-55-01 | www.restaurantpaustian.dk

Prémisse [S] *French/International*
Moltkes Palæ | Dronningens Tværgade 2 | (45-33) 11-11-45 | fax 11-11-68 | www.premisse.dk

Rasmus Oubæk [S] *French*
Store Kongensgade 52 | (45-33) 32-32-09 | www.rasmusoubaek.dk

Sanshin Sushi *Japanese*
Smallegade 20 | (45-38) 33-80-59 | www.sanshin-sushi.com

Schønnemann [S] *Danish*
Hauser Plads 16 | (45-33) 12-07-85

Viva *Mediterranean/Seafood*
Langebro Kaj 570 | (45-27) 25-05-05 | www.restaurantviva.dk

FOOD | DECOR | SERVICE | COST

Dublin

TOP FOOD RANKING

	Restaurant	Cuisine
27	Thornton's Restaurant	Irish/French
	Patrick Guilbaud	French
26	Seasons	Irish/European
25	L'Ecrivain	Irish/New French
	One Pico	French/Irish
	Shanahan's on the Green	American/Steakhouse
24	Mint Restaurant	New French
	Tea Room	Irish/International
23	Balzac	French/Irish
	Chapter One Restaurant	French/International
	O'Connells	Irish
	Poulot's	French/Irish
22	Lobster Pot	Seafood
	Jaipur	Indian
	Eden	Irish
	Jacob's Ladder	Irish/International
21	Mermaid Café	French/American
	Winding Stair	Irish
	Halo	Irish/International
	Roly's Bistro	Irish/French
	Alexis Bar & Grill	French
20	Peploe's	European/Irish
	Brownes	Irish/International
	First Floor	Irish
19	Mackerel	Seafood

NEW Alexis Bar & Grill M *French* — 21 | 18 | 18 | M

Dun Laoghaire | 17-18 Patrick St. | (353-1) 280-8872 | www.alexis.ie

"Very enjoyable" is the verdict on this "delicious" French bistro and "worthwhile new addition" to Dun Laoghaire; throw in a "relaxing" setting with red banquettes, a "charming and friendly staff that treats you like family" and "moderate prices" and "what else could you wish for?"

NEW Balzac *French/Irish* — 23 | 23 | 21 | E

St. Stephen's Green | La Stampa Hotel & Spa | 35 Dawson St. | (353-1) 677-4444 | www.balzac.ie

"One of the loveliest rooms in Dublin" and "the new 'it' spot" is this French-Irish brasserie "in a neat hotel" "on trendy Dawson Street" that serves "proper grown-up food" "worthy of its surroundings"; "vaulted ceilings, tall mirrors" and a Victorian cocktail bar are an "elegant" backdrop for chef Paul Flynn's "excellent" albeit "expensive" cuisine.

Brownes *Irish/International* — 20 | 23 | 23 | E

St. Stephen's Green | Brownes Townhouse Hotel | 22 St. Stephen's Green | (353-1) 638-3939 | fax 638-3900 | www.brownesdublin.com

Set in a stunning listed Georgian townhouse in a "great locale on St. Stephen's Green" is this "elegant" Irish-International with a fireplace and chandeliers; "excellent" dishes and "warm service" make it "popular" with a posh crowd.

Chapter One Restaurant ⓈⓂ *French/International* 23 | 23 | 24 | E

Parnell Square | Dublin Writers Museum | 18-19 Parnell Sq. | (353-1) 873-2266 | fax 873-2330 | www.chapteronerestaurant.com

"You can almost hear Joyce and Yeats reading their work while you're dining on delicious food" at this French-International in the Dublin Writers Museum; considered one of the city's "finest" spots, with a "good value pre-theater menu" from Tuesday-Saturday, it's a "must" for literate libation-lovers who like to salute the "inspirational" setting with the establishment's infamous Irish Coffee.

Eden *Irish* 22 | 21 | 22 | E

Temple Bar | Meeting House Sq. | (353-1) 670-5372 | fax 670-3330 | www.edenrestaurant.ie

"Located in throbbing Temple Bar", this "buzzy" Irish "staple" boasts "sophisticated food", a "modern" setting and "friendly" service; "lots of locals" descend to dine on the legendary 'smokies' (smoked haddock with crème fraîche and cheddar cheese), and in summer the gas-lamp-lit terrace is a "great scene" and place to watch films and shows.

First Floor *Irish* 20 | 19 | 20 | E

Dundrum | Harvey Nichols, Dundrum Town Ctr. | Sandyford Rd. | (353-1) 291-0488 | fax 291-0489 | www.harveynichols.com

Shoppers are buzzing about this Irish in Dundrum's Harvey Nichols department store: fans feel the "wonderful food" and ultramodern setting with LED lighting make it a "fashionable" place "to be seen", but cynics sigh "ho-hum", it "feels like you're eating in an office", so "spend the money on a flight to London and a taxi" to the original Nichs flagship.

Halo *Irish/International* 21 | 23 | 23 | E

Northside | Morrison Hotel | Ormond Quay | (353-1) 887-2420 | fax 878-3185 | www.morrisonhotel.ie

This "dramatic", two-story space with a striking staircase and "beautiful" minimalist design is in the fashionable Morrison Hotel on the banks of the Liffey; corporate types mainline Irish-International dishes, many with organic ingredients, or choose tastes from the tapas menu, and pick up pricey tabs in what, despite a renovation, is still one of the smartest dining rooms in the city.

Jacob's Ladder ⓈⓂ *Irish/International* 22 | 20 | 22 | E

City Center | 4 Nassau St. | (353-1) 670-3865 | fax 670-3868 | www.jacobsladder.ie

"A real winner" "bang in the center of town" is what supporters say about this chef-owned, bi-level Irish-International with "innovative", "enjoyable" cuisine and "solid service"; spectacular Georgian windows dominate the "pleasing" minimalist space and provide a "great view over Trinity College's playing fields."

Jaipur *Indian* 22 | 15 | 17 | M

City Center | 41 S. Great George's St. | (353-1) 677-0999 | fax 677-0979 | www.jaipur.ie

It's "probably the best Indian in Dublin" declare devotees of this "authentic" Asian in a trendy part of the bustling City Center, where low-key decor - light wood, chrome and floor-to-ceiling windows - makes for a "nice environment"; prices are moderate to begin with, but there's a "great early-bird special" too crow wallet-watchers.

L'Ecrivain ☒ *Irish/French* 25 | 23 | 24 | VE

City Center | 109a Lower Baggot St. | (353-1) 661-1919 | fax 661-0617 | www.lecrivain.com

"High-end" Irish-New French that's one of the city's "top picks" for "loquacious" chef-owner Derry Clarke's "excellent, imaginative" fare; "staffers that make you feel like a guest in their home" preside over a quietly luxurious split-level setting that's "full of suits" during the week, while a pianist on Mondays-Saturdays attracts the "special-occasion" crowd.

Lobster Pot, The ☒ *Seafood* 22 | 17 | 21 | E

Ballsbridge | 9 Ballsbridge Terrace | (353-1) 668-0025 | fax 668-0025 | www.thelobsterpot.ie

A local favorite is this long-standing, family-run, "old-school" seafooder (Mornay sauce, anyone?) with "frolicking fresh fish" in Ballsbridge, the embassy district, just south of the City Center; a "veteran staff" presides over a warm, "walking-back-into-a-time-machine" setting with an open fireplace, maritime memorabilia and dessert cart.

Mackerel *Seafood* 19 | 18 | 18 | M

City Center | 78-79 Grafton St. | (353-1) 672-7719 | www.mackerel.ie

Dedicated seafood restaurants are still unusual in Ireland, but this venue in City Center ("on the premises of the historic and original Bewley's Cafe") fills the bill with "delicious" "fresh" fish dishes; the quarters can be "cramped", but "holy mackerel", "not too expensive prices" for Dublin make the place a catch.

Mermaid Café, The *French/American* 21 | 18 | 22 | E

Temple Bar | 69-70 Dame St. | (353-1) 670-8236 | fax 670-8205 | www.mermaid.ie

This "lively" stalwart, on the edge of Temple Bar, is still going strong with "exceptionally well-prepared" French-American fare served by a "professional staff"; the high-ceilinged, open-kitchen setting is simple but that doesn't keep it from being "one of the city's best loved eateries"; N.B. the prix fixe lunch is one of Dublin's biggest bargains.

Mint Restaurant ☒Ⓜ *French* 24 | 20 | 21 | E

Ranelagh | 47 Ranelagh Village | (353-1) 497-8655 | fax 497-9035 | www.mintrestaurant.ie

"Beautifully presented" and "inspired" New French cuisine makes for a "lovely dining experience" in Ranelagh; the small, stylish spot attracts tony types, who tout that it's in mint condition for prime people-watching, particularly at lunchtime; N.B. a post-Survey renovation may outdate the above Decor score.

O'Connells *Irish* 23 | 19 | 19 | M

Ballsbridge | Bewley's Hotel | Merrion Rd. | (353-1) 647-3304 | fax 647-3398 | www.oconnellsballsbridge.com

This "excellent" traditional and modern Irish owned by foodie Tom O'Connell relies on organic "locally sourced ingredients"; some find the sprawling setting in Ballsbridge's Bewley's Hotel a bit like an "airport lounge", but a kitchen that's responsive to dietary needs (most menu items are gluten-free), has reasonable prices, including an "incredible value early-bird", and an appealingly "quirky", affordable wine list win way more yeas than nays.

One Pico ⓢ *French/Irish* 25 | 23 | 23 | VE

City Center | 5-6 Molesworth Pl., Schoolhouse Ln. | (353-1) 676-0300 | fax 676-0411 | www.onepico.com

Set in an 18th-century coach house that's "tucked away" in a lane off St. Stephen's Green is chef-owner Eamonn O'Reilly's French-Irish "gem"; a "subtly elegant setting" is the backdrop for "wonderful", "top-quality" food, "very accommodating service" and "amazing wines"; of course, dining at "one of Dublin's better restaurants" comes at a price.

Patrick Guilbaud ⓢⓜ *French* 27 | 25 | 26 | VE

City Center | Merrion Hotel | 21 Upper Merrion St. | (353-1) 676-4192 | fax 661-0052 | www.restaurantpatrickguilbaud.ie

"Every city has its famous restaurant and this is Dublin's"; at Patrick Guilbaud's "excellent all-round" French in City Center, there's Guillaume Lebrun's "revelatory" cuisine, 500 "world-class wines", "outstanding service" and "amazing", "luxe surroundings" with 20th-century Irish art (and "it doesn't hurt that Bono may be at the next table"); "if you really want to treat someone this is the place", "so go on blow the budget" big, big, big time.

Peploe's *European/Irish* 20 | 20 | 18 | E

St. Stephen's Green | 16 St. Stephen's Green | (353-1) 676-3144 | fax 676-3154 | www.peploes.com

A "delightful addition to the Dublin dining scene", this "buzzing" wine bar features about 150 "fantastic selections" and a "good" though "not inspirational" European-Irish menu; its "perfect location" on the Green and chic "subterranean" space attract an "aspirational" clientele.

Poulot's ⓢⓜ *French/Irish* 23 | 18 | 19 | E

Donnybrook | Mulberry Garden | (353-1) 269-3300 | fax 269-3260 | www.poulots.ie

On the site of the former Ernie's in Donnybrook is this French-Irish from chef-owner Jean-Michel Poulot, whose "delicious" cuisine relies on exceptional local produce, much of it organic, and is backed up by what some say is "the best wine list for value in Dublin"; the setting includes a bright modern interior decorated with contemporary paintings and an exterior with a "lovely" courtyard garden and fountain.

Roly's Bistro *Irish/French* 21 | 17 | 21 | E

Ballsbridge | 7 Ballsbridge Terrace | (353-1) 668-2611 | fax 660-8535 | www.rolysbistro.ie

"As reliable as old boots", this "boisterous" Irish-French "fixture" in Ballsbridge, near the sports stadium, is "bustling" with "lots of locals"; they come for "good plain food" like Dublin Bay prawns and a four-course lunch that's "one of the best values in town" (20 euros).

Seasons *Irish/European* 26 | 25 | 27 | VE

Ballsbridge | Four Seasons Hotel | Simmonscourt Rd. | (353-1) 665-4000 | fax 665-4880 | www.fourseasons.com/dublin

"Exactly what you'd expect from the Four Seasons" is what fans of this Irish-European in Ballsbridge say; "outstanding service", "excellent cuisine" and a "posh" setting with conservatory windows, a fireplace and an abundance of flowers add up to a "top-tier", "high-priced" experience; P.S. some swear the "Sunday brunch here is the best in the world."

Shanahan's on the Green *American/Steak* 25 24 26 VE

St. Stephen's Green | 119 St. Stephen's Green | (353-1) 407-0939 | fax 407-0940 | www.shanahans.ie

"Great steaks but gosh do you pay for them" at this opulent American chophouse "conveniently located" on St. Stephen's Green; "portions are mammoth" ("I hope they have a defibrillator on the premises"), and the glamorous Georgian setting is far from the typical "testosterone"-oriented atmosphere found in most meat meccas; throw in a seafood selection, an "amazing wine list", a celeb clientele and service that exudes "Irish charm" and no wonder it's "loved by the locals"; P.S. be sure to "check out JFK's rocker in the Oval Office bar."

Tea Room *Irish/International* 24 23 20 E

Temple Bar | The Clarence | 6-8 Wellington Quay | (353-1) 407-0813 | fax 407-0820 | www.theclarence.ie

"A cathedral to fine food" in the "über-hip", U2-owned Clarence hotel is this "chic" and "spacious" Irish-International with a 20-ft. "soaring ceiling", "beautiful tall windows", "acres of blond wood" and "heavenly" cuisine; "it's perfect for romance, business" or "people-watching", so if you're big on "buzz" and "you're only in town for a short time", this is the place.

Thornton's Restaurant S M *Irish/French* 27 19 25 VE

St. Stephen's Green | Fitzwilliam Hotel | 128 St. Stephen's Green | (353-1) 478-7008 | fax 478-7009 | www.thorntonsrestaurant.com

Voted No. 1 for Food in the city, chef Kevin Thornton's "highly personal and poetic" Irish-French cuisine, which relies on the "highest quality fresh local ingredients", is "unsurpassed" and served by a "perfect yet friendly" staff; sure, it's "very expensive", but most maintain it's a "great way to start or finish a trip to Dublin"; P.S. a major refurbishment may outdate the above Decor score and make some who found the Fitzwilliam Hotel setting "stark" change their minds.

NEW **Winding Stair** *Irish* 21 20 22 M

City Center | 40 Ormond Quay | (353-1) 872-7320 | www.winding-stair.com

New corporate owners have reopened this former City Center landmark that has a bookstore downstairs and an Irish cafe upstairs; the latter offers "reasonably priced", "good wholesome fresh" food made from "quality ingredients" (many of them organic) and an extensive wine list; the "bright, airy and open" setting is simple, but big windows provide "lovely" "views of the river Liffey."

Other Noteworthy Places

Aya *Japanese*

49-52 Clarendon St. | (353-1) 677-1544 | www.aya.ie

Canal Bank Café *International*

146 Upper Leeson St. | (353-1) 664-2135 | fax 664-2719 | www.canalbankcafe.com

Chili Club *Thai*

1 Annes Ln. | (353-1) 677-3721 | fax 635-1928

DUBLIN

Frank's Bar & Restaurant *International*
Grand Canal Quay | (353-1) 662-5870

La Maison des Gourmets ☒ *French*
15 Castle Market St. | (353-1) 672-7258

Les Frères Jacques ☒ *French*
74 Dame St. | (353-1) 679-4555 | fax 679-4725 | www.lesfreresjacques.com

L'Gueuleton *French*
3 Fade St. | (353-1) 675-3708

Locks ☒ *French/Irish*
1 Windsor Terrace | (353-1) 454-3391 | fax 453-8352 | www.locksrestaurant.ie

Lord Edward, The ☒ *Seafood*
23 Christchurch Pl. | (353-1) 454-2420 | fax 454-2420 | www.lordedward.ie

Saagar *Indian*
16 Harcourt St. | (353-1) 475-5060 | fax 475-5741 | www.saagarindianrestaurants.com

Still Restaurant *Irish*
Dylan Hotel Dublin | Eastmoreland Pl. | (353-1) 660-3000 | fax 660-3005 | www.dylan.ie

Town Bar & Grill *Italian*
21 Kildare St. | (353-1) 662-4724 | fax 662-3857 | www.townbarandgrill.com

FOOD | DECOR | SERVICE | COST

Florence

TOP FOOD RANKING

	Restaurant	Cuisine
27	Enoteca Pinchiorri	Italian
	La Giostra	Tuscan
26	Alle Murate	Tuscan
	Fuor d'Acqua	Seafood
	Cibrèo	Italian
	Taverna del Bronzino	Italian
25	Omero	Tuscan
	Zibibbo	Italian/Mediterranean
	Villa San Michele	Italian
24	Cantinetta Antinori	Italian
	Sabatini	Tuscan
	Ora d'Aria	Tuscan/Mediterranean
	InCanto	Italian
	Il Latini	Tuscan
23	Olio & Convivium	Italian
	Buca Lapi	Tuscan
	Da Ruggero	Tuscan
22	Beccofino	Italian/Seafood
	Enoteca Pane E Vino	Tuscan
21	Cammillo Trattoria	Italian
20	Coco Lezzone	Tuscan
	Paoli	Italian
19	Dino	Tuscan
	Frescobaldi Wine Bar	Tuscan/International
18	Harry's Bar	International

Alle Murate M *Tuscan* 26 | - | 24 | VE

Duomo | 16R Via del Proconsolo | (39) 055-240-618 | fax 055-288-950 | www.artenotai.org

This "lovely, modern" Tuscan with an exceptional wine list is in a new Duomo locale, where a "friendly" staff oversees an "intimate" room with unearthed 14th-century frescoes; the "overall package puts them in a higher class" so expect to pay accordingly.

Beccofino S *Italian/Seafood* 22 | 20 | 21 | E

Santo Spirito | 1R Piazza Degli Scarlatti | (39) 055-290-076 | fax 055-272-8312 | www.beccofino.com

"Trendy", "tasty" Italian seafooder and "hot spot" in Santo Spirito that features a full "creative" menu with meat dishes as well as a wine bar with a "great selection" of vinos and lighter fare; the interior is "spare but chic", and there's also an appealing outdoor area overlooking the Arno.

Buca Lapi S *Tuscan* 23 | 19 | 21 | E

City Center | 1R Via del Trebbio | (39) 055-213-768 | fax 055-284-862 | www.bucalapi.com

At this "hospitable", "old" 1880 Tuscan in the basement of an 11th-century palazzo off tony Tornabuoni, the "famous *bistecca alla fioren-*

tina is the star" and the atmospheric setting with "postered walls still charms"; a few sniff it's "touristy" and say "unless you are a saber-toothed tiger the beef is too rare and big", but they're outvoted.

Cammillo Trattoria *Italian* 21 | 17 | 19 | M

Oltrarno | 57R Borgo Sant Jacopo | (39) 055-212-427 | fax 055-212-963

This Italian "near the Ponte Vecchio" is noted for "excellently executed classic" meat and fish dishes and "efficient", old-world service; the rustic setting and moderate prices make it a "great family" place that's "always crowded"; N.B. closed Tuesday–Wednesday.

Cantinetta Antinori [S] *Italian* 24 | 23 | 23 | E

Duomo | 3 Piazza Antinori | (39) 055-292-234 | fax 055-235-9877 | www.antinori.it

"Owned by the famous wine family", this "wonderful" Italian in a Renaissance building in a "beautiful location" near the Piazza Duomo showcases 60 of their vintages (both by the bottle and the glass); "equally impressive" food is served by a "friendly" staff in a polished, wood-paneled setting filled with the fashionable who like to lunch here; N.B. closed Saturday–Sunday.

Cibrèo [S][M] *Italian* 26 | 21 | 23 | VE

St. Ambrogio | 8R Via Andrea del Verrocchio | (39) 055-234-1100 | fax 055-244-966 | www.cibreo.com

Chef-owner Fabio Picchi's "captivating" St. Ambrogio Italian is "one of the best in Florence" – the food is "original" (just note it's as likely to be "cock's combs and animal organs" as it is a signature ricotta, pesto and potato soufflé) and there's "no pasta" in sight; the tabs are high, but most maintain "even the memory feels satisfying"; N.B. on the same corner there is Picchi's less expensive Trattoria Cibrèo, which shares the same kitchen, as well as a cafe and the Teatro del Sale, with a buffet and entertainment.

Coco Lezzone [S][≠] *Tuscan* 20 | 12 | 19 | M

City Center | 26R Via del Parioncino | (39) 055-287-178 | fax 055-280-349

"Good solid cooking" ("you can make a meal of the *ribollita* that's always bubbling on the stove") and "reasonable prices" are an appealing combo at this "no-frills", family-run Tuscan housed in an antique Roman tower in the City Center; its "jammed communal tables" "can be fun if you don't mind sitting on top of a stranger"; N.B. note that where the wall paint changes color from yellow to white indicates the height the city's infamous flood rose to in 1966; closed Sundays and Tuesday evenings.

Da Ruggero *Tuscan* 23 | 16 | 18 | E

Porta Romana | 89R Via Senese | (39) 055-220-542

At this rustic "little jewel" just outside Porta Romana, the chef-owner's "delicious", "well-prepared" Tuscan trattoria dishes lead loyalists to say "I dream of this place when I'm asleep in NY"; N.B. closed Tuesday–Wednesday.

Dino [S] *Tuscan* 19 | 15 | 17 | E

Santa Croce | 47R Via Ghibellina | (39) 055-241-452 | fax 055-241-378 | www.ristorantedino.it

"It's like being at grandma's all over again" at this "good", classic Tuscan with arches and wood-beamed ceilings housed in a 15th-century building near the Santa Croce church; surprisingly, for a small, family-run spot the wine list is sophisticated and international, but the smart thing is to stick to the luscious local reds.

Enoteca Pane E Vino [S] *Tuscan*

22 | 17 | 19 | E

Oltrarno | 3R Piazza di Cestello | (39) 055-247-6956 | fax 055-421-5009 | www.ristorantepaneevino.it

A "wonderful escape from the tourists" is this creative Tuscan in the Oltrarno district, which is known for its crafts people; an "amazing" 800-bottle wine list complements "excellent" cuisine, which is served in a minimal two-story setting.

Enoteca Pinchiorri [S] [M] *Italian*

27 | 27 | 26 | VE

Santa Croce | 87 Via Ghibellina | (39) 055-242-757 | fax 055-244-983 | www.enotecapinchiorri.com

"If there is a dining room in heaven it's taking lessons" from this Santa Croce Italian, where Annie Féolde's "fantastic mix of flavors" and "masterful cuisine" is voted No. 1 for Food in Florence, partner Giorgio Pinchiorri's "incredible wine cellar" is praised as the "finest in Europe" and an "impeccable" staff presides over a "gorgeous", gardenlike setting with swagged drapes, massive flowers and the best crystal and china; while foes feel it's "more bloated than an old Englishman", most find the "incredible experience" is worth the "obscenely expensive" tab.

Frescobaldi Ristorante & Wine Bar [S] *Tuscan/International*

19 | 18 | 21 | E

Piazza della Signoria | 2-4R Via dei Magazzini | (39) 055-284-724 | fax 055-265-6535 | www.frescobaldiwinebar.it

Frescobaldi family wines – 45 by the bottle as well as the glass – are the focus and there are the "right" entrees and "delightful small dishes" to complement them at this Tuscan-International off Piazza della Signoria; the bright, modern interior is, appropriately enough, frescoed, and when the weather warrants, outdoor tables in a leafy court beckon.

Fuor d'Acqua [S] *Seafood*

26 | 19 | 21 | E

San Frediano | 37R Via Pisana | (39) 055-222-299 | fax 055-228-1816

The darling of the fashion and entertainment set is this San Frediano seafooder where the "best fresh fish in town with a presentation to match" tempt the trendy; a vaulted-brick-ceiling setting with minimalist decor doesn't distract from "star- and people-watching."

Harry's Bar *International*

18 | 21 | 22 | E

City Center | 22R Lungarno Amerigo Vespucci | (39) 055-239-6700 | fax 055-213-100 | www.harrysbarfirenze.it

"You have to go once" for a "well-poured classic cocktail", "great riverfront location" and "civilized" "expat" vibe at this 1953 International that's no relation to the same-named spot in Venice; your burger "may be the most expensive one in Europe", so "down as many Bellinis as possible to ensure blurred vision when the bill arrives."

Il Latini [M] *Tuscan*

24 | 18 | 21 | M

City Center | 6R Via dei Palchetti | (39) 055-210-916 | fax 055-289-794 | www.illatini.com

"Be prepared to queue big time" at this "eternally popular" "true Tuscan" in City Center where "hungry tourists" and locals are "packed in" at communal tables ("it's like eating with one giant Florentine family you never knew you had") to "revel in" gutsy food; "forget about the menu, let the waiter take care of you", sit back and enjoy the "congenial" atmosphere and "inexpensive" prices.

InCanto *Italian* 24 22 22 VE

Ponte Vecchio | Grand Hotel | 1 Piazza Ognissanti | (39) 055-271-61 | fax 055-217-400 | www.starwoodhotels.com

"Grand views" of the Arno and the Ponte Vecchio can be had from this very "expensive" Italian "refuge" in the Grand Hotel; "fine food" and an "excellent wine list" are proferred in an intimate, "inviting" room with leather armchairs and an open kitchen.

La Giostra ◐ *Tuscan* 27 22 24 E

Duomo | 12R Via Borgo Pinti | (39) 055-241-341 | fax 055-226-8781 | www.ristorantelagiostra.com

"A wonderful restaurant with a chef who claims he's royalty" is what supporters say about this Tuscan near the Duomo where Prince Hapsburg Lorena and his "handsome" twin sons serve "delicious" food based on ancient recipes in a small, "romantic" setting where celebrity photos line the walls and "little white lights twinkle from the ceiling"; a few mutter it "oozes as much cheese as charm", but they're outvoted.

Olio & Convivium 🅂 *Italian* 23 21 23 E

Oltrarno | 4 Via Santo Spirito | (39) 055-265-8198 | fax 055-265-6267 | www.conviviumfirenze.it

This classically decorated "tiny gem" with "inventive" Italian food in the Renaissance Palazzo Capponi is good for lunch if you're in the Oltrarno area; it's also a gourmet take-out shop where you can get picnic fixings, wines and a selection of about 40 olive oils.

Omero *Tuscan* 25 21 22 E

Arcetri | 11R Via Pian dei Giullari | (39) 055-220-053 | fax 055-233-6183 | www.ristoranteomero.it

"Take a taxi" and "go when it's light so you can enjoy" the "beautiful views of Florence" from the second dining room or terrace of this "unassuming", 106-year-old Tuscan trattoria in the cool hills of Arcetri, about five kilometers from the City Center; order the "best" fried chicken, rabbit and *bistecca alla fiorentina* and you'll join those who say: "eat here once and you'll want to return forever"; N.B. closed Tuesdays.

Ora d'Aria 🅂 *Tuscan/Mediterranean* 24 21 22 E

Santa Croce | 3 CR Via Ghibellina | (39) 055-200-1699 | fax 055-200-1699 | www.oradariaristorante.com

"Wow" – "amazing food" (from "both their traditional and creative menus"), a "charming locale" in trendy Santa Croce, "elegant" modern decor with "ever-changing art on display" and "lovely service" make this Tuscan-Mediterranean "popular" with the "beautiful and stylish people", particularly after the theater; so "forget about the exchange rate" and focus on the "enchanting evening that awaits."

Paoli *Italian* 20 21 21 E

Duomo | 12R Via dei Tavolini | (39) 055-216-215 | fax 055-216-215

If it's ambiance you're after you'll find it "sitting under tall, incredibly beautiful frescoed vaulted ceilings that make you feel like you're dining in pre-Renaissance times" at this Italian housed in a former church near the Duomo; there are no "fireworks from the kitchen", but the food is "reliable", "service friendly" and the room "spectacular"; N.B. closed Tuesdays.

Sabatini Ⓜ *Tuscan* 24 21 22 VE

Duomo | 9A Via Panzani | (39) 055-282-802 | fax 055-210-293 | www.ristorantesabatini.it

Since 1929 this "traditional", high-profile Tuscan with "excellent" but "expensive" food and "refined service" has been "one of the better Florentine restaurants", and it's conveniently located near the Duomo; fans of the surprisingly "spacious", "formal", wood-paneled room with paintings praise its lovely garden view, but others disdain the "dated setting."

Taverna del Bronzino Ⓢ *Italian* 26 21 26 E

Piazza Indipendenza | 25 Via delle Ruote | (39) 055-495-220 | fax 055-462-0076

"No hype or hipness", just "wonderful food" is found at this Italian set in a 16th-century former artist's studio that's "a bit off the beaten path", near San Marco, where a "wonderful, attentive staff always tries to please the demanding international clientele that frequents" the place.

Villa San Michele *Italian* 25 28 25 VE

Fiesole | Hotel Villa San Michele | 4 Via Doccia | (39) 055-567-8200 | fax 055-567-8250 | www.villasanmichele.com

"This is living" say sybarites about this Italian in Fiesole's Villa San Michele, a former 15th-century monastery with a facade attributed to Michelangelo; sure, the food is "very good", "wine list outstanding", service "exceptional" and the dining areas "beautiful", but what surveyors "really remember is seeing night falling on Florence from a terrace table", "champagne glass in hand"; the less romantic also recall the "astronomical prices."

Zibibbo Ⓢ *Italian/Mediterranean* 25 20 25 E

Careggi | 3R Via di Terzollina | (39) 055-433-383 | fax 055-428-9070

Chef-owner Benedetta Vitali (ex co-founder Cibrèo) is a "magician" when it comes to cooking "great" Italian-Mediterranean cuisine at this "out-of-the-way temple of food" in the Careggi hills, about eight kilometers from the City Center; devotees declare it's "worth the trek" to dine in her modern room with a skylight and Medici tower view on "outstanding" culinary combinations.

Other Noteworthy Places

Angels *Florentine/Mediterranean*

Grand Hotel Cavour | Via del Proconsolo 29/31 | (39) 055-239-8762 | fax 055-239-8123 | www.ristoranteangels.it

Borgo San Jacopo *Italian*

Hotel Lungarno | Borgo San Jacopo 62 | (39) 055-281-661 | fax 055-291-114 | www.lungarnohotels.com

Carmagnini Del'500 Ⓜ *Tuscan*

Via Barberinese 242 | (39) 055-881-9930 | fax 055-881-9611 | www.carmagninidel500.it

Centanni [S][M] *Tuscan*
Centanni Residence | Via di Centanni 8 | (39) 055-630-122 | fax 055-651-0445 | www.residence-centanni.it

Don Chisciotte [S] *Florentine/Seafood*
Via Cosimo Ridolfi 4R | (39) 055-475-430 | fax 055-485-305 | www.ristorantedonchisciotte.com

Il Cavaliere *Tuscan*
Viale Lavagnini 22 | (39) 055-471-914 | fax 055-471-914

Il Cavallino *Tuscan*
Via delle Farine 6R | (39) 055-215-818 | fax 055-214-555

Il Verrocchio *Italian*
Hotel Villa La Massa | Via della Massa 24 | (39) 055-62611 | fax 055-633-102 | www.villalamassa.com

I Quattro Amici *Seafood*
Via Orti Oricellari 29 | (39) 055-215-413 | fax 055-289-767 | www.accademiadelgusto.it

La Panacea [M] *Italian/Seafood*
Via Bosconi 58A | (39) 055-548-972 | fax 055-548-973

Lo Strettoio [S][M] *Tuscan*
Via di Serpiolle 7 | (39) 055-425-0044 | fax 055-425-0044 | www.lostrettoio.com

Oliviero [S] *Tuscan*
Via delle Terme 51R | (39) 055-287-643 | fax 055-230-2407 | www.ristorante-oliviero.it

Onice Lounge & Restaurant [M] *Tuscan/Asian*
Hotel Villa La Vedetta | Viale Michelangiolo 78 | (39) 055-681-631 | fax 055-658-2544 | www.villalavedettahotel.com

Osteria del Caffè Italiano [M] *Tuscan*
11/13 Via Isola delle Stinche | (39) 055-289-080 | fax 055-288-950 | www.caffeitaliano.it

Rossini *Mediterranean*
Lungarno Corsini 4 | (39) 055-239-9224 | fax 055-271-7990 | www.ristoranterossini.it

Targa Bistrot Fiorentino [S] *Italian*
Lungarno Cristoforo Colombo 7 | (39) 055-677-377 | fax 055-676-493 | www.targabistrot.net

Trattoria Donnini *Tuscan*
Via di Rimaggio 22 | (39) 055-630-076 | fax 055-633-228

Ulivo Rosso *Italian*
Via Le Catese 2 | (39) 055-448-1890 | fax 055-448-1953 | www.ulivorosso.com

	FOOD	DECOR	SERVICE	COST

Frankfurt

TOP FOOD RANKING

	Restaurant	Cuisine
25	Gargantua	New French/Mediterranean
	Osteria Enoteca	Italian
24	Restaurant Français	New French
23	Aubergine	Italian/German
	Sushimoto	Japanese
22	M Steakhouse	Steakhouse
20	Medici	Mediterranean
	Erno's Bistro	French
	Edelweiss	Austrian
	Tiger	French/Mediterranean
19	Holbein's	German/International
	Charlot	Italian
	Signatures Veranda	German
	Rama V	Thai
18	Größenwahn	Italian/International
	Opéra	International
17	Die Leiter	International
16	Apfelwein Wagner	German
15	Garibaldi	Italian
14	Central Park Public Pantry	American/International

Apfelwein Wagner ◐ *German* — 16 | 14 | 14 | M

Sachsenhausen | Schweizer Str. 71 | (49-69) 612-565 | fax 611-445 | www.apfelwein-wagner.com

For a taste of "typical Frankfurt", try this "typical apple-wine pub" in Sachsenhausen; the "down-to-earth" digs may be "bleak", the "simple" German fare "unexceptional" ("pork, pork and more pork") and the "rough", "gruff" staffers "uncouth", but "fast service", "moderate prices" and the city's "signature beverage" make it "popular among locals and tourists alike."

Aubergine ⊠ *Italian/German* — 23 | 22 | 23 | E

City Center | Alte Gasse 14 | (49-69) 920-0780 | fax 920-0786 | www.aubergine-frankfurt.de

A small red awning marks this "superb" City Center spot where one can expect "extravagant, freshly prepared" Italian-German fare as well as "attentive service" from a "nice, young, friendly" staff; owner and native Sardinian Paolo Vargiu's "incredible attention to detail" extends from the "excellent" wine list and "tasteful decor" "right down to the Versace plates" that grace the few tables.

Central Park Public Pantry ◐⊠ *American/International* — 14 | 19 | 17 | M

City Center | Kaiserhofstr. 12 | (49-69) 9139-6146 | fax 9139-6148 | www.central-park.com

The flagship of a family of five local venues, this "upscale" spot in City Center – "just off a wonderful street", the Goethestraße, and "near the

Opera House" – exudes a "hip atmosphere", fueled in part by a "fun bar" where a "trendy" crowd congregates; its "eclectic" American-International dishes make it "a place to escape the traditional meat-and-potatoes German" cuisine, and even those who find the casual fare merely "decent" declare "who cares about the food" when you can "look at the staff"?

Charlot *Italian* 19 | 17 | 17 | E

City Center | Opernplatz 10 | (49-69) 287-007 | fax 219-966

"A lot of thought goes into preparing" the "authentic Italian" fare at this "good, consistent" City Center establishment whose regulars report there's "no need to even look at a menu" – the "waiters are pros", so "just tell them what you like and they'll deliver something delicious"; the "small but attractive setting" is patronized "by smart people of all sorts", including a "celebrity crowd", making it "a good place to people-watch" too.

Die Leiter ⊠ *International* 17 | 12 | 12 | E

City Center | Kaiserhofstr. 11 | (49-69) 292-121 | fax 291-645 | www.dieleiter.de

When it opened nearly a quarter-century ago, this "super-centrally located" City Center spot quickly became a trendy destination, and it still attracts "the 'in' crowd" with an "extravagant" International menu of "appetizing" Italian- and Austrian-accented offerings; but foes fault "nothing-special" food, "excessive prices", "sober decor" and an "arrogant" staff that "seems burdened by having to wait on you."

Edelweiss *Austrian* 20 | 15 | 21 | M

Sachsenhausen | Schweizer Str. 96 | (49-69) 619-696 | fax 619-697 | www.edelweiss-ffm.de

"Friendly service" from a "special" staff clad in lederhosen combined with a "relaxed atmosphere" lends a "holiday" feel to this "comfortable" Sachsenhausen pseudo-ski lodge where the "really good flavors" of "authentic Austrian food", including "wonderful dishes like Wiener schnitzel", are accompanied by a selection of "super brews to wash everything down"; N.B. don't miss the large heated terrace.

Erno's Bistro ⊠ *French* 20 | 15 | 21 | VE

Westend | Liebigstr. 15 | (49-69) 721-997 | fax 173-838 | www.ernosbistro.de

"Attentive" service from a "caring" staff overseen by longtime owner Eric Huber sets the tone at this "ultrareliable, top-flight French" in Westend, "a surprising oasis in a city full of heavy food" thanks to chef Valéry Mathis' "small but exquisite menu" of "excellent" fare; not only is it "a welcome break from German cuisine", but the "comfy atmosphere" of its "lively, friendly" digs makes it just the kind of place to which many "would go every day if they could."

Gargantua ⊠ *French/Mediterranean* 25 | 19 | 20 | VE

Westend | Liebigstr. 47 | (49-69) 720-718 | fax 7103-4695 | www.gargantua.de

It's the "creative, well-executed menu" of "incredible" New French-Mediterranean fare from chef-owner and cookbook author Klaus Trebes that makes this "exceptional small bistro" in Westend justifiably "famous", and earns it the ranking of No. 1 for Food in Frankfurt; "very good service", a winning wine list and shady terrace are other reasons it's "well worth" a visit; yes, it's quite expensive, but such an "excellent" experience offers "good value for the money."

Garibaldi ⊠ *Italian* 15 | 15 | 11 | M

City Center | Kleine Hochstr. 4 | (49-69) 2199-7644 | fax 2199-7655

"Always crowded", this "hip spot" in City Center serves up "decent", "authentic Italian" fare "at a good price", but "you don't come here for the food" (or the "disappointing wine list") - rather, you come "to watch" the antics of the crowd and "listen to [the staff] sing 'Happy Birthday' several times an evening"; fun aside, though, some just "don't get what attracts people to" its "loud, smoke-filled" setting and "sometimes confused service."

Größenwahn *Italian/International* 18 | 13 | 15 | M

Nordend | Lenaustr. 97 | (49-69) 599-356 | www.cafe-groessenwahn.de

For "more than 25 years", this "casual" Nordend "favorite" has been a "place for locals" to enjoy "a really nice evening" over a "varied", "creative" menu of Italian-International cuisine (including "fresh, delicious" vegetarian fare) that's "attractively" presented and "reasonably priced"; perhaps the decor is "nothing special" and the "service could be faster", but at least there's "always a smile on the faces" of the "friendly" staffers, ensuring that you "feel good" within the "warm", "cozy" setting.

Holbein's Ⓜ *German/International* 19 | 21 | 16 | E

Sachsenhausen | Städel Kunstmuseum | Holbeinstr. 1 | (49-69) 6605-6666 | fax 6605-6677 | www.holbeins.de

"Beautiful, stylish decor" is the point at this "posh joint" that's "nicely located in the Städel museum" in Sachsenhausen, "a wonderful setting for a great meal" of "tasty" German-International fare made from "particularly fresh ingredients"; still, some complain of "long waits" and suggest that the generally "well-trained staff" is "not accommodating" when "stressed", "leaving the impression that guests are annoying and have to be tolerated"; P.S. "in summer, sit on the terrace" overlooking the gardens.

Medici ⊠ *Mediterranean* 20 | 19 | 19 | E

City Center | Weißadlergasse 2 | (49-69) 2199-0794 | fax 2199-0795 | www.restaurant-medici.de

Most maintain this centrally located City Center Mediterranean housed in an insurance company building is a "popular" and "secure bet for a business lunch or dinner"; for those who find the modern minimalist interior with its massive painting of bare-breasted females a "turnoff", there's alternate alfresco eating out on the terrace.

M Steakhouse ⊠ *Steak* 22 | 15 | 18 | E

Westend | Feuerbachstr. 11A | (49-69) 7103-4050 | www.the-steakhouse.de

"A piece of America in Frankfurt", this Westend steakhouse packs in "lots of English-speaking customers" who come to sample its "delicious" fare - including "really tender" beef, "satisfying jumbo prawns" and "fantastic salads" - served by "good-humored" staffers in a "sparse" setting with "cowboy photos on the walls"; yes, it's "expensive", but most feel the "cost is appropriate given the quality" and "generous portions."

FOOD | DECOR | SERVICE | COST

Opéra *International*

18 | 23 | 17 | E

City Center | Alte Oper | Opernplatz 1 | (49-69) 134-0215 | fax 134-0239 | www.opera-restauration.de

"Don't forget to look at the ceiling" while taking in the "spectacular old-world setting" of this "glamorous site" in a "stunning location" "within the Opera House" in City Center, where a "polite", "professional" staff serves "well-presented" International fare and "expensive wines"; still, critics claim that the "erratic kitchen" produces "good but not great food" that should "be more ambitious to match" the "unbeatable ambiance."

Osteria Enoteca ☒ *Italian*

25 | 18 | 23 | E

Rödelheim | Arnoldshainer Str. 2 | (49-69) 789-2216 | fax 789-2216 | www.osteria-enoteca.de

Chef Carmelo Greco's "fresh", "delicious Italian food" (including "great antipasti") draws urbanites to this bi-level venue in the somewhat "remote suburb" of Rödelheim, where guests must ring a bell to gain access to the romantically lit, off-white dining room; add in a "good wine list" and an "accommodating, attentive" staff and you'll see why many lauders label it "a special-occasion place" that's "a bit out of the way but worth the trip."

Rama V ◐ *Thai*

19 | 15 | 15 | M

City Center | Vilbeler Str. 32 | (49-69) 2199-6488

"A must for Thai lovers", this City Center Siamese sports "an extensive menu" of "authentic" dishes that are "delicious and beautifully prepared"; the "stylish" space, "tastefully decorated with art", is overseen by an "obliging staff" headed by "meticulous" owners whose "attention to detail is apparent in everything they serve", not to mention a "big golden Buddha" who "sits in the back watching you eat."

Restaurant Français ☒ *French*

24 | 22 | 24 | VE

City Center | Steigenberger Frankfurter Hof | Am Kaiserplatz | (49-69) 215-118 | fax 215-119 | www.frankfurter-hof.steigenberger.de

Set "in Frankfurt's dowager hotel", City Center's Steigenberger Frankfurter Hof, this "formal special-occasion restaurant" has been "nicely upgraded" in recent years, and now attracts a "less-stuffy clientele" with its "gourmet New French selections", "excellent service" and "extremely civilized" decor with cream-colored walls and opulent oil paintings; "make sure you have plenty of room on your credit card", though, because "you may feel like royalty but you'll need access to the state treasury to settle the bill."

Signatures Veranda *German*

19 | 16 | 18 | E

City Center | InterContinental Frankfurt | Wilhelm-Leuschner-Str. 43 | (49-69) 2605-2452 | fax 2605-2402 | www.interconti.com

Serving from breakfast through dinner, this "very good" venue in the InterContinental Frankfurt in City Center features "delicious" German fare offered in "ample" à la carte portions or via "great buffets" that are "restocked like magic" by "competent and almost invisible" staffers; still, some surveyors damn with faint praise, purporting it "meets every expectation of a typical hotel restaurant."

Sushimoto M *Japanese* | 23 | 16 | 18 | E

City Center | ArabellaSheraton Grand Hotel | Konrad Adenauer Str. 7 | (49-69) 298-1187 | fax 298-1810 | www.arabellasheraton.com

Guests "wonder if you can eat so well in" Tokyo after a visit to this "unexpected" Japanese in City Center's ArabellaSheraton Grand; despite decor that "isn't world-shaking" and a staff that could use "a better knowledge of German" and English, it's "a must for fans" seeking "fantastic and fresh meals" featuring "excellent sushi" and teppanyaki selections; P.S. those who find the tabs "too high" should check out the more "moderately priced set menu" at lunch.

Tiger S M *French/Mediterranean* | 20 | 19 | 18 | E

City Center | Tigerpalast Varieté | Heiligkreuzgasse 16-20 | (49-69) 920-02250 | fax 9200-2217 | www.tigerpalast.com

The "kitchen deserves high praise" at this "gourmet" French-Med venue in City Center's Tigerpalast Varieté theater, where the "extravagant", "delicious dishes and exclusive wines" come with "plenty of action" in the form of a "surprisingly" "smashing show" ("don't miss" it); additionally, the "cozy setup" is "nicely decorated" and the "obliging staffers" "know what they're doing", making for an "all-around aesthetic" experience that has even some with "tight wallets" conceding they "can't complain about the cost."

Other Noteworthy Places

Alt Byblos ◐ M *Lebanese*
Hanauer Landstr. 7, Zoo Passage | (49-69) 9441-0103 | fax 9441-1765 | www.selected-restaurants.com/alt-byblos

Avocado S *French/Mediterranean*
Hochstr. 27 | (49-69) 294-642 | fax 1337-9455 | www.restaurant-avocado.de

Beyond *Italian/Mediterranean*
Mergenthaler Allee 1 | (49-61) 9677-9360 | www.beyond-ffm.de

Biancalani S *Mediterranean*
Walther-von-Cronberg-Platz 7-9 | (49-69) 6897-7615 | www.biancalani.de

Das Leben ist schön ⇏ *Italian*
Hanauer Landstr. 198 | (49-69) 4305-7870

Dorade *Mediterranean/Seafood*
Carl-von-Noorden-Platz 5 | (49-69) 6319-8383 | fax 6319-8085 | www.dorade.net

Emma Metzler M *French/German*
Schaumainkai 17 | (49-69) 6199-5906 | fax 6199-5909 | www.emma-metzler.com

Exil S ⇏ *German*
Mercatorstr. 26 | (49-69) 447-200 | fax 4898-1888 | www.exil-frankfurt.de

Fischer's M *German*
Am Marktplatz 6 | (49-6171) 52-755 | fax 28-6992 | www.fischers-restaurant.de

Goldman Restaurant & Bar *German/Mediterranean*
Goldman 25hours Hotel | Hanauer Landstr. 127 | (49-69) 4058-6890 | fax 689-890 | www.25hours-hotels.com

Hessler [M] *German*
Hotel Hessler | Am Bootshafen 4 | (49-61) 814-3030 | fax 8143-0333 | www.hesslers.de

Higematsu [S] *Japanese*
Meisengasse 11 | (49-69) 280-688

Ivory Club, The [S] *Indian*
Taunusanlage 15 | (49-69) 7706-7767 | www.the-steakhouse.de

Iwase [S] *Japanese*
Vilbeler Str. 31 | (49-69) 283-992

Jasper's [S] *French*
Schifferstr. 8 | (49-69) 614-117 | fax 623-554 | www.jaspersrestaurant.com

King Kamehameha Suite [S] *French*
Taunusanlage 20 | (49-69) 7103-5277 | fax 7103-5980 | www.king-kamehameha.de

Knoblauch ◐[S]≠ *French*
Staufenstr. 39 | (49-69) 722-828 | fax 729-715 | www.restaurantknoblauchfrankfurt.de

La Stalla di Ugo *Italian/Mediterranean*
Fürstenbergerstr. 179 | (49-69) 5979-7975 | fax 9050-0778

Maaschanz [M] *French*
Färberstr. 75 | (49-69) 622-886 | fax 622-886 | www.maaschanz.de

Maingau Stuben [S][M] *German/International*
Hotel Maingau | Schifferstr. 38-40 | (49-69) 610-752 | fax 620-790 | www.maingau.de

Main Tower Restaurant & Bar [S][M] *International*
Neue Mainzer Str. 52-58 | (49-69) 3650-4777 | fax 3650-4871 | www.maintower-restaurant.de

Meyer's Restaurant & Bar [S] *International*
Grosse Bockenheimer Str. 54 | (49-69) 9139-7070 | fax 9139-7071 | www.meyer-frankfurt.de

Neuer Haferkasten *Italian*
Frankfurter Str. 118 | (49-6102) 35329 | www.neuer-haferkasten.de

Nibelungenschänke ◐≠ *Greek*
Nibelungenallee 55 | (49-69) 554-244 | fax 593-861 | www.nibelungenschaenke.de

Orfeo's Erben *International*
Hamburger Allee 45 | (49-69) 7076-9100 | fax 9708-4793 | www.orfeos.de

Oscar*s ◐ *International*
Steigenberger Frankfurter Hof | Am Kaiserplatz | (49-69) 215-118 | fax 215-119 | www.frankfurter-hof.steigenberger.de

Sachsenhäuser Warte *German*
Darmstädter Landstr. 279 | (49-69) 682-716 | fax 685-362 | www.sachsenhaeuserwarte.de

Sèvres *French*
Hotel Hessischer Hof | Friedrich-Ebert Anlage 40 | (49-69) 7540-2927 | fax 7540-2924 | www.hessischer-hof.de

Silk & Micro [S][M] *International*
CocoonClub | UFO Building, Karl-Benz-Str. 21 | (49-69) 900-200 | fax 900-205-90 | www.cocoonclub.net

Stella 🅂 *Italian*
Galerie Freßgass | Große Bockenheimer Str. 52 | (49-69) 9050-1271 | fax 9050-1669 | www.stella-ffm.de

Surf 'n Turf 🅂 *Seafood/Steak*
Grüneburgweg 95 | (49-69) 722-122 | fax 7140-2810 | www.the-steakhouse.de

Villa Leonhardi *Italian*
Zeppelinallee 18 | (49-69) 789-8847 | fax 7898-8488 | www.villa-leonhardi.de

Villa Merton 🅂 *International*
Union International Club | Am Leonhardsbrunn 12 | (49-69) 703-033 | fax 707-3820 | www.kofler-company.de

Weidemann 🅂 *International*
Kelsterbacher Str. 66 | (49-69) 675-996 | fax 673-928 | www.weidemann-online.de

FOOD | DECOR | SERVICE | COST

Geneva

TOP FOOD RANKING

	Restaurant	Cuisine
29	Domaine de Châteauvieux	New French
26	Auberge du Lion d'Or	French
25	Patara	Thai
24	La Vendée	French
	Chez Jacky	French
	Restaurant du Parc	New French
	La Favola	Italian
	Miyako	Japanese/Sushi
	L'Auberge d'Hermance	French
	Spice's	Asian Fusion
23	L'Entrecôte Couronnée	French
	Vertig'O*	French/Mediterranean
	Il Lago	Northern Italian
	Le Relais de l'Entrecôte	Steakhouse
	Le Chat-Botté	French
22	Roberto	Lombardian
21	L'Olivier de Provence	French
	Le Buffet de la Gare	French/Mediterranean
20	Bistrot du Boeuf Rouge	Lyonnaise
	Thai Phuket*	Thai
	La Perle du Lac	New French
	Tsé-Yang	Chinese
19	Café des Négociants	French/Mediterranean
	L'Arabesque	Lebanese
	Les Armures	French/Swiss
18	Brasserie Lipp	French Brasserie
17	Brasserie de l'Hôtel de Ville	Swiss/French Brasserie
16	Café de Peney	Classic French
	Café des Bains	International
11	Le Baroque	International

Auberge du Lion d'Or ☒ *French* — 26 | 24 | 25 | VE

Cologny | 5 Place Pierre Gautier | (41-22) 736-4432 | fax 786-7462 | www.liondor.ch

"Worth" the trip "outside of town", this "excellent, old-school" inn in Cologny boasts a "contemporary" "gastronomic restaurant" and a "pretty", more casual bistro, "both of which serve fabulous French food"; the setting "overlooking the lake" is "magnificent" and the staff is "impeccable", ensuring "an experience that should not be missed."

Bistrot du Boeuf Rouge ☒ *Lyon* — 20 | 17 | 17 | M

Right Bank | 17 Rue Alfred-Vincent | (41-22) 732-7537 | fax 731-4684 | www.boeufrouge.ch

A bastion of "Lyon in Geneva", this "reliable" Right Bank spot "is the place to go for" that French city's "excellent specialties" (like tripe), as

* Indicates a tie with restaurant above

well as some "local" favorites, all offered "at moderate prices"; the "small dining room" is sometimes "noisy", but its "original decor" featuring scads of quirky bric-a-brac and a collection of water carafes makes it "a fun place to eat."

Brasserie de l'Hôtel de Ville *Swiss/French* 17 | 16 | 16 | E

Old Town | 39 Grand-Rue | (41-22) 311-7030

Its prime Old Town location is the main draw of this "convivial" spot where the "hearty" Swiss-French brasserie fare includes "good cheese fondue" and other "regional specialties"; some say it's "a little too expensive in view of the quality", merely "fair" service and "nothing-fancy" decor, but most agree it's "ok in a pinch."

Brasserie Lipp ◐ *French* 18 | 17 | 15 | E

Left Bank | 8 Rue de la Confédération | (41-22) 311-1011 | fax 312-0104 | www.brasserie-lipp.com

"Modeled on its Paris namesake", this "busy", "buzzy" Left Bank boîte is "everything you'd expect" in a "typical French brasserie" - "noisy" "art nouveau" digs "packed" with patrons at "too-small tables" enjoying "consistently good" "traditional" fare ("shellfish is a specialty") "roughly served" by sometimes "rude" staffers; it also offers "salvation for those who don't eat on a strict Swiss timetable", as it's "seemingly always open"; P.S. you "must dine" on the "terrace overlooking the ramparts of the Old Town."

Café de Peney *French* 16 | 18 | 18 | E

Satigny | 130 Route d'Aire-la-Ville, Peney-Dessous | (41-22) 753-1755 | fax 753-1760

On the banks of the Rhône in the "quaint village" of Peney-Dessous in Satigny, "Geneva's wine country", this "pretty", "welcoming" cafe from "the same owner as the prestigious" Domaine de Châteauvieux up the hill "serves Classic French fare" along with some more "unusual dishes"; a few "disappointed" diners declare the menu offers "little choice" and say certain staffers are "not very friendly", but many appreciate that it's "open seven days a week - definitely a plus."

Café des Bains *International* 16 | 15 | 14 | E

Left Bank | 26 Rue des Bains | (41-22) 321-5798 | fax 321-5838 | www.cafedesbains.com

"A young, hip" crowd congregates at this "small cafe" on the Left Bank, calling it a "cool place to be" thanks to its "innovative" International menu and "trendy" design-conscious, candle-studded interior; less enthusiastic sorts, though, claim "the bill is excessive, considering" the "nothing-exceptional service", "overly smoky" atmosphere and "rather uneven cuisine."

Café des Négociants *French/Mediterranean* 19 | 18 | 17 | E

Carouge | 29 Rue de la Filature | (41-22) 300-3130 | fax 300-3105 | www.negociants.ch

The "wonderful wine list" is a "highlight" of any visit to this "reliable restaurant" in the "fun neighborhood" of "old Carouge", "the SoHo of Geneva"; in fact, guests are "invited" to take "a trip to the cellar" "to pick a bottle themselves" (though the "knowledgeable" sommelier will also "select" for you), and those "charmed" by the subterranean space's "great ambiance" can even dine there on "refined" French-

Med cuisine; still, some say the service is just "satisfactory" and the cost "exorbitant."

Chez Jacky [S] *French* 24 | 15 | 21 | E

Right Bank | 9-11 Rue Necker | (41-22) 732-8680 | fax 731-1297 | www.chezjacky.ch

For a "distinguished dining experience", visit this "great little restaurant" whose "setting slightly off the beaten track" on the Right Bank "adds to its cachet as 'a find'"; eponymous "chef Gruber's truly imaginative" French food offers "value" (regulars recommend you "stick to the excellent, affordable set menu"), and a "friendly staff" further enhances the "pleasant" atmosphere; P.S. "dining on the patio is just wonderful."

Domaine de Châteauvieux [S] [M] *French* 29 | 25 | 27 | VE

Satigny | Domaine de Châteauvieux | Chemin de Châteauvieux 16, Peney-Dessus | (41-22) 753-1511 | fax 753-1924 | www.chateauvieux.ch

"Wow!" is how fans sum up this "deluxe" venue in a "marvelous setting" overlooking the Rhône in Satigny that offers "the best table" around town, ranking No. 1 for Food in greater Geneva; "creative" chef "Philippe Chevrier's alchemy" produces "superb" New French fare, which is paired with a "fantastic wine list" and "impeccably served" by an "attentive, efficient" staff in "a lovely room" with "panoramic countryside views"; true, you'll need "a well-filled billfold", but everyone should experience such a "true gastronomic delight", "even if it's just once."

Il Lago *Italian* 23 | 26 | 23 | VE

Right Bank | Four Seasons Hôtel des Bergues | 33 Quai des Bergues | (41-22) 908-7110 | fax 908-7411 | www.fourseasons.com/geneva

"If you like dining in hotels, this restaurant is as good as they come" say supporters of this Northern Italian in the Four Seasons Hôtel des Bergues on the Right Bank; "excellent" cuisine and a "great wine list" that includes bottles from France, Switzerland and The Boot are proffered in a "beautiful" "formal setting" with extravagant floral displays, paintings and Rhône views; of course, "prices that are off the charts" also make for an "elite" experience.

La Favola [S] *Italian* 24 | 22 | 19 | E

Old Town | 15 Rue Jean Calvin | (41-22) 311-7437 | fax 310-1713 | www.lafavola.com

It's no fairy tale: "a most memorable meal" can in fact be found at this "tiny gem", "a wonderful retreat" "in the heart of Old Town", where "fabulous Italian" "dishes and wines from Ticino" are served with "personalized attention" in a "cute" little "jewel-box" space; though both floors are "sweet", regulars recommend that "those who can navigate the tight staircase" should "make sure to get a table upstairs"; P.S. don't miss "the best tiramisu ever."

La Perle du Lac [M] *French* 20 | 22 | 20 | VE

Right Bank | 128 Rue de Lausanne | (41-22) 909-1020 | fax 909-1030 | www.laperledulac.ch

There's "fine New French" fare at this "divine" Right Bank venue, but it's the "magnificent view" (maybe the "most beautiful" in town) that keeps folks "coming back" to this "perfect location" in a "lovely lakeside setting" surrounded by "charming gardens"; it's "a must in

Geneva" for "all the tourists" for a "casual luncheon outdoors or formal dining indoors" "especially in spring and summer."

L'Arabesque *Lebanese* 19 | 19 | 20 | VE

Right Bank | Hôtel Président Wilson | 47 Quai Wilson | (41-22) 906-6666 | fax 906-6667 | www.hotelpwilson.com

"You might find better Lebanese food" somewhere, "but you won't be able to eat it in more luxury" than at this "exquisite, expensive" dining room in the Right Bank's "upmarket" Hôtel Président Wilson, where an "accommodating" staff serves up "delicious", exotic fare; some say the decor "could use a little refreshing", but most declare it a "lovely spot."

L'Auberge d'Hermance *French* 24 | 23 | 24 | E

Hermance | L'Auberge d'Hermance | 12 Rue du Midi | (41-22) 751-1368 | fax 751-1631 | www.hotel-hermance.ch

Peripatetic patrons who are willing "to drive 15 minutes outside of the city" will be rewarded with an undeniably "great meal" at this "idyllic" French inn ensconced "in the medieval village" of Hermance, where a "friendly, professional" staff will seat you within the "intimate" "antique" dining room, in the "delightful" glass-walled winter garden or on the "beautiful terrace"; wherever you sit, though, expect "attractively presented dishes" from a "superb kitchen."

La Vendée *French* 24 | 17 | 20 | VE

Petit-Lancy | Hostellerie de la Vendée | 28 Chemin de la Vendée | (41-22) 792-0411 | fax 792-0546 | www.vendee.ch

"Inventive" French fare - including especially "well-prepared fresh-fish" dishes - served by a staff with "plenty of savoir faire" makes this "high-quality" destination in a Petit-Lancy hotel "worth the trip", despite its "steep" prices; some suggest the "rather somber" surroundings "don't suit the standing" of such an otherwise "first-class" venue, but all agree "the veranda is very nice."

Le Baroque ☒ *International* 14 | 19 | 12 | E

Left Bank | 12 Place de la Fusterie | (41-22) 311-0515 | fax 311-8804 | www.lebaroque.com

The place to "see and be seen", this "popular" Left Bank venue "gives Geneva a young face" thanks to the "hip, trendy people" who populate its "smart", "noisy" interior; the International fare is "average" and "expensive", and the "unfriendly" service ranges from "basic" to "terrible", but those who consider it "more nightclub than restaurant" know they're "paying for reputation and decor more than the staff or meal."

Le Buffet de la Gare des Eaux-Vives ☒ *French/Mediterranean* 21 | 15 | 17 | E

Left Bank | 7 Avenue de la Gare des Eaux-Vives | (41-22) 840-4430 | www.lebuffetdelagare.ch

"Believe it or not", "haute cuisine" awaits at this "small place" in a "unique" "setting literally next to an old train station" on the Left Bank, where an "amazing selection" of "inventive", "refined" French-Med fare is "well served" along with "good wines"; perhaps the "modern decor" is "nothing special", but there's a "great terrace in summer", and though it's "not cheap", most insist it's "really worth it" - meaning "reservations are a must."

Le Chat-Botté *French* 23 | 22 | 23 | VE

Right Bank | Hôtel Beau-Rivage | 13 Quai du Mont-Blanc | (41-22) 716-6666 | fax 716-6060 | www.beau-rivage.ch

"A favorite for many years", this "elegant" French venue in the Right Bank's Hôtel Beau-Rivage features "enchanting" cuisine and a "very nice wine list", all "effortlessly served" by an "impeccable" staff "in a refined setting" with decor resembling that of a "grand palace"; yes, "it will cost you", but most feel "the quality equals the price", though a few wonder "what's with the hype?", saying the fare would benefit from "a touch of originality."

L'Entrecôte Couronnée Ⓢ *French* 23 | 18 | 19 | E

Right Bank | 5 Rue du Pâquis | (41-22) 732-8445 | fax 732-8446

Of course, this "lively" little French place on the popular Right Bank features an "excellent" namesake entrecôte with "endless frites", but other "quality" dishes (many based on local ingredients like fish fresh from the nearby lake) "will have you coming back for more"; wooden furnishings, mirrors and ceiling fans help produce an appealing archetypal bistro ambiance .

Le Relais de l'Entrecôte Ⓢ *Steak* 23 | 18 | 17 | M

Left Bank | 49 Rue du Rhône | (41-22) 310-6004 | fax 310-6064

"Choice is not the strong" suit at this "single-dish" steakhouse "institution" on the Left Bank, but fans "know why they go" - for the "same quality" entrecôte "with a twist (an addictive sauce that's guaranteed to have you licking the plate)" and "classic frites" that are served at its Paris siblings; "the only disadvantage" is that it's "difficult to get a table" in the "noisy", "cramped" space, but most "don't mind standing in line" when "the meat is divine and the prices fair."

Les Armures *French/Swiss* 19 | 19 | 17 | E

Old Town | Hôtel Les Armures | 1 Rue du Puits-Saint-Pierre | (41-22) 310-3442 | fax 818-7113 | www.hotel-les-armures.ch

Just "steps from all the points of interest in Old Town", this "charming" "longtime favorite" "in the lovely" Hôtel Les Armures is "crowded" with "conventioneers and tourists" seeking "stereotypical" "Swiss-style" dining from a "traditional menu" with "wonderful specialties" such as "great fondue and raclette", along with classic French dishes; be warned, though, that the "overpowering smell" "of melted cheese" may stay with you "for a long" time.

L'Olivier de Provence Ⓢ *French* 21 | 19 | 20 | E

Carouge | 13 Rue Jacques-Dalphin | (41-22) 342-0450 | fax 300-5088 | www.olivierdeprovence.ch

This "real treat" in an 18th-century building overlooking the old fountain on Place du Temple in Carouge welcomes guests with a "cozy, warm" wood-beamed setting in which a "helpful" staff serves "good" classic French fare "with a Mediterranean touch" that reminds patrons of "being in Provence."

Miyako Ⓢ *Japanese* 24 | 18 | 22 | VE

Right Bank | 11 Rue de Chantepoulet | (41-22) 738-0120 | fax 738-1608 | www.miyako.ch

"One of the best Japanese restaurants in Geneva", this Right Bank spot serves up "fresh", "delicious sushi and sashimi", plus "wonderful teppanyaki", to an "international and business clientele" amid "traditional" (some say "a bit stuffy") decor that makes "you think you're in" the East; though the "excellent" staffers are "all very willing to help" ensure that guests "enjoy a nice evening", some still wonder whether the experience "justifies the excessive prices."

Patara *Thai* 25 19 19 E

Right Bank | Hôtel Beau-Rivage | 13 Quai du Mont-Blanc | (41-22) 731-5566 | fax 731-6677 | www.patara-geneve.com

"Part of a high-class chain" with additional locations in Singapore, Taipei and London, this "deluxe" Thai in a "great location" on the Right Bank offers "excellent" (albeit "high-priced") Siamese cuisine delivered by "attentive" staffers in a "pretty setting" replete with ceiling fans, wooden blinds and fresh flowers; still, some purists pout that the fare's "not authentic enough", while others opine that service suffers when it's "overcrowded."

Restaurant du Parc des Eaux-Vives Ⓢ Ⓜ *French* 24 25 20 VE

Left Bank | Hôtel du Parc des Eaux-Vives | 82 Quai Gustave-Ador | (41-22) 849-7575 | fax 849-7570 | www.parcdeseauxvives.ch

"What a view!" exclaim enthusiasts of this "elegant" venue in the Left Bank's Hôtel du Parc des Eaux-Vives; a "wonderful menu" of "superb" New French fare made from "quality ingredients" is presented in a "smart", "classical" interior with "the lake in the background"; true, "you pay for" the "enchanted setting", but the cost-conscious note that the downstairs "brasserie offers excellent food for decent prices"; P.S. "go when the roses are in bloom."

Roberto Ⓢ *Lombardian* 22 18 21 VE

Left Bank | 10 Rue Pierre-Fatio | (41-22) 311-8033

"Viva Roberto!" proclaim proponents of owner Mr. Carugati who have "nothing but positive things to say" about this "high-priced" eponymous "Italian institution in the center of Geneva's" Left Bank, where a "creative menu" of "delicious" Lombardian dishes is served by a "superb staff"; a "power-lunch" "favorite" of "the old-money" "business crowd", its "flashy red" room is "always busy" at midday, so regulars recommend you "go for dinner and relax."

Spice's Ⓢ *Asian Fusion* 24 21 22 VE

Right Bank | Hôtel Président Wilson | 47 Quai Wilson | (41-22) 906-6666 | fax 906-6667 | www.hotelpwilson.com

"If you like great food but want something other than typical French cuisine", this "pleasant surprise" in the Right Bank's Hôtel Président Wilson "is for you"; its "creative", "excellent" Asian fusion cooking is served by an "impeccable" staff in a "hip", "modern" setting with "nice views"; no wonder most insist it's "worth" the "astronomical prices."

Thai Phuket *Thai* 20 18 17 E

Right Bank | 33 Avenue de France | (41-22) 734-4100 | fax 734-4240

"One of Geneva's best Thai addresses", this "solid" Right Bank spot features an "extensive menu" of "exotic" offerings served in a "modern", "no-fuss" space by a "welcoming staff"; some cynics say that the treats are "too tame", "tiny" and "expensive for what you get", but it's still "popular" "with the U.N. crowd" and "people from the other international organizations nearby" for a "business lunch", so midday "reservations are recommended."

Tsé-Yang *Chinese* 20 | 20 | 19 | VE

Right Bank | Grand Hotel Kempinski Geneva | 19 Quai du Mont Blanc | (41-22) 732-5081 | fax 731-0582 | www.kempinski-geneva.com

Set in a "nice location", the Right Bank's Grand Hotel Kempinski, "this fine-dining Chinese" (part of an international chain) draws the bulk of its "clientele from the megahotel and its neighboring businesses", but local foodies also come from farther afield to sample its "sophisticated" fare; even if some find it less than authentic and "outrageously expensive", more maintain "the beautiful view of Lake Geneva", "the Jet d'Eau and Mount Blanc" "tops off the evening."

NEW **Vertig'O** S *French/Mediterranean* 23 | 22 | 24 | VE

Right Bank | Hôtel de la Paix | 11 Quai du Mont-Blanc | (41-22) 909-6066 | fax 909-6001

Alright, you may well get vertigo from the "exorbitant" prices at this new French-Mediterranean that has replaced the former Café de la Paix in the venerable and recently renovated hotel of the same name; still, most maintain "very pleasing cuisine", "excellent service", "stunning" slate-blue and copper contemporary decor and a "beautiful location on the lake shore" make for a "winning" experience; N.B. closed Saturday-Sunday.

Woods *Mediterranean*

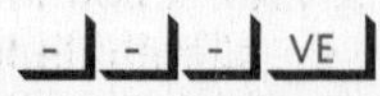

Right Bank | Hotel InterContinental | 7-9 Chemin du Petit-Saconnex | (41-22) 919-3333 | fax 919-3838 | www.interconti.com

Part of the "extensive modernization" of the Right Bank's Hotel InterContinental, this reinvention of the former Les Continents is already being recognized for chef Didier Quesnel's "excellent", "expensive" Mediterranean fare, "correct service" from staffers who "treat guests like VIPs" or "aristocracy" and a dramatic setting by New York-based designer Tony Chi; P.S. "take your Swiss broker here with what you saved on taxes."

Other Noteworthy Places

Auberge de Floris S M *French*

287 Route d'Hermance | (41-22) 751-2020 | fax 751-2250 | www.lefloris.com

Auberge de Pinchat S M *French*

Auberge de Pinchat | 32 Chemin de Pinchat | (41-22) 342-3077 | fax 300-2219 | www.auberge-de-pinchat.ch

Au Renfort M *French*

19 Route du Creux-de-Loup, Sézegnin | (41-22) 756-1236 | fax 756-3337 | www.renfort.ch

Café de Certoux S M *French/Mediterranean*

133 Route de Certoux | (41-22) 771-1032 | fax 771-2843 | www.cafe-certoux.ch

Café de la Réunion S *French*

2 Chemin Sous-Balme | (41-22) 784-0798 | fax 784-3859 | www.restaurant-reunion.ch

GENEVA

Café Nikolaj [S] *French/Seafood*
30 Rue du Rhône | (41-22) 781-3447 | fax 781-0924

Chez Uchino [S][M] *Japanese*
66 Route de Suisse | (41-22) 755-1032

Floortwo: The Grill *International*
Grand Hotel Kempinski Geneva | 19 Quai du Mont-Blanc | (41-22) 908-9081 | www.kempinski-geneva.com

La Chaumière [S][M] *French*
16 Chemin de la Fondelle | (41-22) 784-3066 | fax 784-6048 | www.lachaumiere.ch

La Closerie [M] *Italian/Mediterranean*
14 Place du Manoir | (41-22) 736-1355 | fax 700-0119 | www.lacloserie.ch

La Rôtisserie *French/Swiss*
Hôtel du Lac | 51 Grand Rue | (41-22) 960-8000 | fax 960-8010 | www.hoteldulac.ch

Le Bistrot Dumas [S] *Lyon*
7 Avenue Dumas | (41-22) 347-7422 | fax 347-7462

Le Cigalon [S][M] *Seafood*
39 Route d'Ambilly | (41-22) 349-9733 | www.le-cigalon.ch

Le Dix Vins [S] *French*
29 Rue Jacques-Dalphin | (41-22) 342-4010 | fax 342-0205

Le Grand Quai *French/International*
Swissôtel Métropole Genève | 34 Quai Général Guisan | (41-22) 318-3461 | fax 318-3300 | www.grandquai.ch

Le Loti *French/Mediterranean*
La Réserve Geneve | 301 Route de Lausanne | (41-22) 959-5979 | fax 959-5960 | www.lareserve.ch

Le Patio [S] *French*
19 Boulevard Helvétique | (41-22) 736-6675

Le Socrate [S] *French*
6 Rue Micheli-du-Crest | (41-22) 320-1677

Les Platanes [S] *French*
92 Route de la Plaine, Dardagny | (41-22) 754-1960

Le Tsé-Fung *Chinese*
La Réserve Geneve | 301 Route de Lausanne | (41-22) 959-5899 | fax 959-5960 | www.lareserve.ch

Plein Ciel *French*
Geneva-Cointrin Airport | Main Building, 2nd fl. | (41-22) 717-7676 | fax 798-7768 | www.canonica.com

Restaurant du Cheval Blanc [S][M] *Italian*
1 Route de Meinier | (41-22) 750-1401 | fax 750-3101 | www.restaurant-chevalblanc.ch

Restaurant le Vallon [S] *French*
182 Route de Florissant | (41-22) 347-1104 | fax 346-3111 | www.chateauvieux.ch

Sagano *Japanese*
86 Rue de Montbrillant | (41-22) 733-1150 | fax 733-2755

Sapori *Italian*
Hôtel Richemond | 8-10, Rue Adhémar-Fabri | (41-22) 715-7000 | fax 715-7001 | www.lerichemond.com

Senso Ristorante & Bar *Italian*
56 Rue du Rhône | (41-22) 310-3990 | fax 310-3991 | www.senso-living.ch

Tiffany *French*
Hôtel Tiffany | 1 Rue des Marbriers | (41-22) 708-1606 | fax 708-1617 | www.hotel-tiffany.ch

Windows *International*
Hôtel d'Angleterre | 17 Quai du Mont-Blanc | (41-22) 906-5514 | fax 906-5556 | www.dangleterrehotel.com

		FOOD	DECOR	SERVICE	COST

Hamburg

TOP FOOD RANKING

	Restaurant	Cuisine
25	Haerlin	French/Mediterranean
23	Jacobs	French/Mediterranean
	Landhaus Scherrer	German
	Le Canard Nouveau	Mediterranean/Turkish
	Doc Cheng's	Eurasian
	Fischereihafen	Seafood
	Saliba	Syrian
22	Stock's Fischrestaurant	German/Seafood
	Cox	New French/Med.
20	Tafelhaus	German/International
	Allegria	Austrian
19	Nil	German
18	Die Bank	French
	Windows	French/Mediterranean
17	Matsumi	Japanese/Sushi
	Rive	Mediterranean/Seafood
16	Landhaus Flottbek	German/Mediterranean

Allegria M *Austrian* 20 17 22 M

Eppendorf | Hudtwalcker Str. 13 | (49-40) 4607-2828 | fax 4607-2607 | www.allegria-restaurant.de

"You'll be happy you went" to this "charming place" in Eppendorf, adjacent to the Winterhuder Komödie theater, as the staff is "attentive but not pushy", and will "answer all questions" about the "interesting" Med-influenced Austrian cuisine of "ingenious chef" Alexander Tschebull; the "modern" glass-and-steel setting is "chic [yet] cozy", and there's also delightful summer dining in the garden outside, with a good view of the river Alster.

Cox ◐ *French/Mediterranean* 22 15 18 E

St. Georg | Lange Reihe 68 | (49-40) 249-422 | fax 2805-0902 | www.restaurant-cox.de

Some "satisfied" surveyors are "surprised" by the "creativity" of the "excellent" New French-Med cuisine at this "place to meet people" in St. Georg given its "restrained" decor, which elicits "contradictory opinions" - some term it "tasteful", while others call it "boring"; at least almost all agree that the "smooth-talking" staff offers "good advice" on what to order from the "innovative", if "short, menu."

Die Bank *French* 18 21 18 E

Neustadt | Hohe Bleichen 17 | (49-40) 238-0030 | www.diebank-brasserie.de

"This very hip to be seen place" in Neustadt is in a "fantastic" and "beautiful" converted old bank with high ceilings, crystal chandeliers, a "big cool bar" and "great terrace"; but since many maintain the French food is "middle-of-the-road", "it's best to go for drinks and checking out the scene."

Doc Cheng's ⊠ *Eurasian* 23 22 23 E

Neustadt | Fairmont Hotel Vier Jahreszeiten | Neuer Jungfernstieg 9-14 | (49-40) 349-4333 | fax 3494-2600 | www.hvj.de

An "all-round" winner, this "high-class establishment" in the Fairmont Hotel Vier Jahreszeiten in Neustadt boasts "a nice team - both in" its "show kitchen", where chefs who've "mastered the contrasting flavors" of their "great Eurasian fusion fare" "prepare it in front of you", and on the floor, where "accommodating and polite" staffers "make every effort" to ensure visitors "feel well-cared-for"; rounding out the "top-notch dining" experience is the "posh, stylish Shanghai Express decor", which also helps the "elevated prices" seem "quite appropriate."

Fischereihafen *Seafood* 23 14 19 E

Altona | Große Elbstr. 143 | (49-40) 381-816 | fax 389-3021 | www.fischereihafenrestaurant.de

"Excellent quality and outstanding selection" are hallmarks of this "traditional" ("not trendy") fish house that "does honor to its name" with "skillfully prepared", "classic seafood" that's "as fresh as it comes", served by a "friendly and competent" staff that really "knows the menu"; some say its "dignified" decor is "a bit dowdy" and "could use an update", but all appreciate its "great" dockside location in Altona, complete with a "wonderful view" - ask for a "table right next to the window."

Haerlin ⊠ M *French/Mediterranean* 25 21 25 VE

Neustadt | Fairmont Hotel Vier Jahreszeiten | Neuer Jungfernstieg 9-14 | (49-40) 3494-3310 | fax 3494-2600 | www.hvj.de

Rated No. 1 for Food in Hamburg, this "top spot" in the Fairmont Hotel Vier Jahreszeiten in Neustadt is "distinguished" by chef Christoph Rüffer's "superb" French-Med cuisine, "gracious service" from staffers who are "so attentive they know what you want before you do" and an "excellent location" affording "lovely views of the Alstersee through picture windows"; in short, this "dream" of a place makes "you feel special", even if you're not one of its "famous guests from radio, television and politics."

Jacobs *French/Mediterranean* 23 19 22 VE

Nienstedten | Hotel Louis C. Jacob | Elbchaussee 401-403 | (49-40) 8225-5405 | fax 8225-5444 | www.hotel-jacob.de

"Exquisite" French-Mediterranean fare, an "excellent wine list", a "charming", "confident" staff and "classic decor" combine at this "elegant" establishment in Nienstedten's Hotel Louis C. Jacob; whether you enjoy "top chef Thomas Martin's" "surprisingly" "imaginative dishes" in an interior with a "wonderful collection of oil paintings" or out on the "magnificent tree-shaded terrace overlooking the Elbe river", the experience will "remain in your memory a very long time" - but be sure to bring a "fat wallet."

Landhaus Flottbek ⊠ ⇏ *German/Mediterranean* 16 14 14 E

Flottbek | Hotel Landhaus Flottbek | Baron-Voght-Str. 179 | (49-40) 8227-4160 | fax 8227-4151 | www.landhaus-flottbek.de

"Lots of variety" on a menu of "good" German-Mediterranean dishes means there's "something for everyone" at this "solid restaurant" in the Hotel Landhaus Flottbek; the "rustic", "cottage-style decor" makes for a "pleasant atmosphere", though some complain that "the cost is quite high" for such a "simple" setting.

Landhaus Scherrer Ⓢ *German* 23 | 16 | 20 | VE

Ottensen | Elbchaussee 130 | (49-40) 880-1325 | fax 880-6260 | www.landhausscherrer.de

"Old-world charm, grace and quality abound" at this German in a former country house close to the river Elbe, where an "obliging" staff provides guests with "super recommendations from" the "creative menu's" "wide selection" of "first-class" modern dishes; some suggest its "decor could be better", but more insist that its "homelike atmosphere" makes it "ideal for a cozy get-together"; P.S. those who cry "oh, my poor wallet!" may find relief in its less-"expensive" bistro space.

Le Canard Nouveau Ⓜ *Mediterranean/Turkish* 23 | 20 | 20 | VE

Ottensen | Elbchaussee 139 | (49-40) 8812-9531 | www.lecanard-hamburg.de

"One of the best restaurants in town" also comes with perhaps "the most stunning view of the Elbe River" report respondents about this "excellent" Med with Turkish accents in Ottensen; it's "very expensive" but "always worth it", particularly if you get a seat on the terrace.

Matsumi Ⓢ *Japanese* 17 | 15 | 19 | E

Neustadt | Colonnaden 96, 1st fl. | (49-40) 343-125 | fax 344-219 | www.matsumi.de

Expect "fast and friendly" service from the "attentive" staff at this "snug" spot in Neustadt, where "something different" from the usual comes in the form of "delicious" Japanese cuisine, including some of "the best sushi in the city" (if "the prices are high", "well, good fresh fish costs something"); still, critics "wouldn't give it high marks", claiming the "taste leaves something to be desired" and adding "there's nothing stunning" about the "standard" decor.

Nil ⊭ *German* 19 | 16 | 13 | M

St. Pauli | Neuer Pferdemarkt 5 | (49-40) 439-7823 | fax 433-371 | www.restaurant-nil.de

"All the beautiful people" still crowd this "relaxed yet classy" St. Pauli spot, "for years a trendsetter" with its "fresh", "delicious food" – lately "high-quality", "medium-priced" Med-influenced "new German cuisine"; insiders advise that you "enjoy the stylish", "colorful" gallery above and avoid "the poorly lit basement", while first-timers report that "folks have to be regulars to get a smile" from the merely "civil" staffers whose idea of service seems to be Nil; N.B. closed Tuesdays.

Rive ◐ *Mediterranean/Seafood* 17 | 19 | 17 | E

Altona | Van-der-Smissen-Str. 1 | (49-40) 380-5919 | fax 389-4775 | www.rive.de

"For those romantic moments, a table by the window" or "on the wonderful, sunny [heated] terrace" of this "posh" Med seafooder in Altona "is a must" according to fans of its "fantastic location" and "exceptional view of the Elbe"; there's "something for everyone on its menu" of "fresh", "imaginative creations", though some are "disappointed" with the "simple", "nothing-special decor", "long waits", "ok service" and "high cost", declaring it "better for a light snack and drinks than an evening out."

Saliba *Syrian* 23 | 20 | 19 | E

Altona | Leverkusenstr. 54 | (49-40) 858-071 | fax 858-082 | www.saliba.de

"An adventure for the senses" awaits at this "wonderful" Altona venue, set in a former power station, that offers a break from the "monotonous" with its "delicious" Syrian fare (a "whole new taste experience"); neophytes needn't worry, as the "friendly, patient" staff "provides the necessary information" to those who "don't know" "this exceptional cuisine"; and aesthetes add that its "imaginative, appealing decor" helps take you to "another world."

Stock's Fischrestaurant 🄼 *German/Seafood* 22 | 15 | 21 | M

Poppenbüttel | An Der Alsterschleife 3 | (49-40) 602-0043 | fax 602-2826 | www.stocks.de

"Congratulations to Mr. Stock" say fans of this German seafooder set in a replica of a thatched, half-timbered 18th-century house "pleasantly located near Alstertal" Park in residential Poppenbüttel; "you get the feeling" that the "excellent local fish" "jumped directly out of the water onto your plate with a brief stopover in the frying pan", and you "can't complain" about the moderate cost, so it's no wonder most don't mind that the "simple decor" is a bit "meager."

Tafelhaus ◐🅂 *German/International* 20 | 22 | 18 | E

Övelgönne | Neumühlen 17 | (49-40) 892-760 | fax 899-3324 | www.tafelhaus-hamburg.de

This "wonderful place" blessed with "a great view of the harbor" in Övelgönne "exceeds expectations" with "sober but stylish decor" and "simply delicious" "German specialties" as well as some International dishes; still, surveyors are split over service, with some reporting "no complaints" about "caring" attendants who are "always at hand" and others offering "no special praise" for certain "slow" staffers.

Windows 🅂🄼 *French/Mediterranean* 18 | 19 | 21 | E

Pöseldorf | InterContinental Hamburg | Fontenay 10, 9th fl. | (49-40) 41420 | fax 4142-2290 | www.interconti.com

Set in a "beautiful location" - the penultimate floor of the InterContinental Hamburg hotel - this "expensive" fine-dining venue offers an equally "beautiful experience"; perhaps the "wonderful view over Lake Alster" and the city "tops" the "consistently good" French-Mediterranean cuisine, but most visitors nevertheless report being "thoroughly impressed with the restaurant."

Other Noteworthy Places

Artisan 🅂🄼 *International*

Kampstr. 27 | (49-40) 4210-2915 | fax 4210-2916 | www.artisan-hamburg.com

Brook 🅂 *French/Mediterranean*

Bei den Mühren 91 | (49-40) 3750-3128 | fax 3750-3127 | www.restaurant-brook.de

Calla 🅂🄼 *Eurasian*

Steigenberger Hotel Hamburg | Heiligengeist Brücke 4 | (49-40) 368-060 | fax 3680-6777 | www.hamburg.steigenberger.de

Das Kleine Rote 🅂🄼 *German*

Holstenkamp 71 | (49-40) 8972-6813 | www.das-kleine-rote.de

Das Weisse Haus *International*
Neumühlen 50 | (49-40) 390-9016 | fax 390-8799 | www.das-weisse-haus.de

Henssler & Henssler *Californian/Japanese*
Grosse Elbstr. 160 | (49-40) 3869-9000 | fax 3869-9055 | www.h2dine.de

Il Sole *Italian*
Nienstedtener Str. 2d | (49-40) 8231-0330 | fax 8231-0336 | www.il-sole.de

Jena Paradies *German/French*
Klosterwall 23 | (49-40) 327-008 | fax 327-598 | www.jena-paradies.net

La Fayette *European*
Zimmerstr. 30 | (49-40) 225-630 | fax 225-630 | www.la-fayette-hamburg.de

La Scala *Italian*
Falkenried 54 | (49-40) 420-6295 | fax 4291-3104 | www.ristorante-la-scala.com

L'Auberge *French*
Rutschbahn 34 | (49-40) 410-2532 | fax 450-5015 | www.auberge.de

Le Plat du Jour *French*
Dornbusch 4 | (49-40) 321-414 | fax 410-5857 | www.leplatdujour.de

Osteria Due *Italian/International*
Badestr. 4 | (49-40) 410-1651 | fax 410-1658 | www.osteriadue.de

Petit Delice *International*
Grosse Bleichen 21 | (49-40) 343-470 | www.petitdelice.de

Piment *French/Moroccan*
Lehmweg 29 | (49-40) 4293-7788 | www.restaurant-piment.de

Poletto *Italian*
Eppendorfer Landstr. 145 | (49-40) 480-2159 | fax 4140-6993 | www.poletto.de

Prinz Frederik *French/German*
Hotel Abtei | Abteistr. 14 | (49-40) 442-905 | fax 449-820 | www.abtei-hotel.de

Rexrodt *French/International*
Papenhuder Str. 35 | (49-40) 229-7198 | fax 2271-5289 | www.restaurant-rexrodt.de

Seven Seas *French/Mediterranean*
Süllberg Hotel | Süllbergsterrasse 12 | (49-40) 866-2520 | fax 8662-5213 | www.suellberg-hamburg.de

Sgroi *Italian*
Lange Reihe 40 | (49-40) 2800-3930 | fax 2800-3931 | www.sgroi.de

Stocker *Austrian/International*
Max-Brauer-Allee 80 | (49-40) 3861-5056 | fax 3861-5058 | www.restaurant-stocker.de

Wa Yo *Japanese*
Nippon Hotel | Hofweg 75 | (49-40) 227-1140 | www.wa-yo.de

Zippelhaus *Mediterranean*
Zippelhaus 3 | (49-40) 3038-0280 | fax 321-777 | www.zippelhaus.com

Zum Wattkorn *German*
Hotel Wattkorn | Tangstedter Landstr. 230 | (49-40) 520-3797 | fax 520-9044 | www.wattkorn.de

FOOD | DECOR | SERVICE | COST

Istanbul

TOP FOOD RANKING

	Restaurant	Cuisine
26	Borsa	Turkish
25	Körfez	Seafood/Turkish
	Develi	Turkish
	Seasons Restaurant	Mediterranean
	Tugra	Turkish/Ottoman
	Tike	Turkish
	Balikçi Sabahattin	Seafood
24	Lokanta	Turkish/Finnish
	Ulus 29	Turkish/International
	Laledan	Seafood
23	Feriye Lokantasi	Turkish/Ottoman
	Pandeli*	Turkish/Ottoman
	Del Mare	Seafood
	Kösebasi	Turkish/Mediterranean
	Sunset Grill & Bar	International
22	Paper Moon	Italian
	Mezzaluna	Italian
	Changa/Müzedechanga	Euro. Fusion/International
21	Asitane	Turkish
	Leb-i Derya	Turkish/Mediterranean
20	Yesil Ev	Turkish/International
	Vogue	International/Med.
19	360 Istanbul	Med./International
	Banyan	Asian Fusion
18	Nisantasi Brasserie	International
14	Sarniç Restaurant	Turkish/International

Asitane *Turkish* 21 | 16 | 19 | M

Edirnekapí | Kariye Hotel | Kariye Camii Sokak 18 | (90) 212-534-8414 | fax 212-521-6631 | www.kariyeotel.com

Dine like a sultan - as in Suleiman the Magnificent - for far less than a king's ransom at this "undiscovered gem" inside Edirnekapí's Kariye Hotel that features "authentic", "extensively researched" antique Turkish specialties from royal recipes dating back to 1539; while a few find the onetime Ottoman mansion "stuffy", dining in the "outdoor garden is lovely" and the live music on weekends is "interesting for tourists."

Balikçi Sabahattin/The Fisherman ◐ *Seafood* 25 | 17 | 20 | M

Sultanahmet | Seyit Hasan Koyu Sokak 1 | (90) 212-458-1824 | www.armadahotel.com.tr

"Wonderful", "authentic" and "freshly made mezes", "excellent fish and moderate prices" lure loyalists to this Sultanahmet seafooder in a restored mansion behind the Armada Hotel and "near the Blue Mosque"; menus are nonexistent - all meals are fixed-price and in-

* Indicates a tie with restaurant above

clude drinks and dessert - so just "sit at an outside table", relax and enjoy the "classic Turkish experience."

Banyan *Asian Fusion* 19 | 20 | 20 | M

Nisantasi | Abdi Ipekci Caddesi 40/3 | (90) 212-219-6011
Ortaköy | Muallim Naci Caddesi Salhane Sokak 3 | (90) 212-259-9060
www.banyanrestaurant.com

The Ortaköy branch of this establishment offers front-row views of the area's ornate mosque and "wonderful" Bosphorus and its bridge, making it a popular summertime restaurant/bar hang for a young crowd; the Nisantasi venue is a bit older and has a garden for alfresco eating; both locales offer "tasty" Asian fusion fare and moderate prices.

Borsa ◐ *Turkish* 26 | 16 | 25 | E

Harbiye | Istanbul Lütfi Kirdar Convention & Exhibition Ctr. | (90) 212-232-4201 | fax 212-232-5856 | www.borsarestaurants.com

Voted Istanbul's No. 1 for Food, this Harbiye institution is renowned for "excellent traditional" Turkish cuisine ("best doner kebab in town") ably presented by a courteous staff; the bonus of a "handy address" in the Lütfi Kirdar convention center ("five minutes from major hotels") draws a "businesslike" "older crowd" that also appreciates the "lovely" glassed-in terrace "overlooking the sea and the city."

Changa ☒ *Euro. Fusion/International* 22 | 25 | 21 | E

Taksim | Siraselviler Caddesi 47 | (90) 212-249-1205 | fax 212-249-1348

NEW **Müzedechanga** ◐ M *Euro. Fusion/International*

Emirgan | Sakip Sabanci Museum | Sakip Sabanci Cad. 22 | (90) 212-323-0901
www.changa-istanbul.com

"The F word" - fusion - "still rules" at what some call "Istanbul's best" - and possibly only - multiculti eatery, where "good" International dishes are enhanced by local ingredients; located near the sights and sounds of Taksim, the setting is equally eclectic, with a "historical" art nouveau exterior that belies its extremely stylish "modern" interior - small wonder it's popular with "the city's young movers and shakers"; N.B. the newer Müzedechanga offshoot is in the Sakip Sabanci Museum overlooking the Bosphorous.

Del Mare *Seafood* 23 | 18 | 20 | E

Cengelköy | Kuleli Caddesi 53/4 | (90) 216-422-5762 | fax 216-422-6354 | www.del-mare.com

The menu is extensive, the seafood is "delicious", the "service is kind" and the setting in a historic building is atmospheric at this Cengelköy spot; but it's "dining alfresco in the moonlight" on the expansive terrace with its "fantastic view of the Bosphorus" and bridge that's its "biggest asset" and what leaves most "breathless."

Develi *Turkish* 25 | 13 | 21 | M

Etiler | Tepecik Yolu 22 | (90) 212-263-2571 | fax 212-263-5705
Kalamis | Kalamis Marina | Münir Nurettin Selçuk Caddesi | (90) 216-418-9400 | fax 216-418-9405
Samatya | Gümüsyüzük Sokak 7 | (90) 212-529-0833 | fax 212-529-0811
www.develikebap.com

"Fun, frantic and fabulous", this trio of "outstanding kebab houses" specializing in spicy Southeastern Turkish-style fare is "where the locals go" to fill up for mere "pennies", but it's also "friendly to business travelers" who "can't go wrong" with any of the "multitude of meat selections" ("try the pistachio kebab"); ok, "the decor isn't great" but the Samatya original's "pleasant open-air rooftop" provides a panoramic "view of the harbor."

Feriye Lokantasi *Turkish/Ottoman* 23 24 22 E

Ortaköy | Çiragan Caddesi 124 | (90) 212-227-2216 | fax 212-236-5799 | www.feriye.com

"Summer is the best time" to dine at this "beautiful" converted police station in Ortaköy because you'll want to sit on its "lovely terrace" to take in "one of Istanbul's most spectacular views" of the Bogazici Bridge ("unforgettable at sunset"); the location is so "breathtaking" it's "almost difficult to focus" on the "succulent" Turkish-Ottoman cuisine, comparatively extensive wine list and service that's "as good as it gets."

Körfez *Seafood/Turkish* 25 22 24 VE

Kanlica | Körfez Caddesi 78 | (90) 216-413-4314 | fax 216-413-4306 | www.korfez.com

"Exquisite seafood" (e.g. "fantastic" salt-crusted sea bass) and "gorgeous" views of the Mehmet II Bridge and Rumeli Hisar make dinner at this pricey, nautical-themed Turkish "a great experience"; getting to the waterside villa can be half the "fun", since guests can choose to cross the Bosphorus on the restaurant's "private" ferry.

Kösebasi *Turkish/Mediterranean* 23 16 20 M

Beylikdüzü | Kaya Ramada Plaza Yani ES | (90) 212-886-6699
Fenerbahce | Fuatpasa Caddesi, Kurukahveciler Sokak | (90) 216-363-5856
Levent | Çamlik Sokak 153 | (90) 212-270-2433 | fax 212-270-2433
Macka | Bronz Sokak 5 | (90) 212-230-3868
www.kosebasi.com.tr

"You can't miss" at this modern and "upscale" Turkish-Med chain, a "local favorite" with a "wide array" of "tantalizing", "sizzling" kebabs, "plentiful" meze and a large, affordable wine list; execs from the nearby business districts readily entertain foreign clients here, although a few folks fear the owners have now "opened too many branches" to sustain the high quality.

Laledan *Seafood* 24 27 26 VE

Besiktas | Çiragan Palace Kempinski | Çiragan Caddesi 32 | (90) 212-326-4646 | fax 212-259-6687 | www.ciraganpalace.com

This "stunning" seafooder in the Çiragan Palace Kempinski has respondents rhapsodizing over its patio's "spectacular" Bosphorus views, gardens and elegant interiors ("like dining in a museum"); staffers deliver practically "perfect service" along with "world-class food and wine" to a well-heeled clientele, leaving a dazed few to sigh that with surroundings "so pretty" they "can't remember how the meal was."

Leb-i Derya *Turkish/Mediterranean* 21 22 19 M

NEW **Beyoglu** | Richmond Hotel | Istiklal Caddesi 445 | (90) 212-243-4376 | fax 212-243-4387
Tünel | Kumbaraci Yokusu 115/7 | (90) 212-243-9555 | fax 212-243-9556
www.lebiderya.com

Capitalizing on the city's trend of opening chic eateries on rooftops, this Tünel Turkish-Mediterranean offers "stunning" historic and modern panoramas of "the Bosphorus, Golden Horn, Topkapi Palace and opposite Asian shore", both from its open outdoor terrace and glassed-in interior; the new branch atop the Richmond Hotel is built on the same concept - "amazing" views, "delicious", moderate priced fare and a "low-key but high-powered atmosphere"; P.S. at either one "make a reservation for a table when the sun sets."

Lokanta ◐ *Turkish/Finnish* 24 | 18 | 19 | E

Beyoglu | Mesrutiyet Caddesi 149/1 | (90) 212-245-6070 | fax 212-245-6039 | www.lokantadaneve.com

What lures the thirtysomething crowds to this hip Beyoglu eatery is "talented" chef-owner Mehmet Gürs' "cool take" on Turkish treats, incorporating elements of Finnish cuisine; the modern interior is "understated", but for a truly "magical" experience, savor your fusion fare at a rooftop table overlooking the Golden Horn.

Mezzaluna ◐ *Italian* 22 | 15 | 18 | M

Nisantasi | Abdi Ipekçi Caddesi 38/1 | (90) 212-231-3142 | fax 212-225-9269 | www.mezzaluna.com.tr

With a wood oven producing "wonderful pizzas" and an extensive menu full of "high-quality", affordable *cucina,* this big, colorful Italian mainstay in fashionable Nisantasi remains a "good choice" for an informal meal; the staff can be overwhelmed during the dinner rush, but overall this place is "always satisfactory" - which is why it's "always full."

Nisantasi Brasserie at Beymen *International* 18 | 20 | 20 | E

Nisantasi | Abdi Ipekci Caddesi 23/1 | (90) 212-343-0443 | fax 212-343-0445

"Its perfect location" in Nisantasi, one of Istanbul's toniest shopping neighborhoods, means that "during the season" "getting a table outside this International is more difficult than meeting with the president"; the food is "good" and the chandeliered, art nouveau-style interior is attractive, but the well-heeled "Madison Avenue-type crowd" comes primarily "to hang", "see and be seen."

Pandeli *Turkish/Ottoman* 23 | 20 | 20 | M

Eminönü | Misir Çarsisi 1 | (90) 212-522-5534 | fax 212-522-5534

"Yes, it's a bit touristy" but this "bustling" "traditional" Turkish-Ottoman is nevertheless a "magical place" thanks to its "historic setting", a 17th-century edifice above the entrance to the Egyptian Spice Bazaar in Eminönü; colorfully tiled, domed rooms provide "Old Istanbul atmosphere" plus "excellent views" of the bustling market, and it's conveniently located for shoppers to stop in for a moderately priced midday meal (lunch only is served from noon-4 PM).

Paper Moon ◐ *Italian* 22 | 22 | 21 | VE

Etiler | Akmerkez Residence | Nispetiye Caddesi | (90) 212-282-1616 | fax 212-282-1334

"Playboys, models" and other "beautiful" specimens populate the "scene" at this upscale Italian in Etiler's Akmerkez Residence hotel, so "go for the people-watching" but "stay for the food" too suggest surveyors; "good" pastas, risottos and wood-fired pizzas are served in the modern Milano-"chic" dining room or the garden, but because the experience can be "über-expensive", it's best for those "with expense accounts."

	FOOD	DECOR	SERVICE	COST

Sarniç Restaurant *Turkish/International* 14 | 27 | 18 | E

Sultanahmet | Turing Ayasofya Konaklari Hotel | Sogukçesme Sokak | (90) 212-512-4291 | fax 212-514-0216 | www.ayasofyapensions.com

The "fabulous location" in a 1,600-year-old underground cistern, "unique candlelit" ambiance and live harp music make this Sultanahmet showplace "wonderfully atmospheric" (definitely "a great spot for proposing"); however, the Turkish-International "food is so-so" - and not cheap - so dinner here is far more a feast for the eyes than for the stomach.

Seasons Restaurant *Mediterranean* 25 | 26 | 27 | VE

Sultanahmet | Four Seasons Hotel | Tevkifhane Sokak 1 | (90) 212-638-8200 | fax 212-638-8210 | www.fourseasons.com/istanbul

At the center of what was a "former prison" in Sultanahmet, this "intimate", "peaceful" glass-walled restaurant is now the place to "mingle with Istanbul's upper crust" over "marvelous" and costly Mediterranean meals ("order with abandon - it's all good") enhanced by "excellent Turkish wines"; best of all, report respondents, is the "extraordinary" service from an "attentive" and "friendly" staff, but then again all agree that's "typical Four Seasons quality."

Sunset Grill & Bar *International* 23 | 26 | 25 | VE

Ulus Park | Adnan Saygun Caddesi Yol Sokak 2 | (90) 212-287-0357 | fax 212-287-0358 | www.sunsetgrillbar.com

"Out of the City Center" but nevertheless a "must-go", this Ulus Park destination with "terrace tables overlooking the whole city and the Bosphorus" is "one of Istanbul's best options for summer dining", plus the "magnificent" vistas are visible from the spare, open interior; "great" International eats (e.g. "unbeatable" but "expensive" sushi and steaks) come courtesy of a "wonderful" staff, so in all ways "it's worth the trip."

360 Istanbul ◐ *Mediterranean/International* 19 | 24 | 20 | E

Beyoglu | Istiklal Caddesi 8/311, Misir Apt. 8th fl. | (90) 212-251-1042 | fax 212-251-1048 | www.360istanbul.com

The "food is delicious" but "the main draw is the unbelievable view and the slick decor" declare "hip" habitués of this "trendy" Med-International located on the eighth floor of a 19th-century building in Beyoglu; true to its name, the 360-degree panorama from the glassed-in interior and terrace provides "beautiful" vistas of Old Istanbul and the Bosphorus.

Tike *Turkish* 25 | 18 | 20 | E

Günesli | Koçman Caddesi Ziyal Plaza 38 | (90) 212-630-5930 | fax 212-630-2320 ☒

Kadiköy | Kazim Özalp Caddesi 58 | (90) 216-467-5914 | fax 216-467-5243

Kemerburgaz | Göktürk Mahallesi Sadik Sok. 3A | (90) 212-322-3255 | fax 212-322-1259

Levent | Haci Adil Caddesi 4, Aralik 1 | (90) 212-281-8871 | fax 212-281-6666

Nisantasi | Sair Nigar Sokak 4/A | (90) 212-233-3540

Sultanahmet | Senlikköy Mah Germeyan Sokak | (90) 212-574-0505 | fax 212-574-0666

www.tike.com.tr

"Everyone knows" this burgeoning chain of "upscale kebab houses" assert aficionados who say you've "got to love" its "delicious", "perfectly seasoned" grilled meat skewers, "great vegetarian dishes" and "tasty" meze and salads; all branches' "modern", "trendy" settings and ample alfresco seating appeal to "crowds" of affluent thirtysomethings, as do the indoor and outdoor bars featured at the original Levent location.

Tugra *Turkish/Ottoman* 25 | 28 | 27 | VE

Besiktas | Çiragan Palace Kempinski | Çiragan Caddesi 32 | (90) 212-326-4646 | fax 212-259-6687 | www.ciraganpalace.com

"Mind-blowingly beautiful, ornate and colorful", this "fabulous" jewel box "overlooking the glittering Bosphorus" makes it clear you're "dining in the palace" of a sultan (now the Çiragan Palace Kempinski in Besiktas); similarly exalted are the "wonderful", "perfectly" presented Turkish and Ottoman specialties, a wine list that's among the city's best, "excellent" live piano music performed nightly and tabs that may necessitate dipping into the royal treasury.

Ulus 29 *Turkish/International* 24 | 26 | 22 | VE

Ulus Park | Adnan Saygun Caddesi Yol Sokak 1 | (90) 212-358-2929 | fax 212-265-2242 | www.club29.com

Perched on a hilltop in residential Ulus, this "always 'in'" eatery offers "drop-dead" vistas - not only a "famous" panoramic Bosphorus view of both bridges, but also glimpses of the "beautiful people" who frequent this "elegant" mod-minimalist boîte to dine on "top-level", premium-priced Turkish-International cuisine; after dinner the young, fashionable crowd happily heads to the "fun" adjacent club for late-night dancing.

Vogue ◐ *International/Mediterranean* 20 | 25 | 21 | VE

Besiktas | BJK Plaza | Spor Caddesi 92, 13th fl. | (90) 212-227-4404 | fax 212-227-2545 | www.istanbuldoors.com

Still "in vogue" among "Turkish and foreign yuppies alike", this 10-year-old, minimalist International-Med with a sushi bar boasts "the spectacular views one would expect" from its position "atop a Besiktas Plaza office tower"; veterans advise "get one of the corner tables on the terrace" for a "romantic" (if pricey) "candlelit dinner."

Yesil Ev *Turkish/International* 20 | 23 | 21 | M

Sultanahmet | Yesil Ev Hotel | Kabasakal Caddesi 5 | (90) 212-517-6785 | fax 212-517-6780 | www.istanbulyesilev.com

The name means "green house", which befits this "graceful" replica of an Ottoman mansion's emerald exterior and is also a pun on its "gorgeous", partially glassed-in "private garden", where four seasons of the year the hotel serves "fresh, well-prepared" Turkish-International fare around a cooling fountain; thanks to the "great" Sultanahmet location, plenty of tourists "come in for drinks" and "unbeatable", affordable meze "on a hot day."

Other Noteworthy Places

Bosphorus Palace *International*

Bosphorus Palace Hotel | Yaliboyu Caddesi 64 | (90) 216-422-0003 | fax 216-422-0012 | www.bosphoruspalace.com

Cafe du Levant *French*

Rahmi M Koç Museum | Hasköy Caddesi 27 | (90) 212-369-6607 | fax 212-369-9450 | www.rmk-museum.org.tr

Çiya *Turkish*
Caferaga Mahallesi Guneslibahce Sokak 43 | (90) 216-418-5115 | fax 216-349-1902 | www.ciya.com.tr

da Mario *Southern Italian*
Dilhayat Sokak 7 | (90) 212-265-5196 | fax 212-265-5186 | www.istanbuldoors.com

Divan *Mediterranean/Turkish*
Divan Hotel | Cumhuriyet Caddesi 2 | (90) 212-315-5500 | fax 212-315-5515 | www.divan.com.tr

Doga Balik ◐ *Turkish/Seafood*
Hotel Villa Zurich | Akarsu Yokusu Caddesi 46 | (90) 212-243-3656 | fax 212-293-9144 | www.dogabalik.com.tr

Flamm *Turkish*
Sofyali Sokak 16/1 | (90) 212-245-7604 | www.flamm-ist.com

Galata ☒ *Turkish*
Orhan Apaydin Sokak 11 | (90) 212-293-1139 | fax 212-245-6705 | www.galata.com.tr

Hasan Balikçilar ◐ *Seafood*
Yat Limani | Rihtim Sokak 8 | (90) 212-573-8300

Hünkar Lokantasi ◐ *Turkish*
Nispetiye Caddesi 52 | (90) 212-287-8470 | fax 212-291-7292
Mim Kemal Öke Caddesi 21/1 | (90) 212-225-4665 | fax 212-291-7292

Lacivert ◐ *Mediterranean*
Körfez Caddesi 57/A | (90) 216-413-4224 | fax 216-425-1974 | www.lacivertrestaurant.com

La Maison *French*
La Maison Hotel | Müvezzi Caddesi 63 | (90) 212-227-4263 | fax 212-227-4278 | www.lamaison.com.tr

Loft Restaurant Bar *Mediterranean*
Istanbul Lütfi Kirdar Convention & Exhibition Ctr. | (90) 212-219-6384 | fax 212-232-5856 | www.loftrestbar.com

Mabeyin *Turkish*
Eski Kisikli Caddesi 129 | (90) 216-422-5580 | fax 216-321-4648 | www.mabeyin.com

Maiden's Tower *International*
Kiz Kulesi Island | (90) 216-342-4747 | www.kizkulesi.com.tr

Malta Köskü *Seafood/Turkish*
Yildiz Parki | (90) 212-258-9453 | fax 212-258-9453

Mavi Ev/Blue House *Turkish*
Mavi Ev Hotel | Dalbasti Sokak 14 | (90) 212-638-9010 | fax 212-638-9017 | www.bluehouse.com.tr

Mel's Bebek ☒ *Russian/International*
Çevdetpasa Caddesi Vezirköskü Sokak 2 | (90) 212-257-7040 | fax 212-257-7041

Mia Mensa *Italian*
Kuruçesme Caddesi 64C | (90) 212-263-4214 | www.miamensa.com

Mikla ☒ *International/Turkish*
Marmara Pera Hotel | Mesrutiyet Caddesi 167/185 | (90) 212-293-5656 | fax 212-243-8463 | www.istanbulyi.com

Panorama Ⓢ *International*
Marmara Istanbul | Taksim Meydani | (90) 212-251-4696 | fax 212-244-0509 | www.themarmarahotels.com

Park Fora ◐ *International/Seafood*
Cemil Topuzlu Parki | Muallim Naci Caddesi 134 | (90) 212-265-5063 | fax 212-265-5072 | www.parkfora.com

Park Samdan Ⓢ *International/Turkish*
Mim Kemal Öke Caddesi 18/1 | (90) 212-225-0710

Rumeli Cafe Restaurant *Turkish*
Ticarethane Sokagi 8 | (90) 212-512-0008 | fax 212-513-2404

Safran *Turkish*
InterContinental Ceylan | Asker Ocagi Caddesi 1 | (90) 212-368-4444 | fax 212-368-4499 | www.interconti.com

Wan-na ◐ Ⓢ Ⓜ *Asian/Mediterranean*
Mesrutiyet Caddesi 151 | (90) 212-243-1794 | www.istanbuldoors.com

Zarifi ◐ *Turkish*
Çukurçesme Sok. 13 | (90) 212-293-5480 | fax 212-293-5484 | www.zarifi.com.tr

Zindan Bar Restaurant Ⓢ *Turkish*
Istiklal Caddesi, Oliva Han Geçidi 13 | (90) 212-252-7340

Lisbon

	FOOD	DECOR	SERVICE	COST

TOP FOOD RANKING

	Restaurant	Cuisine
27	Varanda	French
	Ristorante Hotel Cipriani	Italian
	Sua Excelência	Portuguese
24	Gambrinus	International
	Casa da Comida	Portuguese
	Adega Tia Matilde	Portuguese
	O Mercado do Peixe	Seafood
	Olivier	Mediterranean
23	A Travessa	International
	Solar dos Presuntos	Portuguese
22	A Galeria Gemelli	Italian
	Solar dos Nunes	Portuguese
	Valle Flôr	French/Mediterranean
	Pap'Açorda	Portuguese
	A Casa do Bacalhau	Portuguese/Seafood
21	Ad Lib	French/Portuguese
	Conventual	Portuguese
	Tavares Rico	French/International
20	Alcântara Café	International
	BBC – Belém Bar Café*	French/Portuguese
	XL	Portuguese/International
19	Bica do Sapato	International/Sushi
17	Clara	Portuguese/International
15	Kais	International
14	Casa do Leão	Portuguese

A Casa do Bacalhau ⓢ *Portuguese/Seafood* — 22 | 21 | 17 | M

Beato | Rua do Grilo 54 | (351-21) 862-0000 | fax 862-0008 | www.acasadobacalhau.restaunet.pt

You are at the 'House of the Codfish' at this Beato Portuguese specialist serving over 20 "good" versions of the revered local staple; prices are moderate, so if you're bananas for *bacalhau*, this is a good catch.

Adega Tia Matilde ◐ *Portuguese* — 24 | 16 | 21 | M

Praça de Espanha | Rua da Beneficencia 77 | (351-21) 797-2172 | fax 797-9298

Since 1937, locals have been flocking to this "delicious and authentic" Portuguese in Praça de Espanha for classic dishes; the spacious, tiled setting is traditionally decorated, and the price is right.

Ad Lib *French/Portuguese* — 21 | 20 | 21 | E

Liberdade | Hotel Sofitel | Avenida da Liberdade 127 | (351-21) 322-8350 | fax 322-8310 | www.sofitel.com

Supporters spontaneously say this "good, innovative" French-Portuguese in the Hotel Sofitel "adds a bit of global chic to Avenida da

* Indicates a tie with restaurant above

Liberdade", the city's main thoroughfare, making it appropriate either for a business lunch or romantic dinner; it's a "beautiful find" in Downtown Lisbon, but "bring your wallet" because "it's expensive" by local "standards."

A Galeria Gemelli ◐ Ⓢ Ⓜ *Italian* 22 10 16 E

Bairro das Mercês | Rua de São Bento 334 | (351-21) 395-2552 | fax 920-4201 | www.augustogemelli.com

Insiders insist "let owner Augusto Gemelli make the choice" as to what you'll order at this Bairro Mercês "excellent Italian" where many recipes rely on Portuguese products and there is always a "nice surprise on the menu"; the bistro-style room is small but "warm" and welcoming.

Alcântara Café ◐ *International* 20 22 18 E

Alcântara | Rua Maria Luísa Holstein 15 | (351-21) 363-7176 | fax 362-2948 | www.alcantaracafe.com

Even after 18 years it's "still one of the most beautiful rooms in Lisbon" is what supporters say about this "stunning" Alcântara International in "an old industrial setting" with steel beams, ornate mirrors, classic statues, candlelight and a sexy bar; even though it's "more like a nightclub than a restaurant", the food is "surprisingly good", and the crowd is a nice "mix of tourists and locals."

A Travessa ◐ Ⓢ *International* 23 23 22 E

Madragoa | Travessa do Convento das Bernardas 12 | (351-21) 390-2034 | fax 394-0839 | www.atravessa.com

This long-standing International in the 17th-century Convento das Bernardas in Madragoa has "all the charm of a historic location"; a "nice" selection of "excellent Belgian dishes and local Portuguese favorites" is served in an "inviting" setting by a "very polite staff"; regulars recommend on a "warm night have dinner alfresco" on the terrace.

BBC - Belém Bar Café ◐ Ⓢ Ⓜ *French/Portuguese* 20 23 20 E

Belém | Avenida Brasília, Pavilhão Poente | (351-21) 362-4232 | fax 21-362-4243 | www.belembarcafe.com

In a "very beautiful location" in a "happening neighborhood" is this well-frequented French-Portuguese restaurant/bar/club in Belém, a "little far from the City Center" but in a popular redeveloped area with a "good view" of the Tejo river and bridge; a "hip" crowd comes for a "lively" time and an exceptionally "atmospheric" glassed-in setting.

Bica do Sapato Ⓢ *International/Japanese* 19 22 16 E

Santa Apolónia | Avenida Infante D. Henrique, Armazém B, Cais da Pedra | (351-21) 881-0320 | fax 881-0329 | www.bicadosapato.com

"As cool as you can get in Lisbon" is this "trendy", "inventive" Santa Apolónia International with a separate upstairs sushi bar in a "huge waterfront warehouse" that's co-owned by actor John Malkovich; "portions are small" ("the ideal quantity for models") and service could be "friendlier and more attentive", but it's the "grooviest" "place to see local celebs", and there are "beautiful views" of the Tagus River too.

Casa da Comida Ⓢ *Portuguese* 24 23 22 E

Jardim das Amoreiras | Travessa das Amoreiras 1 | (351-21) 388-5376 | fax 387-5132 | www.casadacomida.pt

Among the "tops in town" is this refined, "romantic" Portuguese in a pretty, 18th-century townhouse in Jardim das Amoreiras; start by sipping a crisp white port while perusing the menu in the wood-paneled lounge before moving into the "wonderful" interior garden room and enjoying an "excellent" meal served by a "cordial staff."

Casa do Leão *Portuguese* | 14 | 20 | 18 | E

Castelo de São Jorge | Castelo de São Jorge | (351-21) 888-0154 | fax 887-6329 | www.pousadas.pt

The "best and most historic views of Lisbon" and the Tagus River are from this Portuguese in the 12th-century St. George's Castle, the city's oldest monument; the "nice" atmosphere includes an arched-and-tiled interior, summer dining terrace and pianist, but those amenities can't appease critics who call it a "touristy" place with "unoriginal" food ("how much cod can you eat anyway?") that's "secondary to the scenery."

Clara ☒ *Portuguese/International* | 17 | 20 | 21 | E

Pena | Campo dos Mártires da Pátria 49 | (351-21) 885-3053 | fax 885-2082 | www.lisboa-clara.pt

For over 30 years, this "pretty" Portuguese-International in Pena with "good food", an extensive wine list, "charming management" and a "comfortable setting" in an 18th-century mansion has been particularly popular for business lunches; in winter the fireplace is the focus, while in summer "exquisite garden" dining is the draw.

Conventual ☒ *Portuguese* | 21 | 19 | 21 | E

Bairro das Mercês | Praça das Flores 45 | (351-21) 390-9196 | fax 390-9196

Many of long-standing chef-owner Dina Marques dishes are inspired by old recipes from Portuguese convents or monasteries and the result is "deliciously flavored" "traditional" food; an "attentive" staff presides over the "sedate", white-walled space in the Bairro das Mercês that is, appropriately enough, decorated with "interesting religious art."

Gambrinus ◐ *International* | 24 | 20 | 24 | VE

Baixa | Rua das Portas de Santo Antão 23-25 | (351-21) 342-1466 | fax 346-5032

"Excellent seafood and game" are the focus at this International, "one of the oldest and most traditional restaurants" in the Baixa, where "waiters and customers seem to be longtime friends"; its decor - "dark-paneled rooms", stained glass and leather chairs - appeals to "mostly male" patrons, but everyone exclaims 'holy mackerel' when it comes to the "very expensive" prices.

Kais ◐☒ *International* | 15 | 22 | 16 | E

Santos | Cais da Viscondessa | Rua da Cintura do Porto de Lisboa | (351-21) 393-2930 | fax 393-2939 | www.kais-k.com

This boisterous International with a hot bar scene and "awesome" industrial decor is located in a "beautiful" 19th-century warehouse in Santos; it's too bad the food is "nothing special", and as for the service it's "confusing" - at first "there are so many employees" attending to your table, but "in the end they all forget about you."

Olivier ◐☒ *Mediterranean* | 24 | 15 | 20 | E

Bairro Alto | Rua do Teixeira 35 | (351-21) 343-1405 | www.restaurante-olivier.com

The menu at chef-owner Olivier da Costa's Bairro Alto dinner-only Mediterranean may be limited, but the cuisine is "unique", "sophisticated" and "delicious"; no wonder the charming, "tiny" wood-paneled room with paintings is always "full."

O Mercado do Peixe *Seafood* 24 | 13 | 16 | E

Monsanto | Estrada Pedro Teixeira, Vila Simão, Carmão da Ajuda | (351-21) 361-6070 | fax 362-3023 | www.mercadodopeixe.web.pt

There's a "large diversity" of the "freshest" fish and shellfish on ice to choose from, and then you watch your selection being "grilled to perfection" in front of you at this favorite in Monsanto; aesthetes assert that the plain decor is not the lure, but even they insist the experience is "simple, direct and wonderful."

Pap'Açorda Ⓢ Ⓜ *Portuguese* 22 | 17 | 19 | E

Bairro Alto | Rua da Atalaia 57-59 | (351-21) 346-4811 | fax 342-3765

Still "very popular" and "eternally trendy" "after more than 25 years" is this "Portuguese with a twist" up in the hopping Bairro Alto; dishes like the traditional namesake açorda (a bread stew cooked with shellfish, garlic and coriander) and an "excellent chocolate mousse" have their fans, but it's the "people-watching" that's the real order of the day.

Ristorante Hotel Cipriani *Italian* 27 | 25 | 27 | VE

Lapa | Lapa Palace Hotel | Rua do Pau de Bandeira 4 | (351-21) 394-9494 | fax 395-0665 | www.lapapalace.com

Housed in the lush and "lovely" Lapa Palace Hotel in the "ritzy" embassy area is this "great" Italian with equally highly rated service; the softly lit room is patrician and pretty, plus in summer there's a "nice dining terrace overlooking the garden"; in sum, it's "very elegant" and "very expensive."

Solar dos Nunes ◐ Ⓢ *Portuguese* 22 | 14 | 18 | M

Alcântara | Rua dos Lusíadas 70 | (351-21) 364-7359 | fax 363-1631 | www.solardosnunes.restaunet.pt

At this "Lisbon fixture" in the Alcântara, there's a "large choice" of "delightful" Alentejo specialties; a "friendly" staff, country casual decor and moderate prices add to its appeal.

Solar dos Presuntos ◐ *Portuguese* 23 | 17 | 22 | M

Baixa | Rua das Portas de Santo Antão | (351-21) 342-4253 | fax 346-8468 | www.solardospresuntos.com

"Lots of locals and tourists" hit this "very good" Restaurant Row pioneer in the Baixa for a plethora of "classic" and "simple" Portuguese staples that range from meats to seafood dishes like "perfect paella", all complemented by a substantial wine cellar; "service is excellent", the decor is "traditional" and prices are "acceptable"; P.S. "try to get a table upstairs."

Sua Excelência *Portuguese* 27 | 16 | 22 | E

Lapa | Rua do Conde 34 | (351-21) 390-3614 | fax 396-7585 | www.suaexcelencia.co.nr

"Start with a chilled white port", sit back and let the "interesting" owner "recite the day's offerings" in several languages, including English if necessary, at this "excellent" Portuguese in the Lapa district; an "attentive and polite" staff presides over the small, unpretentious setting with white walls and wooden beams.

Tavares Rico 🅢 *French/International* | 21 | 22 | 19 | E

Chiado | Rua da Misericórdia 35-37 | (351-21) 342-1112 | fax 347-8125 | www.tavaresrico.pt

"Still good after all these years" assert admirers of this 1784 Chiado French-International - maybe that's because its drop-dead opulent interior with gilt, mirrors and chandeliers was recently restored; the finest appointments - Vista Alegre china, Riedel crystal and Christofle silver - ensure this "institution" remains elegant.

Valle Flôr *French/Mediterranean* | 22 | 28 | 23 | VE

Alcântara | Pestana Palace Hotel | Rua Jau 54 | (351-21) 361-5600 | fax 361-5625 | www.pestana.com

"Probably the most beautiful and historic dining room in Lisbon" is this French-Mediterranean with frescoes, boiserie and garden views in the Pestana Palace Hotel, which is also a national monument; chef Aimé Barroyer does a "wonderful job modernizing classic dishes" and the result is an "expensive" but "great experience."

Varanda *French* | 27 | 24 | 27 | VE

São Sebastião da Pedreira | Four Seasons Hotel Ritz | Rua Rodrigo da Fonseca 88 | (351-21) 381-1400 | fax 383-1783 | www.fourseasons.com/lisbon

Voted No. 1 for Food in the city is this "very expensive" French venue that "like most other Four Seasons' restaurants could easily stand on its own without the hotel"; an "impeccable" staff serves "exquisite" food in a luminous room with a view of Eduardo VII park; P.S. the "sumptuous and well-presented lunchtime buffet" is "where all of Lisbon meets."

XL ◐🅢 *Portuguese/International* | 20 | 18 | 20 | E

Lapa | Calçada da Estrela 57-63 | (351-21) 395-6118

At this chef-owned Portuguese-International in the aristocratic Lapa district, "delicious steaks" and "good soufflés" are the stars; a "friendly, helpful" staff and "cool", "informal" vibe make it "a hit with a younger clientele."

Other Noteworthy Places

A Charcutaria 🅢 *Portuguese*
Rua do Alecrim 47A | (351-21) 342-3845

A Commenda *Mediterranean*
Centro Cultural de Belém | Praça do Império | (351-21) 364-8561 | fax 361-2610 | www.cerger.com

A Confraria *Portuguese*
York House Hotel | Rua das Janelas Verdes 32-1º | (351-21) 396-2435 | fax 397-2793 | www.yorkhouselisboa.com

Casanostra 🅜 *Italian*
Travessa do Poço da Cidade 60 | (351-21) 342-5931 | fax 346-7558 | www.casanostra.restaunet.pt

Chafariz do Vinho ◐🅜 *Portuguese/Spanish*
Chafariz da Mãe d'Água | Rua da Mãe d'Água à Praça da Alegria | (351-21) 342-2079 | fax 772-7249 | www.chafarizdovinho.com

Coelho da Rocha 🅢 *Portuguese*
Rua Coelho da Rocha 104 | (351-21) 390-0831

Eleven [S] *Mediterranean*
Jardim Amália Rodrigues | Rua Marquês de Fronteira | (351-21) 386-2211 | fax 386-2214 | www.restauranteleven.com

Espaço Lisboa ◐ *Portuguese*
Rua da Cozinha Económica 16 | (351-21) 361-0212 | fax 361-0211

Estufa Real *Mediterranean/Portuguese*
Calçada do Galvão | Jardim Botânico d' Ajuda | (351-21) 361-9400 | fax 361-9018 | www.estufareal.com

Flores *International/Portuguese*
Bairro Alto Hotel | Praça Luís de Camões 2 | (351-21) 340-8288 | fax 340-8299 | www.bairroaltohotel.com

Il Gattopardo *Italian*
Hotel Dom Pedro Palace | Avenida Eng Duarte Pacheco 24, 3rd fl. | (351-21) 389-6600 | fax 389-6629 | www.dompedro.com

Luca [S] *Italian/International*
Rua de Santa Marta 35 | (351-21) 315-0212 | www.luca.pt

Mezzaluna [S] *Italian*
Rua Artilharia 16 | (351-21) 387-9944 | fax 385-1661 | www.mezzalunalisboa.com

Nariz de Vinho Tinto [M] *Portuguese*
Rua do Conde 75 | (351-21) 395-3035 | fax 397-1222

O Galito [S] *Portuguese*
Rua da Fonte 18D | (351-21) 711-1088

O Mattos [S] *Portuguese/Seafood*
Rua Bulhão Pato 2A | (351-21) 848-3924

O Poleiro [S] *Portuguese*
Rua de Entrecampos 30A | (351-21) 797-6265 | fax 797-6126 | www.opoleiro.restaunet.pt

Pabe *French/Portuguese*
Rua Duque de Palmela 27A | (351-21) 353-5675 | fax 353-6437

Picanha *Brazilian*
Rua das Janelas Verdes 96 | (351-21) 397-5401 | fax 346-9786

Pragma Fausto Airoldi ◐[M] *Italian*
Casino Alameda dos Oceanos | Parque das Nações | (351-21) 892-9040 | fax 894-2189 | www.pragmalx.com

Restaurante El Gordo ◐ *Spanish/Portuguese*
Rua de São Boaventura 16 | (351-21) 342-4266 | fax 342-4266

Speakeasy ◐[S] *International/Portuguese*
Cais das Oficinas | Armazém 115, Rodra Conde d'Óbidos | (351-21) 390-9166 | fax 390-9167 | www.speakeasy-bar.com

Terraço *Portuguese*
Hotel Tivoli Lisboa | Avenida da Liberdade 185 | (351-21) 319-8900 | fax 319-8950 | www.tivolihotels.com

Terreiro do Paço [S] *Portuguese*
Praça do Comercio | (351-21) 031-2850 | fax 031-2859 | www.terreiropaco.com

Vela Latina [S] *International/Portuguese*
Doca do Bom Sucesso | (351-21) 301-7118 | fax 301-9311 | www.velalatina.pt

London

See our Zagat *London Restaurants* Survey for full coverage.

TOP FOOD RANKING

	Restaurant	Cuisine
28	Chez Bruce	British
	Gordon Ramsay/68 Royal	French
	Hunan	Chinese
	Square, The	French
	Pétrus	French
	Pied à Terre	French
27	La Trompette	European/French
	Le Gavroche	French
	River Café	Italian
	Nobu London	Japanese/Peruvian
	Capital	French
	Morgan M*	French
	Enoteca Turi	Italian
	Defune	Japanese
	Rasoi Vineet Bhatia*	Indian
26	L'Atelier Robuchon/La Cuisine	French
	Roussillon	French
	Zuma	Japanese
	Theo Randall	Italian
	Assaggi	Italian
	Miyama	Japanese
	Foliage	European/French
	Club Gascon	French
	Mosimann's (club)	International
	Nobu Berkeley St.	Japanese/Peruvian
	Umu	Japanese
	Tom Aikens	French
	Jin Kichi	Japanese
	Aubergine	French
	Zafferano	Italian
	Nahm	Thai
25	Gordon Ramsay/Claridge's	European
	Quirinale	Italian
	Clarke's	British
	Quilon	Indian
	Locanda Locatelli	Italian
	Yauatcha	Chinese
	Latium	Italian
	Amaya	Indian
	Moro	Mediterranean
	J. Sheekey	Seafood
	Orrery	French
	Greenhouse, The	French

* Indicates a tie with restaurant above

		FOOD	DECOR	SERVICE	COST
Ledbury	French				
Kai Mayfair	Chinese				
Maze	French				
Tamarind	Indian				
St. John	British				
Roka	Japanese				
Zaika	Indian				

Amaya ◐ *Indian* 25 | 24 | 21 | VE

Belgravia | 15-19 Halkin Arcade, Motcomb St., SW1 (Knightsbridge) | (44-20) 7823 1166 | fax 7259 6464 | www.realindianfood.com

"As Nobu is to Japanese, this is to Indian" gush groupies of this "gorgeous", "glitzy" Belgravia eatery - "low lighting and candles everywhere" - whose "tasty, grilled" small plates and "curries with class" make "a refreshing departure from the usual"; some pout the "pricey" "portions are small", but most of the "manicured clientele" maintains this colony of the Chutney Mary empire is "a serious find in London's high-end food stakes."

Assaggi Ⓢ *Italian* 26 | 15 | 23 | VE

Notting Hill | 39 Chepstow Pl., 1st fl., W2 (Notting Hill Gate) | (44-20) 7792 5501 | fax 0870-051 2923

The "mood is set by the exuberant maitre d' who explains the menu with gusto and passion" at this "exquisite Italian" in a "spartan" room "above a pub" in Notting Hill; the "simple, rustic" dishes are "magnificently executed" and "beautifully served" - all of which explains why it's so "very hard to get a table."

Aubergine Ⓢ *French* 26 | 20 | 24 | VE

Chelsea | 11 Park Walk, SW10 (Gloucester Rd./South Kensington) | (44-20) 7352 3449 | fax 7351 1770 | www.auberginerestaurant.co.uk

From its low-key "side street location" in Chelsea, this "quaint place subtly exerts its culinary clout" through chef William Drabble's "seductive" New French food - the "pièce de résistance is the degustation menu" - "executed with style" and served by an "attentive, yet unobtrusive" staff; a few malcontents "expect more for this kind of cash", but most maintain this is "a model for how haute cuisine should be"; P.S. the lunch prix fixe is a relative "bargain."

NEW Bincho Yakitori Ⓢ Ⓜ *Japanese* - | - | - | E

South Bank | Oxo Tower | Barge House St., SE1 (Blackfriars/Waterloo) | (44-20) 7803 0858

Sited on the airy second floor of the iconic Oxo Tower on the South Bank, and offering impressive views across the Thames, this informal Japanese newcomer shuns fancy decor and focuses instead on traditional yakitori and kushiyaki cuisine, with an emphasis on flame-grilled and skewered fare; the varied, well-explained choice of sakes, shochus, beers and fine-grade teas overshadows a limited wine section.

Capital Restaurant, The *French* 27 | 22 | 26 | VE

Knightsbridge | Capital Hotel | 22-24 Basil St., SW3 (Knightsbridge) | (44-20) 7591 1202 | fax 7225 0011 | www.capitalhotel.co.uk

"A tiny piece of heaven in the middle of Knightsbridge" is how "discerning diners" view this "serene", "understated" hotel New French that "gives one the impression of eating in a rich relative's dining room" while being waited on by a near-"perfect" staff; chef Eric Chavot's cuisine is "a real treat" "not to be missed" - even if it does require "a second mortgage" on the *maison*; all told, a capital experience, though perhaps "not for the young and hip."

Chez Bruce *British* 28 21 25 VE

Wandsworth | 2 Bellevue Rd., SW17 (Wandsworth Common B.R.) | (44-20) 8672 0114 | fax 8767 6648 | www.chezbruce.co.uk

"Simply no restaurant can match the quality for the quid" of this "Wandsworth wonder", which has knocked off Gordon Ramsay at 68 Royal Hospital Rd. as London's No. 1 for Food with its "reliably fantastic", "flawlessly executed" Modern British cuisine; "everything [else] about it is class" too - the "knowledgeable" but "never intrusive" staff, "the extensive wine list and possibly the largest selection of cheese in town"; the "cozy" room can be "cramped", but really, "the only problem is getting a reservation" ("even for long-term customers").

Clarke's 🅂 *British* 25 18 24 VE

Kensington | 124 Kensington Church St., W8 (Notting Hill Gate) | (44-20) 7221 9225 | fax 7229 4564 | www.sallyclarke.com

After almost a quarter-century, Sally Clarke's Kensington corner continues to be "consistently classy" "without the fuss often associated with high-end" places; her Modern British menus - now "with a choice of entrees" - are "still fresh" and "fabulous", the "service exceptional" and the "atmosphere pleasant" (if you "sit upstairs"); the "limited" number of offerings "aren't for everybody", but overall, this is possibly "the most reliable restaurant in London."

Club Gascon 🅂 *French* 26 21 22 VE

Smithfield | 57 W. Smithfield, EC1 (Barbican/Farringdon) | (44-20) 7796 0600 | fax 7796 0601 | www.clubgascon.com

"Never has the phrase 'quality over quantity' been more true" than with the "well-constructed", "exquisitely presented" small plates offered at this "charming Gallic experience" in an old Smithfield tea house; featuring "foie gras more ways than most people have had hot dinners", backed by an "excellent Gascon wine list", it's "perfect for a business or a romantic dinner (no small feat)"; "the bill piles up quickly", but "you won't remember what it cost, only how nice it was to be there."

Defune *Japanese* 27 16 20 VE

Marylebone | 34 George St., W1 (Baker St./Bond St.) | (44-20) 7935 8311 | fax 7487 3762

There are those who "refuse to have sushi anywhere else" than this "serene", "friendly" Marylebone Japanese, maintaining its "marvellous, freshest" victuals are "perfect in size and consistency"; "you'll be shocked how much you're spending", especially since the "decor's nothing fancy", but "if you have an expense account, give it a try."

Enoteca Turi 🅂 *Italian* 27 19 23 E

Putney | 28 Putney High St., SW15 (Putney Bridge) | (44-20) 8785 4449 | fax 8780 5409 | www.enotecaturi.com

"We have to keep reminding ourselves this is just across the Thames, not in the hills in Tuscany" say fans of this rustic ristorante that's "just about the best Italian in London"; the fare "never fails to impress" and there's "a phenomenal wine list too"; "tables are too close", but "personal attention from the owner and his wife ensures" a "pleasant evening."

Foliage *European/French* 26 23 26 VE

Knightsbridge | Mandarin Oriental Hyde Park | 66 Knightsbridge, SW1 (Knightsbridge) | (44-20) 7201 3723 | fax 7235 2001 | www.mandarinoriental.com

"Beautiful in every respect" maintain admirers of the Mandarin Oriental's dining room where "culinary wizard Chris Staines" produces Classic French-Modern European cuisine "with vision, zest and skill", which is served by a "gracious staff" in Adam Tihany-designed premises ("light, with big windows"); though the "cost is equal to trans-Atlantic airfare", "it's worth every posh penny"; P.S. "ask for a window table" to savor the "splendid view of Hyde Park."

Gordon Ramsay at Claridge's *European* 25 24 24 VE

Mayfair | Claridge's Hotel | 45 Brook St., W1 (Bond St.) | (44-20) 7499 0099 | fax 7499 3099 | www.gordonramsay.com

"His kitchen might be hell, but the food is heavenly" at TV star/chef Gordon Ramsay's "art deco fantasy" ("red drapes, swirly light fixtures") in Claridge's Hotel, where the team led by exec toque Mark Sargeant is "inspired to deliver" "ever-so-imaginative" Modern European "refined classics" with "old-world charm"; sure, it's a "budget-buster" and, some believe, "a bit of a let-down lately", but most hail it as a "heady wonderland experience"; P.S. "lunch provides 80% of the experience at 20% of the cost."

Gordon Ramsay at 68 Royal Hospital Rd. ⊠ *French* 28 24 28 VE

Chelsea | 68 Royal Hospital Rd., SW3 (Sloane Sq.) | (44-20) 7352 4441 | fax 7592 1213 | www.gordonramsay.com

"Dine at the altar of the master", Gordon Ramsay - a "superlative experience" for "serious foodies" in "crisp, chic" Chelsea quarters; the "rich and complex", "hellishly good" New French cuisine is ferried by a "suave staff" that delivers the "royal treatment" (manager Jean-Claude Breton "deserves to be as famous as Gordon"); it's "eye-wateringly expensive" - perhaps one reason why it was edged out as No. 1 for Food in London this year - but all in all, Ramsay's "flagship is sailing high."

Greenhouse, The ⊠ *French* 25 23 24 VE

Mayfair | 27A Hay's Mews, W1 (Green Park) | (44-20) 7499 3331 | fax 7499 5368 | www.greenhouserestaurant.co.uk

In the "secluded setting" of a "hidden Mayfair mews", this "enchanting" eatery from restaurateur Marlon Abela (Umu) is lauded for a "gorgeously prepared" New French menu that "mixes slightly quirky flavors with standard ones", "presented with flair" by a staff that's "excellent without being stifling"; true, it can be "difficult to get past the price tag", but you could economize with the wine, as the "simply stunning" list contains "both full and half-bottles."

NEW **Haiku** ⊠ *Pan-Asian* - - - E

Mayfair | 15 New Burlington Pl., W1 (Oxford Circus) | (44-20) 7494 4777 | www.haikurestaurant.com

This hip new Pan-Asian sits in a cul-de-sac "just off Regent Street, hidden" behind huge wood blinds; it's spread over three dark floors, each with a single-technique kitchen that produces raw, steamed or sizzling fare; there's also a "bar area for the 'been-shopping-on-Bond-Street-and-my-Choos-are-killing-me' crowd."

Hunan Ⓢ *Chinese* 28 | 14 | 22 | E

Pimlico | 51 Pimlico Rd., SW1 (Sloane Sq.) | (44-20) 7730 5712 | fax 7730 8265

The trick is to let chef-owner Mr. Peng "know what you like and it will keep coming" at this "fine choice for the Chinese connoisseur" in Pimlico; admirers call it "incomparable" for its Hunanese dishes "dependant on the day's market" and delivered in "tasty little bites"; just be prepared to "ignore the cold surroundings" and "remember to say when you are full - otherwise they will keep feeding you!"

Jin Kichi Ⓜ *Japanese* 26 | 10 | 17 | M

Hampstead | 73 Heath St., NW3 (Hampstead) | (44-20) 7794 6158 | fax 7794 6158 | www.jinkichi.com

Almost every critic calls it "cramped", but what this Hampstead "survivor" "lacks in space, it makes up for in quality", with an "outstanding" "range of choices" of Japanese cuisine ("the yakitori grill bar is the true star here"); "be sure to book in advance" as it is "hard to get into."

J. Sheekey ◐ *Seafood* 25 | 21 | 23 | VE

Covent Garden | 28-32 St. Martin's Ct., WC2 (Leicester Sq.) | (44-20) 7240 2565 | fax 7497 0891 | www.j-sheekey.co.uk

The "peerless seafood has barely stopped breathing" at this "discreet" Theatreland "bastion" where "the warmly lit, woody interior complements the conviviality"; throw in "unerring service" and a "chance to celeb-spot" amongst all "the thespians after a show", and this "slick outfit" "is "rightly revered", "like her sister, The Ivy."

Kai Mayfair *Chinese* 25 | 21 | 22 | VE

Mayfair | 65 S. Audley St., W1 (Bond St./Marble Arch) | (44-20) 7493 8988 | fax 7493 1456 | www.kaimayfair.co.uk

Embark on a "dining adventure" at this "delightful spot in quiet Mayfair", where "Chinese food for grown-ups" takes "the concept of originality to extremes"; the setting - "beautiful", "if a bit corporate" - proves Asian eateries "can be posh", and the staff pays "meticulous attention to detail"; sure, it's "crazy expensive", but many say it's "the best of its kind."

NEW La Petite Maison Ⓢ *Mediterranean* - | - | - | E

Mayfair | 54 Brooks Mews, W1 (Bond St.) | (44-20) 7495 4774 | www.lpmlondon.co.uk

After 19 years as one of the Côte d'Azur's more celeb-filled haunts, the Nice original has spawned its first offshoot, this bustling newcomer unveiled by an owner of Zuma in V-shaped Mayfair mews digs; its open kitchen produces Mediterranean dishes dominated by French and Ligurian brasserie-style classics as well as many shared plates.

NEW L'Atelier de Joël Robuchon ◐ *French* 26 | 24 | 24 | VE

Covent Garden | 13-15 West St., WC2 (Leicester Sq.) | (44-20) 7010 8600

NEW La Cuisine *French*

Covent Garden | L'Atelier de Joël Robuchon | 13-15 West St., WC2 (Leicester Sq.) | (44-20) 7010 8600

Super-chef Joël Robuchon has "hit town with his fantastic creativity" at this "thrilling" Theatreland yearling; there's a "chic" red/black eatery with a "wall of green plants" and counter seating, and up above, a "black and white kitchen"-themed restaurant, La Cuisine, both offering different iterations of "divine *nouvelle cuisine française*"; given the "minuscule mains", it's all too "pricey" and "pretentious" pessimists protest, but "if you really want to impress, this is where to come"; P.S. there's also a "boudoirlike bar" on the top floor.

Latium ☒ *Italian* 25 | 19 | 24 | E

Fitzrovia | 21 Berners St., W1 (Goodge St.) | (44-20) 7323 9123 | fax 7323 3205 | www.latiumrestaurant.com

"They pack them in" to this "real find" in Fitzrovia, where diners are "welcomed professionally", then fed "impeccable Italian dishes", including "various types of ravioli"; though the "tempting wine list can rack up the bill", a "reasonable" meal "can be had with study."

La Trompette *European/French* 27 | 21 | 25 | VE

Chiswick | 5-7 Devonshire Rd., W4 (Turnham Green) | (44-20) 8747 1836 | fax 8995 8097 | www.latrompette.co.uk

Surveyors "sound the trumpets" for this "hidden" "blessing for Chiswick locals" (sister of Chez Bruce), an "elegant" venue with "expertly prepared" Modern European-New French cooking, a "wine list to dive into" and "attentive, but not cloying service"; while the "fixed-price menus make for excellent cost control", it's "great to impress for business or that second date (may be a bit flashy for a first)."

Ledbury, The *French* 25 | 23 | 24 | VE

Notting Hill | 127 Ledbury Rd., W11 (Notting Hill Gate/Westbourne Park) | (44-20) 7792 9090 | fax 7792 9191 | www.theledbury.com

After "a stunning debut" in 2005, this "elegant" Notting Hill sister of The Square "continues to please" with "inventive" New French cuisine that, while occasionally "over-the-top", hits "orgasmic" levels; "nicely spaced" tables that "strike the perfect balance between buzzy and so loud you can't have a conversation" and "gracious service" add appeal.

Le Gavroche ☒ *French* 27 | 24 | 26 | VE

Mayfair | 43 Upper Brook St., W1 (Marble Arch) | (44-20) 7408 0881 | fax 7491 4387 | www.le-gavroche.co.uk

"As expensive as it gets, but as fabulous as it can be" sums up Michel Roux Jr.'s "magnificent" Mayfair "bastion" of haute cuisine in a "sumptuous" "snug basement setting with a real sense of exclusivity"; the "*superbe*" kitchen doesn't "miss a beat" and "every detail is attended to" by an "exemplary" staff; modernists may mutter "this 1950s rendition of fancy French" "needs updating", but the overwhelming opinion is "the old style still works."

Locanda Locatelli *Italian* 25 | 22 | 22 | VE

Marylebone | Hyatt Regency London - The Churchill | 8 Seymour St., W1 (Marble Arch) | (44-20) 7935 9088 | fax 7935 1149 | www.locandalocatelli.com

"Leave the family-style for another day - this is the place" for a "posh" experience attest *amici* of Italian "icon Giorgio Locatelli's" "outstanding, inventive" Northern Italian *cucina* in a Portman Square hotel; it's "popular with the glitterati", causing some to sigh "I'm not famous enough to get much service", but nearly everyone else would "eat here often - if it weren't so horrifically expensive."

Maze *French* 25 | 21 | 23 | VE

Mayfair | 10-13 Grosvenor Sq., W1 (Bond St.) | (44-20) 7107 0000 | fax 7107 0001 | www.gordonramsay.com

"The great man does tapas" at this highly hyped two-year-old in "Gordon Ramsay's stable" in Grosvenor Square, where "creative" Asian-inflected New French small plates make a "fantastic way to sample different flavors without popping buttons"; cynics snap the yellow-beige "decor lacks character" and the "knowledgeable" "service is uneven", but most are "enthusiastic" about this "exciting concept" (just "be prepared to be a-mazed at the cost").

Miyama *Japanese* 26 | 12 | 20 | E

Mayfair | 38 Clarges St., W1 (Green Park) | (44-20) 7499 2443 | fax 7491 1569 | www.miyama.co.uk

This "simple little place on a side street" in Mayfair is "a favorite of the Japanese expat community", serving "exquisite", "excellent sushi and sashimi the size of which will break your chopsticks"; an attentive staff" makes amends for "decor that could use some work."

Morgan M 🄼 *French* 27 | 17 | 22 | VE

Islington | 489 Liverpool Rd., N7 (Highbury & Islington) | (44-20) 7609 3560 | fax 8292 5699 | www.morganm.com

"A real mecca for food lovers", "dedicated chef"-owner Morgan Meunier's "hidden gem" offers Islingtonians "the rare pleasure of an eponymous restaurant with the namesake firmly in control"; the experience involves "delectable" New French fare (including an "outstanding vegetarian" tasting menu), plus a "staff that's trained to please"; P.S. the "refurbishment provides a better", more formal setting.

Moro 🅂 *Mediterranean* 25 | 18 | 20 | E

Clerkenwell | 34-36 Exmouth Mkt., EC1 (Angel/Farringdon) | (44-20) 7833 8336 | fax 7833 9338 | www.moro.co.uk

"The oohs and ahhs of eating" the "exotic" Med cuisine - "bursting with flavor" and "true to the Moorish spirit" - add to the "deafening noise" at this Exmouth Market eatery ("the harsh interior" doesn't help); even if the staff is "not always able to keep up with the crowds", the place is "great for a gaggle of girls or a fun night with clients."

Mosimann's 🅂 *International* 26 | 26 | 25 | VE

Private club; inquiries: (44-20) 7235 9625

"Civilized beyond civilization as it is today", this Belgravia club offers "a supreme dining experience from start to finish"; within the "dazzling" space (a 19th-century former church) with "many enchanting [private] rooms", guests experience "masterful" International cooking, "world-class wines" and "interactive but not intrusive waiters"; the "only downside is you need to have a member take you."

Nahm *Thai* 26 | 20 | 23 | VE

Belgravia | Halkin Hotel | 5 Halkin St., SW1 (Hyde Park Corner) | (44-20) 7333 1234 | fax 7333 1100 | www.nahm.como.bz

"If you are a fan of Thai cuisine" - and "your bank account is sufficient" - you'll find the "intricate" menu at this Belgravia hotel eatery "extraordinarily interesting" and even "inspiring"; some call the marble-floored, "minimalist" "decor cold, but warm, pleasant servers" make this a "good special-occasion restaurant."

Nobu Berkeley St. ◐ *Japanese/Peruvian* 26 | 21 | 20 | VE

Mayfair | 15 Berkeley St., W1 (Green Park) | (44-20) 7290 9222 | fax 7290 9223 | www.noburestaurants.com

There's always "quite a scene going on" at the Nobu empire's number-two Mayfair outpost - "hipper than the one at the Met" - where celebrities and "hedge-fund zillionaires come to play", whether it be in the "brilliant bar" or "bright dining room upstairs"; supporters still swoon over "sushi like you've never tasted before" and the Japanese-Peruvian cuisine that's "divine", if "extremely expensive"; however, the "rush 'em in, rush 'em out policy is not appreciated."

Nobu London *Japanese/Peruvian* 27 | 20 | 21 | VE

Mayfair | Metropolitan Hotel | 19 Old Park Ln., W1 (Hyde Park Corner) | (44-20) 7447 4747 | fax 7447 4749 | www.noburestaurants.com

Even after 10 years, Nobu Matsuhisa's "sizzling" Old Park Lane "flagship is firing on all cylinders", with an "exotically marvelous" Japanese-Peruvian menu that "exceeds expectations"; ok, the "stark" decor "could do with a splash of paint", the "efficient staff sometimes seems harassed" and "booking a table takes creativity"; but few deny this "celestial" spot - rammed with "A- through C-list celebs" - is "definitely a treat, especially if someone else drops the credit card."

NEW **Olivomare** ☒ *Italian/Seafood* - | - | - | E

Belgravia | 10 Lower Belgrave St., SW1 (Victoria) | (44-20) 7730 9022

This Belgravia newcomer is set in bright, gleaming premises where, apart from one wall bedecked with fishy modern artwork, everywhere is pristine white; the sophisticated Sardinian seafood menu is not long, but offers a wide selection of species.

Orrery *French* 25 | 23 | 23 | VE

Marylebone | 55 Marylebone High St., W1 (Baker St./Regent's Park) | (44-20) 7616 8000 | fax 7616 8080 | www.orreryrestaurant.co.uk

Flooded in natural light, this "spacious" Marylebone New French offers a "serene setting" for "understated, yet refined" and "tantalizing" tasting menus - culminating in a "divine cheese tray" - "served by a professional", if slightly "stiff" staff; ornery souls may sniff it's "not life-changing", and you definitely "feel the money flying from your wallet", but it's "worth every penny" for most.

Pétrus ☒ *French* 28 | 25 | 26 | VE

Belgravia | Berkeley Hotel | Wilton Pl., SW1 (Hyde Park Corner) | (44-20) 7235 1200 | www.gordonramsay.com

"Luxuriate in Marcus Wareing's sublime creations" - the epitome of New French "cooking at its most cutting edge", backed by "wines that live up to the restaurant's name" - at this "beautiful" Belgravia venue where an "utterly professional" staff "provides tip-top service"; perhaps it's *un peu* "pretentious", with "eye-popping prices", but it's also "everything a modern fine-dining institution should be" - "so pick a special occasion, forget the cost and book it."

Pied à Terre ☒ *French* 28 | 22 | 25 | VE

Fitzrovia | 34 Charlotte St., W1 (Goodge St.) | (44-20) 7636 1178 | fax 7916 1171 | www.pied-a-terre.co.uk

"Hats off to chef Shane Osborne for the culinary masterpieces" he creates at this "small" but "stunning" New French in Fitzrovia; from the "star wine list" to the "extremely knowledgeable servers", it has "everything you could possibly want in a restaurant" (except perhaps the decor - "chic, but nothing eye-grabbing"), and so it's "worth the prices" - "you'll pay, but you'll leave *la terre* for *le ciel*!"

Quilon *Indian* 25 | 19 | 21 | E

Victoria | Crowne Plaza London St. James Hotel | 41 Buckingham Gate, SW1 (St. James's Park/Victoria) | (44-20) 7821 1899 | fax 7828 5802 | www.quilon.co.uk

"In its own way, great" say those familiar with this "modern"-looking Indian in a "corporate" hotel south of St. James's Park; it's applauded for "amazing" Keralan cooking that's "true to the region" - though "quite pricey" compared to more standard subcontinental sites.

Quirinale [S] *Italian* 25 | 20 | 25 | E

Westminster | 1 Great Peter St., SW1 (Westminster) | (44-20) 7222 7080 | fax 7233 3080 | www.quirinale.co.uk

"Combining an elegant simplicity with high-quality service", this "Westminster favorite gets the vote" - as well as attracts "the occasional MP" - for "divine" Italian cooking "plus the best selection of cheeses"; although the "comfortable" cream-colored setting can be "a bit quiet", the "intimate" basement makes it feel "like a club."

Rasoi Vineet Bhatia [S] *Indian* 27 | 19 | 23 | VE

Chelsea | 10 Lincoln St., SW3 (Sloane Sq.) | (44-20) 7225 1881 | fax 7581 0220 | www.vineetbhatia.com

With an "exquisite Indian" menu of "dishes that tempt and surprise", chef-owner Vineet Bhatia's "charming" Chelsea townhouse (recently given a light refurb) is "always a pleasure", smoothed along by "superb service"; if a few flinch at the "high-end prices", even they are "entertained" by this "epicurean delight."

NEW **Rhodes W1 Restaurant** [S] [M] *British* - | - | - | VE

Marylebone | Cumberland Hotel | Great Cumberland Pl., W1 (Marble Arch) | (44-20) 7479 3737 | fax 7479 3888 | www.rhodesw1.com

The combination of chef Gary Rhodes' sophisticated Modern British menu (including a small-plates offering) and designer Kelly Hoppen's glammed-up decor (dominated by weeping willow-like beaded chandeliers) creates a dramatic setting for this swanky new venue in the Cumberland Hotel (though it has its own entrance on Bryanston Street).

NEW **Ristorante Semplice** [S] *Italian* - | - | - | E

Mayfair | 10 Blenheim St., W1 (Bond St.) | (44-20) 7495 1509

Given its luxe but "tasteful" decor of polished ebony and gold walls, leather seats and a Murano chandelier, it's hard to believe this Mayfair space used to house a fish 'n' chip shop; now a Northern Italian calls it home, with rich and richly priced dishes "of great promise."

River Café *Italian* 27 | 22 | 24 | VE

Hammersmith | Thames Wharf | Rainville Rd., W6 (Hammersmith) | (44-20) 7386 4200 | fax 7386 4201 | www.rivercafe.co.uk

With "joyful" "unfussy dishes that showcase exquisite ingredients to beautiful effect", this Italian "evergreen" "never fails to delight", even after 20-plus years; the "decor and ambiance display a similar lack of pretension, and the informally clad staff clearly enjoys working here";

yes, the Thames-side Hammersmith "location is a problem", but it's "so worth the trip" - especially if you can "sit on the terrace (the view's as good as the food)."

Roka ◐ *Japanese* 25 | 20 | 19 | VE

Fitzrovia | 37 Charlotte St., W1 (Goodge St./Tottenham Court Rd.) | (44-20) 7580 6464 | fax 7580 0220 | www.rokarestaurant.com

"Zuma's little sister" on Charlotte Street - a "sexy", "sophisticated room of pale wood and glass" - is "notable in its own right", with a "fantastic robata grill" ("see the chefs at work") and "positively sublime" Japanese dishes at "high prices when everything is so tempting"; "haphazard service" irks some, but all "love lounging in the Shochu" bar downstairs with its "dangerous cocktails."

Roussillon ☒ *French* 26 | 23 | 25 | VE

Pimlico | 16 St. Barnabas St., SW1 (Sloane Sq./Victoria) | (44-20) 7730 5550 | fax 7824 8617 | www.roussillon.co.uk

"Deserves to be better known than it is" say fans of this "quiet" Pimlico place with a pleasantly "informal" feel ("like walking into someone's lounge"); but there's nothing casual about chef/co-owner Alexis Gauthier's "high-end, creative" New French cooking that "emphasizes vegetables"; with perks like "pampering" service and a "fabulous wine list with one of the smartest sommeliers", it's "worth going on a special occasion - or just to treat yourself."

NEW Skylon *European* - | - | - | E

South Bank | Royal Festival Hall | Belvedere Rd., SE1 (Waterloo) | (44-20) 7654 7800 | www.skylonrestaurant.co.uk

Named after an iconic attraction from the 1951 Festival of Britain, this confident newcomer in the newly revamped Royal Festival Hall offers a dramatic panoramic view across the Thames; a casual, hardwood-floored grill and smarter, retro-looking restaurant - both serving different incarnations of a Modern European menu from chef Helena Puolakka - act as stylish bookends to an airy cocktail bar in the center of the cavernous space.

Square, The *French* 28 | 24 | 26 | VE

Mayfair | 6-10 Bruton St., W1 (Bond St./Green Park) | (44-20) 7495 7100 | fax 7495 7150 | www.squarerestaurant.com

"Fantastic food", "faultless service", "my favorite" fawn fans of this "grown-up", "elegant eatery off Bond Street" that maintains its edge with an "inventive take on Classic French" food, a "gigantic wine list" and "understated" decor that has gotten "warmer after a makeover"; "though the set lunch is reasonable, it's very expensive for dinner" - better "bring your Black Amex" - but that doesn't stop it from being one of "the best all-rounders in London."

St. John ☒ *British* 25 | 16 | 20 | E

Smithfield | 26 St. John St., EC1 (Farringdon) | (44-20) 7251 0848 | fax 7251 4090 | www.stjohnrestaurant.com

"Eating a pig's eyeball was never so much fun" swear supporters of this "snout-to-tail" Smithfield Modern Brit, "after 14 years still trendsetting" in its use of animal "innards in all their glory"; some beef that the "bare-white" "dreary decor" detracts, but the only moan of most is that "the best 'bits' often sell out quickly."

	FOOD	DECOR	SERVICE	COST
Tamarind	25	21	23	VE
Theo Randall at The InterContinental	26	21	24	VE
Tom Aikens	26	22	24	VE
Umu	26	25	23	VE
Wild Honey	-	-	-	E
Yauatcha	25	22	17	E

Tamarind ◐ *Indian*

Mayfair | 20 Queen St., W1 (Green Park) | (44-20) 7629 3561 | fax 7499 5034 | www.tamarindrestaurant.com

"Deservedly popular" for over a decade, this "regal" Mayfair "milestone" "serves the who's who" with "nouvelle Indian" fare; highly "helpful waiters" will guide you through the "wonderfully spiced", simultaneously "earthy and ephemeral dal dishes"; but you better "not mind spending the rupees" - a typical "takeaway curry house this is not."

NEW **Theo Randall at The InterContinental** *Italian*

Mayfair | InterContinental Park Ln. | 1 Hamilton Pl., W1 (Hyde Park Corner) | (44-20) 7318 8747 | www.theorandall.com

Although it's still "unknown to many", this newly renovated hotel restaurant is "a change for the positive at Hyde Park Corner"; the "wonderful", "innovative Italian food" is "in the tradition of the River Café" (the ex-home of the eponymous chef), and is served by a "genial" staff; only the room - "slick" but "somewhat sterile" - sets some back.

Tom Aikens Ⓢ *French*

Chelsea | 43 Elystan St., SW3 (South Kensington) | (44-20) 7584 2003 | fax 7584 2001 | www.tomaikens.co.uk

The "most imaginative food on the planet" enthuse "the shirt-sleeved expense-account crowd" enamored by the "creative pairings" (both food and wine) offered in "huge portions" by "elegant servers" at this Chelsea New French; critics cavil it's "self-consciously clever" cooking "from the chemistry-set school of cuisine", and views on the monochrome decor range from "austere" to "smart"; either way, "eating here is a true experience"; P.S. the tasting menu is "the way to go."

Umu Ⓢ *Japanese*

Mayfair | 14-16 Bruton Pl., W1 (Bond St.) | (44-20) 7499 8881 | www.umurestaurant.com

"It always feels special" at this "stylish" Mayfair specialist in *kaiseki* (traditional Japanese tasting menus); devotees drool over the "delicate" dishes, especially the "exquisite experience" of "fish that still tastes of the sea", served with "finesse" "within a somber, well-appointed room"; even the few who "don't get the hype", calling it "really overpriced", admit it's a "perfect" "place to impress."

NEW **Wild Honey** Ⓢ Ⓜ *British*

Mayfair | 12 St. George St., W1 (Oxford Circus) | (44-20) 7758 9160

Owners Anthony Demetre and Will Smith have opened this newcomer in clublike, wood-paneled Mayfair premises; it serves innovative Modern British cooking at commendable prices for the quality and neighborhood, and also offers a clever oenological policy of making the 80-strong wine list available in mini-carafe size (about two large glasses) to encourage experimentation.

Yauatcha ◐ *Chinese*

Soho | 15 Broadwick St., W1 (Piccadilly Circus) | (44-20) 7494 8888 | fax 7287 6959

Owner "Alan Yau delivers" with this "sexy" split-level Soho Chinese that attracts a "noisy" crowd of London's "most attractive yuppies"; "interesting" teas and "exquisite" pastries abound in the ground-floor cafe, while down the "dark" staircase lies "dim sum as theater" with "innovative" delicacies like "melt-in-the-mouth venison puffs" washed down with "standout cocktails"; the only "shame" is the "snippy servers'" "conveyor-belt attitude to turning tables."

Zafferano *Italian* 26 | 20 | 22 | VE

Belgravia | 15 Lowndes St., SW1 (Knightsbridge) | (44-20) 7235 5800 | fax 7235 1971 | www.zafferanorestaurant.com

"*Bellissima*" bellow believers in this Belgravia venue, for 18 years a "consistently high, very high, in fact" "standard-bearer" for The Boot's *cucina* ("go around truffle season" or try the "fantastic lobster linguini" anytime); true, tables are "tight" and the "tariffs high", leading a few to wonder "is it worth it?", but the plethora of celebrities, "local hedge fund mangers and your friendly neighborhood Russian tycoon dining" here seems to suggest *sì*.

Zaika *Indian* 25 | 24 | 21 | E

Kensington | 1 Kensington High St., W8 (High St. Kensington) | (44-20) 7795 6533 | fax 7937 8854 | www.zaika-restaurant.co.uk

In between its "creative" "fusion cuisine" (try a "divine chocolate samosa") and its vaulted-ceiling, "ethereal atmosphere, light years from the hustle of Kensington", this "modern" Indian "spoils you for the local" curry house; even so, hostiles huff its "high prices are hard to justify."

Zuma *Japanese* 26 | 24 | 21 | VE

Knightsbridge | 5 Raphael St., SW7 (Knightsbridge) | (44-20) 7584 1010 | fax 7584 5005 | www.zumarestaurant.com

If you can breach the "obnoxious reservation system", you too can join the "ultrathin women, middle-aged bankers" "and expense-account types" at this "buzzy to the extreme" Knightsbridge "nouveau Japanese"; ranging from rave-worthy robata to "superb" sushi, the "food's mind-blowing" - and "it's easy to blow a fortune" on it as well; but despite that, and a "staff not quite up to" handling the "hot, heaving" scene, this hipster still seems "sensational."

Other Noteworthy Places

Cinnamon Club ☒ *Indian*

Old Westminster Library | 30-32 Great Smith St., SW1 (Westminster) | (44-20) 7222 2555 | fax 7222 1333 | www.cinnamonclub.com

ffiona's M *British*

51 Kensington Church St., W8 (High St. Kensington/Notting Hill Gate) | (44-20) 7937 4152 | www.ffionas.com

Galvin Bistrot de Luxe *French*

66 Baker St., W1 (Baker St.) | (44-20) 7935 4007 | fax 7486 1735 | www.galvin.myzen.co.uk

Glasshouse, The *British*

14 Station Parade, TW9 (Kew Gdns.) | (44-20) 8940 6777 | fax 8940 3833 | www.glasshouserestaurant.co.uk

Hakkasan ◐ *Chinese*

8 Hanway Pl., W1 (Tottenham Court Rd.) | (44-20) 7927 7000 | fax 7907 1889

Harry's Bar ◐☒ *Italian*

26 S. Audley St., W1 (Green Park) | (44-20) 7408 0844 | fax 7493 6366

Ivy, The ◐ *British/European*
Private club; inquiries: (44-20) 7836 4751

Kiku *Japanese*
17 Half Moon St., W1 (Green Park) | (44-20) 7499 4208 | fax 7409 3359 | www.kikurestaurant.co.uk

La Fromagerie Café *European*
2-4 Moxon St., W1 (Baker St.) | (44-20) 7935 0341 | fax 7935 0341 | www.lafromagerie.co.uk

Lanes *International*
Four Seasons Hotel | Hamilton Pl., W1 (Green Park/Hyde Park Corner) | (44-20) 7499 0888 | fax 7493 6629 | www.fourseasons.com/london

Le Caprice ◐ *British/European*
Arlington Hse. | Arlington St., SW1 (Green Park) | (44-20) 7629 2239 | fax 7493 9040 | www.le-caprice.co.uk

L'Oranger Ⓢ *French*
5 St. James's St., SW1 (Green Park) | (44-20) 7839 3774 | fax 7839 4330 | www.loranger.co.uk

Mark's Club Ⓢ *British/French*
Private club; inquiries: (44-20) 7499 2936

Morton's Ⓢ *French*
Private club; inquiries: (44-20) 7518 2982

Wilton's Ⓢ *British/Seafood*
55 Jermyn St., SW1 (Green Park/Piccadilly Circus) | (44-20) 7629 9955 | fax 7495 6233 | www.wiltons.co.uk

Yoshino Ⓢ *Japanese*
3 Piccadilly Pl., W1 (Piccadilly Circus) | (44-20) 7287 6622 | fax 7287 1733 | www.yoshino.net

Ziani *Italian*
45 Radnor Walk, SW3 (Sloane Sq.) | (44-20) 7351 5297 | fax 7244 8387 | www.ziani.uk.com

Madrid

TOP FOOD RANKING

	Restaurant	Cuisine
28	Santceloni	Mediterranean
27	Zalacaín	International
	Goizeko Kabi/Wellington	Basque
26	Príncipe de Viana	Basque/Navarraise
	Combarro	Seafood/Galician
	Viridiana	International
	La Terraza del Casino	Spanish
	El Chaflán	Mediterranean
25	Horcher	International
	Jockey	International
	El Amparo	Basque
	Goya	Spanish/International
	Kabuki	Japanese/Mediterranean
24	Asia Gallery	Chinese
	Arce	Basque
	El Pescador	Seafood
	La Broche	Mediterranean
	La Trainera	Seafood
23	El Bodegón	Basque
	El Olivo	Mediterranean
	Shiratori	Japanese
	Lavinia Espacio	Mediterranean
	Rubaiyat	Brazilian/Steakhouse
22	Tse-Yang	Chinese
	Botín Restaurante	Castilian
	Balzac	Mediterranean
	Club 31	International
	La Tapería	Spanish/Tapas
	L'Albufera	Valencian
	Taberna del Alabardero	Basque/Tapas
21	Lágrimas Negras	Spanish
	Casa Lucio	Castilian
	La Bola	Madrilian
	Thaï Gardens	Thai
20	Teatro Real	Mediterranean
	Alkalde	Basque/Tapas
	Europa Decó*	Mediterranean
	Las Cuatro Estaciones*	International
	Lhardy*	Spanish/International
	José Luis	Tapas/Basque
	Al-Mounia	Moroccan
19	Annapurna	Indian
	Café Saigon	Chinese/Vietnamese
	Pan de Lujo	Spanish Fusion
18	Nodo	Japanese/Mediterranean

* Indicates a tie with restaurant above

	Pedro Larumbe	Spanish
	Teatriz	International
16	Café de Oriente	Basque/Tapas
	Mumbai Massala	Indian
14	Iroco	International
11	El Espejo	Basque/French

Alkalde ◐ *Basque* 20 13 17 E

Salamanca | Jorge Juan 10 | (34) 91-576-3359 | fax 91-781-4010 | www.alkalderestaurante.com

"Good" traditional and modern Basque dishes as well as tapas are all available at this 1963 pioneer in a "nice location in Salamanca"; but while some find its candlelit setting with stained-glass windows and "beamed ceilings" "welcoming" and atmospheric, others opine it's "antiquated."

Al-Mounia Ⓢ Ⓜ *Moroccan* 20 19 17 E

Salamanca | Recoletos 5 | (34) 91-435-0828 | www.almounia.es

"*Mechui* like mama used to make" if your mom was Moroccan is on the menu, along with tagines, couscous and an order-ahead entire roast lamb, at this "excellent" Salamanca stalwart; a "dreamlike Arabic setting" - tiles, crystal lamps and oriental carpets - adds to the "unique" experience.

Annapurna ◐ Ⓢ *Indian* 19 17 19 E

Chamberí | Zurbano 5 | (34) 91-319-8716 | fax 91-308-3249 | www.annapurnarestaurante.com

The "best Indian food in Madrid" is found at this Chamberí "classic" where an "excellent" staff presides over a spacious terra-cotta room with arches and an appealing interior garden patio.

Arce ◐ Ⓢ *Basque* 24 16 21 E

Centro | Augusto Figueroa 32 | (34) 91-522-0440 | fax 91-522-5913 | www.restaurantearce.com

Admirers advise on planning for an interactive evening at this "fine" modern Basque in El Centro, where "attentive" chef-owner Iñaki Camba may "come out of the kitchen and help you design your meal", which can be complemented with wine from an impressive 900-bottle list; the cozy, "comfortable" setting reminds some of "eating at home."

Asia Gallery ◐ *Chinese* 24 24 24 E

Centro | Hotel Westin Palace | Plaza las Cortes 7 | (34) 91-360-0049 | fax 91-360-8100 | www.palacemadrid.com

"It's hard to find Asian food this good in Spain" say supporters of this Chinese in the Hotel Westin Palace; an "amazing", "luxurious" setting with silks and antiques and "great service" add to the experience, making it "ideal for a romantic evening."

Balzac ◐ Ⓢ *Mediterranean* 22 19 21 E

Retiro | Moreto 7 | (34) 91-420-0177 | fax 91-429-8370

"An epicurean delight" is how devotees describe the cuisine at this "inventive", "modern" Med in the Retiro, near the Prado Museum; "pleasing" service and a series of softly lit, minimally decorated rooms with modern art provide an "enjoyable atmosphere."

Botín Restaurante ◐ *Castilian* 22 | 22 | 21 | E

Centro | Cuchilleros 17 | (34) 91-366-4217 | fax 91-366-8494 | www.casabotin.com

"Although touristy, it's no trap" assert admirers of this 1725 Castilian "institution" and former Hemingway haunt off Plaza Mayor that bills itself as "the oldest restaurant in the world"; the food is "great" ("particularly roast suckling pig, baby lamb" and "mouthwatering Iberian ham"), the "warren of rickety rooms" is "atmospheric" and service is "gracious", making it "a must-see" and "must-do" in Madrid.

Café de Oriente ◐ *Basque* 16 | 20 | 17 | E

Centro | Plaza de Oriente 2 | (34) 91-541-3974 | fax 91-547-7707 | www.grupolezama.es/cafeoriente

"Snag a table on the terrace" at this Basque for the "best location in Madrid" for "people-watching" and a "dazzling" "view of the Royal Palace"; but since the food is "average and expensive" and "service is spotty", most say stick to tapas or cocktails.

Café Saigon ◐ *Chinese/Vietnamese* 19 | 21 | 18 | M

Salamanca | Maria de Molina 4 | (34) 91-563-1566 | fax 91-377-2103 | www.elcafesaigon.com

This sprawling split-level Salamanca Chinese-Vietnamese has glam colonial decor, a gilded staircase, high ceilings and "very good" food; a local celeb clientele (including the Royal Family) and moderate prices are additional pluses.

Casa Lucio ◐ *Castilian* 21 | 14 | 18 | E

La Latina | Cava Baja 35 | (34) 91-365-3252 | fax 91-364-1714 | www.casalucio.es

"Abundant", "very good" food is found at this popular Castilian in Latina, where an "attentive" staff serves "classic" dishes like the *huevos estrellados* appetizer; the "rustic" decor is "antiquated" and there can be "long waits", but it "continues to be a mandatory stop" for the "beautiful people" and visiting celebs like Tom Cruise.

Club 31 ◐ *International* 22 | 21 | 24 | VE

Centro | Alcalá 58 | (34) 91-532-0511 | www.club31.net

For almost 50 years, this "pricey" but "excellent" International near Puerta de Alcalá has been "*the* place for a power lunch"; there's "lots of business being done" in the handsome dining room, whose dress code no longer dictates jacket-required attire in winter.

Combarro ◐ *Seafood/Galician* 26 | 18 | 21 | E

Tetuán | Reina Mercedes 12 | (34) 91-554-7784 | fax 91-534-2501 | www.combarro.com

Many surveyors say this Tetuán establishment is the "best place in town" for simply prepared seafood with a Galician accent; it imports its fin fare from its own fish farm in that region along with local wines like the crisp Albariños; the "bill can add up", but "you'll leave satisfied."

El Amparo ☒ *Basque* 25 | 22 | 22 | VE

Salamanca | Calle Puigcerdá 8 | (34) 91-431-6456 | fax 91-575-5491 | www.arturocantoblanco.com

"It really doesn't get much better than this" "outstanding" Basque in the "ritzy" Salamanca district, where "perfectly prepared" modern cuisine and an "excellent wine list" are proffered by a solidly rated staff in a "relaxing", "romantic" triplex setting.

El Bodegón ⊠ *Basque* 23 | 21 | 21 | E

Salamanca | Pinar 15 | (34) 91-562-8844 | www.grupovips.com

Housed in a stone cottage in Salamanca is this Basque bastion serving "quality" "classic" cooking; "top-notch service" and a comfortable and "tasteful dining room" with wood beams and "beautiful art" make it "excellent for entertaining clients."

El Chaflán *Mediterranean* 26 | 22 | 24 | VE

Chamartín | Hotel Aristos | Avenida de Pío XII 34 | (34) 91-350-6193 | fax 91-345-1023 | www.elchaflan.com

One of the most talked about restaurants in town is cutting-edge chef Juan Pablo Felipe's "inventive" modern Mediterranean, which makes the most of white Alba truffles in autumn; housed in the Hotel Aristos, the "minimalist" pale-green-and-white space is enlivened by a skylight and gleaming open kitchen.

El Espejo ◐ *Basque/French* 11 | 25 | 13 | M

Salamanca | Paseo de Recoletos 31 | (34) 91-308-2347 | fax 91-593-2223 | www.restauranteelespejo.com

The tiled-and-mirrored belle epoque setting is "gorgeous" and there's an "utterly charming and romantic" "glass pavilion" that looks onto Salamanca's lively and lovely Paseo de Recoletos, but since the Basque-French food is barely "passable" and service is only "ok", most maintain stick to drinks and "people-watching."

El Olivo ◐⊠ *Mediterranean* 23 | 18 | 22 | E

Chamartín | General Gallegos 1 | (34) 91-359-1535 | fax 91-345-9183 | www.elolivorestaurante.es

As its name implies, this "first-class" Mediterranean in Chamartín is devoted to olives as well as their oils (there's a trolley of them for sampling and for sale) and the ingredient turns up in "subtle and delicate" dishes, even including a signature ice cream; a "kind" staff, "comfortable" setting and swell selection of 120 sherries are added attractions.

El Pescador ◐⊠ *Seafood* 24 | 15 | 20 | E

Salamanca | José Ortega y Gasset 75 | (34) 91-402-1290 | fax 91-401-3026

"Fabulous fresh seafood" like "big-as-a-whale sole" is the lure at this long-standing "no-attitude" spot in Salamanca; the "casual nautical decor" could use "refurbishing", but that doesn't keep the likes of the Royal Family from frequenting the place.

Europa Decó ◐ *Mediterranean* 20 | 21 | 20 | E

Centro | Urban Hotel | Carrera San Jerónimo 34 | (34) 91-787-7770 | fax 91-787-7799 | www.derbyhotels.com

The "exceptional" "modern minimalist" decor at this Mediterranean in the Urban Hotel includes striking primitive antiques from Papua New Guinea, Africa and Asia; it's a "posh" place that attracts a "fashionable" "mix of clean-cut bankers, high-flying creative types and look-at-me's", but a few gourmands grouse "you don't go there for the food."

	FOOD	DECOR	SERVICE	COST

Goizeko Kabi ◐ ☒ *Basque* | 27 | 19 | 20 | VE

Tetuán | Comandante Zorita 37 | (34) 91-533-0214 | fax 91-555-1666

Goizeko Wellington ◐ ☒ *Basque*

Salamanca | Wellington Hotel | Villanueva 34 | (34) 91-577-0138 | fax 91-577-6026

www.goizekogaztelupe.com

"A bastion of the fur-wearing Tetuán ladies and their banking husbands" is this very expensive Basque that boosters boast is "one of the best choices in town", with "fine food" and a "great wine list"; P.S. those who find the ambiance here "stuffy" prefer the newer, more modern and relaxed branch in the Wellington Hotel.

Goya *Spanish/International* | 25 | 26 | 26 | VE

Retiro | Hotel Ritz | Plaza de la Lealtad 5 | (34) 91-701-6767 | fax 91-701-6776 | www.ritzmadrid.com

This "grand" Spanish-International on the ground floor of the Ritz comes with "pampering" service that's a "tribute to the art of fine dining"; the interior, with its chandeliers and palms, evokes "old-world elegance to the nth degree", and in summer, eating in the "garden is magical"; like one of its namesake's paintings, its cost is "excessive", but the "well-heeled" clientele doesn't dwell on such mundane matters.

Horcher ☒ *International* | 25 | 24 | 26 | VE

Retiro | Alfonso XII 6 | (34) 91-522-0731 | fax 91-523-3490 | www.restaurantehorcher.com

Family-owned International dowager with a German accent near Retiro Park that's been turning out "classic" cuisine like stroganoff and game dishes since 1943; an "excellent" solicitous staff ("in his heyday Franco would not have been treated better") works an "old-world" room with floral fabrics and porcelain figurines; of course, you pay for a "formal evening out" like this "big time"; N.B. jacket and tie required.

Iroco ◐ *International* | 14 | 19 | 14 | M

Salamanca | Velázquez 18 | (34) 91-431-7381 | fax 91-576-1633 | www.grupovips.com

"*Muy* hip" and still "one of the coolest Madrid spots" is this 13-year-old International in Salamanca; the "attractive" "modern" interior appeals to fashionistas, "but if you sit on the fabulous terrace you can better excuse the mediocre food and service"; insiders advise stick to the weekend brunch or "order something that it's not easy to fail with."

Jockey ◐ ☒ *International* | 25 | 23 | 25 | VE

Chamberí | Amador de los Ríos 6 | (34) 91-319-2435 | fax 91-319-2435 | www.restaurantejockey.net

This "old-school", über-expensive International in Chamberí has been putting itself through its paces since 1945 and still draws a formally dressed crowd of the "who's who of the Madrid business and aristocratic worlds"; they come for "classic" cuisine, a "great wine list", "attentive service" and a "clubby" setting with paintings and prints; N.B. jacket and tie required.

José Luis ◐ *Basque* | 20 | 11 | 16 | E

Chamartín | Rafael Salgado 11 | (34) 91-457-5036 | www.joseluis.es

Many tout this 1960 institution across from the Bernabeu football stadium as having the "best tapas in town", plus there are full-fledged

Basque entrees; the decor is only "average" but service is "fast" and the atmosphere is "friendly."

Kabuki ◐ ☒ *Japanese/Mediterranean* 25 | 16 | 19 | E

Chamartín | Presidente Carmona 2 | (34) 91-417-6415

For the "best toro in town" and other "top-quality sushi", loyalists head to this chef-owned Japanese-Mediterranean in Chamartín, where a "charming" and "friendly" staff presides over a small, minimalist black-and-yellow setting that spills over onto an appealing terrace in summer.

La Bola ≠ *Madrilian* 21 | 17 | 19 | M

Centro | Bola 5 | (34) 91-547-6930 | fax 91-541-7164 | www.labola.es

"*The* place" for "delicious" *cocido Madrileño,* a famous regional chickpea stew with meat and vegetables that's cooked and presented in little "clay-fired pots", is this Madrilian in Centro; the "star dish" is served in an "inviting" 1870 tavern setting with old photos, dark wood and tile; moderate prices add to the establishment's mellow atmosphere.

La Broche ☒ *Mediterranean* 24 | 24 | 23 | VE

Chamberí | Miguel Ángel Hotel | Miguel Ángel 29-31 | (34) 91-399-3437 | fax 91-399-3778 | www.labroche.com

Top toque and Ferran Adrià disciple Sergi Arola's modern Med in the Miguel Ángel Hotel is "controversial": aficionados admire his "unbelievable imagination" and "exquisite and daring" deconstructed dishes, while detractors declare them "weird" and the puzzled plead "who wants to eat rooster combs?"; note that the "stark white setting" "couldn't be more minimalist", and the tab is about the "price of a Picasso"; N.B. closed Saturday and Sunday.

Lágrimas Negras ☒ *Spanish* 21 | 22 | 21 | VE

Chamartín | Hotel Puerta America | Avenida de América 41 | (34) 91-744-5405 | fax 91-744-5401 | www.hotelpuertamerica.com

This fashionable Spanish in the Puerta America "upholds the European tradition of great hotels hosting great restaurants" according to admirers who call it "Madrid's answer to intelligent cuisine"; they also praise noted interior designer Christian Liaigre's colorfully dramatic setting, which includes "a great deck in summer with beautiful views" of the city.

L'Albufera ◐ *Valencian* 22 | 17 | 18 | E

Tetuán | Meliá Castilla Hotel | Capitán Haya 45 | (34) 91-567-5197 | fax 91-567-5051 | www.meliacastilla.solmelia.com

Those who think rice is nice make a dash for this Valencian in a hotel in Tetuán, where it turns up in a variety of "excellent" entrees like the "delicious authentic paellas"; the "inviting" dining room gives on to a pleasant patio that's welcoming in spring.

Las Cuatro Estaciones ☒ *International* 20 | 18 | 21 | E

Chamberí | General Ibáñez de Ibero 5 | (34) 91-553-6305 | fax 91-535-0523

If your quest is for a "quiet" meal, this International in Chamberí with "carefully designed" acoustics should fill the bill; "reliable" and "refined" cuisine is served in a neutrally toned setting by an "excellent" staff.

	FOOD	DECOR	SERVICE	COST

La Tapería ◐ *Spanish* 22 | 16 | 15 | M

Centro | Paseo del Prado 22 | (34) 91-429-4094 | www.accua.com/lataperia

Some say "the best place to have a small bite" is this "excellent", informal Spanish tapas spot across from the Prado Museum; a 19th-century split-level space with columns and arches and moderate prices attract a colorful crowd.

La Terraza del Casino 🅂 *Spanish* 26 | 24 | 25 | VE

Puerta del Sol | Casino de Madrid | Alcalá 15 | (34) 91-532-1275 | fax 91-523-4436 | www.casinodemadrid.es

"You'll feel like a king" (or at least "Cary Grant") dining in a "breathtaking" rooftop room in one of the city's oldest "exclusive" clubs just off the Puerta del Sol; El Bulli's touted Ferran Adrià is the consulting chef, and his "high-quality", "high-tech" deconstructed Spanish dishes with foams are complemented by "great wines" and served by an "incredibly attentive" staff in a see-and-be-seen-in space; it's "quite expensive" but the experience is "incomparable."

La Trainera 🅂 *Seafood* 24 | 15 | 19 | E

Salamanca | Lagasca 60 | (34) 91-576-0575 | fax 91-575-0631 | www.latrainera.es

For "simple, satisfying and consistently excellent" "classical" dishes like clams and the signature turbot, fanatics flock to this sprawling seafooder in Salamanca; just be warned that its "unassuming" decor - "wood paneling" and a "nautical theme" with ships' lanterns and wheels - "belies how expensive it is."

NEW Lavinia Espacio Gastronómico 🅂 *Mediterranean* 23 | 19 | 22 | E

Salamanca | Calle José Ortega y Gasset 16 | (34) 91-426-0599 | fax 91-426-0598 | www.lavinia.es

This new, lunch-only Mediterranean is on the mezzanine of a prestigious, well-established Salamanca wine shop (with branches in Paris and Kiev) that bills itself as the largest in Europe; it offers "well-prepared, imaginative" dishes served by a "lovely, friendly staff", but since the international "wines are very impressive", with a two-story display of some 4,500 bottlings, oenophiles often opt for teaming up a tipple or two - priced at less than the usual restaurant markup - with tapas at the bar.

Lhardy 🅂 *Spanish/International* 20 | 19 | 20 | E

Centro | Carrera de San Jerónimo 8 | (34) 91-522-2207 | fax 91-523-1171 | www.lhardy.com

A cosmopolitan crowd is still coming to this 1839 Centro-area Spanish-International, "one of Madrid's oldest restaurants"; dishes like the signature *cocido* (the typical local stew) are served in an "old-fashioned but atmospheric" and "exquisite" setting with burnished wood and chandeliers by a "helpful and dedicated staff"; N.B. several of the private rooms are gorgeous, and there's a charming gourmet take-out shop on the ground floor.

Mumbai Massala *Indian* 16 | 23 | 18 | E

Salamanca | Recoletos 14 | (34) 91-435-7194 | www.mumbaimassala.com

"At last you can get chicken tikka in Madrid" enthuse admirers of this "attractive", "upmarket" Indian in Salamanca with silver chairs, silk cushions and saris on the wall; but foes feel that the "food is nothing to write home about" and "for the price they should do much better."

Nodo ◐ *Japanese/Mediterranean* 18 | 18 | 15 | E

El Viso | Velázquez 150 | (34) 91-564-4044 | www.restaurantenodo.es

One of the city's first fusion restaurants is this "surprisingly cosmopolitan" Japanese-Med in leafy El Viso, whose "famous" signature dish is tuna *tataki* with white garlic sauce; it's popular so the minimalist setting can get "noisy" and "tight" - "you'll find out more about the table next to you than you will about the person you're with" - and don't expect to pay Nodo.

NEW **Pan de Lujo** *Spanish Fusion* 19 | 22 | 17 | VE

Salamanca | Calle Jorge Juan 20 | (34) 91-436-1100 | www.pandelujo.es

Surveyors are split over this new, reserve-well-in-advance Salamanca Spanish fusion "hottie" frequented by "chic", well-heeled habitués: fans fawn over "one of the trendiest spots in town" "to see and be seen" and its "great decor", which includes a sexily lit reflecting pool, cascades of greenery and glassed-in walls; but critics pan its "exorbitantly priced" "bland food" and "abysmal service."

Pedro Larumbe ☒ *Spanish* 18 | 20 | 18 | E

Salamanca | Serrano 61 | (34) 91-575-1112 | fax 91-576-6019 | www.larumbe.com

Among "the most beautiful settings in all of Europe" assert aesthetes about this creative Spanish housed in the former historic ABC Newspaper building in Salamanca; one salon has an "elegant belle epoque interior", another art deco decor, plus there's a lovely tiled room with a spectacular stained-glass roof and magical terrace too; still, the eponymous chef-owner's cuisine gets mixed reviews, with fans praising the "fine food" but foes declaring it only "ok."

Príncipe de Viana ◐ ☒ *Basque/Navarraise* 26 | 18 | 25 | VE

Chamartín | Manuel de Falla 5 | (34) 91-457-1549 | fax 91-457-5283

"They don't take risks" at this "classic" Basque-Navarraise in Chamartín, but "top ingredients" and "extremely fresh, tasty and delicate food" make it "one of Madrid's perennial greats"; an older crowd appreciates the comfortable split-level space and serious service and can cope with the "pricey" tabs.

NEW **Rubaiyat** *Brazilian/Steak* 23 | 20 | 20 | E

Chamartín | Juan Ramón Jiménez 37 | (34) 91-359-5696 | fax 91-359-1000 | www.rubaiyat.es

At this new, big and bustling Brazilian steakhouse in Chamartín, carnivores commend "some of the best meat in Madrid", "very good desserts", the "only real caipirinha cocktail in Spain" and an impressive wine list, all presented by an "excellent" staff; for detractors who declare the bright modern setting is "lacking charm" ("there can be a kids' birthday party atmosphere"), there's a shaded terrace garden alternative.

Santceloni ☒ *Mediterranean* 28 | 25 | 28 | VE

Chamberí | Hotel Hesperia | Paseo de la Castellana 57 | (34) 91-210-8840 | fax 91-210-8896 | www.restaurantesantceloni.com

Voted No. 1 for Food in Madrid is star chef Santi Santamaría's (of the acclaimed Can Fabes outside Barcelona) "fantastic", "cutting-edge"

Med that's "never over the top" in the Hotel Hesperia; the staff is the "best", plus there's a "great wine list, good sommelier advice" and a "chic" white skylit setting that provides well-spaced tables and "lots of privacy"; not surprisingly, such an "extraordinary experience" is "very, very expensive."

Shiratori *Japanese* 23 | 21 | 23 | E

Salamanca | Avenida de la Castellana 36-38 | (34) 91- 577-3733

After the long-standing Suntory shuttered its doors in 2004, its former manager and chef upgraded its interior and opened this "centrally located" renamed Japanese in Salamanca; for "those who cannot do without sushi in Spain" or without sashimi or teppanyaki for that matter, it's an "upscale", "well-managed" option.

Taberna del Alabardero *Basque* 22 | 19 | 18 | E

Centro | Felipe V 6 | (34) 91-547-2577 | fax 91-542-8102 | www.grupolezama.es

You'll be "in the middle of the action if you sit outside and watch the people" on their way to the Royal Palace or the Opera at this Basque bastion with "delicious" "typical" entrees and tapas; service can be "perfunctory", but the 19th-century tavern-style setting is warm and welcoming.

Teatriz *International* 18 | 24 | 17 | E

Salamanca | Hermosilla 15 | (34) 91-577-5379 | fax 91-431-6910 | www.grupovips.com

"The perfect setting for a romantic evening" is this Salamanca International designed by Philippe Starck and set in a "luxurious former theater" whose "stage is a gorgeous bar"; the "good" food only plays a supporting role here, but the "crowd is hip" and the "vibe is hot."

Teatro Real *Mediterranean* 20 | 24 | 21 | E

Centro | Plaza de Oriente | Felipe V s/n | (34) 91-516-0670 | www.arturocantoblanco.com

Located inside the Opera House, the Teatro Real, is this couldn't-be-more-convenient Med where the menu changes with each new production; but the real diva here is the wonderfully "over-the-top" decor - red velvet, wooden columns and a sparkling star-studded ceiling make for a truly theatrical evening.

Thaï Gardens *Thai* 21 | 25 | 19 | E

Salamanca | Jorge Juan 5 | (34) 91-577-8884 | fax 91-578-3137 | www.thaigardensgroup.com

"It's a trip to paradise" from the moment you see this Salamanca Thai, with its ornate palacelike entrance with a Buddha and "beautiful" "atmospheric" interior; "unexpectedly" "excellent and exquisite" traditional and modern dishes are served by an "efficient and polite staff", plus it's "good for big groups."

Tse-Yang *Chinese* 22 | 18 | 23 | E

Salamanca | Hotel Villa Magna | Paseo de la Castellana 22 | (34) 91-431-1888 | fax 91-431-2286 | www.madrid.hyatt.com

"If you're in Madrid and dying for Chinese", this Cantonese-Mandarin in the Hotel Villa Magna "is the place"; just be prepared to pay the price for a "memorable" meal in a luxurious setting with red silk walls, ornate wooden chairs and sculptures.

	FOOD	DECOR	SERVICE	COST
Viridiana	26	18	21	VE
Zalacaín	27	24	27	VE

Viridiana ◐ [S] *International*

Retiro | Juan de Mena 14 | (34) 91-523-4478 | fax 91-523-4274 | www.restauranteviridiana.com

Fans of chef-owner Abraham García and his "innovative-in-all-senses" International near Retiro Park say he's been doing "superb" "fusion cuisine in his own inimitable style for nigh on 20 years", making it almost "impossible not to be surprised here"; an "attentive professional" staff presides over a black-and-white setting dominated by stills from the Buñuel film for which it is named; considered "one of Madrid's best", it's "worth taking out a mortgage for."

Zalacaín [S] *International*

Salamanca | Álvarez de Baena 4 | (34) 91-561-4840 | fax 91-561-4732 | www.restaurantezalacain.com

"It's seldom that a restaurant can keep its standards up for more than 30 years", but this "winner" in Salamanca has; "innovative" International cuisine using the best seasonal ingredients is served by an "excellent professional" staff in a "handsome" setting with salmon-colored walls and dark wood; you'll need "mucho dollars but you'll see it as a good investment" as it's a gastronomic landmark that "lives up to its large reputation"; P.S. "jackets and ties are mandatory for gents."

Other Noteworthy Places

Alboroque Espacio Exclusivo [S] *Mediterranean*
Casa Palacio | Calle Atocha 32 | (34) 91-389-6570 |
www.alboroque.es

Antojo [S][M] *Spanish*
Calle Ferraz 36 | (34) 91-547-4046 | fax 91-310-0981

Arola Madrid ◐ *Mediterranean*
Argumosa 43 | (34) 91-467-0202 | fax 91-539-2444 |
www.arola-madrid.com

Asador Frontón ◐ *Basque/Navarraise*
Tirso de Molina 7 | (34) 91-369-1617 | fax 91-350-9533
Pedro Muguruza 8 | (34) 91-345-3696 | fax 91-350-9533
www.asadorfronton.com

Asiana [S][M] *International*
Travesía de San Mateo 4 | (34) 91-310-0965 | fax 91-310-0981

Azabara Nueva Fontana ◐ [S] *Mediterranean*
Hernani 75 | (34) 91-417-5979 | www.lanuevafontana.com

Bauzá Restaurante ◐ *Mediterranean/Spanish*
Bauzá Hotel | Goya 79 | (34) 91-435-7545 | fax 91-431-0943 |
www.hotelbauza.com

Bokado ◐ [S][M] *Basque*
Avenida Juan de Herrera 2 | (34) 91-549-0041 | fax 91-455-0282 |
www.bokadogrupo.com

Casa Benigna ◐ *Mediterranean*
Benigno Soto 9 | (34) 91-413-3356 | fax 91-519-4064 |
www.casabenigna.com

Casa d'A Troya [S] *Galician*
Emiliano Barral 14 | (34) 91-416-4455 | fax 91-416-4280

Chantarella Restaurante ◐ [S] *Mediterranean/Spanish*
Doctor Fleming 7 | (34) 91-344-1004

Currito *Basque*
Pabellón de Vizcaya | Avenida Las Provincias s/n | (34) 91-464-5704

Dantxari [S] *Basque/Navarraise*
Ventura Rodríguez 8 | (34) 91-542-3524 | fax 91-547-4029 | www.dantxari.com

Dassa Bassa [S] [M] *International*
Calle Villalar 7 | (34) 91-576-7397 | www.dassabassa.com

El Foque ◐ [S] *Spanish/Seafood*
Suero de Quiñones 22 | (34) 91-519-2572 | fax 91-561-0799 | www.elfoque.com

Entre Suspiro y Suspiro [S] *Mexican*
Caños del Peral 3 | (34) 91-542-0644 | www.entresuspiroysuspiro.com

Gala [S] *Spanish/International*
Espronceda 14 | (34) 91-442-2244 | www.restaurantegala.com

La Manduca de Azagra ◐ [S] *Navarraise*
Sagasta 14 | (34) 91-591-0112 | www.lamanducadeazagra.com

La Máquina ◐ *Seafood*
Sor Ángela de la Cruz 22 | (34) 91-572-3318 | fax 91-570-4409

La Misión ◐ [S] *Mediterranean*
José Silva 22 | (34) 91-519-2463 | fax 91-519-2470 | www.lamision.es

La Paloma ◐ [S] *French/Basque*
Jorge Juan 39 | (34) 91-575-5141

Los Remos ◐ [S] *Seafood*
Carretera Coruna, Km 12.700, La Florida | (34) 91-307-7230 | www.losremos.es

Lucca ◐ *International/Italian*
Ortega y Gasset 29 | (34) 91-576-2150 | www.grupovips.com

Lur Maitea ◐ [S] *Basque/Seafood*
Fernando el Santo 4 | (34) 91-308-0350 | fax 91-391-3821 | www.lurmaitea.com

Montana ◐ [S] *Mediterranean*
Lagasca 5 | (34) 91-435-9901 | fax 91-426-0418 | www.restaurantemontana.es

NHube ◐ [M] *Mediterranean*
NH Balboa | Núñez de Balboa 112 | (34) 91-563-0324 | fax 91-562-6980 | www.nh-hotels.com

Ølsen ◐ [M] *Scandinavian*
Calle del Prado 15 | (34) 91-429-3659 | fax 91-360-1618 | www.olsenmadrid.com

O'Pazo ◐ [S] *Cantabrian/Seafood*
Reina Mercedes 20 | (34) 91-553-2333 | fax 91-554-9072

Orzán *Galician/Seafood*
Paseo de Extremadura 102 | (34) 91-464-1007 | fax 91-464-1277

Paradís Madrid ◐ [S] *Mediterranean*
Marqués de Cubas 14 | (34) 91-429-7303 | fax 91-429-3295 | www.paradis.es

Sacha ◐ [S] *Spanish*
Juan Ramón Jimenez 37 | (34) 91-345-5952

Sal Gorda ◐ [S] *Spanish*
Beatriz de Bobadilla 9 | (34) 91-553-9506

Taberna Gaztelupe ◐ *Basque*
Comandante Zorita 32 | (34) 91-534-9116 | www.goizekogaztelupe.com

Tras Os Montes [S] *Portuguese*
Senda del Infante 28 | (34) 91-376-5727 | www.trasosmontes.es

Trastévere Café-Restaurante ◐ [M] *Mediterranean*
Mesón de Paños 1 | (34) 91-547-2936 | fax 91-563-4570 |
www.trastevere-madrid.com

Tsunami [S] *Japanese*
Caracas 10 | (34) 91-308-0569 | fax 91-308-0569

Zaranda [S] *Spanish*
Paseo de Eduardo Dato 5 | (34) 91-446-4548 | www.zaranda.es

	FOOD	DECOR	SERVICE	COST

Milan

TOP FOOD RANKING

	Restaurant	Cuisine
29	Il Luogo di Aimo e Nadia	Italian
28	Sadler	Italian
27	Ristorante Cracco	Italian
25	Da Giacomo	Seafood/Tuscan
	Boeucc	Italian/International
	Il Teatro	Italian/Mediterranean
24	Joia	Vegetarian
	Armani/Nobu	Japanese/Peruvian
	Bebel's	Italian/Mediterranean
23	Giannino	Italian
	La Veranda	Italian/International
	Park, The	Italian/Mediterranean
	Dal Bolognese	Emilian
22	Innocenti Evasioni	Italian
	Trussardi alla Scala	Italian/International
	Don Lisander	Lombardian/Milanese
	Trattoria Bagutta	Lombardian/Tuscan
	Bice	Tuscan
	Al Girarrosto	Tuscan
21	Shambala	Thai/Vietnamese
	Alla Cucina delle Langhe	Piedmontese
20	Gold	Tuscan/Mediterranean
	La Briciola	Milanese
15	10 Corso Como Cafè	Italian/International

Al Girarrosto *Tuscan* 22 | 17 | 22 | E

San Babila | Corso Venezia 31 | (39) 02-7600-0481

This "always reliable" Tuscan trattoria with "an efficient" and "knowledgeable staff" is near Milan's commercial center, Piazza San Babila, and is particularly popular for business lunches; the warm interior with watercolors hasn't changed since the Michi family opened the restaurant in 1943, and their four daughters intend to keep it that way; P.S. closed Saturdays, "but it's one of the few good restaurants here open for Sunday dinner."

Alla Cucina delle Langhe ⊠ *Piedmontese* 21 | 15 | 19 | E

Garibaldi | Corso Como 6 | (39) 02-655-4279 | fax 02-2900-6859

A "very fashionable" crowd frequents this sprawling stalwart on trendy Corso Como, where "excellent", "honest" food from the Langhe district in the Piedmont is complemented by a "good selection" of the area's red wines and a "warm welcome" from the owners.

Armani/Nobu *Japanese/Peruvian* 24 | 22 | 21 | VE

Montenapoleone | Via Pisoni 1 | (39) 02-6231-2645 | fax 02-7231-8674 | www.armaninobu.it

"What could possibly be more chic" than this "internationally acclaimed" Japanese-Peruvian housed in a stylish Armani shop in the heart of the fashion district in Montenapoleone?; "excellent", "inventive" and "artistic" cuisine, "hip" Eastern decor with screens and natural wood and a "stylish crowd" lead customers to conclude "beautiful food, people and ambiance", but "terrible prices."

Bebel's *Italian/Mediterranean* 24 | 19 | 20 | E

Brera | Via San Marco 38 | (39) 02-657-1658 | fax 02-3651-3881

This long-standing, popular Italian-Med on the edge of the Brera district serves "fantastic authentic" grilled meat, fish and pizzas to locals like Miuccia Prada; the long, narrow room has art nouveau accents and stained-glass windows, plus there are "wonderful market displays" of the day's "fresh vegetables, seafood and cheeses."

Bice ⊠ *Tuscan* 22 | 19 | 21 | VE

Montenapoleone | Via Borgospesso 12 | (39) 02-7600-2572 | fax 02-7601-3356 | www.bicemilano.it

"Good things never change" at this 1926 Montenapoleone Tuscan, the original "flagship" of a third-generation, family-run franchise; "loyal patrons" like its "reliable", "classic" cuisine and "chic" clientele and setting, but cynics shrug at the "rich, tourist-trap" prices and conclude "better for ogling - I kept tripping over all the tall models' feet - than eating."

Boeucc *Italian/International* 25 | 22 | 24 | VE

Duomo | Piazza Belgioioso 2 | (39) 02-7602-0224 | fax 02-796-173 | www.boeucc.com

This "distinguished" 1696 Italian-International, near the Duomo, with "311 years of experience" excels with "excellent" "classic" dishes, a "wine list that's a bible of Italian vintages", "impeccable service" and an "exquisite setting" with antique columns and vaulted ceilings; a few sniff it's "stuffy", but "power brokers and beautiful people" pronounce it "the only choice for business dinners and special occasions"; N.B. closed Saturdays.

Da Giacomo *Seafood/Tuscan* 25 | 20 | 23 | E

Porta Vittoria | Via Pasquale Sotto Corno 6 | (39) 02-7602-3313 | fax 02-7602-4305 | www.dagiacomoristorante.it

The "seafood-laced spaghetti is a triumph" at this long-standing Tuscan fish house near Porta Vittoria, but you can also order *bistecca alla fiorentina* complemented by a "serious" wine list that's strong on that region's reds; an "in" crowd of fashionistas and arty types frequents the gracious space with arches and mosaic-tiled floors.

Dal Bolognese ⊠ *Emilian* 23 | 19 | 20 | E

Repubblica | Piazza della Repubblica 13 | (39) 02-6269-4843

This hot Emilian next door to the stylish Hotel Principe di Savoia is a "posh" "place to see and be seen", just like its legendary flagship in Rome; foodies may fume about "unexciting" cuisine, but that doesn't stop fashionistas from praising the "delightful" dishes, then hitting its smoky bar, surveying the scene and declaring it a "must when in Milan."

Don Lisander ⊠ *Lombardian/Milanese* 22 | 18 | 20 | E

Piazza della Scala | Via Alessandro Manzoni 12A | (39) 02-7602-0130 | fax 02-784-573 | www.ristorantedonlisander.it

Near the newly restored Teatro alla Scala Opera House is this "historical" Lombardian with "good, reliable" "classic" Milanese dishes; whether eating in the "cozy interior in winter", the former chapel of an aristocratic family, or in the "marvelous garden in summer", it's "delightful."

NEW Giannino ◐ *Italian* 23 20 21 E

Repubblica | Via Vittor Pisani 6 | (39) 02-6698-6998 | fax 02-6710-1211 | www.giannino.it

A Milan landmark since 1899, this Italian has changed hands (and even addresses), but its new Repubblica incarnation that opened last year is still offering "excellent" traditional fare and "first-class service"; its "cool New York-style interior" and expansive terrace are also a "hangout" for "beautiful women and soccer players."

NEW Gold *Tuscan/Mediterranean* 20 25 21 VE

Porta Venezia | Via Carlo Poerio 2/A | (39) 02-757-7771 | fax 02-757-7720 | www.dolcegabbanagold.it

If you're going for the Gold, you'll need to "bring plenty of it to pay for your meal" at this "trendy" new Porta Venezia Tuscan-Med with a first-floor restaurant, ground-floor bistro and small food shop; owned by fashion darlings Dolce & Gabbana, it emphasizes glitz not gourmet food, so look for "stylish-till-it-hurts" sparkling yellow accents "everywhere – on the walls, toilets, tables" and even in some of the dishes.

Il Luogo di Aimo e Nadia ⊠ *Italian* 29 20 28 VE

Bande Nere | Via Montecuccoli 6 | (39) 02-416-886 | fax 02-4830-2005 | www.aimoenadia.com

Voted No. 1 for Food in Milan is Aimo and Nadia Moroni's "superb from start to finish" "innovative" and expensive Italian with top-notch ingredients, "sparkling, fresh" flavors, the "best wine list" and "incredible service"; it's a "bit out of the way" in Bande Nere and some don't care for "the room decorated with modern art", but proponents proclaim don't let that keep you from "one of the most rewarding eating experiences of your life."

Il Teatro ⊠ *Italian/Mediterranean* 25 26 26 VE

Montenapoleone | Four Seasons Hotel | Via Gesù 8 | (39) 02-7708-1435 | fax 02-7708-5000 | www.fourseasons.com/milan

"Everything is exceptional" at this Italian-Med in the Four Seasons Hotel – from chef Sergio Mei's "superb creative cuisine" and "excellent wines" to the "reliably efficient" service and "warm, comfortable" and "serene setting"; of course, it's so "blindingly expensive", "it will cost you your shirt", but you're in Milan so "just visit Zegna for another."

Innocenti Evasioni ⊠ *Italian* 22 20 20 E

Certosa | Via Privata della Bindellina | (39) 02-3300-1882 | fax 02-3300-1882 | www.innocentievasioni.com

At this intimate Italian in Certosa there's "excellent", "innovative cuisine", an "extensive wine list" and "friendly but discreet service"; the "warm and welcoming", rustically "romantic" room with well-spaced tables overlooks "a wonderful garden" with Asian accents and adds to the opinion that dining here is "a treat for all the senses."

Joia ⊠ *Vegetarian* 24 18 24 VE

Porta Venezia | Via Panfilo Castaldi 18 | (39) 02-2952-2124 | fax 02-204-9244 | www.joia.it

Wags wager the "best place to go with a model on a diet" is probably chef-owner Pietro Leemann's "very pricey" vegetarian in Porta

Venezia, where "beautifully presented" "creative" cuisine "with a lively twist" is served in a wood-and-stone setting that reflects his attraction to an Asian aesthetic.

La Briciola Ⓢ *Milanese* 20 | 18 | 18 | E

Brera | Via Solferino 25 | (39) 02-655-1012 | fax 02-653-699 | www.labriciola.com

Owner Gianni Valveri knows everyone in town so even after 30 years his spacious Milanese "favorite" in Brera is still "trendy" and "full of beautiful young Italians"; it's "good for carpaccio and beef and the women at the next table."

La Veranda ◐ *Italian/International* 23 | 26 | 25 | VE

Montenapoleone | Four Seasons Hotel | Via Gesù 8 | (39) 02-7708-1478 | fax 02-7708-5000 | www.fourseasons.com/milan

The less-formal sister of the Four Seasons' Il Teatro is this Italian-International in Montenapoleone, the center of Milan's fashion scene; "good across-the-board" is the verdict on "excellent food" (with light choices for the style-conscious clientele), a "gracious" staff and an "airy setting" with frescoes and a "great view" of a cloistered courtyard.

Park, The Ⓢ *Italian/Mediterranean* 23 | 25 | 23 | VE

Duomo | Park Hyatt Milan | Via Tommaso Grossi 1 | (39) 02-8821-1234 | fax 02-8821-1235 | www.milan.park.hyatt.com

On the ground floor of the luxurious Park Hyatt Milan, this Italian-Mediterranean makes a strong "modern" design statement with expanses of cool, cream travertine marble and black leather banquettes; "creative and delicious" dishes and "the nicest staff in town" add up to a "high-end" and "enjoyable" experience.

Ristorante Cracco Ⓢ *Italian* 27 | 22 | 24 | VE

(fka Cracco-Peck)

Duomo | Via Victor Hugo 4 | (39) 02-876-774 | fax 02-861-040

Chef Carlo Cracco is no longer affiliated with the nearby prestigious gourmet shop Peck, but his experimental recipes and innovative techniques continue to make this "top-class" Italian a "temple of modern cuisine"; a "wonderful wine list" and "amazingly knowledgeable staff" are added pluses; a few fault the cellar setting, but most maintain the elevated eating experience offsets it and the "expensive" prices.

Sadler Ⓢ *Italian* 28 | - | 24 | VE

Navigli | Via Ascanio Sforza 77 | (39) 02-5810-4451 | fax 02-5811-2343 | www.sadler.it

"One of the best restaurants in town" is what supporters say about this "wonderful" Italian "institution" that after 21 years in a tiny Navigli space has moved to new digs in that same neighborhood; celebrity chef-owner Claudio Sadler's "excellent", "creative" cuisine with "well-balanced flavors" is complemented by an extensive wine list and a "friendly and efficient staff."

Shambala ◐ *Thai/Vietnamese* 21 | 26 | 19 | E

Ripamonti | Via Ripamonti 337 | (39) 02-552-0194 | fax 02-5681-6101 | www.shambalamilano.it

It's decidedly out of the way in Ripamonti, about a 15-minute cab ride from the City Center, but if for some reason you must have Thai-

Vietnamese instead of Milanese, this "excellent" fusion venue features dishes like *branzino* cooked in banana leaves; the interior is "impressive", with "lots of candles and cushions of every color", but "the garden is the best place you can go on a hot summer night."

10 Corso Como Cafè ◐ *Italian/International* 15 | 23 | 15 | E

Garibaldi | Corso Como 10 | (39) 02-2901-3581 | fax 02-2900-0760

"See and be seen" is the order of the day at Carla Sozzani's (sister of long-standing *Italian Vogue* editor-in-chief Franca) "trendy" Italian-International that's part of her gallery/bookstore/boutique emporium in Garibaldi; slim sorts live off the "cool atmosphere" or indulge in brunch, lunch or cocktails in the jasmine-scented garden; of course, it's "style over substance" and "the food is not up to the same standards as the decor or guests' clothes", but for fashionistas it's a heavenly "hang."

Trattoria Bagutta ☒ *Lombardian/Tuscan* 22 | 19 | 19 | E

San Babila | Via Bagutta 14 | (39) 02-7600-2767 | fax 02-4577-1401 | www.bagutta.it

Since 1924, this big, "vibrant" San Babila trattoria has been feeding cultural icons and business leaders from a Lombardian-Tuscan menu and the result has been "consistently good over the years", particularly the "wonderful pastas and antipasti"; the setting is "charming", with wood-beamed ceilings and walls lined with frescoes and photos, but the alfresco-oriented advise "sit in the garden if the weather permits."

Trussardi alla Scala ☒ *Italian/International* 22 | 23 | 21 | E

Piazza della Scala | Piazza della Scala 5 | (39) 02-8068-8201 | fax 02-8068-8287 | www.trussardiallascala.com

Set in Piazza della Scala and with a great view of its legendary and now restored opera house is this Italian-International in the Trussadi building, which is owned by the fashion family; patrons are "singing the praises" of chef Andrea Berton's "terrific" cuisine, which is served in a "spectacular" contemporary red-and-white setting with columns and leather seating.

Other Noteworthy Places

Acanto *International/Italian*

Hotel Principe di Savoia | Piazza della Repubblica 17 | (39) 02-62301 | fax 02-659-5838 | www.hotelprincipedisavoia.com

Alfredo Gran San Bernardo ☒ *Milanese*

Via Borgese 14 | (39) 02-331-9000 | fax 02-2900-6859

Al Porto ☒ *Seafood*

Piazzale Generale Cantore | (39) 02-8940-7425 | fax 02-832-1481 | www.acena.it/alportodimilano

Antica Trattoria della Pesa ☒ *Milanese*

Viale Pasubio 10 | (39) 02-655-5741 | fax 02-2901-5157

Arrow's ☒ *Italian/Seafood*

Via Mantegna 17/19 | (39) 02-341-533 | fax 02-3310-6496

Casanova Grill *Mediterranean*

Westin Palace Hotel | Piazza della Repubblica 20 | (39) 02-63361 | fax 02-654-485 | www.westin.com/palacemilan

D'O - La Tradizione in Cucina *Italian*
Via Magenta 18 | (39) 02-936-2209 | fax 02-936-2209

Don Carlos *Italian*
Grand Hotel et de Milan | Via Manzoni 29 | (39) 02-7231-4640 | fax 02-8646-0861 | www.ristorantedoncarlos.it

Finger's *Brazilian/Japanese*
Via San Gerolamo Emiliani 2 | (39) 02-5412-2675 | fax 02-5412-2675

Forma *Italian*
Piazza Tito Lucrezio Caro 1 | (39) 02-4547-4688 | fax 02-4547-4689 | www.formafoto.it

Fuji *Japanese*
Via Montello 9 | (39) 02-655-2517 | fax 02-2900-3592

Gianni e Dorina *Ligurian/Tuscan*
Via Guglielmo Pepe 38 | (39) 02-606-340 | www.gianniedorina.com

Gref *Italian*
Via Marco D'Oggiono 6 | (39) 02-5810-4107 | www.gref.it

Gustibus *Italian*
Via Lorenteggio 269 | (39) 02-415-0556 | fax 02-415-2056 | www.gustibus.it

Hong Kong *Chinese*
Via Schiaparelli 5 | (39) 02-6707-1790 | fax 02-6707-1917

Il Baretto *International*
Via Senato 7 | (39) 02-781-255 | fax 02-782-382

Il Ristorante *Italian*
Bulgari Hotel | Via Privata Fratelli Gabba 7B | (39) 02-805-8051 | fax 02-805-805-222 | www.bulgarihotels.com

Il Sambuco *Seafood*
Hotel Hermitage | Via Messina 10 | (39) 02-3361-0333 | fax 02-3361-1850 | www.ilsambuco.it

I Malavoglia *Sicilian*
Via Lecco 4 | (39) 02-2953-1387 | fax 02-2040-2722 | www.ristorante-imalavoglia.com

L'Altra Isola *Milanese*
Via E. Porro 8 | (39) 02-6083-0205

Liberty *Italian*
Viale Montegrappa 6 | (39) 02-2901-1439 | fax 02-3705-3744 | www.il-liberty.it

Light *International*
Via Maroncelli 8 & Tito Speri | (39) 02-6269-0631 | fax 02-2901-0579 | www.lightlounge.it

Livet *Italian*
Piazza della Stazione di Porta Genova 3 | (39) 02-8324-1463 | fax 02-8324-1463 | www.livetrestaurant.com

L'Ulmet *Italian*
Via Disciplini 17 | (39) 02-8645-2718 | fax 02-7200-2486 | www.lulmet.it

Mistral *Mediterranean*
Viale Monte Nero 34 | (39) 02-5501-9104 | www.ristorantemistral.it

Nepentha *International*
Piazza Diaz 1 | (39) 02-804-837 | fax 02-804-837

Nuovo Macello Ⓢ⊄ *Milanese*
Via Cesare Lombroso 20 | (39) 02-5990-2122 | fax 02-5990-2122 | www.trattoriadelnuovomacello.it

Orti di Leonardo Ⓢ *Italian*
Via Aristide De Togni 6-8 | (39) 02-498-3197 | fax 02-498-3476

Osteria della Cagnola Ⓢ *Italian*
Via Domenico Cirillo 14 | (39) 02-331-9428 | fax 02-331-9428

Rigolo Ⓜ *Milanese/Tuscan*
Largo Treves | (39) 02-8646-3220 | fax 02-8646-3220 | www.rigolo.it

San Fruttuoso di Camogli Ⓢ *Ligurian/Seafood*
Viale Corsica 3 | (39) 02-7611-0558 | fax 02-3655-4405

Moscow

TOP FOOD RANKING

	Restaurant	Cuisine
25	Mario	Italian
24	Palazzo Ducale	Italian
23	Café Pushkin	Russian/French
	Cantinetta Antinori	Tuscan
22	Vogue Café	International
21	Bistrot	Italian
	Cheese	Italian
	Uzbekistan	Uzbeki/Chinese
20	Galereya	International
	Shinok	Ukrainian
	Vanil	French/Japanese
19	White Sun of the Desert	Uzbeki/Chinese
	Scandinavia	Scandinavian
18	Café des Artistes	European/Med.
	CDL	Russian/Italian
	Maharaja	Indian

NEW Bistrot ◐ *Italian* 21 | 21 | 17 | VE

Savvinskaya naberezhnaya | Bolshoi Savvinskiy pereulok 12/2 | (7-495) 248-4045 | fax 291-5606 | www.restsindikat.com

The setting and menu of the award-winning Bistrot in Italy's Forte dei Marmi inspired this new collaboration in the up-and-coming neighborhood of Savvinskaya naberezhnaya between the owner of the aforementioned Tuscan and some Russian restaurateurs; the result is a "great looking" re-created two-storied villa with a courtyard and fountain, serene white-and-cream decor, working fireplaces and candlelight that's a backdrop for "very good food" from The Boot; but wallet-watchers note "as always, Moscow restaurants are overpriced."

Café des Artistes ◐ *European/Mediterranean* 18 | 19 | 18 | E

Tverskaya | Kamergersky pereulok 5/6 | (7-495) 692-4042 | fax 692-5271 | www.artistico.ru

Its "great location" close to Tverskaya ulitsa and opposite the Moscow Art Theater makes this European-Med ideal for a pre- or post-play dinner; the "food is good not great", but it's a "reliable" place with a romantic, candlelit art nouveau setting displaying the works of local artists, and in summer its "relaxing" sidewalk cafe on a pedestrians-only street is a prime perch for "people-watching" and "taking in the local scene."

Café Pushkin ◐ *Russian/French* 23 | 27 | 23 | E

Tverskaya | Tverskoy bulvar 26a | (7-495) 629-5590

This "delicious", "classic" Russian-French "must" is set in a "richly decorated mansion" in Tverskaya that's overseen by an "attentive", graceful staff that's been trained by a ballet-master; the "magical" multilevel space consists of a first floor decorated like a "beautiful" 19th-century chemist's shop that's open 24/7 so "you can indulge in caviar and champagne at 6 AM", and a "more expensive" and formal "upstairs Imperial library" where jackets are required; either way, it's "high-priced and touristy", but most say don't miss the chance to hang with an "illustrious" clientele of "movers, shakers and mafia."

Cantinetta Antinori ◐ *Tuscan* 23 23 20 VE

Arbat | Denezhny pereulok 20 | (7-495) 241-3771 | fax 241-3325 | www.antinori.it

"The latest hangout for oligarchs" is this "fashionable" Tuscan in the Arbat, an affiliate of the Florence-based namesake original; Antinori family wines (100 by the bottle and 30 by the glass) are complemented by "superb" "authentic" cuisine and a rustically chic setting with a fireplace; for some "it's hard to justify the price", but sybarites simply cite the "buzz" and say "when you're sick of sour cream and borscht, this is the place."

CDL ◐ *Russian/Italian* 18 24 20 VE

Sadovoe Ring | Povarskaya ulitsa 50 | (7-495) 291-1515 | fax 202-3419 | www.cdlrestaurant.ru

Set in an 1899 Sadovoe Ring building that formerly housed the Soviet Writers' Union, this Russian-Italian exudes "tremendous history", "lots of cachet" and "impressive decor" - richly burnished interiors with oak paneling, tapestries and chandeliers; "traditional food" and "exquisite service" make for an "impressive", very expensive "taste and feel of old Moscow" and "for a super evening if you have the time."

Cheese ◐ *Italian* 21 20 17 VE

Tsvetnoy Boulevard | Sadovaya-Samotechnaya ulitsa 16/2 | (7-495) 650-7770 | www.cheese-restaurant.ru

So you've always wanted to know what it's like to sit inside a huge, hollow chunk of cheese? well, here's your chance because that's what the first-floor decor of this Italian near Tsvetnoy Boulevard looks like; an open kitchen turns out expensive, "high-quality" dishes like octopus carpaccio and "great pasta"; for a less-cheesy experience, head for the more conventionally decorated burgundy-colored dining room upstairs.

Galereya ◐ *International* 20 21 18 E

Boulevard Ring | Petrovka ulitsa 27 | (7-495) 937-4544 | fax 937-5668 | www.novikovgroup.ru

"If you like beautiful women who are taller than you are" and "would give Claudia and Giselle inferiority complexes", then head to the Boulevard Ring and one of the "trendiest" spots in town owned by Russian restaurant czar Arkady Novikov; the "beautifully presented" International food is "fine" and the gallerylike space with changing artwork is dramatic, but the "crowd is better" and it's open 24/7; "it costs an arm and a leg", but scenesters sniff "who cares?"

Maharaja *Indian* 18 10 18 M

Kitai Gorod | Starosadsky pereulok 2/1 | (7-495) 621-9844 | www.maharaja.ru

Proponents pronounce this basement-level stalwart in the Kitai Gorod area, the old center of the city, the "best Indian in Moscow" for "authentic" and "tasty" cooking; the decor is nonexistent, but that doesn't stop the crowds - "mostly expats" and their families - from coming back for moderately priced meals.

Mario ◐ *Italian* 25 | 15 | 19 | VE

Presnya | Klimashkina ulitsa 17 | (7-495) 253-6505

Voted No. 1 for Food in the city and judged by many to be the "best Italian" in town, this split-level spot in Presnya offers "excellent" pasta and fish dishes; outside there's an expansive summer garden and Ferraris and Lamborghinis in the parking lot, inside there's glam owner Tatiana Kurbatskaya and a clubby, salon vibe that attracts rich young Russians who all seem to know each other; "prices are outrageous" and the "service is like the weather, but the kitchen is Gibraltar."

Palazzo Ducale ◐ *Italian* 24 | 22 | 21 | VE

Tverskaya | Tverskoy bulvar 3/1 | (7-495) 789-6404 | fax 203-0149

"Great pasta for the price of caviar" can be had at this über-expensive, "authentic" Italian in Tverskaya run by the owner of Mario; while a few fume about it being a "poseur paradise", most maintain a "wine list strong on Tuscan reds", "top-notch service" and "rich decor" evocative of a Venetian palace with paintings, mirrors, chandeliers and a gilded, gondola-shaped bar make it "a good place for romantic dinners."

Scandinavia *Scandinavian* 19 | 16 | 18 | E

Tverskaya | Malye Palashevsky pereulok 7 | (7-495) 937-5630 | fax 937-5631 | www.scandinavia.ru

A "popular expat place" in Tverskaya that's "consistently good" is this Scandinavian with a "varied menu" that ranges from herring to halibut; a "friendly" staff presides over a "sleek, chic" but cozy Swedish country house setting, and in summer its "famous garden" with a less-expensive menu is "one of the best outdoor hangouts in Moscow."

Shinok ◐ *Ukrainian* 20 | 23 | 18 | E

Presnya | 1905 Goda ulitsa 2 | (7-495) 255-0888 | www.shinok.ru

To say this 24-hour Ukrainian in Presnya has the most "unique decor of any restaurant in the world" may be an understatement since it consists of a glassed-in "faux farmhouse in the center" filled with "live domestic animals" like cows, hens and horses tended to by a lady who sits and knits when not otherwise occupied with her charges; the rustic food is "filling" and "satisfying", but clearly it plays second fiddle to the setting.

Uzbekistan ◐ *Uzbeki/Chinese* 21 | 25 | 20 | E

Tsvetnoy Boulevard | Neglinnaya ulitsa 29/14 | (7-495) 623-0585 | fax 623-2469 | www.uzbek-rest.ru

This Uzbeki-Chinese near Tsvetnoy Boulevard shares space and the same menu with sister restaurant The White Sun of the Desert; a "cavernous" palatial space filled with sofas, pillows and carpets makes guests "feel like a sultan" and encourages lingering over "tasty" dishes; a summer garden and belly dancing add to the indolent atmosphere.

Vanil *French/Japanese* 20 | 19 | 18 | VE

Kropotkinskaya | Ostozhenka ulitsa 1/9 | (7-495) 202-3341 | fax 201-5228 | www.novikovgroup.ru

Admirers enamored of this "trendy" French-Japanese fusion in posh Kropotkinskaya assert "if you bring your better half here for a date all your sins will be forgotten", thanks to pricey but "very good" food and a comfortable, candlelit modern setting with brick walls, banquettes and views of the reconstructed 19th-century Christ the Savior Cathedral.

Vogue Café ◐ *International* 22 19 19 E

Bolshoy Theatre | Kuznetsky most ulitsa 7/9 | (7-495) 623-1701 | www.novikovgroup.ru

Not surprisingly, given its moniker and affiliation with the Russian magazine of the same name, the "fashionable" flock to this "trendy" International, another venue from Moscow restaurant magnate Arkady Novikov, located near the Bolshoi Theatre; a few sniff it's more for "meeting than eating", but proponents praise "very good food" that's fairly priced for "such quality" and the "stylish" setting.

White Sun of the Desert, The ◐ *Uzbeki/Chinese* 19 23 18 E

Tsvetnoy Boulevard | Neglinnaya ulitsa 29/14 | (7-495) 209-6015 | www.bsp-rest.ru

Named after and inspired by a cult Soviet film, this Uzbeki-Chinese theme restaurant near Tsvetnoy Boulevard shares space and the same menu with its sibling, Uzbekistan; a kitschy setting - a tree trunk, life-size papier-mâché soldiers and wizened hookah smokers - is the bizarre backdrop for "fresh and authentic" dishes that feature some "startling options" like an "entire roast lamb on a spit" that you can pre-order.

Other Noteworthy Places

Aist ◐ *Italian/Russian*
Malaya Bronnaya ulitsa 8/1 | (7-495) 736-9131 | www.novikovgroup.ru

Anatoly Komm S M *International*
Kutuzovskiy prospekt 12 | (7-495) 725-5575 | fax 725-5574

Antonio ◐ *Italian/French*
1905 Goda ulitsa 2 | (7-495) 255-1025 | www.tabanton.ru

Bochka ◐ *Russian*
1905 Goda ulitsa 2 | (7-495) 252-3041 | fax 252-3041

Cafe Cipollino ◐ *Mediterranean*
Soimonovskiy proezd 7/1 | (7-495) 291-6576 | www.cipollino.ru

Carré Blanc *French*
Seleznevskaya ulitsa 19/2 | (7-495) 258-4403 | www.carreblanc.ru

Casual ◐ *French/Italian*
1-st Obidenskiy pereulok 3 | (7-495) 775-2310

China Club ◐ *Chinese/French*
Krasina ulitsa 21 | (7-495) 232-2778 | fax 232-6520 | www.novikovgroup.ru

Goodman *Steak*
Bolshaya Tulskaya 13 | (7-495) 775-9888
Kievskaya ulitsa 2 | (7-495) 775-9888
Leninsky prospekt 57 | (7-495) 775-9888
Novinsky bulvar 31 | (7-495) 775-9888 ◐
Tverskaya ulitsa 23/1 | (7-495) 775-9888 ◐
www.goodman.ru

Gorki ◐ *Russian/Italian*
1-aya Tverskaya-Yamskaya ulitsa 3 | (7-495) 775-2456 | www.gorki.su

Kavkazskaya Plennitza *Georgian*
Mira prospekt 36 | (7-495) 680-5111 | fax 680-7688 | www.rectoran.ru

La Maree *French/Seafood*
Petrovka ulitsa 28 | (7-495) 694-0930

Market ◐ *Asian/Seafood*
Sadovaya-Samotechnaya ulitsa 18/1 | (7-495) 650-3488 | www.novikovgroup.ru

Most, The ◐🅂 *French*
Kuznetsky most ulitsa 6/3 | (7-495) 660-0706

Nabi ◐ *Chinese/Vietnamese*
Maliy Afanasievskiy pereulok 4 | (7-495) 291-4060 | fax 291-5606 | www.restsindikat.com

Nedalny Vostok ◐ *Pan-Asian*
Tverskoy bulvar 15/2 | (7-495) 694-0641 | fax 739-5765 | www.novikovgroup.ru

Nostalgie Art Club *French*
Chistoprudny bulvar 12a | (7-495) 916-9478 | fax 956-9130 | www.nostalgie.ru

Oblomov ◐ *Russian*
Monetchikovsky 1-y pereulok 5 | (7-495) 953-6828 | fax 953-5593 | www.restoran-oblomov.ru

Pavillion ◐ *Russian/European*
Patriarchiy pereulok 7 | (7-495) 203-5110 | www.restoran-oblomov.ru

Porto Maltese ◐ *Mediterranean/Seafood*
Pravdy ulitsa 21 | (7-495) 506-2131
Leninskiy prospekt 11 | (7-495) 506-2131
Bolshaya Spasskaya ulitsa 8 | (7-495) 506-2131
www.portomaltese.ru

Semifreddo Mulinazzo 🅂 *Italian*
Rossolimo ulitsa 2 | (7-495) 248-6169 | www.semifreddo-restaurant.com

Sem Pyatnits/Seven Fridays ◐ *Russian/French*
Vorontsovskaya ulitsa 6/1 | (7-495) 912-1218 | www.fhouse.ru

Shafran ◐ *Lebanese*
Spiridonevsky pereulok 12/9 | (7-495) 737-9500 | www.restoran-shafran.ru

Shatush ◐ *Chinese*
Gogolevsky bulvar 17 | (7-495) 637-4071 | fax 637-4071 | www.shatush.ru

Sirena *Seafood*
Bolshaya Spasskaya ulitsa 15 | (7-495) 208-1412 | fax 208-4203 | www.novikovgroup.ru

Turandot ◐ *Chinese/Japanese*
Tverskoy bulvar 26/5 | (7-495) 739-0011 | fax 204-4279

Vertinsky ◐ *Chinese/Russian*
Ostozhenka ulitsa 3/4 | (7-495) 202-0570 | www.vertinsky.com

Vesna ◐ *Italian/Japanese*
Novy Arbat ulitsa 19/1 | (7-495) 783-6966 | www.novikovgroup.ru

Villa ◐ *Tuscan*
Myasnitskaya ulitsa 48 | (7-495) 625-4715 | fax 625-9240 | www.villa.su

Yoko ◐ *International/Pan-Asian*
Soymonovsky proezd 5 | (7-495) 290-1217 | fax 739-5765 | www.novikovgroup.ru

Zolotoy ◐ *International/Russian*
Kutuzovsky prospect 3 | (7-499) 243-6540 | fax 495-291-5606 | www.restsindikat.com

FOOD DECOR SERVICE COST

Munich

TOP FOOD RANKING

	Restaurant	Cuisine
27	Tantris	International
25	Vue Maximilian	Bavarian/International
	Schuhbeck's	Bavarian
	Boettner's	International
24	Königshof	New French/International
	Mark's	Med./International
	Dallmayr	Mediterranean/Seafood
23	Sushibar	Japanese/Sushi
	Retter's	German
	Acquarello	Italian
22	Fleming's Koscher	Kosher
	Paulaner am Nockherberg	German
	Käfer-Schänke	Italian/International
	Hippocampus	Italian
	Austernkeller	French/Seafood
21	Mangostin Asia	Pan-Asian
20	Brenner	Mediterranean
	Garden*	Mediterranean
19	Weichandhof	Bavarian/International
	Geisel's Vinothek	Italian/Mediterranean
18	Lenbach	International
	Terrine	French Bistro
	Weisses Brauhaus	German/Austrian
17	Weinhaus Neuner	International
	Schumann's	International
15	Nymphenburger Hof	Austrian/International
	Chinesischen Turm	German/International

Acquarello *Italian* 23 | 15 | 21 | VE

Bogenhausen | Mühlbaurstr. 36 | (49-89) 470-4848 | fax 476-464 | www.acquarello.com

Touted by some as "the best Italian in town", this small spot in residential Bogenhausen draws diners with "excellent" fare that "reflects the creativity of the chef", served by "friendly" staffers who are "knowledgeable" about the expansive wine list; despite its "good reputation", though, detractors cite "too-expensive" eats and "dismal decor" bordering on "kitsch" as evidence that it may be "overhyped"; P.S. the special menus available on Truffle Evenings during the fall are especially "worth" sampling.

Austernkeller *French/Seafood* 22 | 19 | 21 | E

Innenstadt | Stollbergstr. 11 | (49-89) 298-787 | fax 223-166 | www.austernkeller.de

This "favorite" in the Altstadt section of Innenstadt has been serving up "quality" French cuisine for more than 25 years; the "romantic" in-

* Indicates a tie with restaurant above

terior manages to be a bit "opulent", despite its "cellar" setting, and the service is reliably "friendly", but the "highlight" that keeps regulars returning is the "fantastic seafood", such as "excellent lobster Thermidor" and (as the name indicates) some of "the best" oysters in town – including a platter of 24 featuring four varieties in season.

Boettner's ☒ *International* 25 | 22 | 26 | VE

Innenstadt | Pfisterstr. 9 | (49-89) 221-210 | fax 2916-2024

For a "terrific slice of old Munich", locals head to this elegant Innenstadt International (in a "great location" in the historic Altstadt section) that's been run by the same family for more than a century; its "innovative chef brings the world to" German palates with his "grand selection of specialties", and the "attentive, competent" staff also helps ensure that its "beautiful" interior is the "perfect place for a really good meal."

Brenner ◐ *Mediterranean* 20 | 23 | 20 | E

Innenstadt | Maximilianstr. 15 | (49-89) 452-2880 | fax 4522-8811 | www.brennergrill.de

Set behind the opera house, in the Altstadt section of Innenstadt, this former royal stable has been restored and modernized, creating a bright, expansive space with "big" pillars and vaulted ceilings; the "unparalleled" interior is divided into "various dining areas", with chefs at a "large open grill" cooking up up Med specialties for a chic clientele that "enjoys" the "satisfying" fare.

Chinesischen Turm Restaurant & Biergarten *German/International* 15 | 16 | 12 | M

Schwabing | Englischer Garten 3 | (49-89) 3838-730 | fax 3838-7373 | www.chinaturm.de

"A trip to Munich would not be complete without an afternoon spent" in the "beautiful", "truly Bavarian" beer garden of this landmark in Schwabing, whose "special" "Chinese Tower" serves as the backdrop for what most maintain is only "standard", "self-serve" German fare; the restaurant's interior offers an International menu that's generally considered "much better" foodwise, but then you miss out on the "festive" "Oktoberfest experience."

Dallmayr *Mediterranean/Seafood* 24 | 20 | 21 | E

Innenstadt | Dienerstr. 14-15 | (49-89) 213-50 | fax 213-5443 | www.dallmayr.de

An Innenstadt "institution", this "upmarket" venue in the Altstadt section features a "gourmet emporium" "downstairs" that's "akin to a food museum" thanks to a "tremendous selection of delicacies", some of "the finest coffee" in town and a champagne-and-oyster bar for "hedonists" seeking "paradise"; "upstairs", there's a "top-notch restaurant" serving "delicious" Mediterranean and seafood dishes, which are complemented by a "posh" setting and "smart" service – but "don't expect to get a table without a reservation, even for lunch."

NEW **Fleming's Koscher Restaurant** *Kosher* 22 | 19 | 22 | E

Innenstadt | St.-Jakobs-Platz 18 | (49-89) 202-400-333 | fax 400-334 | www.flemings-hotels.de

"The chopped liver can actually compete with your own *bubbe*'s" boast boosters of this new spot in Innenstadt that claims to be the only glatt kosher restaurant in Bavaria; Israeli and Eastern European specialties are also served "by a knowledgeable staff" in an expansive "modern" setting located within the Jewish community center.

Garden *Mediterranean* 20 | 19 | 19 | E

Innenstadt | Bayerischer Hof | Promenadeplatz 2-6 | (49-89) 212-0993 | fax 212-0906 | www.bayerischerhof.de

Both the "beautiful" terrace and the menu at this Innenstadt spot sport "Mediterranean flair" in the midst of "oh-so-traditionally German" surroundings; while some surveyors are split on the service ("expert" vs. "unfriendly") and find the "modest" interior "dowdy", the majority maintains the overall experience "leaves a lasting impression."

Geisel's Vinothek *Italian/Mediterranean* 19 | 21 | 19 | E

Innenstadt | Hotel Excelsior | Schützenstr. 11 | (49-89) 5513-7140 | fax 5513-7121 | www.geisel-hotels.de

"Nice for oenophiles", this "lovely hotel restaurant" in Innenstadt is all about vintages, and "friendly, service-oriented" staffers are "dedicated" to providing "good recommendations" about the "excellent list's" "extraordinary variety" of labels (more than 400) from all over the world; a "nice", "down-to-earth" Italian-Med menu and "cozy", "country" dining room with vaulted, frescoed ceilings add to the "outstanding" ambiance.

Hippocampus *Italian* 22 | 21 | 21 | E

Bogenhausen | Mühlbauerstr. 5 | (49-89) 475-855 | fax 4702-7187 | www.hippocampus-restaurant.de

"Anyone with a hippocampus" will remember that it's expensive joke jesters about this Italian in Bogenhausen, but "always fresh" and "absolutely delicious" cuisine keeps the crowds returning and the place "quite popular"; the "exquisite" setting consists of dark-walnut paneling, marble floors and bronze art nouveau lamps, as well as a torch-lit terrace in summer.

Käfer-Schänke 🅂 *Italian/International* 22 | 20 | 19 | E

Bogenhausen | Prinzregentenstr. 73 | (49-89) 416-8247 | fax 416-8623 | www.feinkost-kaefer.de

"Excellent Italian food" and "out-of-the-ordinary" International dishes are served in an "old-world", country house-style dining area or in one of 12 "beautiful" private rooms at this "classic" in suburban Bogenhausen; the service is generally "friendly", even if it "sometimes takes too long" when things get "hectic", but "great people-watching" helps pass the time; P.S. "don't miss their gourmet store downstairs", "the ultimate German delicatessen."

Königshof *French/International* 24 | 21 | 24 | E

Innenstadt | Hotel Königshof | Karlsplatz 25 | (49-89) 551-360 | fax 5513-6113 | www.geisel-hotels.de

With "superior" New French-International creations courtesy of chef Martin Fauster and "accommodating" service from a "discreet" staff, this "fine-dining" venue in the Hotel Königshof offers an "elegant experience" befitting a "king's court"; the "exclusive ambiance" is enhanced by "plush" design details, a dramatic view of Innenstadt's Karlsplatz and live piano music on Friday and Saturday evenings; P.S. the prix fixe "gourmet dinner, including wines with each course, is spectacular."

	FOOD	DECOR	SERVICE	COST

Lenbach *International* | 18 | 20 | 18 | E |

Innenstadt | Ottostr. 6 | (49-89) 549-1300 | fax 5491-3075 | www.lenbach.de

"Hip comes to Munich" in the form of this 19th-century Innenstadt palace-turned-"modern" urban ode to the Seven Deadly Sins thanks to the "über-trendy" design of Sir Terence Conran; a "fast", "friendly", "pretty" staff serves International dishes (including "great sushi") that are "varied" and "fanciful" - though some quip "you may need to view them with a magnifying glass"; the "catwalk atmosphere" and late-night hours also help keep it "in vogue."

Mangostin Asia *Pan-Asian* | 21 | 19 | 16 | E |

Thalkirchen | Maria-Einsiedel-Str. 2 | (49-89) 723-2031 | fax 723-9847 | www.mangostin.de

"Unusual atmosphere and unusually delicious" Pan-Asian fare make it "easy to think you're in a different country" at this Thalkirchen "jewel" near the zoo, where "authentic", "attractive" dishes are delivered within a trio of Japanese-, Thai- and Colonial-style dining rooms (or outside in the beer garden); some cynics say "it's past its prime" and find the service "lacking", but most maintain it's "a real joy", especially for its "great" dinner and Sunday brunch buffets.

Mark's *Mediterranean/International* | 24 | 21 | 24 | VE |

Innenstadt | Mandarin Oriental | Neuturmstr. 1 | (49-89) 2909-8862 | fax 222-539 | www.mandarinoriental.com

Chef Mario Corti's "inspired" Med-International cuisine is "perfectly executed and flawlessly" delivered by a "well-trained, friendly" staff at this "awesome place" in the Mandarin Oriental hotel, in the Altstadt section of Innenstadt; a few find the "quiet, elegant" dining room a "little boring" and say the "surreal prices" make for "excessive" tabs, but the monthly changing, six-course menu (including wine) and the special late-night, three-course dinner offered during the Opera Festival in summer are especially "worth a try."

Nymphenburger Hof *Austrian/International* | 15 | 14 | 18 | E |

Maxvorstadt | Nymphenburger Str. 24 | (49-89) 123-3830 | fax 123-3852 | www.nymphenburgerhof.de

A "pleasant stop" in "picturesque" Maxvorstadt, this Austrian-International boasts outdoor garden seating, occasional live piano music, a selection of local beers and a staff that's "fast and attentive"; the "traditional" (some say "ordinary") dishes and "unobtrusive" style of the dining room draw a conservative crowd, as well as ticket-holders for the Volkstheater, which is within walking distance.

Paulaner am Nockherberg *German* | 22 | 20 | 18 | M |

Giesing | Hochstr. 77 | (49-89) 459-9130 | fax 459-913-200 | www.nockherberg.com

The Paulaner brewery folks are behind the "authentic Bavarian feel" of this "typical beer garden" in Giesing and they continue to have one of the largest Oktoberfest tents each year (it's "enormous" as are all those "liter brews everyone's drinking"); suds aside, though, the moderately priced, "good German" fare - such as "well-made" and well-priced Weißwurst and roast pork - is itself "worth stopping" for.

	FOOD	DECOR	SERVICE	COST

NEW Retter's Ⓢ Ⓜ *German* — 23 | 18 | 22 | E

Innenstadt | Frauenstr. 8 | (49-89) 2323-7923 | fax 2323-7921 | www.retters.de

Oenophile Nicole Retter has opened this new German restaurant/wineshop in Innenstadt, and while the cuisine is "creative" and "inspired" (often by the ingredients in the adjacent Viktualienmarkt or food market), it's the potential "great pairings" with any of 250 "excellent" selections by the bottle and 25 by the glass that's generating the buzz; the setting is a handsome, wood-paneled townhouse with ample garden seating in summer.

Schuhbeck's Restaurant in den Südtiroler Stuben Ⓢ *Bavarian* — 25 | 20 | 25 | VE

Innenstadt | Platzl 6 + 8 | (49-89) 216-6900 | fax 2166-9025 | www.schuhbeck.de

"Traditional Bavarian cuisine" is given a "contemporary cutting edge" (read: "not so heavy") at this gourmet spot, owned by "famous" TV-chef Alfons Schuhbeck, just next door to the Hofbräuhaus in the Altstadt section of Innenstadt; "clever" food combinations, "exceedingly attentive" service and a "superb" wine selection may come at a price that's even "beyond expense-account" status, but it adds up to one of "the best restaurants in Munich" for a truly "adult dining" experience.

Schumann's ◐ *International* — 17 | 17 | 18 | E

Innenstadt | Odeonsplatz 6+7 | (49-89) 229-060 | fax 228-5688 | www.schumanns.de

"He's done it again" say fans of renowned mixologist Charles Schumann, chef-owner of this "trendy" Hofgarten spot in the Altstadt section of Innenstadt; the "simple" International "bar food" is "solid" enough and the servers are "friendly" even when it's "too busy", so despite the fact that it's "a bit pricey for the quality", the crowds keep returning to this veritable "cocktail heaven amid the beer halls of Munich" for a spirited experience and "great people-watching."

Sushibar *Japanese* — 23 | 19 | 21 | E

NEW **Innenstadt** | Maximilianstr. 34 | (49-89) 2554-0645 Ⓢ ⊄

Schwabing | Marschallstr. 2 | (49-89) 3889-9606

www.sushibar-muc.de

Like the name says, sushi is showcased here at this small specialist that some say serves the "freshest raw fish in town", including sashimi; the setting is light, modern and urbane, and the location is in one of the quieter quarters of tourist hot spot Schwabing; N.B. the new Maximilian Strasse offshoot opened post-Survey.

Tantris Ⓢ Ⓜ *International* — 27 | 23 | 26 | VE

Schwabing | Johann-Fichte-Str. 7 | (49-89) 361-9590 | fax 3619-5922 | www.tantris.de

Austrian chef Hans Haas incorporates regional influences and culinary trends at his "outstanding" International out in Schwabing, earning it the ranking of No. 1 for Food in Munich; his "superb" daily changing prix fixe menus are paired with sommelier Paula Bosch's "inspired wines" and complemented by "remarkable service" ("you'll feel like a king!"), so though a few fault the "truly weird" "over-the-top" decor and "outrageous" prices, most insist "you get what you pay for" at this "classic."

Terrine ☒Ⓜ *French* 18 | 15 | 24 | E

Maxvorstadt | Amalienpassage | Amalienstr. 89 | (49-89) 281-780 | fax 280-9316 | www.terrine.de

"Attentive" service creates a "warm atmosphere" at this "little" stalwart near the university in Maxvorstadt, making it "great" for a relaxing evening of "excellent wine" and "tasty" French dishes, served either in the "unobtrusive" bistro interior or out on the terrace; though it shares the same ownership with the highly rated and more expensive Tantris, its "fairly priced" prix fixe menus offer real "value", leaving some amazed that you can "get something so good for so little"; a post-Survey chef and decor change may outdate the above scores.

Vue Maximilian *Bavarian/International* 25 | 23 | 25 | VE

Innenstadt | Hotel Vier Jahreszeiten Kempinski | Maximilianstr. 17 | (49-89) 2125-2125 | fax 2125-2222 | www.vue-maximilian.de

This venue in the historic Hotel Vier Jahreszeiten Kempinski takes its name from the wonderful view of Maximilian Strasse, the city's most beautiful and exclusive boulevard; the redone interior, a lighter, less "stuffy" room than what went before, is a "lovely" but "very expensive" backdrop for "top-notch" Bavarian-International cuisine, which relies on local and seasonal ingredients.

Weichandhof *Bavarian/International* 19 | 17 | 21 | M

Obermenzing | Betzenweg 81 | (49-89) 891-1600 | fax 8911-6012 | www.weichandhof.de

"Everyone should visit" this "good place to dine" along the river Würm in rural Obermenzing, where the "attentive" staff "never stops being friendly" and the "fine" Bavarian-International fare includes "good wild game dishes"; perhaps the "cozy", "rustic" refurbished farmhouse setting with a beer garden is "slightly outmoded" by city standards, but most feel that's more than compensated for by modest prices.

Weinhaus Neuner ☒ *International* 17 | 16 | 18 | M

Innenstadt | Herzogspitalstr. 8 | (49-89) 260-3954 | www.weinhaus-neuner.de

"Accommodating" service and original vaulted ceilings contribute to the "cozy" vibe at this "typical tavern" in "the heart of" the Altstadt section of Innenstadt that serves up International fare at moderate prices; as befits its status as a former royal wine cellar, the emphasis is on pairing vintages with the meal – something of a novelty in a country where most "come to drink beer."

Weisses Brauhaus *Austrian/German* 18 | 16 | 14 | M

Innenstadt | Tal 7 | (49-89) 290-1380 | fax 2901-3815 | www.weisses-brauhaus.de

"Home-brewed" wheat beer "constantly flows" at this brewery "right next to Marienplatz", where "well-prepared" German and Austrian fare – both "traditional" ("sausages and roast pork") and "unusual" ("innards") – is served in "typical" Bavarian dining rooms; as its "many local" patrons advise, "don't be scared by" the staff's "trademark" "gruffness" – "they're just teasing" all the tourists, so sit back and enjoy the native "charm."

Other Noteworthy Places

Acetaia *Italian/Mediterranean*
Nymphenburger Str. 215 | (49-89) 1392-9077 | fax 1392-9078 | www.restaurant-acetaia.de

Al Pino *Italian*
Franz-Hals-Str. 3 | (49-89) 799-885 | fax 799-872 | www.al-pino.de

Anna ◐ *International*
Anna Hotel | Schützenstr. 1 | (49-89) 599-940 | fax 5999-4333 | www.annahotel.de

Barista ◐⊭ *International/Italian*
Fünf Höfe | Kardinal-Faulhaber-Str. 11 | (49-89) 2080-2180 | fax 2080-2181

Blauer Bock ☒ *Bavarian/International*
Sebastiansplatz 9 | (49-89) 4522-2333 | fax 4522-2330 | www.restaurant-blauerbock.de

Ederer ☒ *Bavarian/Mediterranean*
Fünf Höfe | Kardinal-Faulhaber-Str. 10 | (49-89) 2423-1310 | fax 2423-1312 | www.restaurant-ederer.de

G-Munich *International*
Geyerstr. 52 | (49-89) 7474-7999 | fax 7474-7929 | www.g-munich.de

Halali ☒ *International*
Schönfeldstr. 22 | (49-89) 285-909 | fax 282-786 | www.restaurant-halali.de

Islay ☒ *Mediterranean*
Thierschstr. 14 | (49-89) 2916-3700 | fax 2916-2311 | www.islay-whiskeybar.de

Kam Yi *Chinese*
Rosenheimer Str. 32 | (49-89) 448-1366 | fax 448-1301

Landersdorfer & Innerhofer ☒ *Austrian/International*
Hackenstr. 6-8 | (49-89) 2601-8637 | fax 2601-8650
Ledererstr. 17 | (49-89) 2323-7789 | fax 2102-0594
www.landersdorferundinnerhofer.de

La Rocca ☒ *Italian*
Maximilianstr. 35 | (49-89) 2421-7778 | fax 2421-7779

Le Faubourg ☒ *French*
Kirchenstr. 5 | (49-89) 475-533 | www.le-faubourg.de

Les Cuisiniers ☒ *French/Mediterranean*
Reitmorstr. 21 | (49-89) 2370-9890 | fax 2370-9891 | www.lescuisiniers.de

Le Stollberg ☒ *French*
Stollbergstr. 2 | (49-89) 2424-3450 | fax 2424-3451 | www.lestollberg.de

Le Sud *French*
Bismarckstr. 21 | (49-89) 3308-8783 | fax 3308-8742 | www.le-sud.de

Makassar ☒⊭ *French*
Dreimühlenstr. 25 | (49-89) 776-959 | fax 7466-5441 | www.makassar.de

Prinzregent *Bavarian/Mediterranean*
Hotel Prinzregent an der Messe | Riemer Str. 350 | (49-89) 945-390 | fax 9453-9566 | www.prinzregent.de

Rüen-Thai *Thai*
Kazmairstr. 58 | (49-89) 0172-809-0119 | fax 503-239

Schwarz & Weiz ◐ *International*
Dorint Sofitel Bayerpost München | Bayerstr. 12 | (49-89) 599-480 | fax 599-481-000 | www.sofitel.com

Tabacco ◐⊠ *European/Steak*
Hartmannstr. 8 | (49-89) 227-216 | www.bartabacco.de

Vinaiolo *Italian*
Steinstr. 42 | (49-89) 4895-0356 | fax 4591-1795 | www.vinaiolo.de

Vinorant Alter Hof ◐ *German/International*
Alter Hof 3 | (49-89) 2424-3733 | www.alter-hof-muenchen.de

Paris

See our Zagat *Paris Restaurants* Survey for full coverage.

TOP FOOD RANKING

	Restaurant	Cuisine
28	Taillevent	Haute Cuisine
	Pierre Gagnaire	Haute Cuisine
	Alain Ducasse	Haute Cuisine
	Le Cinq	Haute Cuisine
	Guy Savoy	Haute Cuisine
27	Le Grand Véfour	Haute Cuisine
	Hiramatsu	Haute Cuisine
	L'Ambroisie	Haute Cuisine
	Le Bristol	Haute Cuisine
	L'Astrance	New French
	Isami	Japanese/Sushi
	Les Ambassadeurs	New French
	Michel Rostang	Classic French
	Lasserre	Haute Cuisine
	L'Atelier Joël Robuchon	Haute Cuisine
26	Pavillon Ledoyen	Haute Cuisine
	L'Arpège	Haute Cuisine
	La Table de Robuchon	Haute Cuisine
	Jacques Cagna	Haute Cuisine
	Le Meurice	Haute Cuisine
	Caviar Kaspia	Russian
	Apicius	Haute Cuisine
	Les Elysées	Haute Cuisine
	Le Pré Catelan	Haute Cuisine
	Relais d'Auteuil	Haute Cuisine
	L'Ami Louis	French Bistro
25	Relais Louis XIII	Haute Cuisine
	La Tour d'Argent	Haute Cuisine
	Carré des Feuillants	Haute Cuisine
	Gérard Besson	Classic French
	Kinugawa	Japanese/Sushi
	La Table du Lancaster	Haute Cuisine
	La Marée	Seafood
	Stella Maris	Classic French
	L'Espadon	Classic French
	L'Avant Goût	New French
	Salon d'Hélène	Southwest French
24	Le Duc	Seafood
	Le Céladon	Classic French
	Le Florimond*	Classic French
	Le Violon d'Ingres*	French Bistro
	La Cave Gourmande	French Bistro
	La Truffière	Haute Cuisine

* Indicates a tie with restaurant above

Les Ormes	Haute Cuisine
Le Clos des Gourmets	New French
L'Ostéria	Italian
Sormani	Italian
La Luna	Seafood
Benoît	Lyon
Laurent	Haute Cuisine

Alain Ducasse au Plaza Athénée ⊠ *Haute Cuisine* 28 | 28 | 28 | VE

8e | Hôtel Plaza-Athénée | 25, av Montaigne (Alma Marceau/ Franklin D. Roosevelt) | (33-1) 53 67 65 00 | fax 53 67 65 12 | www.alain-ducasse.com

"The world's superstar chef" – "if God cooked, this would be the food" – lives up to his reputation at his Plaza-Athénée home, an "opulent" "18th-century space done modern" for which "every superlative is appropriate" (i.e. "the pinnacle of Haute Cuisine"); kudos, too, for the "exemplary" servers, even if they do "emphasize expensive wines"; the place is "prodigiously" pricey, "but who cares – everybody needs to splurge" once (and you get a free treat to take home for breakfast).

Apicius ⊠ *Haute Cuisine* 26 | 24 | 25 | VE

8e | 20, rue d'Artois (George V/St-Philippe-du-Roule) | (33-1) 43 80 19 66 | fax 44 40 09 57 | www.relaischateaux.com

"Surrounded by gardens in the heart of [the 8th], the locale is a show-stopper" swoon supporters of chef-owner Jean-Pierre Vigato's Haute Cuisine "hidden gem", which occupies a "marvelous" "mansion that dates from the 18th century"; "the food's as great as ever" – a mix of classic and "audacious dishes" (e.g. the order-in-advance duck with chocolate) – and the "delightful staff" is "unpretentious"; of course, it's "very expensive", but habitués "haven't had a bad meal yet."

Benoît *Lyon* 24 | 21 | 22 | E

4e | Hôtel de Ville | 20, rue St-Martin (Châtelet-Les Halles) | (33-1) 42 72 25 76 | fax 42 72 45 68 | www.alain-ducasse.com

Since this "ultimate" belle epoque-era bistro "close to Les Halles" is one of the best-loved "time capsules" in Paris, anxiety greeted the news that gastro-entrepreneurs Alain Ducasse and Thierry de la Brosse had bought it; but steady scores suggest it's "still wonderful and worth the money" – a lot of money – for "delicious", "decadent" Lyonnais "classics" ("make sure you have nap time planned"); "service is lively", but "don't cross the maitre d'", or you'll be "rushed into the side room with all of the Americans."

Carré des Feuillants ⊠ *Haute Cuisine* 25 | 21 | 24 | VE

1er | 14, rue de Castiglione (Concorde/Tuileries) | (33-1) 42 86 82 82 | fax 42 86 07 71 | www.carredesfeuillants.fr

You can "order with confidence since everything is fabulous" at this "super-chic" Haute Cuisine table in the 1st, where "chef-owner Alain Dutournier's Southwest-inspired cuisine" "enthralls" with its "innovative", "subtle" flavors; surveyors also smile on the staff – "formal, but not at all snobby", and if the "modern decor" that mixes "splendid Venetian chandeliers" with exposed-steel beams leaves some "indifferent", most deem dinner here well "worth all those euros."

Caviar Kaspia *Russian* 26 | 21 | 24 | VE

8e | 17, pl de la Madeleine (Madeleine) | (33-1) 42 65 33 32 | fax 42 65 66 26 | www.kaspia.fr

"Unchanged, and even better than 50 years ago", the "best address in Paris for caviar" "with a gorgeous view on the side" caters to a "*très* trendy clientele" with "over-the-top" Russian decor and cuisine - though the formula that most follow is "fish eggs, spoon, mouth, vodka, repeat (maybe smoked salmon for variety)"; the "exceptional service" and "romantic" Place de la Madeleine ambiance ensure a "delightful" time, even if you must "sell your Fabergé eggs to come here."

Gérard Besson *Classic French* 25 | 21 | 23 | VE

1er | 5, rue du Coq-Héron (Louvre-Rivoli/Palais Royal-Musée du Louvre) | (33-1) 42 33 14 74 | fax 42 33 85 71 | www.gerardbesson.com

"Gérard Besson is one of the great underrated talents cooking today", perhaps because "polished classicism, not innovation" is his culinary style; but most "have no complaints" about his Classic French in the 1st, even those who've "been going here for 20 years"; supporters swoon over his "wonderful" dishes and "delicious desserts that have to be consumed, despite you're being full to bursting", served by a "sublime" staff in "warm surroundings"; it's "expensive but worth every euro cent."

Guy Savoy, Restaurant *Haute Cuisine* 28 | 25 | 27 | VE

17e | 18, rue Troyon (Etoile) | (33-1) 43 80 40 61 | fax 46 22 43 09 | www.guysavoy.com

He may be "locating in Las Vegas", but chef-owner Guy Savoy's table in the 17th is "reason alone to go to Paris", because this "spectacular" Haute Cuisine site has it all: "original" dishes in which "every flavor sings", staffers who are "trained observers, or perhaps mind-readers", and attractive "minimalist" decor dominated by modern art; "bring an armored car full of money" because the tabs are "over the top", but then, this is "one of the best restaurants in Paris" - even, "arguably, the world."

Hiramatsu *Haute Cuisine* 27 | 22 | 25 | VE

16e | 52, rue de Longchamp (Trocadéro/Boissière) | (33-1) 56 81 08 80 | fax 56 81 08 81 | www.hiramatsu.co.jp

"Almost perfection" proclaim proponents of this Haute Cuisine table in the 16th that, despite the Japanese name, carries "creative and conceptually fascinating" New French dishes; "light, delicate and often transparent", they're "beautifully presented by a lovely staff"; although some "preferred the old address on the Ile Saint-Louis", the current "elegant, minimalist" "digs are beautiful and offer more tables" too.

Hôtel Amour *New French* - | - | - | M

9e | Hôtel Amour | 8, rue Navarin (St-Georges) | (33-1) 48 78 31 80 | fax 48 74 14 09 | www.hotelamour.com

Co-owned by Thierry Costes, this late-night newcomer in the funky Hôtel Amour is one of the hottest young spots in town; inside, there's an eye-catching collection of flea-market Danish Modern tables and chairs mixed with collector's pieces by esteemed designers Charlotte Perriand and Jean Prouvé; outside, there's a fountain splattering in the back garden; all around are easygoing, moderately priced New French eats.

Isami [S][M] *Japanese* — 27 | 10 | 16 | E

4[e] | 4, quai d'Orléans (Pont-Marie) | (33-1) 40 46 06 97

Despite the "dull decor" and "indifferent service", no surveyor seems to be able to resist "the best sushi in Paris" ("melts in your mouth, not in your hand"), which "means reservations are essential" if you want a place at this "jewel box-sized" Japanese in the 4th that charges "jewelry prices for each bite"; however, "once you are in, you will feel as if you are in Tokyo" - especially if you go for the "chef-recommended plate"; P.S. sit at the counter, which "lets you contemplate the maestro" chef at work.

Jacques Cagna [S] *Haute Cuisine* — 26 | 23 | 23 | VE

6[e] | 14, rue des Grands-Augustins (Odéon/St-Michel) | (33-1) 43 26 49 39 | fax 43 54 54 48 | www.jacquescagna.com

"Housed in an attractive old beamed building in Saint-Germain", for some 40 years this vet has seduced those in search of a "romantic" experience with "elegantly hearty" Haute Cuisine, served "with Parisian flair" by a staff that's "attentive, but doesn't crowd you"; modernist mavens may find its "classical" approach "a little outdated" - and there's nothing nostalgic about the prices - but the majority is "moved", especially since chef-owner "Jacques Cagna himself speaks to every table", "a welcome touch."

Kinugawa [S] *Japanese* — 25 | 14 | 18 | E

1[er] | 9, rue du Mont-Thabor (Tuileries) | (33-1) 42 60 65 07 | fax 42 60 57 36

8[e] | 4, rue St-Philippe-du-Roule (St-Philippe-du-Roule) | (33-1) 45 63 08 07

NEW **Kinugawa & Hanawa** [S] *Japanese*

8[e] | 26, rue Bayard (Franklin D. Roosevelt) | (33-1) 45 63 08 07 kinugawa.free.fr

A sizable Asian clientele persuades many surveyors that this trio of sushi specialists, which also delivers delicate dishes from Kyoto and Tokyo, is "almost as good as what you'll find in Japan" - and certainly among "the best in Paris"; both the "sublime" sashimi and the "excellent" cooked fare are "charmingly served", "but the prices cut like a samurai's sword", and the "traditional" digs "feel kind of musty."

La Cave Gourmande - le Restaurant de Mark Singer [S] *Bistro* — 24 | 15 | 22 | M

19[e] | 10, rue du Général Brunet (Botzaris/Danube) | (33-1) 40 40 03 30 | fax 40 40 03 30

"Maybe it's a bit out of the way for the average tourist", but gourmands gush it's "well worth the Homeric effort to find" this bistro in the far reaches of the 19th, thanks to the "splendid market-driven", "inventive" cuisine concocted "with much thought to taste, texture and presentation" by chef-owner Mark Singer, an "American in Paris"; "efficient service" and an "affordable, sharp wine list" make up for the "modest setting."

La Gazzetta [S][M] *Mediterranean/New French* — - | - | - | M

12[e] | 29, rue de Cotte (Ledru-Rollin) | (33-1) 43 47 47 05 | fax 43 47 47 17 | www.lagazzetta.fr

Up-and-coming young Swedish chef Petter Nilsson (ex Troisgros, in the Rhône Valley) is attracting gourmets from all over town to this trendy but reasonably priced trattoria not far from Bastille; his nervy

New French-Med menu (example: a starter of caramelized endive with horseradish and fresh almond purée) unfolds in a low-lit loftlike space with parquet floors, framed posters and a vibe that's hip but relaxed, like the service.

La Luna Ⓢ *Seafood* 24 | 17 | 18 | E

8e | 69, rue du Rocher (Villiers/Europe) | (33-1) 42 93 77 61 | fax 40 08 02 44

Seafood-loving surveyors proclaim this small site behind the Gare Saint-Lazare "one of the best for fish in Paris" - plus a "*baba au rhum* that can't be beat"; all's "expertly prepared" and served, but wallet-watchers wail "for these prices, they can afford to improve the decor" a bit - though others find the gray-and-red-toned digs "pretty enough."

La Marée Ⓢ *Seafood* 25 | 17 | 21 | VE

8e | 1, rue Daru (Ternes/Courcelles) | (33-1) 43 80 20 00 | fax 48 88 04 04 | www.lamaree.fr

For more than 40 years this "haute" seafooder in the 8th has hooked politicians and other big *poissons* with "fish of the highest quality", prepared in both classic and "inventive" ways, "and incredible desserts"; with "professional service" and an "elegant" setting of Flemish paintings and stained-glass windows, it is "expensive - and worth it"; N.B. its recent acquisition by the Frères Blanc group may outdate the scores.

L'Ambroisie Ⓢ Ⓜ *Haute Cuisine* 27 | 26 | 26 | VE

4e | 9, pl des Vosges (Chemin-Vert/St-Paul) | (33-1) 42 78 51 45

You may well feel "as if you'd drunk the nectar of the gods" after a "transporting" trip to this small site in the 4th; it's "the epitome of class from a bygone era", from the "superb", "sophisticated" Haute Cuisine to the decor that recalls the Renaissance - "inlaid stone-parquet floors and Aubusson tapestries hanging on honey-hued walls"; "beneath the Gallic bravado, the staff has hearts of gold"; naturally, this heavenly experience commands "astronomical prices."

L'Ami Louis Ⓜ *Bistro* 26 | 16 | 20 | VE

3e | 32, rue du Vertbois (Arts et Métiers/Temple) | (33-1) 48 87 77 48

When seeking out this "superlative bistro" in the 3rd, bring an appetite, as portions of the Classic French fare ("foie gras served in actual slabs", "roast chicken as rich as a steak") are "so big that sharing is a matter of survival"; true, the room "won't win any decor awards", and some sniff the staff seems "self-important" (though the savvy smile that's just "part of the shtick"); even "*amis* of Louis" lament the tabs - "it may be cheaper to buy a ranch - but you won't leave hungry or unhappy."

L'Arpège Ⓢ *Haute Cuisine* 26 | 23 | 25 | VE

7e | 84, rue de Varenne (Varenne) | (33-1) 47 05 09 06 | fax 44 18 98 39 | www.alain-passard.com

"It's not your typical" Haute Cuisine haven, "but if you're looking for a simple, product-based approach to food", an "ethereal culinary experience" awaits at this address in the 7th; aided by a "symphony of service", red meat-eschewing chef Alain Passard "gets more flavor out of vegetables than you'd think possible"; a few foes find the decor and staff "kinda cold" and the "prices exorbitant", but scores side with the supporters; P.S. "don't let them stick you in the dungeon (cellar)."

Lasserre [S] *Haute Cuisine* 27 | 28 | 27 | VE

8e | 17, av Franklin D. Roosevelt (Franklin D. Roosevelt) | (33-1) 43 59 02 13 | fax 45 63 72 23 | www.restaurant-lasserre.com

"Very, very civilized", this bastion of "traditional French Haute Cuisine" in the 8th is still a crowd-pleaser, mainly because it makes a meal a "magical experience"; chef Jean-Louis Nomicos' food is "exquisite (if also exquisitely priced)", the "service hums like a finely tuned engine" and when the "gorgeous" "dining room ceiling is opened to the star-lit sky, it just doesn't get any more romantic"; P.S. "gentlemen, don't forget your jackets."

L'Astrance [S] [M] *New French* 27 | 21 | 24 | VE

16e | 4, rue Beethoven (Passy) | (33-1) 40 50 84 40

Assuming you can snag a reservation ("it takes Houdini to get in"), "a superb eating experience" awaits at this "small hideout in the posh 16th", where "genius" chef/co-owner Pascal Barbot's New French cooking is a "gorgeous" "daily invention, based on the morning market"; there's also "super-smart service" and "sophisticated yet cozy" digs; while "no longer a great value" (in fact, it's quite expensive), it's "worth it" for "the most creative cuisine in Paris."

La Table de Joël Robuchon *Haute Cuisine* 26 | 20 | 24 | VE

16e | 16, av Bugeaud (Victor Hugo) | (33-1) 56 28 16 16 | fax 56 28 16 78 | www.joel-robuchon.com

Because "Joël Robuchon is brilliant", a "*très chic* crowd" willingly pays "*très chic* prices" for his "breathtaking" Haute Cuisine venture in the 16th; offered in both regular and "small tasting portions", "the food seems similar to that at his Atelier", but "you can reserve a table" here; malcontents murmur the "modern decor is a little bland", but others like the lack of "glitz"; and when you add in the "professional" servers and a sommelier who's "a master in his own right", the total is a "remarkable experience."

La Table du Lancaster *Haute Cuisine* 25 | 25 | 23 | VE

8e | Hôtel Lancaster | 7, rue de Berri (George V/Franklin Roosevelt) | (33-1) 40 76 40 18 | fax 40 76 40 00 | www.hotel-lancaster.fr

Gastronomes are "delighted to have [Rhone Valley chef] Michel Troisgros in Paris" overseeing this "great addition to the restaurant scene" in an "elegant" boutique hotel near the Champs; the "intimate, luxurious" "Asian-inspired setting" is an apt backdrop for the "interesting tastes" from around the globe; both the Haute Cuisine and the "friendly service" can be "strained", but "the few disappointments" are offset by "superb gustatory moments."

L'Atelier de Joël Robuchon ● *Haute Cuisine* 27 | 22 | 22 | VE

7e | Hôtel Pont Royal | 5, rue de Montalembert (Rue du Bac) | (33-1) 42 22 56 56 | fax 42 22 97 91 | www.joel-robuchon.com

"A must for any foodie", this "relaxed", "hip bar counter/upscale diner" in the 7th from "one of the great chefs of our time" has an "innovative" Haute Cuisine menu that showcases "a fusion of flavors" served small plates-style; "the waiters are a fun bunch", if "too fast" ("order a lot", "slow the kitchen down"); "while not cheap, it's a bargain" for a trip down "Robuchon memory lane"; P.S. those "perturbed by" the "long waits", rejoice: "they take reservations" for certain hours.

La Tour d'Argent M *Haute Cuisine* 25 | 28 | 26 | VE

5e | 15-17, quai de la Tournelle (Cardinal Lemoine/Pont Marie) | (33-1) 43 54 23 31 | fax 44 07 12 04 | www.latourdargent.com

Dining at this Haute Cuisine "legend" is "pure theater", thanks to its "enchanting setting" with "an unparalleled view of Notre Dame" in the 5th; the numbered "duck is a must", accompanied by a bottle from the "fabled" *cave* (reserve ahead to "tour it after dinner"); some sniff this tower is "for the birds" and arguably "Paris' most expensive, elegant tourist trap", but the savvy "go at lunch - that's when the natives go, and the tab is much kinder."

La Truffière S M *Haute Cuisine* 24 | 23 | 23 | E

5e | 4, rue Blainville (Cardinal Lemoine/Place Monge) | (33-1) 46 33 29 82 | fax 46 33 64 74 | www.latruffiere.com

"Truffles, great wine, great cheese - this is the life" sigh those seduced by this "elegant", "extremely *romantique*" 17th-century vaulted cellar in the 5th, where the Haute Cuisine menu offers fungus "in abundance", as well as *fromage* "from a tray so huge the waiters have trouble rolling it around the room"; a few warn to "watch the wine list or it can get very expensive", and be mindful that, while it might feel like "old-world Paris" here, "you may very well run into your neighbors from Ft. Worth."

Laurent S *Haute Cuisine* 24 | 26 | 23 | VE

8e | 41, av Gabriel (Champs-Elysées-Clémenceau) | (33-1) 42 25 00 39 | fax 45 62 45 21 | www.le-laurent.com

"In a magnificent garden right next to the Champs", this "elegant" Haute Cuisine establishment holds sway; while "preferable in summer for its outdoor terrace", it's always "exceptional", with its "excellent" if "traditional" fare and "discreet, well-behaved" (though slightly "stuffy") staff; it's "worth the cost" even if "you may have to sell off a few T-bonds to pay the bill - or else you can do as many of the other high-powered patrons do and order the prix fixe menu, available at both lunch and dinner."

L'Avant Goût S M *New French* 25 | 15 | 19 | M

13e | 26, rue Bobillot (Place d'Italie) | (33-1) 53 80 24 00 | fax 53 80 00 77 | www.lavantgout.com

"If you're willing to make the trip to the 13th, this bustling bistro will never disappoint - and sometimes it'll stun" say supporters; the New French cuisine is "original", even "surprising" ("where else would we have been inspired to try a pig pot-au-feu?"), and "for a heck of a price" too; while the "minimally decorated" dining room has been redone, still "the tables are mighty close together" and service swings from "smiling" to "surly."

Le Bristol *Haute Cuisine* 27 | 27 | 26 | VE

8e | Hôtel Le Bristol | 112, rue du Faubourg St-Honoré (Miromesnil) | (33-1) 53 43 43 40 | fax 53 43 43 01 | www.lebristolparis.com

"Eric Frechon is the resident culinary genius here" at the Bristol, cooking "updated Haute Cuisine" that's "classic but creative"; while the food "is worth the trip alone", the dining rooms - a round oak-paneled salon in winter and a garden pavilion in summer - are both "stunningly beautiful", and the service is "surprisingly not haughty" for a place that offers one of the "most refined dining experiences in the world"; even the "heavy-on-the-wallet prices" don't stop it from being "sublime in every way."

Le Céladon Ⓢ *Classic French* 24 | 25 | 23 | E

2e | Hôtel Westminster | 15, rue Daunou (Opéra) | (33-1) 47 03 40 42 | fax 42 61 33 78 | www.leceladon.com

Near the ritzy Place Vendôme, the plush dining room of the Hôtel Westminster "serenely" serves up "superb" Classic French fare in an "elegant", "classical setting"; since the "excellent prix fixe" is a "relative bargain given the quality of the food and service", executives find it "fantastic for a business lunch", but it's also a good "stop for an after-dinner drink and chat with the wonderful master bartender."

Le Chateaubriand Ⓢ Ⓜ *New French* - | - | - | M

11e | 129, av Parmentier (Goncourt/Parmentier) | (33-1) 43 57 45 95 | fax 43 57 45 95

To sample the Asian-accented, produce-driven New French cooking that's all the rage right now, hoof it over to this funky, hugely popular bistro in the Oberkampf quarter, where a vintage grocery store-turned-dining room is the newest setting for rising-star chef Iñaki Aizpitarte; a native of the Basque country, he describes his cooking style as "*cuisine de vagabonde*", a reference to his international travels, and it results in dishes with clean but unexpected combinations of flavors - e.g. asparagus with tahini foam and sesame-seed brittle.

Le Cinq *Haute Cuisine* 28 | 29 | 28 | VE

8e | Four Seasons George V | 31, av George V (Alma Marceau/George V) | (33-1) 49 52 71 54 | fax 49 52 71 81 | www.fourseasons.com/paris

"For an incredible experience - what royalty must feel like every day" - surveyors tout this "enchanting" "temple of Haute Cuisine" with its "oasis of flowers" in the George V; the staff is so "faultless" it's like "items appear at the table as though your server never left", and the dishes are "the stuff culinary dreams are made of"; true, it's a "traditional" place, and "you might be left a peasant" by the prices - but dining's "as good as it gets" here.

Le Clos des Gourmets Ⓢ Ⓜ *New French* 24 | 20 | 22 | M

7e | 16, av Rapp (Alma Marceau/Ecole Militaire) | (33-1) 45 51 75 61 | fax 47 05 74 20 | www.closdesgourmets.com

"It's really worth the trip" to the quiet residential 7th in order to sit down in this "lovely room (even if the tables are really close together)"; run by a "husband-and-wife team that keeps clients coming back", it serves "exquisite, refined" New French dishes, especially on the "inventive prix fixe" whose "supplements are worth the splurge"; all this "in a price range" that'll make you "spoiled forever."

Le Duc Ⓢ Ⓜ *Seafood* 24 | 16 | 22 | VE

14e | 243, bd Raspail (Raspail) | (33-1) 43 20 96 30 | fax 43 20 46 73

Ah, but life is good when you're seated in front of "a buttery *sole meunière* served in a room resembling a ship of the French line" - as you are at this "sedate" but "sublime" seafooder in Montparnasse; after nigh on 40 years, perhaps the "tired" hull needs overhauling, but "watching waiters fillet the fish is great fun", so plenty are pleased to put into port at "one of the top" *poisson* palaces in Paris.

Le Florimond ☒ *Classic French* 24 | 18 | 24 | M

7e | 19, av de la Motte-Picquet (Ecole Militaire) | (33-1) 45 55 40 38 | fax 45 55 40 38

Surveyors just "can't say enough about this wonderful restaurant, which serves sublime, non-fussy Classic French fare with genuine affection not only for the food, but for its patrons"; reviewers revisit the "cozy" digs in the 7th for the "luscious stuffed cabbage", along with "attentive service even when it's crowded"; "entirely nonsmoking", it's especially a "great option for Saturday night, when many of the good places in Paris are closed."

Le Grand Véfour ☒ *Haute Cuisine* 27 | 28 | 27 | VE

1er | Palais Royal | 17, rue de Beaujolais (Palais Royal-Musée du Louvre) | (33-1) 42 96 56 27 | fax 42 86 80 71 | www.grand-vefour.com

This "historic" Haute Cuisine "heaven" in the Palais Royal gardens is "a glittering jewel box" that offers a "culinary experience beyond compare"; chef Guy Martin's cooking is "awesome in every way", and as you wait for each "divine" course, you can gaze at brass plaques with the names of famous patrons past, like Colette and Victor Hugo; you too "are treated like royalty" "upon entering this bastion of epicurean bliss", so, even if it costs a fortune, "for a few hours, it's good to be the king."

Le Meurice ☒ *Haute Cuisine* 26 | 28 | 25 | VE

1er | Hôtel Meurice | 228, rue de Rivoli (Concorde/Tuileries) | (33-1) 44 58 10 55 | fax 44 58 10 76 | www.meuricehotel.com

In the 1st, "one of the most beautiful dining rooms in Paris" is the setting for one of the "best meals in town" fawn fans of the "remarkable" Yannick Alléno's "highly inventive" Haute Cuisine, delivered by waiters who treat patrons "like royalty" amid the "gorgeous" marbled, mirrored and mosaic room that "screams opulence"; "considering the decor, food and service, this is a bargain", but "if you're on a budget", "the terrific lounge is half the price for the same chef's" cuisine.

Le Pré Catelan ☒ M *Haute Cuisine* 26 | 28 | 25 | VE

16e | Bois de Boulogne, Route de Suresnes (Pont-de-Neuilly/Porte Maillot) | (33-1) 44 14 41 14 | fax 45 24 43 25 | www.lenotre.fr

Given its setting "in a fairy-tale park" with a "sumptuous" "fireplace in the winter" and a "terrace in the summer", some might suspect this vet of turning into "a tourist trap" - but instead, almost all are "thrilled" by the "truly wonderful experience", thanks to chef Frédéric Anton's "amazing" Haute Cuisine with a light, contemporary touch and the "classy" service; while the "outrageously expensive" bill makes it preferable "if someone else is paying", this is "the perfect splurge"; N.B. it is slated to unveil a new look in fall 2007, which may outdate the Decor score.

NEW **Le Rech** ☒ M *Classic French/Seafood* - | - | - | E

17e | 62, av des Ternes (Charles de Gaulle-Etoile/Ternes) | (33-1) 45 72 29 47 | fax 45 72 41 60 | www.rech.fr

Ever since gastronaut chef Alain Ducasse netted this circa-1925 Classic French fish house near the Place des Ternes in the 17th, its been high tide here - the menu's been completely revamped and the catch of the day is not only finer but prepared with a lot more imagination; while the duplex art deco interior's been freshened up, such classics as the well-aged Camembert and giant éclair have been retained, much to the delight of newly returning devotees.

Les Ambassadeurs S M *New French* 27 29 27 VE

8e | Hôtel de Crillon | 10, pl de la Concorde (Concorde) | (33-1) 44 71 16 16 | fax 44 71 15 03 | www.crillon.com

This "incredible" New French in the Crillon is "fabulous in every way", especially since the arrival of chef Jean-François Piège, who's brought "fun and whimsy" to the fare; his "delectable delights" contrast with the "staggeringly grand" surrounds; "from the gilded barges for ferrying [champagne] to the tiny stools for handbags" to the "phenomenal service that's formal, but friendly (for France)", this is "the closest you'll get to living like Louis XV - and you'll wish you had his wealth, when the bill comes."

Les Elysées S *Haute Cuisine* 26 25 24 VE

8e | Hôtel Vernet | 25, rue Vernet (Charles de Gaulle-Etoile/George V) | (33-1) 44 31 98 98 | fax 44 31 85 69 | www.hotelvernet.com

The "phenomenal service" and glass-domed "ceiling designed by Gustave Eiffel" - yes, of Tower fame - create a genteel atmosphere at this "delightful" Haute Cuisine table in the 8th; unlike some celebrity chefs, toque Eric Briffard (ex Plaza Athénée) "is actually in the kitchen cooking and checking on his diners", which is why his contemporary dishes are so "refined" and full of "wonderful flavors"; in short, this is one to add "to your little black book" even if "it's expensive."

NEW **Le Sensing** S *Haute Cuisine* - - - E

6e | 19, rue Brea (Vavin) | (33-1) 43 27 08 80 | fax 43 26 99 27 | www.restaurant-sensing.com

Chef-restaurateur Guy Martin is aiming to wow the senses with his slickly designed new Haute Cuisine venture in Montparnasse - all minimalist and modern, with tobacco-colored walls, limestone floors and a curving wrought-iron staircase; in the kitchen, Rémi Van Peteghem, Martin's former second at Grand Véfour, produces a contemporary yet sensual tasting-plates mix-and-match menu for a mélange of media types, fashionistas and gastronauts; service from young waiters in well-cut dark suits displays a definite dash.

Les Ombres *New French* - - - VE

7e | Musée du Quai Branly | 27, quai Branly, Portail Debilly (Alma Marceau) | (33-1) 47 53 68 00 | fax 47 53 68 18 | www.elior.com

Located on the fifth floor of the Musée du Quai Branly (a showcase for Asian, African and North and South American art), this New French is the most glamorous debutante to have appeared in Paris for some time; architect Jean Nouvel, who designed the museum, also created the sleek look of the dining room and its terrace, right down to the streamlined stainless-steel cutlery and curvy rattan chairs; the happy surprise is that young chef Arno Busquet's menu lives up to the setting's magical city views.

Les Ormes S M *Haute Cuisine* 24 17 21 E

7e | 22, rue Surcouf (Invalides/La Tour-Maubourg) | (33-1) 45 51 46 93 | fax 45 50 30 11 | www.restaurant-les-ormes.com

Faithful foodies have followed their "favorite" toque, Stéphane Molé, from the fringes of the 16th to these digs "near the Eiffel Tower", trumpeting his "thoughtful, delicious" Haute Cuisine and a prix fixe menu that's a "great bargain"; still, some nostalgists are "not sure he should have moved", saying the fancy address has made the place "a little starchy" ("service hasn't quite caught up to the chef, but it's improving").

L'Espadon *Classic French* 25 | 27 | 26 | VE

1er | Hôtel Ritz | 15, pl Vendôme (Concorde/Opéra) | (33-1) 43 16 30 80 | fax 43 16 33 75 | www.ritzparis.com

"Forget harsh reality just outside the walls of this prestigious palace" – aka the Hôtel Ritz's dining room – "a bastion of tradition where all is abundant silver, crystal and fresh flowers"; chef Michel Roth's Classic French cuisine is the "pinnacle of refinement", with its "delectable" dishes doled out by "doting and experienced waiters"; "it may not be cutting-edge, it might be a bit stuffy and it [definitely] will empty your wallet – but it won't be anything less than excellent."

Le Violon d'Ingres S M *Bistro* 24 | 21 | 21 | M

7e | 135, rue St-Dominique (Ecole Militaire) | (33-1) 45 55 15 05 | fax 45 55 48 42 | www.leviolondingres.com

Chef-owner Christian Constant transports fans (including "a lot of Americans") to "foodie heaven" at his "chic" table in the 7th; his constant supervision of the kitchen ensures "near perfection" on the plate, while wife Catherine oversees service in the "long, narrow" dining room; dissenters deem it "disappointing" ("we observed it's different if you are 'known'") but most marvel at "this most memorable meal"; N.B. a post-Survey menu switch from Haute Cuisine to upscale bistro fare, plus new brasserie-chic decor, is not reflected in the above scores.

L'Ostéria S *Italian* 24 | 11 | 15 | E

4e | 10, rue de Sévigné (St-Paul) | (33-1) 42 71 37 08 | fax 48 06 27 71

It's "missing a sign on the door" (the better to "keep out the vulgar crowds"), but those in-the-know make tracks to this "masterful" Marais site for "perhaps the best Italian food in Paris" including "clouds masquerading as gnocchi" and "sublime" risotto; regrettably, it's "deliriously expensive" ("food as rich as the clientele"), "service can be hectic and the room is small"; N.B. scores don't reflect an ownership change post-Survey.

Michel Rostang S *Classic French* 27 | 23 | 26 | VE

17e | 20, rue Rennequin (Péreire/Ternes) | (33-1) 47 63 40 77 | fax 47 63 82 75 | www.michelrostang.com

Surveyors "swoon" over "dishes that sparkle with taste" by this "grand chef"-owner whose Classic French in the 17th is "one of the best in Paris" (especially in winter, when it becomes "a truffle lover's paradise"), enhanced by a "serious wine list" and "superb sommelier"; the wood-paneled, "rich setting" seems "grandmotherly" to some, but others feel "right at home", thanks to "flawlessly graceful service", and devotees declare that "coming back each time is like putting on a warm glove."

Pavillon Ledoyen S *Haute Cuisine* 26 | 27 | 25 | VE

8e | 8, av Dutuit (Champs-Elysées-Clémenceau/Concorde) | (33-1) 53 05 10 01 | www.ledoyen.com

In a "parklike setting, with lush verdant views from its sumptuous dining room", this pavilion off the Champs is a "temple of good food and refinement" – not to mention "romantic as hell"; the Napoleon III-style decor is "dripping with elegance", the Haute Cuisine is "fit for the gods" and the staff "makes you feel like royalty"; "sometimes it's overrun with special events", but it's "a must" if you're going to propose - just be warned "dinner will be as expensive as the engagement ring."

Pierre Gagnaire *Haute Cuisine* 28 25 27 VE

8^e^ | Hôtel Balzac | 6, rue Balzac (Charles de Gaulle-Etoile/George V) | (33-1) 58 36 12 50 | fax 58 36 12 51 | www.pierre-gagnaire.com

"Before you die, go" to this Haute Cuisine table in the 8th, "a place to push your palate and explore new sensations" with a chef-owner who, "mad scientist-like", combines "tastes that blow your mind away"; within a "chic" "Scandi-Asian setting of blond woods and gray" tones, near-"faultless service" presents a "dizzying" number of dishes "almost too overwhelming to comprehend"; alas, the "huge" bill registers all too well, "but the price is justified", since "Pierre is still without peer."

Relais d'Auteuil "Patrick Pignol" Ⓢ Ⓜ *Haute Cuisine* 26 20 23 VE

16^e^ | 31, bd Murat (Michel-Ange-Molitor/Porte d'Auteuil) | (33-1) 46 51 09 54 | fax 40 71 05 03

A "*belle* clientele from the neighborhood" near the Porte d'Auteuil and French Open fans with a hunger for Haute Cuisine know that, though this warm-colored corner "doesn't have the aura of the big names", it remains "one of the best culinary experiences in Paris", thanks to a "family's passion" for "perfection", from M'sieur Pignol's "exquisite" cooking to Madame's "kind service"; P.S. the game and "truffle dishes in season will bring you to your knees."

Relais Louis XIII Ⓢ Ⓜ *Haute Cuisine* 25 24 24 VE

6^e^ | 8, rue des Grands-Augustins (Odéon/St-Michel) | (33-1) 43 26 75 96 | fax 44 07 07 80 | www.relaislouis13.com

Patrons pledge fealty to this "sleeper" in the 6th for classic Haute Cuisine in a "lovely old house" with 17th-century paintings, where Louis XIII was proclaimed king; the current sovereign, chef-owner Manuel Martinez, produces "astounding" fare that's "expensive" but "worth every euro", as is the "wonderful" wine list; the "accommodating staff" and "formal" ambiance make it "fantastic to celebrate any grand occasion", "to luxuriate with a lover" or even "to take grandma."

Salon d'Hélène Ⓢ Ⓜ *Southwest French* 25 20 19 E

6^e^ | 4, rue d'Assas (Sèvres-Babylone) | (33-1) 42 22 00 11 | fax 42 22 25 40

The "more relaxed (and lower-priced) eatery of top chef Hélène Darroze" draws an "ever-so-chic young set" from the stylish 6th who call her "tapas system" "sensational", featuring "a wide selection" of Southwestern French small plates "creatively paired and plated" (ok, so "a few combinations border on the bizarre, but most are deliciously successful"); some salon-goers slam the "frosty" service and "uncomfortable seating" ("ask for a banquette when you reserve") but don't be put off - "the place is really worth it."

Senderens *Brasserie/New French* - - - VE

8^e^ | 9, pl de la Madeleine (Madeleine) | (33-1) 42 65 22 90 | fax 42 65 06 23 | www.senderens.fr

Chef-owner Alain Senderens created a stir when he decided to "reinvent" Lucas Carton in the 8th as a brasserie; the "chic" decor now features metallic leather chairs, an undulating fabric ceiling and Corian-topped tables, the New French menu runs to "modern" dishes like curried lamb shoulder and service is "more casual"; lovers of the old landmark "will be shocked" by this "legend downscaled to reality", but fans urge "take a chance and go."

Sormani ☒ *Italian* 24 | 18 | 21 | VE

17e | 4, rue du Général Lanrezac (Charles de Gaulle-Etoile) | (33-1) 43 80 13 91 | fax 40 55 07 37

"Everyone raves" that this "institution" near the Etoile is one of "the best Italians in Paris"; with "divine" dishes often "bathed in truffles", it's "as close to Italy as you are going to get without going there" (but don't expect an economic advantage, since the "prices are astounding"); the Venetian-style, "lively red decor partially offsets" the "oppressive" air generated by the number of "business and older patrons."

NEW Spring ☒ *Bistro* - | - | - | M

9e | 28, rue de la Tour d'Auvergne (Anvers) | (33-1) 45 96 05 72

Before going out on his own with this 16-seater, Chicago native Daniel Rose cooked with the likes of Paul Bocuse and Yannick Alléno at Le Meurice; now, with the help of a single waitress, he nightly produces a contemporary bistro menu in a cozy room decorated with Asian puppets that's putting a spring into the step of the bobos who frequent this trendy part of the 9th.

Stella Maris ☒ *Classic French* 25 | 20 | 22 | E

8e | 4, rue Arsène Houssaye (Charles de Gaulle-Etoile) | (33-1) 42 89 16 22 | fax 42 89 16 01

Tateru Yoshino - "a remarkable chef" who trained with the likes of Robuchon and Gagnaire - brings "creativity" and a Japanese "mastery of technique" to Classic French cuisine in his small place in the 8th; admirers assert his interpretation of such national treasures as tête de veau and lièvre à la royale is "irreproachable", the "service exceptional" and a "successful" "recent face-lift" has warmed the "formerly cold" decor; given all this, "prices aren't so bad."

Taillevent ☒ *Haute Cuisine* 28 | 28 | 28 | VE

8e | 15, rue Lamennais (Charles de Gaulle-Etoile/George V) | (33-1) 44 95 15 01 | fax 42 25 95 18 | www.taillevent.com

Again voted Paris' No. 1 for Food, this "mythic" site in the 8th is "as much a landmark as the Eiffel Tower"; chef Alain Solivérès' classic Haute Cuisine is "exquisite", "no detail is missed" by "consummate host"-owner Jean-Claude Vrinat's staff ("I was squinting because I'd forgotten my glasses, and a waiter presented various pairs on a silver tray") and the "sumptuous" setting now boasts "a refreshing contemporary style"; "reservations are not only required but difficult", but the "memories will last the rest of your life."

Other Noteworthy Places

Auberge du Champ de Mars ☒ *Classic French*

18, rue de l'Exposition (Ecole Militaire) | (33-1) 45 51 78 08

Au Bon Accueil ☒ *Bistro*

14, rue de Monttessuy (Alma Marceau/Ecole Militaire) | (33-1) 47 05 46 11 | fax 45 56 15 80

Au Trou Gascon [S] *Southwest French*
40, rue Taine (Daumesnil) | (33-1) 43 44 34 26 | fax 43 07 80 55 | www.autrougascon.fr

Chen Soleil d'Est [S] *Chinese*
15, rue du Théâtre (Charles Michels) | (33-1) 45 79 34 34 | fax 45 79 07 53

Chez Michel ◐[S] *New French*
10, rue de Belzunce (Gare du Nord/Poissonnière) | (33-1) 44 53 06 20 | fax 44 53 61 31

Dominique Bouchet [S] *Haute Cuisine*
11, rue Treilhard (Miromesnil) | (33-1) 45 61 09 46 | fax 42 89 11 14 | www.dominique-bouchet.com

Goumard *Seafood*
9, rue Duphot (Madeleine) | (33-1) 42 60 36 07 | fax 42 60 04 54 | www.goumard.fr

La Braisière [S] *Gascony*
54, rue Cardinet (Malesherbes) | (33-1) 47 63 40 37 | fax 47 63 04 76

La Cerisaie [S] *Southwest French*
70, bd Edgar-Quinet (Edgar Quinet/Montparnasse) | (33-1) 43 20 98 98 | fax 43 20 98 98

L'Angle du Faubourg [S] *New French*
195, rue du Faubourg St-Honoré (Charles de Gaulle-Etoile/Ternes) | (33-1) 40 74 20 20 | fax 40 74 20 21 | www.taillevent.com

Le Chiberta [S] *New French*
3, rue Arsène Houssaye (Charles de Gaulle-Etoile) | (33-1) 53 53 42 00 | fax 45 62 85 08 | www.lechiberta.com

Le Christine ◐ *Bistro*
1, rue Christine (Odéon/St-Michel) | (33-1) 40 51 71 64 | fax 43 26 15 63

L'Epi Dupin [S] *Bistro*
11, rue Dupin (Sèvres-Babylone) | (33-1) 42 22 64 56 | fax 42 22 30 42

L'Obélisque *Classic French*
Hôtel de Crillon | 10, pl de la Concorde (Concorde) | (33-1) 44 71 15 15 | fax 44 71 15 02 | www.crillon.com

L'Os à Moëlle ◐[S][M] *Classic French*
3, rue Vasco de Gama (Lourmel) | (33-1) 45 57 27 27 | fax 45 57 28 00

Mon Vieil Ami [M] *Bistro*
69, rue St-Louis-en-l'Ile (Pont-Marie) | (33-1) 40 46 01 35 | fax 40 46 01 36 | www.mon-vieil-ami.com

Passiflore [S] *Asian/Classic French*
33, rue de Longchamp (Boissière/Trocadéro) | (33-1) 47 04 96 81 | fax 47 04 32 27 | www.restaurantpassiflore.com

FOOD | DECOR | SERVICE | COST

Prague

TOP FOOD RANKING

	Restaurant	Cuisine
26	Allegro	Italian/Mediterranean
25	Aquarius	Czech/Mediterranean
	David	Czech/International
	V Zátiší	Czech/International
	Essensia	Asian/International
24	Flambée	French/International
	U Zlaté Hrušky	Czech/International
	Rybí trh	International/Seafood
	U Modré Ruze	Czech/International
23	U Modré Kachnicky	Czech
	Kampa Park	International/Seafood
	Mlýnec	International
	Oliva	Mediterranean
	Coda	Mediterranean
	La Perle de Prague*	New French
	Bellevue	Czech/International
22	Hergetova Cihelna	International/Czech
	Pravda	International
	Pálffy Palác	International
21	C'est La Vie	International/Seafood
	Square*	Italian/Spanish
	Alcron	Seafood
	U Vladare	Czech/International
	Barock	Asian/Mediterranean
20	Cowboys	Steakhouse
	La Provence*	Provençal
	Sarah Bernhardt*	French/International
	U Pinkasu*	Czech
	Zlatá Praha*	Czech/International
	Brasserie M	French Brasserie/Seafood
19	Radost FX	International/Vegetarian
	Potrefená husa	Czech/International
15	Francouzská	Czech/French

Alcron, The ⑧ *Seafood* 21 | 19 | 22 | E

New Town | Radisson SAS Alcron Hotel | Stěpánská 40 | (420) 222-820-000 | fax 222-820-100 | www.radissonsas.com

A "private" refuge for well-heeled travelers, businessmen and in-the-know locals, this "wonderful little seafood restaurant" in New Town's Radisson SAS Alcron Hotel is home to chef Jirí Stift, who fans feel is "great with fish", as evidenced by dishes like sea bass roasted in salt crust; his creations are served in an "art deco setting" sporting a "lovely" curved mural, but those who are "a bit jaded" judge the atmosphere "not very warm."

* Indicates a tie with restaurant above

FOOD | DECOR | SERVICE | COST

Allegro *Italian/Mediterranean* 26 | 24 | 27 | VE

Old Town | Four Seasons Hotel | Veleslavínova 2A | (420) 221-426-880 | fax 221-426-000 | www.fourseasons.com/prague

"Not your typical hotel dining" room, this "truly first-rate" Old Town venue "wows" with an "ultimate experience" that's just as "wonderful" "as you'd expect" from the Four Seasons; indeed, it's ranked No. 1 for Food in Prague for "genius chef Vito Mollica's" "fantastic" Italian-Med cuisine, "beautifully presented" in "a lavish environment" by "meticulous", "charming" staffers who treat guests "as visiting royalty"; P.S. "come early to get a window seat" for a "particularly" "spectacular view" of "the Vltava River's Charles Bridge" and the "fairy-tale" castle.

Aquarius *Czech/Mediterranean* 25 | 23 | 19 | E

Little Quarter | Alchymist Grand Hotel & Spa | Tržište 19 | (420) 257-286-019 | fax 257-286-010 | www.alchymisthotel.com

This Czech-Med is located in the Little Quarter's Alchymst Grand Hotel & Spa, four richly and romantically refurbished 16th-century buildings; "great" cuisine and a "fantastic" setting - a vaulted, mirrored space that opens to a courtyard on one side - make for "an enchanting experience", plus the practial pronounce "the price is very good value"; N.B. there's live jazz on Saturdays.

Barock *Asian/Mediterranean* 21 | 23 | 21 | E

Old Town | Parízská 24 | (420) 222-329-221 | fax 222-321-933 | www.barockrestaurant.cz

"Still hip" and "happening", this "trendy little" Old Town "hangout" in a "great location near the luxury shopping in the Jewish Quarter" is known for "nice eye candy" thanks to its posse of "lively young" patrons and photos of "supermodels" adorning the walls of its "stylish" interior; service is "friendly", and the "flavorful options" on its "well-executed" Asian-accented Mediterranean menu (including an extensive sushi selection) offer a "terrific break from the routine."

Bellevue *Czech/International* 23 | 23 | 24 | VE

Old Town | Smetanovo nábrezí 18 | (420) 222-221-443 | fax 222-220-453 | www.zatisigroup.cz

"An incredible dining experience" is in store for guests of this "grand" Old Town venue who enjoy a "magnificent view of the river, Charles Bridge and Prague Castle" as "impeccable" staffers deliver "delicious", "up-to-date" Czech-International cuisine; some suggest the same can't be said about the somewhat "faded" decor, but more maintain the "elegant setting" is "stylish and romantic", saying they'd "happily return again and again."

Brasserie M *French/Seafood* 20 | 17 | 18 | M

New Town | Vladislavova 17 | (420) 224-054-070 | fax 224-054-440 | www.brasseriem.cz

"Great portions" of "delicious" fare with an emphasis on seafood lead loyalists of this French brasserie in New Town to say they "would definitely come again"; "good service", "more than fair prices" and a warm and expansive setting with an open kitchen and red accents add to its appeal.

C'est La Vie *International/Seafood* 21 19 21 E

Little Quarter | Rícní 1 | (420) 721-158-403 | www.cestlavie.cz

"A favorite for locals and tourists alike", this International-seafooder in the historic Little Quarter has a cozy, atmospheric interior with nooks and crannies, but it's the "beautiful" riverside terrace setting with its view of the Charles Bridge and boats that leave lifers proclaiming "we'll be back."

Coda *Mediterranean* 23 23 23 E

Little Quarter | Hotel Aria | Tržište 9 | (420) 225-334-761 | fax 225-334-792 | www.aria.cz

The "beautiful Hotel Aria" "comes through" with this Mediterranean "hot spot" on its premises that offers "exceptional food" and "exceedingly friendly service"; the rich red dining room is "sexy", but the "great view" from the "gorgeous" terrace includes St. Nicholas Church, Prague Castle and a medley of romantic terra-cotta rooftops.

Cowboys *Steak* 20 22 21 M

Old Town | Nerudova 40 | (420) 257-530-438 | fax 257-535-820 | www.kampagroup.com

Meat lovers want to be steered to Old Town, just below Prague Castle, to this latest venture from the successful Kampa Group, for relatively affordable "American-style" steaks; the striking interior with vaulted brick ceilings and cowskin-covered booths is dramatic, but it's "the rooftop terrace offering one of the best views of Prague" that really ropes respondents in.

David *Czech/International* 25 22 24 E

Little Quarter | Tržište 21 | (420) 257-533-109 | fax 257-533-109 | www.restaurant-david.cz

For "a fantastic trip to another era", step inside the "country-style dining rooms" of "this relaxing haven" "tucked into a hillside" "in a quiet corner of" the Little Quarter, where "carefully prepared", "delicious" Czech-International cuisine (including "hearty, traditional game dishes") is "augmented by an excellent wine list"; fans also "can't say enough good things about" the "gracious" service and "charming", "tiny space", insisting you're guaranteed a "most memorable" meal.

NEW **Essensia** *Asian/International* 25 25 25 VE

Little Quarter | Mandarin Oriental Hotel | Nebovidská 459/1 | (420) 233-088-888 | fax 233-088-668 | www.mandarinoriental.com

"A cut above the competition" and "one of the best" "places to take business clients" is this new Asian-International in the Mandarin Oriental Hotel, which is housed in a converted 14th-century monastery and courtyard; "brilliant" cuisine is served in a series of five "beautiful", softly lit vaulted rooms by an "attentive staff"; it's pricey, but pragmatists point out "expensive eating in Prague would be considered cheap in London or Paris."

Flambée ◐ *French/International* 24 25 26 E

Old Town | Husova 5 | (420) 224-248-512 | fax 224-248-513 | www.flambee.cz

"Truly a treasure", this "gem" of a French-International in Old Town is manned by a "hospitable", "attentive staff" that "puts you at ease" the moment you descend to its "distinctive Gothic cellar", which "dates back to the 11th century" but has been updated with modern accents including "elegant red-velvet seating"; "great chef" Dušan Jakubec's "culinary art reaches the highest standards", and when coupled with the "impeccable service" and "striking" setting more than justifies the "astronomical" prices.

Francouzská *Czech/French* 15 22 18 VE

Old Town | Obecní Dum | námestí Republiky 5 | (420) 222-002-770 | fax 222-002-778 | www.francouzskarestaurace.cz

"Breathtaking art nouveau architecture" and a "great historical location" are the claims to fame of this "expensive" Czech-French venue in the right wing of the Municipal House, on the edge of the Old Town; fans feel its proximity to the in-house halls makes it "perfect for a little something post-" or "pre-concert", but foes say it's a "shame" the "decor is better than the dishes", adding that certain "not-too-friendly" staffers "need to change their attitude."

Hergetova Cihelna *Czech/International* 22 25 21 E

Little Quarter | Cihelná 2b | (420) 296-826-103 | fax 257-535-820 | www.kampagroup.com

The "fantastic view of the Charles Bridge" from its "window seats and terrace" "is alone worth the visit" to this "special treat" "with an amazing location" "in an old brick factory" "on the riverbank" in the Little Quarter; within the "*très chic*" atmosphere of its "dramatic yet romantic setting", a "modern" menu of "excellent" International offerings "as well as regional Czech dishes" is served by a "very good" staff, making it "a must stop when in town."

Kampa Park *International/Seafood* 23 24 22 E

Little Quarter | Na Kampe 8B | (420) 296-826-102 | www.kampagroup.com

Perennially "popular", this "renowned" "favorite" "beautifully located" on the Little Quarter's "historic Kampa Island" (right "under the famous Charles Bridge") offers two terraces for "contemporary fine dining at the water's edge"; loyalists also laud the "lovely" interior and "inventive", "top-quality" International menu focusing on "properly cooked fish entrees", but surveyors are split on the "efficient" staffers, with some swearing they "couldn't be more friendly" and others opining that they "need an attitude adjustment."

La Perle de Prague ☒ *French* 23 25 22 VE

New Town | Tancící Dum | Rašínovo nábrezí 80 | (420) 221-984-160 | fax 221-984-179 | www.laperle.cz

"Both the beautiful views and good cocktails will make you giddy" at this "fantastic location atop" 'The Dancing House', architect Frank "Gehry's whimsical" creation in New Town; some say the "surroundings are far better than" the "overpriced" fare, but more insist the "excellent" New French cuisine – offered in a "funky", "contemporary" interior with "pampering service" – "matches the splendor of" the "amazing" vistas of the winding river, Old Town and Prague Castle on the horizon.

La Provence *Provençal* 20 19 18 E

Old Town | Stupartská 9 | (420) 296-826-155 | fax 224-816-692 | www.kampagroup.com

"A little bit of Paris in Prague", this brasserie "located in a hip area" in "the twisty cobbled streets" of Old Town "is decked out in French

Provençal charm" - from its "super" "comfort food" to its "excellent" selection of "fine wines" to its "interesting decor"; the "upstairs is a popular place to meet for a pre-dinner drink", but insiders advise "eat downstairs" in the "basement-level" dining room, "a haven in the cold winter."

Mlýnec *International* 23 21 21 E

Old Town | Novotného Lávka 9 | (420) 221-082-208 | fax 221-082-391 | www.zatisigroup.cz

With its "great location" on a pier "at the foot of the Charles Bridge" in Old Town, this "superb" spot offers "very nice views" to accompany its "wonderful food" and "top-flight service"; the "interesting" International "menu challenges the traditional Prague palate" since there's "nothing local" on it, but the "good quality wine list" does feature some Moravian selections.

NEW **Oliva** ☒ *Mediterranean* 23 21 22 M

New Town | 4 Plavecká | (420) 222-520-288 | www.olivarestaurant.cz

In-the-know locals have taken to this "stylish" Mediterranean newcomer in New Town that, like the name says, pays homage to the olive and its oil in some of its "delicious" dishes and also in the pale-green color on its walls; "fresh food", "friendly owners" and fair prices make many say they "wish this favorite were in their neighborhood."

Pálffy Palác *International* 22 24 19 E

Little Quarter | Valdštejnská 14 | (420) 257-530-522 | fax 257-530-522 | www.palffy.cz

"Difficult to find but worth the effort", this delightful" "favorite" features a "romantic", "candlelit" setting "in an old nobleman's palace close to the castle" in the Little Quarter, where "excellent" International food is served along with "good local wines" by an "able" staff; P.S. the "ancient building" also houses a "music conservatory", so sometimes "you dine to the sounds" of its students.

Potrefená husa *Czech/International* 19 20 17 M

Old Town | Bílkova 5 | (420) 222-326-626 | www.potrefenahusa.com

Located on the ground floor of an unusual Cubist building, this Old Town venue offers equally "interesting" Czech-International fare; most find the "spacious" digs "tastefully furnished", though some say they're "a bit severe", as are certain "hard-faced" members of the staff.

Pravda *International* 22 23 22 E

Old Town | Parízská 17 | (420) 222-326-203 | fax 222-312-042 | www.pravdarestaurant.cz

Set "on smart" "Parízská Street, next to the Old-New Synagogue" "in the Jewish Quarter" of Old Town, this "classy" International "celebrates tastes from all over the world"; the "simple", "modern, open space offers views of the bustling" thoroughfare ("during the summer months the outdoor tables" provide particularly "great people-watching"), and "excellent cocktails" add to the "lively", "trendy" vibe.

Radost FX ◐⊄ *International/Vegetarian* 19 17 17 M

New Town | Belehradská 120 | (420) 224-254-776 | fax 224-254-776 | www.radostfx.cz

A "lively, young" crowd "speaks highly about this" bastion of "bohemian cool" in New Town, a "hip chameleonlike" venue - equal parts "funky cafe", lounge and nightclub – with an "innovative" International menu of "great vegetarian" "comfort food" that "even a meat eater could love"; perhaps the "relaxed" staff "could move a little faster", but the "economical" prices make it a "good value"; P.S. "all the Americans go for the great brunch."

Rybí trh *International/Seafood* 24 | 19 | 23 | E

Old Town | Týnský Dvur 5 | (420) 224-895-447 | fax 224-895-449 | www.rybitrh.cz

You might not expect "simply divine" "seafood in a land-locked country", but you'll find it at this Old Town "fish market/restaurant" set "on the charming Týnský Dvur courtyard"; its "excellent" International menu offers a "great choice" of "creatively prepared" fin fare, the savvy staff has a knack for "fulfilling unspoken wishes" and the "understated" interior is appropriately decorated with "nice aquariums"; as for the cost, surveyors wax philosophical, saying "what can you do? – quality is expensive."

Sarah Bernhardt *French/International* 20 | 24 | 22 | E

Old Town | Hotel Paris | U Obecniho domu 1 | (420) 222-195-195 | fax 224-225-475 | www.sarah-bernhardt.cz

"Don't miss" this "stunning dining room" "in the venerable Hotel Paris" in Old Town, an exemplar of "art nouveau elegance" whose "outstanding decor" provides a "lovely" backdrop for "extremely refined service" and an "excellent" menu of "classic" French-International cuisine that truly "satisfies"; befitting the fact that it's "named after actress Sarah Bernhardt", it's "a nice place to go after the theater."

Square *Italian/Spanish* 21 | 20 | 19 | E

Little Quarter | Malostranské námestí 5/28 | (420) 296-826-104 | fax 257-532-107 | www.kampagroup.com

"While touring old Prague", visit this "good, reliable venue" in the Little Quarter, where "excellent, modern" Italian-Spanish cuisine (including "outstanding" tapas) and "fabulous drinks" are offered in a setting that's "hip" "yet still intimate", with large windows that allow guests to "enjoy the activity in the Square" outside; some say the "service is slightly rushed", but at least the "efficient" staffers are "among the friendliest" in town; P.S. its "great patio" affords "awesome people-watching."

U Modré Kachnicky *Czech* 23 | 23 | 21 | E

Little Quarter | Nebovidská 6 | (420) 257-320-308 | fax 257-317-427

U Modré Kachnicky II *Czech*

Old Town | Michalská 16 | (420) 224-213-418

www.umodrekachnicky.cz

"Those wanting to taste the true local flavor" of Prague "must stop" for a "cultural experience" 'At the Blue Duckling' (the English translation of this "quaint" and "cozy" Little Quarter "stalwart's" name); like "someone's grandmother's house", its "rustic" rooms are "quirky" but "comfortable", providing a "charming" setting in which to "relish" "exceedingly well-done" "homestyle Czech cooking" with "an emphasis on game" and "regional specialties", proffered by a "warm, gracious" staff; N.B. there's a newer offshoot in the Old Town.

U Modré Ruze *Czech/International* 24 21 22 E

Old Town | Rytírská 16 | (420) 224-225-873 | fax 224-222-623 | www.umodreruze.cz

"Step down into" the "lovely subterranean setting" of this "first-class establishment" (whose name means 'At The Blue Rose') "located in a 15th-century cellar" in Old Town, where "authentic Czech cuisine" and some International offerings are backed up by a "small but reliable wine list" with "good [domestic] selections" at "moderate prices"; the "charming" barrel-vaulted stone walls lend "a medieval feel" to the setting, which is made all the more "romantic" by "a great piano player."

U Pinkasu *Czech* 20 14 15 M

New Town | Jungmannovo námestí 16 | (420) 221-111-150 | fax 221-111-153 | www.upinkasu.cz

"Drop in for" "huge portions" of "delicious, home-cooked", "folksy" fare from a "classic Czech" menu, washed down with "ample draughts of highly regarded [native] beer", at this New Town outpost of "authentic Prague" that was "supposedly the first bar to sell Pilsner Urquell" when it opened back in 1843; the service is "standard" and the decor "old", but "rubbing elbows with the friendly locals" makes for a "pleasant" atmosphere.

U Vladare ◐ *Czech/International* 21 18 19 M

Little Quarter | Maltézské námestí 10 | (420) 257-534-121 | fax 257-532-926 | www.uvladare.cz

"Near the Charles Bridge" in the Little Quarter, this "charming" venue offering "excellent" Czech-International cuisine occupies "one of the oldest restaurant spaces in Prague", having been home to various eating establishments since 1776; perhaps the "service is not the best", but at least the staff is "friendly" and you can choose between three settings - the cozy antiques-filled dining room, the low-ceilinged wine cellar or the earthy club area.

U Zlaté Hrušky *Czech/International* 24 23 21 M

Castle Quarter | Nový svet 3 | (420) 220-514-778 | fax 233-085-412 | www.uzlatehrusky.cz

"A golden find", this "cozy, quaint" "sleeper a little off the beaten track" in the Castle Quarter, "on a beautifully picturesque and quiet cobbled street", boasts a "menu offering traditional Czech food" (including "wonderful game and fish") as well as some International fare; the "pleasantly furnished, comfortable" interior "immediately transports one to another century", and is peopled by "lots of locals", all enjoying the "authentic" cuisine and "gracious service."

V Zátiší *Czech/International* 25 20 23 E

Old Town | Liliová 1 | (420) 222-221-155 | fax 222-220-629 | www.zatisigroup.cz

Think all Czech "cuisine is heavy"? - you'll "think again" after sampling the "excellent local specialties" "exquisitely cooked" with an International, "modern take" at this "lovely restaurant" "just off Betlemska Square" in the Old Town; its "feasts are fit for bohemian royalty" thanks to "creative" cuisine, "first-rate wines", "impeccable service" and an "intimate" setting; a few feel "there are equally good places" charging "much less money", but most insist it's "a truly wonderful dining experience" worthy of "a prompt return visit."

Zlatá Praha *Czech/International* 20 22 22 E

Old Town | InterContinental Praha | námestí Curieovych 43/5 | (420) 296-631-111 | fax 224-811-216 | www.icprague.com

Perched atop the InterContinental Praha, this Czech-International offers a "fabulous view" of the Jewish Quarter and the Old Town, as well as "professional service" from a "cultivated" staff; while many "gourmets enjoy" its fare, those who feel the food is "expensive for what it is" and "not as impressive as" the "absolutely beautiful" panoramic vista advise that there are "more charming" places "just around the corner."

Other Noteworthy Places

ADA *Czech/French*
Hotel Hoffmeister | Pod Bruskou 7 | (420) 251-017-133 | fax 251-017-120 | www.hoffmeister.cz

Amici Miei *Italian*
Vezenská 5 | (420) 224-816-688 | fax 224-812-577 | www.amicimiei.cz

Aromi *Italian/Seafood*
Mánesova 78/442 | (420) 222-713-222 | fax 222-713-444 | www.aromi.cz

Box Block *International*
Carlo IV | Senovázné námestí 13 | (420) 224-593-040 | fax 224-593-000 | www.boscolohotels.com

Casanova *Italian/Seafood*
Saská 3 | (420) 257-535-127 | www.casanovarestaurant.cz

Cervená Tabulka *Czech/International*
Lodecká 4 | (420) 224-810-401 | www.cervenatabulka.cz

Divinis Wine Bar *Italian*
Týnská 19 | (420) 224-808-318 | fax 224-808-318

Gourmet Club *Czech/International*
Hotel Palace | Panská 12 | (420) 224-093-110 | fax 224-221-240 | www.palacehotel.cz

Hanavský Pavilon *International*
Letenské Sady 173 | (420) 233-323-641 | fax 233-323-641 | www.hanavskypavilon.cz

La Bodeguita del Medio ◐ *Cuban*
Kaprova 5 | (420) 224-813-922 | fax 224-814-819 | www.bodeguita.cz

La Casa Argentina ◐ *Argentinean/International*
Dlouhá 35/ 730 | (420) 222-311-512 | fax 222-313-096 | www.argentinarestaurant.cz

La Veranda *International*
Elišky Krásnohorské 2/10 | (420) 224-814-733 | fax 224-814-596 | www.laveranda.cz

Le Papillon *French/International*
Hotel Le Palais | U Zvonarky 1 | (420) 234-634-111 | fax 234-634-635 | www.palaishotel.cz

Les Moules ◐ *Belgian*
Parízská 19/203 | (420) 222-315-022 | fax 222-315-029 | www.lesmoules.cz

PRAGUE

Le Terroir *French/International*
Vejvodova 1 | (420) 222-220-260 | www.leterroir.cz

Nostress *French/Asian*
Dušní 10 | (420) 222-317-007 | fax 222-317-004 | www.nostress.cz

Restaurante Brasileiro ◐ *Brazilian*
U Radnice 8/13 | (420) 224-234-474 | fax 224-234-480
Slovanský Dum | Na Príkope 22 | (420) 221-451-200 | fax 221-451-201
www.ambi.cz

Resto Café Le Patio *French/International*
Národní 22 | (420) 224-934-375 | fax 224-934-549 | www.patium.com

Sushi Bar, The *Japanese*
Zborovská 49 | (420) 603-244-882 | www.sushi.cz

Svatá Klára *International*
U Trojského zámku 35 | (420) 233-540-173 | fax 233-358-113 |
www.svataklara.cz

Tokyo *Japanese/Korean*
Srbská 2 | (420) 233-326-670 | fax 233-326-794

U Patrona *French/International*
Drazického námestí 4 | (420) 257-530-725 | fax 257-530-723 |
www.upatrona.cz

U Zlaté Studne *Czech/International*
Hotel U Zlaté Studne | U Zlaté Studne 166/4 | (420) 257-533-322 |
fax 257-535-044 | www.zlatastudna.cz

Zvonice ◐ *Czech/French*
Jindrišská vez | Jindrišská ulice | (420) 224-220-009 | fax 224 220 028 |
www.restaurantzvonice.cz

Rome

TOP FOOD RANKING

	Restaurant	Cuisine
26	Vivendo	Italian
	La Pergola	Italian/Mediterranean
	Alberto Ciarla	Seafood
	La Rosetta*	Seafood
	Agata e Romeo	Roman
	Mirabelle	Italian
	Sora Lella*	Roman
25	Al Vero Girarrosto	Tuscan
	Quinzi e Gabrieli	Seafood
	Antico Arco	Italian
	L'Altro Mastai*	Mediterranean
	Baby	Neapolitan/Med.
24	Il San Lorenzo	Neapolitan/Seafood
	Il Convivio Troiani	Italian
	Piperno	Roman/Jewish
	Da Tullio	Tuscan
	I Sofa' di Via Giulia	Italian/Mediterranean
	Antica Pesa	Roman
	Camponeschi	Italian
	Vecchia Roma	Roman
	Imàgo	International/Italian
23	La Terrazza	Italian/Mediterranean
	Nino	Tuscan
	Brunello	Italian/Mediterranean
	Romolo nel Giardino	Roman
	Checchino dal 1887	Roman
	Ròmilo*	Roman
	Il Matriciano	Roman
	Al Ceppo	Roman/Marchigiana
	Al Moro	Italian
	Acquolina Hostaria	Italian/Seafood
	La Campana	Roman
	Il Bacaro	Italian
	Paris*	Roman/Jewish
	Ambasciata d'Abruzzo	Roman/Abruzzese
	Checco er Carretiere	Roman
	Dal Bolognese	Emilian
	Colline Emiliane	Emilian
	Costanza	Italian
	Al Presidente	Roman
22	Sabatini	Roman
	Taberna de' Gracchi	Italian
	Hostaria dell'Orso	Italian
	Sapori del Lord Byron*	Italian/Seafood
	La Carbonara	Roman

* Indicates a tie with restaurant above

	Le Jardin de Russie	Italian/Mediterranean
	Crudo	Mediterranean
	Da Alceste al Buongusto	Seafood
	Da Fortunato al Pantheon	Roman
	I Due Ladroni	Neapolitan
21	Girarrosto Fiorentino	Tuscan
	Pierluigi	Italian
	Al Bric	Italian
20	Green T.	Chinese
	Otello alla Concordia	Roman
	Giggetto al Portico d'Ottavia	Roman/Jewish
19	'Gusto	International
	Les Etoiles	Italian
	Casina Valadier	Italian
18	Café de Paris	Italian
	Harry's Bar	International/Med.

NEW Acquolina Hostaria ◐ Ⓢ *Italian/Seafood* 23 | 21 | 21 | E

Flaminia | Via Antonio Serra 60 | (39) 06-333-7192 | fax 06-333-7192 | www.acquolinahostaria.com

The Troiani brothers of Rome's highly rated Il Convivio Troiani have opened this new Italian seafooder and "'in' place for locals" in Flaminia, a trendy section north of the city center; "excellent fish" dishes based on the "freshest" catch of the day are treated in both traditional and "imaginative" ways and backed up by an "expansive wine" list; the split-level space is contemporary, but some prefer "eating outside" on the leafy terrace.

Agata e Romeo Ⓢ *Roman* 26 | 22 | 24 | VE

Esquilino | Via Carlo Alberto 45 | (39) 06-446-6115 | fax 06-446-5842 | www.agataeromeo.it

"Superior ingredients" help make for "brilliant" "creative" interpretations of Roman cuisine at this tiny, "family-run delight" where wife Agata Parisella is the chef, husband Romeo Caraccio is the host-sommelier and daughter Mariantonietta delivers the delicious goods; "a perfect meal" is complemented by an "outstanding wine list" and a "chic but cozy setting"; beside the expensive tabs, the only downside is the near-the-train-station location in Esquilino; N.B. closed Saturday-Sunday.

Alberto Ciarla ◐ Ⓢ *Seafood* 26 | 20 | 24 | VE

Trastevere | Piazza San Cosimato 40 | (39) 06-581-8668 | fax 06-5833-0162 | www.albertociarla.com

The "food practically flops off your plate and into your mouth it's so fresh" at this "great", old famous seafooder that specializes in raw fish (*crudo*) in Trastevere; some find the decor - black walls, sofas and mirrors - "tacky", but proponents point out the space has been updated and insist "if you get the right spot it can be romantic" or head for the outdoor area.

Al Bric ◐ Ⓜ *Italian* 21 | 19 | 18 | E

Campo dei Fiore | Via del Pellegrino 51/52 | (39) 06-687-9533 | www.albric.it

"It's expensive but it has one of the best cheese selections in town" along with a "spectacular wine list" (over 1,000 labels) is what surveyors say about this "creative" Italian near Campo dei Fiore owned by wine producer and importer Roberto Marchetti; the viniferous theme continues with the wine-crate-covered walls.

Al Ceppo M *Roman/Marchigiana* 23 | 18 | 21 | E

Parioli | Via Panama 2 | (39) 06-841-9696 | fax 06-8530-1370 | www.ristorantealceppo.it

At this "class act" in chic residential Parioli frequented by "upscale locals", particularly for Sunday lunch, the "excellent" menu is a mix of two regions, Rome and the Marches; for those who find the decor tired, there's seating on a veranda facing a garden courtyard.

Al Moro *Italian* 23 | 17 | 20 | E

Trevi Fountain | Vicolo delle Bollette 13 | (39) 06-678-3495 | fax 06-6994-0736

A former Fellini haunt and still a "favorite watering hole for Rome's film moguls, pols and bigwigs in general" is this 1929 Italian "in a charming location in an alley near the Trevi Fountain"; "high-quality" ingredients, a "killer wine list", "friendly service" and a "clublike atmosphere" make it "an all-around great choice."

Al Presidente M *Roman* 23 | 18 | 21 | M

Trevi Fountain | Via in Arcione 95 | (39) 06-679-7342 | fax 06-679-7342 | www.alpresidente.it

Just down the street from the Trevi Fountain is this long-standing chef-owned spot, which offers "delicious", reasonably priced Roman dishes, seafood specialties and an extensive wine list; it's "pleasant" to dine here, especially when you can sit outside on the piazza and get a glimpse of the back of the Quirinal Palace, Italy's White House and the site that inspired the restaurant's name.

Al Vero Girarrosto Toscano *Tuscan* 25 | 20 | 23 | E

Via Veneto | Via Campania 29 | (39) 06-482-1899 | fax 39-06-482-1899 | www.alverogirarrostotoscano.com

This "wonderful" Tuscan right behind the Via Veneto and only steps from Villa Borghese is "a true classic" that's been serving "abundant antipasti" and "the best steak Florentine" since 1969; "gracious service" and a "warm" and "cozy" basement setting combine to make customers feel "at home the minute they walk in."

Ambasciata d'Abruzzo *Roman/Abruzzese* 23 | 18 | 20 | M

Parioli | Via Pietro Tacchini 26 | (39) 06-807-8256 | fax 06-807-4964 | www.ambasciatadiabruzzo.com

"A bit off the beaten path" in Parioli, the upscale residential and embassy area, is this "nothing-fancy-just-plain-good" Roman-Abruzzese with "extra-generous portions", beginning with "awesome antipasti" and going on to the likes of "silken pastas" and roast suckling pig; "warm service", a "pleasant", rambling setting and "prices that won't break the bank" bring in locals, tourists and some Hollywood celebs alike.

Antica Pesa *Roman* 24 | 20 | 20 | E

Trastevere | Via Garibaldi 18 | (39) 06-580-9236 | fax 06-5833-1518 | www.anticapesa.it

"Be sure to bring an empty stomach" to this "terrific" Roman "taste treat" in Trastevere; though it dates back to 1922, its menu focuses on "excellent" modern interpretations of traditional ingredients like lamb; the "wonderfully romantic" setting - contemporary frescoes on the walls, a fireplace, enchanting garden and exceptional wine cellar - has become a celebrity hang since its recent association with Robert De Niro's Tribeca Film Festival and the new Rome Film Fest.

Antico Arco ◐ⓢ *Italian* 25 | 20 | 23 | E

Gianicolo | Piazzale Aurelio 7 | (39) 06-581-5274 | fax 06-581-5274 | www.anticoarco.it

It's "off the beaten path", up in the Janiculum Hill near the American Academy, but the "young and the beautiful are all here" at this popular, "innovative" Italian with "decently priced" "divine food", "exceptional wines" and "gracious service"; it's "minimalist in a NYC Village kind of way", there's a "hip vibe" and the experience is "special from entrance to exit."

Baby Ⓜ *Neapolitan/Mediterranean* 25 | 24 | 25 | E

Parioli | Aldrovandi Palace Hotel | Via Ulisse Aldrovandi 15 | (39) 06-321-6126 | fax 06-322-1435 | www.aldrovandi.com

This "great" Neapolitan-Med in the Aldrovandi Palace Hotel in Parioli is the baby of star chef Alfonso Iaccarino, whose celebrated flagship restaurant, Don Alfonso 1890, is near the Amalfi Coast; "excellent", "creative" cuisine is "enriched by the finest ingredients" and served by a "great staff" in a "fantastic setting", whose "crisp white decor" and "view of a swimming pool" "make it feel like the Caribbean" and a "great date place."

NEW Brunello Lounge & Restaurant Ⓜ *Italian/Mediterranean* 23 | 22 | 22 | VE

Via Veneto | Regina Hotel Baglioni | Via Veneto 70/A | (39) 06-4890-2867 | fax 06-4201-2130 | www.brunellorestaurant.com

This very *Dolce Vita* new venue in the Via Veneto's Regina Hotel Baglioni is named after the statusy Tuscan red so it's no surprise the "wines are wonderful" in both the lounge ("a must for checking out the sophisticated bar scene in Rome") and the jacket-required Italian-Mediterranean restaurant, which is turning out "elegant" cuisine; admirers find the decor "unique", while critics call it "strange", but all are in accord about the "high prices", which seem to suit the international jet-set crowd it's catering to.

Café de Paris ◐ *Italian* 18 | 20 | 18 | E

Via Veneto | Via Vittorio Veneto 90 | (39) 06-481-5631 | fax 06-4201-1090 | www.cafedeparis-roma.com

When you want "atmosphere", sit in the glassed-in veranda "with a glass or two of wine" and "watch the world go by" at this Italian on the Via Veneto, across from the Excelsior Hotel, that was once the headquarters of la dolce vita; of course the "lackluster" "food isn't as fabulous as the location" or the "people-watching", but new owners may remedy that.

Camponeschi ◐ⓢ *Italian* 24 | 23 | 23 | VE

Piazza Farnese | Piazza Farnese 50 | (39) 06-687-4927 | fax 06-686-5244 | www.ristorantecamponeschi.it

"*Bella Italia* at its very best" is found at this "top-class", "they-do-everything-well", expensive Italian facing Michelangelo's Palazzo Farnese; there's "excellent food", "superb service" and the "elegant setting", with hand-painted boiserie, is one of the most "romantic" rooms in Rome, but sitting outside looking at the exquisite square is also appealing; N.B. their wine bar next door serves the family's own wines along with about 500 others.

Casina Valadier *Italian* | 19 | 23 | 21 | VE

Villa Borghese | Piazza Bucarest | (39) 06-6992-2090 | fax 06-679-1280 | www.casinavaladier.it

"One of the most breathtaking views of Rome" can be had from the terrace of this three-level, 1850 Italian on Villa Borghese's Pincio Hill that was recently restored and reopened after closing a decade ago; "quality food" is served in an elegant, "atmospheric" setting with ancient brick walls and frescoed ceilings.

Checchino dal 1887 ◐ S M *Roman* | 23 | 17 | 21 | E

Testaccio | Via di Monte Testaccio 30 | (39) 06-574-6318 | fax 06-574-3816 | www.checchino-dal-1887.com

"If you have intestinal fortitude" and don't find offal awful, this 1887 Roman in Testaccio, the old slaughterhouse area, may be for you; the fifth generation of the Mariani family cooks "wonderfully prepared", lightened versions of "traditional" dishes that often include organ meats or cast-off animal parts (like the tail); a "fantastic wine list" and "trip-back-in-time setting" complete the earthy experience.

Checco er Carretiere *Roman* | 23 | 20 | 21 | E

Trastevere | Via Benedetta 10-13 | (39) 06-580-0983 | fax 06-588-4282

Owned by the Porcelli family since 1935, this "big, bustling and boisterous" Roman in the heart of Trastevere serves up "solid" "authentic" dishes like deep-fried vegetables and roast lamb; the rustic, two-story setting is "warm" and "homey", but alfresco fans prefer the "delightful patio in nice weather."

Colline Emiliane M *Emilian* | 23 | 13 | 20 | M

Trevi Fountain | Via degli Avignonesi 22 | (39) 06-481-7538 | fax 06-481-7538

For decades locals have been eating at this small, family-run Emilian near the Trevi Fountain because of its "delicious comfort food" and freshly baked desserts; it's far from "fancy", but it's "definitely a bargain."

Costanza S *Italian* | 23 | 20 | 22 | M

Campo dei Fiore | Piazza del Paradiso 63-65 | (39) 06-686-1717 | fax 06-686-5167 | www.hostariacostanza.com

At this cavernous, brick-walled, vaulted stalwart in Campo dei Fiore, "a food-crazy part of the city", the moderately priced menu spans many regions of Italy and the food is "excellent"; but insiders insist its interior can't be beat for its "wonderful" atmosphere, for you are sitting in a portion of the ancient ruins of the Theatre of Pompeii, circa 63 B.C.

Crudo ◐ *Mediterranean* | 22 | 20 | 21 | E

Campo dei Fiore | Via degli Specchi 5 | (39) 06-683-8989 | fax 06-683-8952 | www.crudoroma.it

"Don't believe the name - there's nothing crude about this" "hot" Campo dei Fiore Mediterranean whose name translates as 'raw', which is how many of the "excellent" meat, fish and vegetable dishes are prepared "from great local ingredients", while others are marinated or barely seared; a "friendly staff" presides over the minimalist upstairs restaurant, while the downstairs lounge draws a cocktail-crowd with its cushy leather sofas.

Da Alceste al Buongusto ◐ Ⓢ *Seafood* 22 | 20 | 19 | E

Piazza Navona | Corso Rinascimento 70 | (39) 06-686-1312 | fax 06-686-1312

This seafood specialist in a "good location" just outside of Piazza Navona ("but without the confusion that's there") receives a fresh catch early every evening from Anzio, a port an hour south of Rome, where the original Alceste has been the reigning piscine palace for 50 years; the "simple" bright white interior is welcoming and there's also sidewalk seating.

Da Fortunato al Pantheon Ⓢ *Roman* 22 | 19 | 21 | E

Pantheon | Via del Pantheon 55 | (39) 06-679-2788 | fax 06-679-3683 | www.ristorantefortunato.it

For over 30 years, politicians and tourists in-the-know ("it's a stop of mine every time") have been frequenting this "dependable" Roman in a "great location in the heart" of the city; there are four wood-paneled dining rooms, but a seat on the little patio outside will provide you with a glimpse of the glorious Pantheon.

Dal Bolognese Ⓜ *Emilian* 23 | 19 | 20 | E

Piazza del Popolo | Piazza del Popolo 1 | (39) 06-361-1426 | fax 06-322-2799

"All of Rome passes through" this 65-year-old Emilian "classic" and its alfresco patio "perfectly positioned" on the Piazza del Popolo; "great" traditional food like *tagliatelle al ragu* and the trolley of boiled meats merit almost as much attention as the "wonderful people-watching"; a few snipe that "service can be snippy", but for most it's a "must."

Da Tullio Ⓢ *Tuscan* 24 | 18 | 23 | E

Piazza Barberini | Via San Nicola da Tolentino 26 | (39) 06-474-5560 | fax 06-481-8564 | www.tullioristorante.it

"Simple" Tuscan near Piazza Barberini that's "been in business forever for good reason" - "well-prepared" "authentic" dishes like *ribollita* and *bistecca alla fiorentina,* which are complemented by a "great" regional wine list.

Giggetto al Portico d'Ottavia Ⓜ *Roman/Jewish* 20 | 15 | 17 | M

The Ghetto | Via del Portico d'Ottavia 21A | (39) 06-686-1105 | fax 06-683-2106 | www.giggettoalportico.com

"Authentic Roman-Jewish soul food" like the famous deep-fried artichokes and stuffed zucchini blossoms is found at this third-generation, family-run, moderately priced trattoria located in the Ghetto; the rambling rooms are warm and rustic, but many feel the best seat in the house is outside, with a view of the ruins of Ottavia's portico.

Girarrosto Fiorentino *Tuscan* 21 | 21 | 22 | E

Via Veneto | Via Sicilia 46 | (39) 06-4288 0660 | fax 06-4201 0078 | www.girarrostofiorentino.it

This long-standing Tuscan is known for its "simple and tasty" *salumi* and T-bone steak, which are complemented by an exceptional wine list heavy on Chiantis and super-Tuscans; an "attentive staff" presides over a warm, wood-paneled setting that is "popular" with visitors from Via Veneto's nearby luxury hotels.

Green T. ⊠ *Chinese* 20 21 16 E

Pantheon | Via del Pié di Marmo 28 | (39) 06-679-8628 | fax 06-679-8628 | www.green-tea.it

Rome's first Chinese for gourmets has debuted in a *centralissimo* position between the Pantheon and Piazza Venezia; the food is "sophisticated" and the co-owner is an Italian sommelier who has managed to match his select list of wines from The Boot with his Asian wife's culinary culture; "service could be better", but the "super-gorgeous" setting - several sexily lit small rooms with oriental antiques, as well as a tiny Zen garden courtyard - "stylishly" distracts.

'Gusto ◐ *International* 19 20 17 M

Via del Corso | Piazza Augusto Imperatore 9 | (39) 06-322-6273 | fax 06-3265-2829 | www.gusto.it

Still "trendy" with a "hip, young vibe", this "good" International off Via del Corso lets you choose a food for your mood; it's a complex that contains an upscale fusion restaurant, a pizzeria with a salad bar at lunch, an *osteria* with Roman specialties and tapas portions, a wine bar with jazz, a gourmet shop/*enotecca* and the latest addition - a cafe/bar featuring only fish and vegetables with all-day takeout; plus there are kitchen and cheese boutiques; it's "crowded" and service can be "marginal", but enthusiasts urge "go for the 'Gusto."

Harry's Bar ◐⊠ *International/Mediterranean* 18 21 20 VE

Via Veneto | Via Veneto 150 | (39) 06-484-643 | fax 06-488-3117 | www.harrysbar.it

"Bellini, panini and people-watching on the Via Veneto" are the point at this "clubby", 1958 International-Med "watering hole" "where you can feel the history"; it's "overpriced", "there are loads of Yanks" and some say "it's lost some of its charm", but most maintain "everyone has to go here at least once just to say they've been."

Hostaria dell'Orso ◐⊠ *Italian* 22 23 22 E

Piazza Navona | Via dei Soldati 25C | (39) 06-6830-1192 | fax 06-6821-7063 | www.hdo.it

Celeb chef Gualtiero Marchesi's Italian in a historic 15th-century building where beautiful frescoes mix with more modern decor is well-located near Piazza Navona; fans cite "excellent" cuisine and "great service" and say the "piano bar" adds to the "enchanted evening", but detractors decry the "overwrought, overpriced food."

I Due Ladroni ◐⊠Ⓜ *Neapolitan* 22 19 20 E

Piazza Navona | Piazza Nicosia 24 | (39) 06-686-1013 | fax 06-689-6299 | www.dueladroni.com

One of the few restaurants in Rome "open late for post-performance dining" is this Neapolitan known for the "freshest, simplest seafood" and "homemade mozzarella"; the wood-paneled interior with antique mirrors is "charming and romantic", but the outdoor seating on the Piazza Nicosia would be more pleasant if it weren't also used as a car park.

Il Bacaro ⊠ *Italian* 23 19 20 M

Pantheon | Via degli Spagnoli 27 | (39) 06-687-2554 | fax 06-687-2554 | www.ilbacaro.com

"Nothing says romance like a candlelit dinner by the Pantheon" and that's what you'll experience at this "cozy", "intimate", ivy-covered creative Italian in a 16th-century building with a few tables outside; it's the "perfect spot to take your Italian or American sweetheart", though a few of the jaded jeer it's been discovered by "tourists looking for a bargain."

Il Convivio Troiani ☒ *Italian* 24 | 22 | 23 | VE

Piazza Navona | Vicolo dei Soldati 31 | (39) 06-686-9432 | fax 06-686-9432 | www.ilconviviotroiani.com

The brothers Troiani "have consistently had one of Rome's best restaurants" is what surveyors say about this Italian near Piazza Navona; "outstanding" traditional and creative dishes, "attentive service" and a "classy", "soigné setting" - three rooms with frescoes or paintings - add up to a "pleasurable" evening; of course, the bill also adds up to "very expensive."

Il Matriciano *Roman* 23 | 16 | 20 | M

Prati | Via dei Gracchi 55 | (39) 06-321-2327 | fax 06-321-2327

Some say the "best" moderately priced place "for a big plate of pasta for lunch" is this sprawling, "popular" Roman in Prati, very close to the Vatican, where the signature *alla 'amatriciana* is the order of the day and used to draw the likes of Marcello Mastroianni; there are five rustic, wood-paneled rooms to choose from, but most are happiest eating outside; N.B. closed Wednesdays in winter, Saturdays in summer.

NEW **Il San Lorenzo** ◐ *Neapolitan/Seafood* 24 | 20 | 21 | E

Campo dei Fiore | Via dei Chiavari 4/5 | (39) 06-686-5097 | fax 06-686-5097

This new Neapolitan seafood specialist "conveniently located" near Campo dei Fiore "wins a lot of points" - there's "excellent food", "respectful service" and "very pretty" multilevel dining rooms dotted with modern art, as well as an oyster-shell-studded bar where you can sip a glass of champers with your crustaceans; no wonder most maintain "it's a must when you are in Rome."

Imàgo *International/Italian* 24 | - | 25 | VE
(fka Hassler Rooftop)

Trinitá dei Monti | Hotel Hassler | Trinità dei Monti 6 | (39) 06-699-34726 | fax 06-678-9991 | www.hotelhasslerroma.com

"A must for everyone who can afford it" declare devotees of the Hotel Hassler's International-Italian with "a commanding rooftop view of the Eternal City" from its "perch atop the Spanish steps"; "delicious" "creative food, an impressive wine list" and "wonderful service" also add to the "romantic", "rarefied experience"; it's a "super-swank" hang for "the glitterati", so be prepared for "over-the-top prices for an over-the-top" evening; N.B. a post-Survey redo and name change make for a more modern and luminous setting but the rest remains the same.

NEW **I Sofa' di Via Giulia** ◐ *Italian/Mediterranean* 24 | 22 | 22 | E

Piazza Farnese | St. George Hotel | Via Giulia 62 | (39) 06-686-611 | fax 06-686-1230 | www.stgeorgehotel.it

"Great food" is found at this Italian-Mediterranean in the new luxury St. George Hotel, "excellently located" on central Rome's loveliest street, Via Giulia; a "wonderful staff" presides over an elegant setting that mixes minimalist modern decor with classic touches in travertine, plus there's a tranquil courtyard garden for warm-weather dining.

	FOOD	DECOR	SERVICE	COST
La Campana	23	16	20	M
La Carbonara	22	19	20	M
L'Altro Mastai	25	24	24	E
La Pergola	26	26	26	VE
La Rosetta	26	20	23	VE
La Terrazza	23	26	24	VE

La Campana M *Roman*

Piazza Navona | Vicolo della Campana 18 | (39) 06-686-7820 | fax 06-686-7820

It's a good thing "the passage of time isn't traceable" at this "simple", "solid" Roman near Piazza Navona that started as a pilgrim's canteen in 1527; the clientele is still coming for moderately priced "authentic" fare that includes all the local specialties, from A(rtichokes) to Z(abaglione), served by a "brusque but knowledgeable staff" in a typical, brightly lit trattoria setting.

La Carbonara *Roman*

Campo dei Fiore | Campo dei Fiori 23 | (39) 06-686 4783 | fax 06-9727 4086 | www.la-carbonara.it

A "lively and loud" crowd convenes at this Roman institution in a "great location" right on Campo dei Fiore for "good" "traditional", moderately priced dishes like the namesake *penne alla carbonara*; while most of your fellow diners will be tourists, grab a seat outside to check out the not-to-be-missed market setting and "passing scene."

L'Altro Mastai S M *Mediterranean*

Piazza Navona | Via Giraud 53 | (39) 06-6830-1296 | fax 06-686-1303 | www.laltromastai.it

Supporters of rising star chef Fabio Baldassarre, a former protégé of La Pergola's acclaimed Heinz Beck, say his four-year-old Mediterranean near Piazza Navona is among "the best in Rome today"; a "formal" setting with modern art, marble and mosaics is the backdrop for his brand of innovative fine dining; N.B. a move to a new location at Via delle Terme di Traiano, 4a, in the Colosseum area, is scheduled for winter 2008.

La Pergola S M *Italian/Mediterranean*

Monte Mario | Cavalieri Hilton | Via Alberto Cadlolo 101 | (39) 06-3509-2152 | fax 06-3509-2165 | www.cavalieri-hilton.it

"A German chef in an American hotel serving Italian-Med food results in one of the finest dining experiences imaginable" assert admirers of Heinz Beck and his "exceptional cuisine" at the Cavalieri Hilton; there's also an "impressive wine list", "outstanding staff" and "beautiful" rooftop room, which provides "an amazing view of Rome"; a few mutter about its "out-of-the-way" Monte Mario locale and "tad-over-the-top" ways – there's gold cutlery and a "mineral water menu with 40 choices" – but they're outvoted.

La Rosetta S *Seafood*

Pantheon | Via della Rosetta 8 | (39) 06-686-1002 | fax 06-6821-5116 | www.larosetta.com

For "mind-blowing" fish with a Sicilian accent, finatics urge you to try this family-owned stalwart with a "wonderful location near the Pantheon", where a "solicitous staff" presides over a "cozy, convivial" setting with frescoes; "prices are insane", but that doesn't prevent a jet-set crowd from streaming through the door.

La Terrazza *Italian/Mediterranean*

Trinitá dei Monti | Hotel Eden | Via Ludovisi 49 | (39) 06-4781-2752 | fax 06-481-4473

There's a "romantic" and "unbelievable" "knockout view of Rome" from this Italian-Mediterranean on the Hotel Eden's rooftop; there's also "wonderful food, wine and service" as well as a "lovely piano bar with great cocktails", so "although prices are as lofty" as the vista, most maintain "it's worth the splurge."

Le Jardin de Russie *Italian/Mediterranean* 22 | 27 | 22 | VE

Piazza del Popolo | Hotel de Russie | Via del Babuino 9 | (39) 06-3288-8870 | fax 06-3288-8888 | www.roccofortehotels.com

"A private courtyard garden retreat populated by celebs" is flourishing at this Italian-Mediterranean in the "chic" Hotel de Russie; the "pricey" food is "surprisingly good", plus "it's a perfect people-watching" and "evening-cocktails" spot in a "stunning setting" "just steps from Piazza del Popolo."

Les Etoiles *Italian* 19 | 24 | 18 | VE

Prati | Hotel Atlante Star | Via Vitelleschi 34 | (39) 06-689-3434 | fax 06-687-2300 | www.atlantehotels.com

"The terrace, the stars, the eye-candy staff - now this is a great place" enthuse aesthetes about this Italian on the Hotel Atlante Star's rooftop; but the practical point out while the food is "good", it can't compete with the "lovely view of Rome and St. Peter's dome."

Mirabelle *Italian* 26 | 24 | 24 | VE

Via Veneto | Hotel Splendide Royal | Via di Porta Pinciana 14 | (39) 06-4216-8838 | fax 06-4216-8870 | www.mirabelle.it

An "absolutely spectacular" "view over Rome" and the Villa Medici gardens "caps what is an excellent evening" sigh sybarites about this Italian atop the Hotel Splendide Royal; chef Giuseppe Sestito's "superb" cuisine, "first-class service" and a "beautiful" room make for a "perfect" and "extremely expensive" "marriage."

Nino *Tuscan* 23 | 17 | 21 | E

Spanish Steps | Via Borgognona 11 | (39) 06-679-5676 | fax 06-678-6752

Mercifully, "nothing has changed for years" at this 1939 "gem" that "still delivers" "in the heart of Rome's shopping area", near the Spanish Steps; the "classic" Tuscan dishes are "delicious" (the house wine and extra-virgin olive oil are also produced on the owner's estate in that region), and the overall "old-world ambiance" is "warm, welcoming" and "best suited to lunch."

Otello alla Concordia 🅢 *Roman* 20 | 14 | 18 | M

Spanish Steps | Via della Croce 81 | (39) 06-679-1178 | fax 06-6992-5200 | www.otelloallaconcordia.com

"Chaos reigns" at this typical "family-run" trattoria that's "flooded with tourists" along with natives and "centrally located" near the Spanish Steps; "reliable" Roman fare and "moderate prices" have made it a "perennial favorite" since 1948.

Paris 🅜 *Roman/Jewish* 23 | 21 | 20 | M

Trastevere | Piazza San Callisto 7A | (39) 06-581-5378 | fax 06-581-5378 | www.ristoranteparis.com

"In the heart of Trastevere" is this "good" Roman-Jewish stalwart where "you can put together" a "classic" meal with dishes like lightly "fried zucchini flowers" and artichokes; "fair prices" and delightful alfresco dining add to the "pleasant experience."

Pierluigi ◑ [M] *Italian* — 21 | 16 | 18 | M

Campo dei Fiore | Piazza dé Ricci 144 | (39) 06-686-1302 | fax 06-6880-7879 | www.pierluigi.it

"Popular" and "always crowded", this 68-year-old Italian trattoria near the Campo dei Fiore features "simple" food and "decent prices"; to feel like a "true Roman" "eat outside" on the picturesque piazza.

Piperno [M] *Roman/Jewish* — 24 | 18 | 21 | E

The Ghetto | Monte de' Cenci 9 | (39) 06-6880-6629 | fax 06-6821-9595 | www.ristorantepiperno.it

"For the best fried artichokes and stuffed zucchini blossoms", "forget your cholesterol problems" and head for this 1860 Roman-Jewish "must" that's a "bit hard to find" in front of historic Palazzo Cenci in the Ghetto; the rooms are looking a "bit worn", but dining out on the small outdoor space on the piazza is pleasing.

Quinzi e Gabrieli [S] *Seafood* — 25 | 18 | 19 | VE

Pantheon | Via delle Coppelle 5/6 | (39) 06-687-9389 | fax 06-687-4940 | www.quinziegabrieli.it

"The freshest seafood money can buy in Rome" is found at this "fashionable" fish house, near the Pantheon, where "exquisite", "unbelievably expensive" dishes are served raw or lightly cooked at the table; a "serene" room is decorated with murals of three seaport cities, and there's also appealing outdoor eating for the alfresco-oriented.

Ròmilo [S] *Roman* — 23 | 20 | 20 | E

Campo Marzio | Via di Campo Marzio 13 | (39) 06-689-3499 | fax 06-689-3499

This "eclectic, excellent" Roman in Campo Marzio, which is "not far from Parliament", is popular with pols; an "enjoyable experience" can be had in the "plain but elegant" interior or out on the side terrace.

Romolo nel Giardino della Fornarina [M] *Roman* — 23 | 22 | 22 | E

Trastevere | Via di Porta Settimiana 8 | (39) 06-581-8284 | fax 06-581-3043 | www.romololafornarina.com

One of the most romantic "walled garden" terraces in the city is found at this "lovely", ivy-covered Roman in a 16th-century Trastevere building where Raphael's mistress, La Fornarina, once resided; today the original owner's daughter continues to cook the kind of "good" "traditional favorites" that first drew devotees 50 years ago.

Sabatini *Roman* — 22 | 21 | 21 | E

Trastevere | Piazza Santa Maria in Trastevere 13 | (39) 06-581-2026 | fax 06-589-8386

You "keep waiting for someone to yell cut" at this Roman "in a charming outdoor setting in Piazza Santa Maria" in Trastevere that's "like being in a movie", with "church bells, kids playing and older women strolling arm and arm"; pros praise its "consistently good" seafood pastas, but the disappointed declare it a "tourist trap."

Sapori del Lord Byron [S] *Italian/Seafood* — 22 | 25 | 23 | VE

Parioli | Hotel Lord Byron | Via Giuseppe de Notaris 5 | (39) 06-322-0404 | fax 06-322-0405 | www.lordbyronhotel.com

"Elegant, expensive and out of the way" sums up this Italian seafooder in the posh Hotel Lord Byron in residential Parioli; "very good" regional dishes like roast lamb with tomatoes, mint and pecorino cheese are served in an "intimate, impressive" setting that is frequented by local aristos and hotel guests.

Sora Lella ☒ *Roman* 26 | 20 | 21 | E

Isola Tiberina | Via di Ponte Quattro Capi 16 | (39) 06-686-1601 | fax 06-686-1601 | www.soralella.com

This long-standing, "family-run" Roman is set on Isola Tiberina, an island on the Tiber River, and features traditional dishes such as *rigatoni all'amatriciana* as well as more creative ones like leg of lamb with artichokes and pecorino cheese - all backed up by an extensive wine list.

Taberna de' Gracchi ☒ *Italian* 22 | 18 | 21 | E

Prati | Via dei Gracchi 266-268 | (39) 06-321-3126 | fax 06-322-1976 | www.tabernagracchi.com

Less than a 15-minute walk through Prati's shopping district from the Vatican is this "good solid" stalwart serving regional dishes and multiple tasting menus from all over Italy; there's one large, traditionally decorated dining room with wood paneling and white walls and several smaller ones for more intimate meals.

Vecchia Roma *Roman* 24 | 21 | 21 | E

The Ghetto | Piazza Campitelli 18 | (39) 06-686-4604 | fax 06-686-4604 | www.ristorantevecchiaroma.com

"To feel like you are really in Rome, come here" to this "wonderful" stalwart, on the edge of the Ghetto, and order "delicious" dishes like "grilled baby calamari"; the interior boasts "beautiful hand-painted murals", but romantics revel in the softly lit, "quiet" piazza where "eating outside is a joy"; N.B. closed Wednesdays.

Vivendo ☒ *Italian* 26 | 27 | 25 | VE

Piazza della Repubblica | St. Regis Grand Hotel | Via Vittorio Emanuele Orlando 3 | (39) 06-4709-2736 | fax 06-474-7307

Voted No. 1 for Food in Rome is this Italian in the "magnificent" St. Regis Grand Hotel, where "exceptional" "creative" cuisine is served by a "flawless staff" in a "lovely", quietly "lavish" room with satin fabrics and contemporary paintings; it all adds up to an experience that's quite expensive and "exquisite in every way."

Other Noteworthy Places

Andrea ☒ *Italian*

Via Sardegna 26-28 | (39) 06-482-1891 | fax 06-482-8151

Antico Bottaro *International/Italian*

Passeggiata di Ripetta 15 | (39) 06-323-6763 | fax 06-323-6763 | www.anticobottaro.it

Asador Café Veneto ◐ *Argentinean/Italian*

Via Vittorio Veneto 116 | (39) 06-482-7107 | fax 06-4201-1240

Charly's Sauciere ☒ *French*

Via San Giovanni in Laterano 270 | (39) 06-7049-5666 | fax 06-7707-7483

Cicilardone a Monte Caruso ☒ *Italian*

Via Farini 12 | (39) 06-483-549 | fax 06-484-436 | www.montecaruso.com

Coriolano *Italian*

Via Ancona 14 | (39) 06-4424-9863 | fax 06-4424-7724

El Toulá 🅂 *Venetian*
Via della Lupa 29B | (39) 06-687-3498 | fax 06-687-1115 | www.toula.it

George's 🅂 *International/Italian*
Via Marche 7 | (39) 06-4208-4575 | fax 06-4274-5204 | www.georgesristorante.it

Giardino dell'Uliveto *Mediterranean/Seafood*
Cavalieri Hilton | Via Alberto Cadlolo 101 | (39) 06-3509-2149 | fax 06-3509-2134 | www.cavalieri-hilton.it

Gli Angeletti *Italian*
Via dell'Angeletto 3A | (39) 06-474-3374 | www.gliangeletti.com

Il Pagliaccio 🅂 *Mediterranean*
Via dei Banchi Vecchi 129 | (39) 06-6880-9595 | fax 06-6821-7504 | www.ristoranteilpagliaccio.it

Il Simposio di Costantini 🅂 *Italian*
Piazza Cavour 16 | (39) 06-321-1502 | fax 06-3211-1131 | www.pierocostantini.it

Jeff Blynn's *American/Italian*
Viale Parioli 103C | (39) 06-807-0444 | fax 06-807-0444

La Cantina di Ninco Nanco ◐🄼 *Italian*
Via Pozzo delle Cornacchie 36 | (39) 06-6813-5558 | www.ninconanco.it

L'Acino Brillo 🄼 *Italian*
Piazza S. Eurosia 2 | (39) 06-513-7145 | fax 06-443-60682 | www.acinobrillo.it

L'Arcangelo 🅂 *Italian*
Via Giuseppe Giocchino Belli 59-61 | (39) 06-321-0992 | fax 06-321-0992 | www.ristorantidiroma.com/arcangelo

L'Ortica 🅂 *Italian*
Via Flaminia Vecchia 573 | (39) 06-333-8709 | fax 06-333-8709

Maremoto *Seafood*
Aleph Hotel | Via di San Basilio 15 | (39) 06-4229-0040 | fax 06-4229-0000 | www.boscolohotels.com

Papà Baccus 🅂 *Tuscan*
Via Toscana 36 | (39) 06-4274-2808 | fax 06-4201-0005 | www.papabaccus.com

Papà Giovanni 🅂 *Roman*
Via dei Sediari 4 | (39) 06-686-5308 | fax 06-686-5308 | www.ristorantepapagiovanni.it

Pauline Borghese *Italian*
Grand Hotel Parco Dei Principi | Via G. Frescobaldi 5 | (39) 06-854-421 | fax 06-884-5104 | www.parcodeiprincipi.com

Riccioli Café ◐🅂 *Mediterranean/Seafood*
Via delle Coppelle 13 | (39) 06-6821-0313 | fax 06-687-2595 | www.ricciolicafe.com

San Teodoro 🅂 *Italian*
Via dei Fienili 49-51 | (39) 06-678-0933 | fax 06-678-6965

Sette *Italian*
Radisson SAS Hotel | Via Filippo Turati 171 | (39) 06-444-841 | fax 06-4434-1396 | www.eshotel.it

Taverna Angelica *Italian*
Piazza Amerigo Capponi 6 | (39) 06-687-4514 | www.tavernaangelica.it

Trattoria [S] *Sicilian*
Via del Pozzo delle Cornacchie 25 | (39) 06-6830-1427 | fax 06-6821-5361 | www.ristorantetrattoria.it

Trattoria Jovinelli [S] *Italian*
Via Guglielmo Pepe 39 | (39) 06-4434-0940

Uno e Bino [M] *Italian*
Via degli Equi 58 | (39) 06-446-0702

FOOD DECOR SERVICE COST

Stockholm

TOP FOOD RANKING

	Restaurant	Cuisine
28	Paul & Norbert	French/Swedish
	Wedholms Fisk	Swedish/Seafood
27	F12	International
26	Lux Stockholm	Swedish/International
	Ulriksdals Wärdshus	Swedish/International
	Vassa Eggen	International
25	Eriks Bakficka	Swedish/International
24	Operakällaren	French/International
	Pontus!	Swedish/Seafood
	Leijontornet	Scandinavian
	Edsbacka Krog	Swedish/French
23	Prinsen	Swedish/French
22	Kungsholmen	International
	Den Gyldene Freden	Swedish
	Eriks Gondolen	Swedish/French
	Restaurangen™	Swedish/International
21	Clas på Hörnet	French/Swedish
	Grands Veranda	Swedish/International
20	Sturehof	Swedish/Seafood
19	Pontus by the Sea	French/Swedish
	KB	Swedish
	Rolfs Kök	Swedish/Mediterranean
	Berns Asian	Asian
17	Undici Restaurant & Bar	Swedish/Italian

Berns Asian *Asian* 19 24 18 E

Norrmalm | Berns Hotel | Berzelii Park | (46-8) 5663-2222 | fax 5663-2323 | www.berns.se

"You have to love" the "fabulously over-the-top" interior of "this massive place" in Norrmalm; its "trendy, aristocratic" crowd ensures there's always "excitement in the air", but even they admit you "go for the drinks" and "scene", as service is only "adequate" and the "competent" kitchen's Asian fare can sometimes be "an afterthought."

Clas på Hörnet ☒ *French/Swedish* 21 20 20 E

Södermalm | Hotel Clas på Hörnet | Surbrunnsgatan 20 | (46-8) 165-136 | www.claspahornet.se

This "charming" French-Swedish in a "quaint" 1731 Södermalm inn serves "tasty" traditional fare, with an emphasis on fish; a "lovely" candlelit Gustavian-style setting overlooking a garden and "stellar service" lead loyalists to say "this is the place to go for an adult evening."

Den Gyldene Freden ☒ *Swedish* 22 24 23 E

Gamla Stan | Österlånggatan 51 | (46-8) 249-760 | fax 213-870 | www.gyldenefreden.se

"Beautiful old-world surroundings" dating from the 18th century define this "charming, historic" Gamla Stan "favorite" "in a cellar in the

Old Town"; almost "everyone loves this place" for its combination of "cozy" ambiance, traditional local dishes (plus some International offerings) and "efficient service", even if some say it's "too bad" it's "getting a little staid" and "somewhat touristy" of late; P.S. "the Swedish Academy dines there on Thursdays."

Edsbacka Krog ⊠ *Swedish/French* 24 | 20 | 22 | VE

Sollentuna | Sollentunavägen 220 | (46-8) 963-300 | fax 964-019 | www.edsbackakrog.se

"A tribute to the art of food", this "exquisite" restaurant in a 17th-century building "is surely worth the journey" to Sollentuna, "on the outskirts of town", as its "top" staff "delivers a symphony of exceedingly well-balanced" dishes from an "excellent" Swedish-French menu; a stellar wine cellar and an idyllic setting further enhance the "extraordinary experience."

Eriks Bakficka *Swedish/International* 25 | 17 | 24 | E

Östermalm | Fredrikshovsgatan 4 | (46-8) 660-1599 | fax 663-2567 | www.eriks.se

"Owned by one of Sweden's best chefs", Erik Lallerstedt, "this charming bistro" is "a favorite haunt of locals" in the "expensive residential quarter" of Östermalm - indeed, the "well-heeled" guests seem to "all know each other" as they gather within its "more formal dining room" or "cozier bar section" to enjoy "fine" Swedish-International cuisine; true, it's "a little pricey", but insiders insist it offers "excellent value."

Eriks Gondolen ◐⊠ *Swedish/French* 22 | 26 | 22 | VE

Södermalm | Stadsgården 6 | (46-8) 641-7090 | fax 641-1140 | www.eriks.se

Though it's the "fantastic atmosphere" and "breathtaking view of Stockholm" (including "spectacular" vistas of "the harbor" and "Old Town") that "really make it stand out", advocates avow you'll also "enjoy a fine meal" of "wonderful" Swedish-French cuisine and "excellent service" at this "great place to watch the sunset" suspended high above Södermalm; even those who feel the "very expensive" fare is "not outstanding" and "only secondary to" the venue's visual delights declare do "come for a drink" and "mingle at the nice bar."

F12 ⊠ *International* 27 | 22 | 24 | VE

Norrmalm | Fredsgatan 12 | (46-8) 248-052 | www.f12.se

A "favorite" for many, this "consistently excellent and stylishly" "mod locale" in Norrmalm is run by "people who care about food" - namely "talented" chef-owners Melker Andersson (a "god in Stockholm") and Danyel Couet, whose "flavorful" International fare is served by an "incredibly friendly and helpful staff" in a "first-rate setting"; still, some who resent "very expensive", "tiny portions" warn that "you may not like" their "innovative approach", which allows guests "to assemble their meal from a number of small dishes."

Grands Veranda *Swedish/International* 21 | 23 | 22 | E

Norrmalm | Grand Hôtel | Södra Blasieholmshamnen 8 | (46-8) 679-3586 | fax 611-8686 | www.grandhotel.se

"For a true Grand Hôtel experience", supporters suggest you "snag a table with" a "to-die-for view" of "the Royal Palace, the parliament building" "and the harbor" at this Swedish-International in Norrmalm; "the service is excellent", and "they always have" a "wonderful smörgåsbord" "filled with" so many "tempting foods" that "it's easy to fill *yourself* to bursting" – though those with less voracious appetites aver there's "nothing wrong with their à la carte menu" of "delicious, high-quality food", either.

KB *Swedish* — 19 | 21 | 21 | E

Norrmalm | Smålandsgatan 7 | (46-8) 679-6032 | fax 611-3932 | www.konstnarsbaren.se

"When visiting Stockholm", locals say, stop at this "cozy" "artists' hangout" in an "excellent" Norrmalm location that's "still lots of fun" after more than 70 years; regulars "enjoy the art in the dining room" even more than the "great traditional *husmanskost*" (down-home Swedish fare), which "perhaps could be more inspired"; it "gets a little hectic and noisy late" in the evening, but it's "perfect as a business lunch place."

NEW **Kungsholmen** *International* — 22 | 22 | 20 | E

Kungsholmen | Norr Mälarstrand | (46-8) 5052-4450 | fax 5052-4455 | www.kungsholmen.com

Swedish restaurant guru Melker Andersson of the highly rated F12 "has done it again" with this "trendy" International in Kungsholmen, right on the waterfront, where patrons mix and match their meal from a variety of seven "upmarket" "gourmet food courts" serving everything from sushi to soups and salads; throw in a "delightful setting" that includes a terrace where you can have "drinks by the sea where the sun never sets" and no wonder a "hip crowd congregates" here.

Leijontornet [S] *Scandinavian* — 24 | 27 | 23 | VE

Gamla Stan | Victory Hotel | Lilla Nygatan 5 | (46-8) 5064-0080 | fax 5064-0085 | www.leijontornet.se

An "authentic medieval room" in an "Old Town cellar" is the "wonderful setting" of this "great place to eat" in Gamla Stan's "small, high-class" Victory Hotel ("don't just eat at the restaurant – stay at the hotel too"); as if the "fabulous" environment weren't enough, you can also expect "splendid art from the kitchen" in the form of "superb" Scandinavian cuisine, served by a "staff that tries hard to please"; no wonder most predict you'll "enjoy the experience."

Lux Stockholm [S] [M] *Swedish/International* — 26 | 19 | 22 | E

Kungsholmen | Primusgatan 116 | (46-8) 619-0190 | www.luxstockholm.com

Set "in a tastefully redone" "old Electrolux building" (hence the name) on Lilla Essingen island near Kungsholmen, "just outside central Stockholm", this "amazing" venue peopled by a "hip, beautiful staff and clientele" is "so trendy it hurts", but even the "cool atmosphere" "can't match the fabulous", "first-class modern Swedish"-International fare or "warm", "attentive service"; its "spacious dining room" is "beautifully minimalist" to some, "a bit too austere" for others, but all adore the "gorgeous view."

Operakällaren [S] [M] *French/International* — 24 | 27 | 23 | VE

Norrmalm | The Royal Opera House | Karl XII:s Torg | (46-8) 676-5801 | fax 676-5872 | www.operakallaren.se

"One can only say bravo!" about this "magnificent" "landmark" "in the lovely" Royal Opera House in Norrmalm that's "so popular it's almost a cliché now" thanks to the hordes of "hip see-and-be-seen" people who "go for the scene" and to "check out the latest fashions"; most report the "grand" "opulent" interior, "delicious" French-International fare and "classic", "formal" service are also "superb", and "worth every penny" of the "astronomical price" here ("no, you can't sing for your supper").

Paul & Norbert ☒ *French/Swedish* 28 | 23 | 25 | VE

Östermalm | Strandvägen 9 | (46-8) 663-8183 | www.paulochnorbert.se

"Truly" a "favorite", this "dining delight" in Östermalm is rated No. 1 for Food in Stockholm on the strength of its "superb" French-Swedish cuisine created by "excellent chef" Norbert Lang; you'll also "enjoy wonderful service" from an "exceptional" staff, a "nice atmosphere" and a "great wine selection", making it a "satisfying" "place for a private, romantic" "meal of a lifetime" that will "never be forgotten" - "but bring a lot of krona because you'll need them"; N.B. if you'd like an interactive evening, you can be a cook for the night and prepare your own meal alongside Lang.

Pontus! ☒ *Swedish/Seafood* 24 | - | 23 | VE

(fka Pontus in the Green House)

Norrmalm | Brunnsgatan 1 | (46-8) 5452-7300 | www.pontusfrithiof.com

"Relax and enjoy" a "fantastic" experience at this Swedish seafooder, a bastion of "great dining" whose habitués "humbly bow to chef" Pontus Frithiof and his "artful kitchen" for delivering "delicious" dishes; other pluses are some "reasonably priced gems on the wine list" and a "friendly staff", so admirers advise "if you have the money to spare", "don't miss it"; N.B. post-Survey, the restaurant moved from Gamla Stan to this new location in Norrmalm.

Pontus by the Sea *French/Swedish* 19 | 21 | 21 | E

Gamla Stan | Skeppsbrokajen, Tullhus 2 | (46-8) 202-095 | fax 220-828 | www.pontusfrithiof.com

Once just a "wonderful summer restaurant", Pontus Frithiof's "expensive" Gamla Stan spot "in the heart of the Old Town" now offers its "friendly service" year-round and, as befits its setting "by the sea", continues to be known for a "solid" French-Swedish menu starring "colorful plates" of "perfectly cooked fish" dressed with "delicate sauces"; for many, though, "it's all about" the "excellent view", as there's "something amazing about dining next to the water."

Prinsen *Swedish/French* 23 | 22 | 23 | E

Norrmalm | Mäster Samuelsgatan 4 | (46-8) 611-1331 | www.restaurangprinsen.se

"The food is excellent and the service is accommodating" at this Norrmalm "classic that never disappoints" with its "innovative" Swedish-French fare, whether enjoyed "at one of the outside tables" or within the "impressive interior" of its "more formal" "wood-paneled dining room"; it's a "power-lunch" favorite for "the cognoscenti of the financial industry" as well as a "terrific evening" haunt of "tourists", and though it's "a bit on the expensive side", most insist it "always gives you value for your money."

Restaurangen™ ☒ *Swedish/International* 22 | 21 | 18 | E

Norrmalm | Oxtorgsgatan 14 | (46-8) 220-952 | fax 220-954 | www.restaurangentm.com

Supporters of "sampling" swear by the "Scandinavian-tapas concept" of this Norrmalm Swedish-International (from the "same owner as

F12") "where you order by numbers" - choosing three, five or seven "tasty, small" "courses, each" "well-paired" with a "different wine" "that complements its flavor"; it "is a fun way to try a variety" of "great food" that's "not the usual fare", and the "noisy room" packed with "pretty people" adds to the experience ("if only I could eat like this every night").

Rolfs Kök ◐ *Swedish/Mediterranean* 19 | 19 | 20 | E

Norrmalm | Tegnérgatan 41 | (46-8) 101-696 | www.rolfskok.se

This casual "old favorite" Swedish-Med in Norrmalm is "still going strong" say some who cite fare that is "fresh and beguiling", an "excellent" staff and a modern, open-kitchen setting that caused a buzz when it was built in the late '80s; the less-enthused lament food that is "not always exciting", a once-bold minimalist design that is now only "alright" and downright "cramped" quarters.

Sturehof ◐ *Swedish/Seafood* 20 | 18 | 18 | E

Stureplan | Sturegallerian 42 | Stureplan 2 | (46-8) 440-5730 | www.sturehof.com

A "smart", "stylish crowd" of locals and "hip tourists" hails this "huge, fun place" "conveniently located" "in the hub of Stockholm's cool Stureplan district" for its "high-quality" "traditional Swedish" menu with a "seafood specialty" and "friendly, professional" staff (including "sommeliers knowledgeable" about the "nice wine list"); three "lively" bars and a generally "buzzing atmosphere" mean it's "too bustling" "for those who like quiet dining", but "lively" sorts love the "great people-watching" - especially from the "wonderful terrace in summertime."

Ulriksdals Wärdshus *Swedish/International* 26 | 23 | 26 | VE

Solna | Ulriksdals Slottspark | (46-8) 850-815 | fax 850-858 | www.ulriksdalswardshus.se

"Well worth every minute of travel" to its "out-of-the-way" but "choice location" - "in the country by a bay" within the "peaceful and relaxing" park of Ulriksdals Castle in Solna - this "gem" is "a rite of passage" "when visiting Stockholm" thanks to "excellent" Swedish-International cuisine (including a "fine smörgåsbord" served weekends and holidays); throw in a "superb wine cellar" and "formal" service from a "thoughtful and courteous staff" and no wonder fans insist this "favorite" is "perfect for festive occasions."

Undici Restaurant & Bar [S] [M] *Swedish/Italian* 17 | 12 | 14 | E

Östermalm | Sturegatan 22 | (46-8) 661-6617 | www.undici.se

Fans of this "friendly" "bar and restaurant" close to Humlegården Park in Östermalm find its "fusion of Northern Swedish and Italian dishes" "surprisingly good", though foes feel the fare is "not always successful" and the decor of its "run-down" "interior is minimal" at best; still, the fact that it's "owned by former soccer player Tomas Brolin" means "you might spot someone famous."

Vassa Eggen [S] *International* 26 | 17 | 23 | VE

Stureplan | Elite Hotel Stockholm Plaza | Birger Jarlsgatan 29 | (46-8) 216-169 | www.vassaeggen.com

Named after W. Somerset Maugham's novel *The Razor's Edge*, this "eggstravagant" venue in the Elite Hotel Stockholm Plaza in Stureplan showcases "stunning" International cuisine (gourmets "strongly recommend the six-course dinner with corresponding wines - a rare experience"); still, some find the food "overly fancy", even "a little pretentious", and the service somewhat "impersonal", while others opine that the "sterile" setting is "not very attractive"; N.B. a scheduled major renovation may outdate the above Decor score.

Wedholms Fisk *Swedish/Seafood* 28 | 21 | 26 | VE

Norrmalm | Nybrokajen 17 | (46-8) 611-7874 | fax 678-6011 | www.wedholmsfisk.se

"Do not leave Stockholm before" visiting this "old-school" Swedish seafooder on Norrmalm's Nybrokajen wharf, where the "first-rate" "chef rightly trusts his ingredients" (namely, "fresh", "fantastic fish"), which results in "superb, simply prepared" "traditional dishes" that are "not too elaborate" but truly "exceptional"; perhaps "the decor is rather plain" and the "atmosphere quiet" (like a "hospital waiting room" some quip), but the "efficient" staff provides "excellent service" - yet another reason to "book in advance."

Other Noteworthy Places

Divino Ristorante & Bar *Tuscan/Sicilian*
Karlavägen 28 | (46-8) 611-0269 | fax 611-1204 | www.divino.se

Esperanto *French/International*
Kungstensgatan 2 | (46-8) 696-2323 | www.esperantorestaurant.se

GQ Gastronomisk Intelligens *French/Swedish*
Kommendörsgatan 23 | (46-8) 5456-7430 | fax 662-2506 | www.gqrestaurang.se

Marie Laveau *French/Italian*
Hornsgatan 66 | (46-8) 668-8500 | www.marielaveau.se

Mistral *Swedish/International*
Lilla Nygatan 21 | (46-8) 10-12-24 | fax 10-12-17

Restaurang Stockholm *Swedish/International*
Centralplan 1 | (46-8) 202-049 | fax 613-6255 | www.restaurangstockholm.se

Riche *French/Swedish*
Birger Jarlsgatan 4 | (46-8) 5450-3560 | fax 5450-3569 | www.riche.se

Spring *Asian/International*
Karlavägen 110 | (46-8) 783-1500 | fax 783-1520 | www.spring.se

Stallmästaregården Hotel & Restaurant *Swedish*
Norrtull | (46-8) 610-1300 | fax 610-1340 | www.stallmastaregarden.se

Teatergrillen *French/Swedish*
Nybrogatan 3 | (46-8) 5450-3565 | fax 5450-3569 | www.teatergrillen.se

Tranan *Swedish*
Karlbergsvägen 14 | (46-8) 5272-8100 | www.tranan.se

Wärdshuset Ulla Winbladh *Swedish*
Rosendalsvägen 8 | (46-8) 663-0571 | fax 663-0573 | www.ullawinbladh.se

FOOD DECOR SERVICE COST

Venice

TOP FOOD RANKING

	Restaurant	Cuisine
27	Vini da Gigio	Venetian
26	Da Ivo	Tuscan/Venetian
	Osteria Da Fiore	Italian/Seafood
	Corte Sconta	Venetian/Seafood
25	Fortuny	Italian
	Club del Doge	Venetian/Mediterranean
	De Pisis*	Italian
	Osteria alle Testiere*	Italian/Seafood
	Al Covo	Seafood
24	Do Leoni	Italian/Seafood
	Fiaschetteria Toscana	Venetian
	La Cusina	Venetian/International
	Cip's Club	Venetian
	Hostaria da Franz	Venetian
	Ai Gondolieri	Venetian
	Antico Pignolo	Venetian/Seafood
23	La Terrazza	Italian/International
	Vecio Fritolin	Venetian/Seafood
	L'Osteria di Santa Marina	Venetian
	Il Ridotto	Italian/Seafood
	Antico Martini	Venetian
22	Do Forni	Venetian
	Naranzaria	Asian/Venetian
	Acquapazza	Italian/Seafood
	Grand Canal	Venetian
21	Harry's Dolci	Venetian
	Al Graspo de Ua	Venetian/Seafood
20	La Caravella	Venetian
19	Harry's Bar	International/Venetian
17	Quadri	Italian/International

Acquapazza Ⓜ *Italian/Seafood* 22 19 18 M

San Marco | Campo Sant'Angelo 3808 | (39) 041-277-0688 | fax 041-277-5421 | www.veniceacquapazza.it

This "affordable" Italian seafooder with an Amalfi Coast accent is in a "lovely" Campo Sant' Angelo setting with antique columns; still a few say "pushy service can spoil some of the magic."

Ai Gondolieri *Venetian* 24 19 23 E

Dorsoduro | Fondamenta de l'Ospedaleto 366 | (39) 041-528-6396 | fax 041-521-0075 | www.aigondolieri.com

Carnivores who can't catch a break in this seafood-loving city head to this Venetian in residential Dorsoduro, near the Guggenheim foundation, where "only land creatures are served" like the signature calf's liver, plus pork, lamb and "wonderful risottos"; an "impeccable yet

* Indicates a tie with restaurant above

warm and friendly" staff presides over a "low-key, comfortable" rustic setting; N.B. closed Tuesdays.

Al Covo *Seafood* 25 | 20 | 23 | E

Castello | Campiello della Pescaria 3968 | (39) 041-522-3812 | fax 041-522-3812

"Amazingly fresh" and "superb" Adriatic seafood is the focus at this "warm-and-welcoming" stalwart in Castello that's run by a "great" Italo-American couple with "high standards", chef Cesare Benelli and his wife, hostess and pastry chef, "delightful Diane"; the room is small but flower-filled and there's a dining terrace with a sweet view of the square; N.B. closed Wednesday–Thursday.

Al Graspo de Ua 🄼 *Venetian/Seafood* 21 | 19 | 20 | E

San Marco | San Marco 5094A | (39) 041-520-0150 | fax 041-520-9389 | www.algraspodeua.it

Fans of this 1911 Venetian seafooder that's almost hidden under the porticos of the Rialto Bridge praise its "reliable" cooking, "wonderful wines", "service that couldn't be better" and "nice atmosphere", but opponents opine it's "overpriced" and "touristy."

Antico Martini ◐ *Venetian* 23 | 22 | 22 | VE

San Marco | Campo San Fantin 1983 | (39) 041-522-4121 | fax 041-528-9857 | www.anticomartini.com

It's "ideal for dinner after the fat lady has sung at the Fenice Opera house next door" is what un-PC admirers assert about this "wonderfully located" "landmark" Venetian with "outrageously expensive" but "memorable" meals; a "refined crowd" fills a "lovely", rosy room with Persian carpets and paintings, plus there's a "romantic terrace" and a late-night piano bar; N.B. closed Tuesdays.

Antico Pignolo *Venetian/Seafood* 24 | 22 | 25 | E

San Marco | Calle dei Specchieri 451 | (39) 041-522-8123 | fax 041-520-9007

"Convenient to St. Mark's Square" is this "good, dependable" Venetian seafooder with a "fantastic wine list", "outstanding service" and a big, beautiful garden for "delightful" outdoor dining; while wallet-watchers warn "bring buckets of euros", the philosophical simply shrug "but that's Venice."

Cip's Club *Venetian* 24 | 25 | 26 | VE

Isola della Guidecca | Hotel Cipriani | Isola della Giudecca 10 | (39) 041-520-7744 | fax 041-240-8519 | www.hotelcipriani.com

Everyone wants to join this "wonderful", dinner-only club in the Cipriani with its "great view of St. Mark's Square" and the lagoon; "go only when the weather is good", "take the hotel's private power boat over" to the Isola della Giudecca, "sit outside on the terrace" and order something from the "tasty" Venetian menu along with "a glass of champagne"; of course, you'll "need a big bank roll", but for most it's a "must."

Club del Doge *Venetian/Mediterranean* 25 | 26 | 26 | VE

San Marco | Hotel Gritti Palace | Campo Santa Maria del Giglio 2467 | (39) 041-794-611 | fax 041-520-0942 | www.starwoodhotels.com

"Why die when you can go to heaven here?" at this "stunning and elegant" Venetian-Med in the "grand" Hotel Gritti Palace that's "beautifully situated on the Grand Canal"; the "glorious view" from the veranda, "great food" and the "best service" add up to an extremely "expensive" but "transporting experience."

Corte Sconta ⓢ Ⓜ *Venetian/Seafood* 26 | 17 | 20 | E

Castello | Calle del Pestrin 3886 | (39) 041-522-7024 | fax 041-522-7513 | www.ristorantibuonaaccoglienzavenezia.it

"Unfussy" but "exceptional seafood" from "passionate owners" is the lure at this "off-the-beaten-path" Venetian near the Arsenale, the city's historic shipyard; the round of briny appetizers is legendary and the *moeche* (soft-shell crab) "sublime", leading surveyors to say a "first-rate meal" makes for a "memorable" and expensive evening.

Da Ivo ⓢ *Tuscan/Venetian* 26 | 21 | 23 | VE

San Marco | Ramo dei Fuseri 1809 | (39) 041-528-5004 | fax 041-520-5889

It's "cool to arrive by gondola", but this "top" Tuscan-Venetian is also just a five-minute walk from St. Mark's Square; "gracious" chef-owner Ivo Natali prepares "wonderful" dishes like "huge, excellent *bistecca alla fiorentina*" or fresh Adriatic seafood, "pops out of the kitchen to ensure your pleasure" and presides over a "tiny, atmospheric, low-lit" "romantic" room that leads devotees to decree "just leave me here forever."

De Pisis *Italian* 25 | 24 | 25 | VE

San Marco | Il Palazzo at the Hotel Bauer | San Marco 1459 | (39) 041-520-7022 | fax 041-520-7557 | www.bauervenezia.com

"The view, the food, the romance" and "the gracious service" leave sybarites sighing over this über-"expensive" Italian in the "grand" 18th-century Il Palazzo at the Hotel Bauer; the interior is opulent, and the "breathtaking terrace" vista of the Grand Canal and St. Mark's basin is better than namesake Italian artist De Pisis might have ever imagined.

Do Forni ◐ *Venetian* 22 | 19 | 19 | E

San Marco | Calle dei Specchieri 457 | (39) 041-523-0663 | fax 041-528-8132 | www.doforni.it

Surveyors are split on this big, pricey, "always-packed" Venetian classic "conveniently located" "just off Piazza San Marco"; loyalists like its huge menu with lots of "good, hearty" meat and seafood dishes and the dining rooms with burnished-wood-and-brass "Orient Express decor", but detractors declare the experience "crowded, loud" and "touristy."

Do Leoni *Italian/Seafood* 24 | 23 | 23 | E

Schiavoni | Hotel Londra Palace | Riva degli Schiavoni 4171 | (39) 041-520-0533 | fax 041-522-5032 | www.hotelondra.it

"Excellent cuisine and high-quality service" are the hallmarks of this Italian seafooder in the Hotel Londra Palace; the "beautiful" contemporary interior is stylish but soothing, and in warm weather the terrace is great for "people-watching" and a panoramic view that goes from the Grand Canal to the Lido.

Fiaschetteria Toscana *Venetian* 24 | 17 | 21 | E

Cannaregio | San Giovanni Grisostomo 5719 | (39) 041-528-5281 | fax 041-528-5521 | www.fiaschetteriatoscana.it

Name to the contrary (it was once an outlet for Tuscan wines), this is a true, family-run Venetian in Cannaregio, and one of the tops in the city, serving "divine dishes" like tagliolini with lobster, risottos and other "fantastic" fish-oriented appetizers and entrees; "the decor is better downstairs, but the staff is charming no matter where you sit" in the "warm", "winning" place; N.B. closed Tuesdays.

Fortuny *Italian* 25 | 26 | 25 | VE

(fka Cipriani)

Isola della Guidecca | Hotel Cipriani | Isola della Giudecca 10 | (39) 041-520-7744 | fax 041-240-8519 | www.hotelcipriani.com

This "fabulous, famous" and "formal" Italian in the Hotel Cipriani recently changed its name, but still "has everything that makes Venice memorable - the view, the water, the romance"; the "impressive" experience starts with the "short private shuttle-boat ride from St. Mark's Square" and goes on to an "excellent staff" serving "exquisite" Italian cuisine in a "beautiful" room with mirrors or out on a "magical" terrace; even those who complain about "outrageous prices" urge "eat here once before you die just to say you did."

Grand Canal *Venetian* 22 | 25 | 21 | E

San Marco | Hotel Monaco | Calle Vallaresso 1332 | (39) 041-520-0211 | fax 041-520-0501 | www.hotelmonaco.it

The restored Hotel Monaco and its Venetian restaurant got a modern makeover, but the view from the outdoor dining terrace "right on the Grand Canal" remains one of "the best" in town; the food is "excellent", but some insiders aver it's better for lunch than dinner due to the more relaxed mood at midday.

Harry's Bar *International/Venetian* 19 | 19 | 18 | VE

San Marco | Calle Vallaresso 1323 | (39) 041-528-5777 | fax 041-520-8822 | www.cipriani.com

It's Cipriani's "original" 1931 "mythic bar", the birthplace of the Bellini and former Hemingway hang in San Marco, and it's still packing "tourists" in, however controversially: the mellow cite the International-Venetian's "history and scene" and shrug just stick to the signature cocktail, but the many who are no longer wild about Harry hiss "what a disappointment - we came in search of the legendary, found the ordinary and paid stratospherically."

Harry's Dolci M *Venetian* 21 | 22 | 22 | E

Isola della Guidecca | Isola della Giudecca 773 | (39) 041-522-4844 | fax 041-522-2322 | www.cipriani.com

Surveyors are sweet on this Venetian, a slightly "cheaper" offshoot of Harry's Bar that features the same famous *dolci* (desserts) as the original; proponents also point out the "great waterside location" on the Giudecca Canal is "to die for" and the "short vaporetto trip" there gets you away from the madding San Marco crowd; N.B. closed Monday-Tuesday and mid-October-Easter.

Hostaria da Franz *Venetian* 24 | 18 | 25 | E

Castello | Fondamenta San Giuseppe 754 | (39) 041-522-0861 | fax 041-241-9278 | www.hostariadafranz.com

"They serve wonderful food and treat you like long-lost rich relatives" at this father-and-son-run Venetian "gem" in Castello, near the Biennale Gardens; "fresh, delicious" dishes, "superb service" and a "great" summertime setting with outdoor tables along a tiny canal make it a big "pleaser"; N.B. closed mid-November-mid-February.

	FOOD	DECOR	SERVICE	COST

NEW Il Ridotto *Italian/Seafood* 23 20 21 E

Castello | Camp San Filippo e Giacomo 4609 | (39) 041-520-8280 | fax 041-277-5203

In a city "where a good meal can be difficult to find", this Italian newcomer in Castello specializing in seafood is a "gem" say supporters who cite "outstanding tastes" and a "mind-blowing wine list"; the tiny contemporary space is a bit "cramped" but that doesn't keep eating here from being a "truly exceptional experience."

La Caravella *Venetian* 20 20 20 E

San Marco | Hotel Saturnia | Larga XXII Marzo 2398 | (39) 041-520-8901 | fax 041-520-7131 | www.hotelsaturnia.it

"Good, reliable" Venetian cuisine is served by an "excellent staff" at this stalwart in the Hotel Saturnia, near St. Mark's Square; the "quiet", "cozy and dimly lit", wood-paneled space resembles an antique sailing ship (*caravella*), but many prefer to dine in the "delightful" courtyard garden in summer.

La Cusina *Venetian/International* 24 24 23 VE

San Marco | The Westin Europa & Regina | Larga XXII Marzo 2159 | (39) 041-240-0001 | fax 041-523-1533 | www.westin.com/europaregina

This "very good" Venetian-International in The Westin Europa & Regina boasts a "beautiful" backdrop - a "grand view of the Grand Canal" from its terrace and an interior that's a series of elegant, intimate rooms filled with marble and Murano glass.

La Terrazza *Italian/International* 23 26 24 VE

San Marco | Hotel Danieli | Riva degli Schiavoni 4196 | (39) 041-522-6480 | fax 041-520-0208 | www.starwoodhotels.com

Romantics say "request a window table" or eat outside on the terrace at this "absolutely stunning" Italian-International with "spectacular views" of the Grand Canal, the lagoon and the Island of San Giorgio from the rooftop of the "opulent Hotel Danieli"; opinions on the food ("wonderful" vs "average") and service ("terrific" vs. "stuffy") vary, but there's consensus that the astronomical tab would be "VE even for Bill Gates."

L'Osteria di Santa Marina S M *Venetian* 23 20 20 M

Castello | Campo Santa Marina 5911 | (39) 041-528-5239 | fax 041-528-5239 | www.osteriadisantamarina.it

At this chef-owned Venetian in Castello, there are "fairly priced", "delicious" traditional dishes as well as "beautifully presented imaginative combinations" with an emphasis on "exceptional seafood", all backed up by an "extensive wine list"; the wooden interior is "charming", and there's a terrace for candlelit dining.

Naranzaria M *Asian/Venetian* 22 21 21 E

Rialto | San Polo 130 | (39) 041-724-1035 | fax 041-724-1035 | www.naranzaria.it

"Italy and the Far East come together" on an Asian-Venetian menu that includes sushi, couscous and seafood with polenta at this tiny, trendy new wine bar on the opposite side of the Rialto Bridge; the "beautiful" bi-level 14th-century setting includes vaulted stone ceilings and arched windows, but outdoor tables provide "picturesque" views of the Grand Canal.

	FOOD	DECOR	SERVICE	COST

Osteria alle Testiere [S][M] *Italian/Seafood* 25 | 18 | 24 | E

Castello | Calle del Mondo Novo 5801 | (39) 041-522-7220 | fax 041-522-7220 | www.osterialletestiere.it

An "outstanding" "place for lovers of good fish" is this popular, "minuscule" Italian off Campo Santa Maria Formosa; "wonderfully prepared", "intriguingly flavored" dishes are served by a "top-notch" staff in a casual setting, making enthusiasts exclaim it's "not to be missed."

Osteria Da Fiore [S][M] *Italian/Seafood* 26 | 22 | 24 | VE

San Polo | Calle del Scaleter 2202A | (39) 041-721-308 | fax 041-721-343 | www.dafiore.net

Among the very "best in Venice" is the Martini family's "innovative" Italian piscine palace in San Polo that some wish could be the "location of their last meal on earth"; "wonderful" cuisine that's "all about the ingredients", "gracious service" and a "comfortable yet elegant setting" add up to a feeling of "pure joy" for most; N.B. not to be confused with the similarly named Trattoria da Fiore near San Marco or Ristorante Osteria da Fiore in Santa Croce.

Quadri [M] *Italian/International* 17 | 25 | 19 | VE

San Marco | Piazza San Marco 120 | (39) 041-522-2105 | fax 041-520-8041 | www.quadrivenice.com

"Streams of tourists" head for this first-floor Italian-International and its "prime location" and "perfect view" overlooking "stunning" Piazza San Marco; the opulent, 1844 red interior is "breathtaking", but the "food's not great" and you'll "pay dearly" for it; still, romantics retain "golden memories" of the orchestra music drifting up from the square and of "old Europe at its most charming."

Vecio Fritolin [M] *Venetian/Seafood* 23 | 22 | 23 | E

Rialto | Calle della Regina 2262 | (39) 041-522-2881 | www.veciofritolin.it

They are famous for their *fritolini* (little deep fried fish) at this "top-notch", "classic" Venetian seafooder near the Rialto bridge, but there are also "delicious pastas", homemade breads and desserts, all served by a "helpful staff"; a "great" Northern Italian wine list and warm, wood-lined 16th-century interior add to the "always-a-pleasure" experience.

Vini da Gigio [M] *Venetian* 27 | 19 | 25 | E

Cannaregio | Fondamenta San Felice 3628A | (39) 041-528-5140 | fax 041-522-8597 | www.vinidagigio.com

A "little difficult to find" but "oh what a find" is this family-run Venetian in Cannaregio that's Voted No. 1 for Food in the city; "terrific" "simply and honestly prepared" meat and fish dishes and an "out-of-this-world wine list" are proferred in a "down-to-earth" setting by a "friendly" staff; it's "not the fanciest or most expensive" spot, but it is a "wonderful experience"; N.B. closed Monday–Tuesday.

Other Noteworthy Places

Aciugheta *Venetian*

Campo San Filippo e Giacomo 4357 | (39) 041-522-4292 | fax 041-520-8222 | www.aciugheta-hotelrio.it

Ai Mercanti [S] *Italian*

Calle dei Fuseri, Corte Coppo 4346A | (39) 041-523-8269 | fax 041-523-8269 | www.aimercanti.com

Alla Vecia Cavana *Venetian/Seafood*
Rio Terà SS Apostoli 4624 | (39) 041-528-7106 | fax 041-523-8644 | www.veciacavana.it

Antica Besseta *Venetian*
Salizada de Cà Zusto 1395 | (39) 041-721-687 | fax 041-721-687

Antiche Carampane *Italian*
Rio Terà delle Carampane 1911 | (39) 041-524-0165 | fax 041-524-0165 | www.antichecarampane.com

Bentigodi *Venetian*
Calle Sele 1423 | (39) 041-716-269

Cà dei Frati *Mediterranean*
San Clemente Palace Hotel | Isola di San Clemente 1 | (39) 041-244-5001 | fax 041-244-5800 | www.sanclemente.thi.it

Canova *Italian*
Luna Hotel Baglioni | Calle Larga dell'Ascensione 1243 | (39) 041-528-9840 | fax 041-528-7160 | www.baglionihotels.com

La Colomba *Venetian/International*
Piscina di Frezzeria 1665 | (39) 041-522-1175 | fax 041-522-1468 | www.sanmarcohotels.com

Le Bistrot de Venise *Venetian*
Calle dei Fabbri 4685 | (39) 041-523-6651 | fax 041-520-2244 | www.bistrotdevenise.com

Ribò *Venetian*
Fondamenta Minotto 158 | (39) 041-524-2486

Vini Da Arturo *Italian*
Calle degli Assassini 3656 | (39) 041-528-6974

	FOOD	DECOR	SERVICE	COST

Vienna

TOP FOOD RANKING

	Restaurant	Cuisine
28	Steirereck	Austrian/International
26	Imperial	Austrian/International
25	Coburg	Austrian/International
24	Demel	Austrian/International
	Walter Bauer	Austrian/International
	Mraz & Sohn	Austrian/International
	Korso bei der Oper	Austrian/French
	Kim Kocht	Asian/International
	Drei Husaren	Austrian/International
23	Julius Meinl am Graben	French/International
	Zum weiß. Rauchfangkehrer	Austrian
22	Österreicher im MAK	Viennese
	DO & CO	Austrian/International
	Plachutta	Austrian
	Goldene Zeiten	Chinese
21	Fabios	Italian/Mediterranean
	Indochine 21*	French/Vietnamese
	Mörwald im Ambassador	International
	Ella's	Greek
	Vestibül	Austrian/International
	Wrenkh*	Vegetarian
	Weinkellerei Artner	Austrian
20	Procacci	Italian
	Zum Schwarz. Kameel*	Austrian/International
19	Cantinetta Antinori	Northern Italian
	Hansen	Mediterranean
18	Café Landtmann	Austrian
	Babu	Asian/Mediterranean
17	Wein & Co Bar	International
16	Sky	Austrian/International
13	Bar Italia Lounge	Italian/International

Babu ◐ *Asian/Mediterranean* 18 | 23 | 12 | E

Alsergrund | Stadtbahnbögen 181-184 | (43-1) 479-4849

An "ideal mixture of bar and restaurant" that combines "the old and the new", this spot in Alsergrund offers "unusual" Asian-Med cuisine in the vault of a fin de siècle tramway updated with leather-and-wood decor; the "trendy" vibe attracts a crowd of "young people from all over the world" who remain undaunted by "unfriendly" service or "high" tabs.

Bar Italia Lounge ◐ *Italian/International* 13 | 18 | 13 | M

Mariahilf | Mariahilfer Str. 19-21 | (43-1) 585-2838 | fax 581-7611 | www.baritalia.net

"Panini and drinks by day" and a "great scene at night" await at this "cute" Mariahilf Italian-International where shoppers and museum-

* Indicates a tie with restaurant above

goers stop in for coffee and light bites in the ground-level cafe and "beautiful people" groove to "excellent music" from a DJ in the lounge in the evening; the prices are "reasonable", though some argue that the fare is really "only snacks."

Café Landtmann ◐ *Austrian* 18 | 20 | 17 | E

Innere Stadt | Dr. Karl Lueger Ring 4 | (43-1) 2410-0120 | fax 532-0625 | www.landtmann.at

You expect to "see Dr. Freud at the next table" at this famous "grand old coffeehouse" in Innere Stadt where "authentic Viennese coffee" and "traditional" Austrian fare are served by "friendly" waiters in a "lovely", "splendidly historical" space; though not as pricey as psychoanalysis, it is "expensive"; P.S. the outdoor terrace offers "great people-watching opportunities."

Cantinetta Antinori *Italian* 19 | 18 | 20 | E

Innere Stadt | Jasomirgottstr. 3-5 | (43-1) 533-7722 | fax 533-7722-11 | www.antinori.it

"Firenze on the Danube" is how fans describe this Innere Stadt outpost of a "high-class" Northern Italian chainlet owned by famous Tuscan vintners, where "fabulous wines" and "dependable" fare are served in a "refined" space in the shadows of St. Stephan's Cathedral; critics, though, complain that the dishes "don't justify the prices", and while the service earns praise from many, others feel it can be "too intrusive."

Coburg [S][M] *Austrian/International* 25 | 22 | 23 | VE

Innere Stadt | Palais Coburg | Coburgbastei 4 | (43-1) 5181-8800 | fax 5181-8818 | www.palaiscoburg.at

"Expensive, but justifiably" so, this Austrian-International housed in Innere Stadt's "breathtaking" Palais Coburg hotel showcases chef Christian Petz's "excellent" cuisine, which is expertly paired with "outstanding" selections from an "incredible wine cellar"; a "young but well-trained" staff provides "courteous" service amid "elegant" surroundings, and for many, dining on the "beautiful" terrace overlooking the Stadtpark is an "unparalleled" experience.

Demel *Austrian/International* 24 | 22 | 10 | E

Innere Stadt | Kohlmarkt 14 | (43-1) 5351-7170 | fax 535-1717-26 | www.demel.at

"Expand your waistline and thin out your wallet" at this "posh" "pastry nirvana" on the Innere Stadt's tony Kohlmarkt, where a "fantastic array" of "beautifully decorated" cakes (some 50 varieties) and other desserts are showcased in "world-famous window displays"; the Austrian-International menu, by contrast, is "unimpressive", and service can be "iffy", so many prefer to just sit back with some "fabulous" "*kaffee und kuchen*" and "watch master bakers at work."

DO & CO Albertina ◐ *Austrian/International* 22 | 21 | 20 | E

Innere Stadt | The Albertina | Albertinaplatz 1 | (43-1) 532-9669 | fax 532-9669-500

DO & CO Stephansplatz ◐ *Austrian/International*

Innere Stadt | Stephansplatz 12 | (43-1) 535-3969 | fax 535-3959 www.doco.com

A "reliable mix of Austrian and International cuisine" (including "superb Japanese" dishes) "prepared in front of you" along with "stunning views of St. Stephan's Cathedral" and the beautiful Stephansplatz attract a "well-dressed crowd" to this "see-and-be-seen" spot atop the Haas Haus in Innere Stadt; the "modern, urban" interior has a "NY feel" and the service is "competent" and "friendly"; N.B. it has a younger sibling in the Albertina museum.

Drei Husaren *Austrian/International* 24 | 23 | 23 | VE

Innere Stadt | Weihburggasse 4 | (43-1) 5121-0920 | fax 512-109-218 | www.drei-husaren.at

"Everything is top-drawer" at "Vienna's most famous" venue (circa 1933) in Innere Stadt near Stephansplatz, where you "feel like a Kaiser" (but you also better "have his bank account") thanks to "terrific" Austrian-International cuisine, including an "incredible hors d'oeuvre cart", "polite", "efficient" service and a "refined", "old-fashioned" setting with live music; while some find it "stuffy" and "not what it once was", for others it's still a "real experience."

NEW **Ella's** *Greek* 21 | 21 | 19 | M

Innere Stadt | Judenplatz 9 | (43-1) 535-1577 | www.ellas.at

Owner Eleftherios Dermitzakis' new modern Hellenic in Innere Stadt has surveyors salivating over its "exceptional fare" (including "eyebrow-raising food combinations" such as foie gras with Granny Smith sorbet) and moderate prices; the "modern, minimalist" space features white tablecloths and black banquettes set against deep-red and orange walls, but in the summer "make a reservation for outside" on the "beautiful" terrace on Judenplatz.

Fabios *Italian/Mediterranean* 21 | 21 | 20 | VE

Innere Stadt | Tuchlauben 6 | (43-1) 532-2222 | fax 532-2225 | www.fabios.at

"You can always meet the people who count" at this "hot spot" in Innere Stadt, just a short walk from Graben, where "authentic" Italian-Med cuisine is served by a "friendly" staff in a "trendy, modern" space with "large tinted windows", lots of "dark wood" and leather, and a "simple but elegant" lounge; still, some find the "masculine" setting "oppressive" and the service "overbearing", while wallet-watchers warn you're "paying for the atmosphere" and "good location."

Goldene Zeiten *Chinese* 22 | 21 | 20 | E

Innere Stadt | Dr. Karl Lueger-Platz 5 | (43-1) 513-4747 | www.goldenezeiten.at

This Chinese may be the "best there is in Vienna" say supporters who praise the chef-owner, who peppers his "authentic" menu with elaborate Shanghainese and Szechuan dishes, which are complemented by an extensive wine list that sparkles with some rare Austrian vintages; recently relocated from the suburbs to Innere Stadt, the bright new modern digs feature butter-yellow walls and soaring ceilings that are punctuated by enormous red lamps.

Hansen *Mediterranean* 19 | 23 | 19 | E

Innere Stadt | Wipplingerstr. 34 | (43-1) 532-0542 | fax 532-0542-10 | www.hansen.co.at

"It's like sitting in a greenhouse" at this Med in the basement of the old stock exchange on Innere Stadt's Ringstrasse, decorated in the motif of a Roman covered market, with a marble floor, skylights and a "beautiful indoor garden" courtesy of the "flower shop next door"; while the "imaginative" weekly menu and "patient" service win praise, many just "come here for the decor."

Imperial *Austrian/International* 26 | 26 | 27 | VE

Innere Stadt | Hotel Imperial | Kärntner Ring 16 | (43-1) 5011-0356 | fax 5011-0410 | www.starwoodhotels.com

"You're treated like an emperor" at this "superlative" Austrian-International housed in Innere Stadt's "grand" Hotel Imperial that provides "friendly", "flawless" service and "outstanding" cuisine in a "plush", wood-paneled Victorian room with Hapsburg portraits; a "marvelous pianist adds to the mood" of "old-world elegance and charm", making it a "slice of heaven on earth" for many - albeit at "hellish prices."

Indochine 21 *French/Vietnamese* 21 | 19 | 19 | E

Innere Stadt | Stubenring 18 | (43-1) 513-7660 | fax 513-7660-16 | www.indochine.at

Across the street from the Museum für Angewandte Kunst (MAK) in Innere Stadt, this French-Vietnamese is a "nice change of pace" "from Viennese and Italian cooking", offering "delectable" dishes with "unusual taste combinations" and "competent" service in a "trendy" yet "comfortable" "cafelike" room with bamboo accents and Buddhist icons; the only complaint is that it's "overpriced."

Julius Meinl am Graben *French/International* 23 | 17 | 21 | E

Innere Stadt | Graben 19 | (43-1) 532-3334-6000 | fax 532-3334-2090 | www.meinlamgraben.at

For a "culinary adventure", a "cosmopolitan clientele" gravitates to Graben and this "upmarket" French-International on the second floor of "Vienna's leading gourmet store", which carries nearly "everything the heart desires"; a "courteous staff" serves chef Joachim Gradwohl's "innovative" fare in a "lovely" room with "stunning views" of the street, though some find it hard to "escape the fact that it is a supermarket."

Kim Kocht *Asian/International* 24 | 18 | 20 | E

Alsergrund | Lustkandlgasse 6 | (43-1) 319-0242 | fax 319-0242 | www.kimkocht.at

A "gourmet experience" awaits at this boîte in Alsergrund near the Volksoper, where chef-owner Sohyi Kim's "inventive" Asian-International cuisine emphasizing organic ingredients is "unbelievably tasty and healthy" and "needs are fulfilled immediately" by a "courteous" staff; "even first-time visitors feel at home" here - those who can get into the "mini" (24-seat) space, that is, which leads some to gripe that it's "impossible to get a table unless you know her well."

Korso bei der Oper *Austrian/French* 24 | 25 | 25 | VE

Innere Stadt | Hotel Bristol | Mahlerstr. 5 | (43-1) 5151-6546 | fax 5151-6575 | www.luxurycollection.com

The "best bet after the opera" is this "classic, opulent" nearby venue in Innere Stadt's Hotel Bristol, where celeb chef "Reinhard Gerer has reinvented Viennese cuisine" via his "superb" Austrian-French creations; service is "polished and professional", the wine list "excellent" and the "beautifully appointed" room evokes "old Vienna" in all its "elegance" - so "don't look at the prices and enjoy a special evening."

	FOOD	DECOR	SERVICE	COST

Mörwald im Ambassador *International* 21 17 21 E

Innere Stadt | Ambassador | Neuer Markt 5/Kärnter Str. 22 | (43-1) 9616-1161 | fax 9616-1160 | www.moerwald.at

Freunden give a "big thank you" to the chef of this "wonderful" International that also offers a "first-class choice" of wines at "reasonable prices" in the Ambassador hotel in Innere Stadt; moreover, the staff is "not intrusive" yet "always there" in the "upscale" space that's at once "modern" and "cozy"; P.S. "don't miss" the winter garden.

Mraz & Sohn ☒ *Austrian/International* 24 21 19 E

Brigittenau | Wallensteinstr. 59 | (43-1) 330-4594 | fax 01-350-1536 | www.mraz-sohn.at

This "excellent, high-quality" Austrian-International may be located in the downscale neighborhood of Brigittenau, but foodies flock to the 45-seater to sample the creations of chef Markus Mraz, a molecular gastronomy pioneer in Vienna; the "casual" setting belies such sophisticated touches as a legendary wine list and choice selection of cheeses.

Österreicher im MAK ◐ *Viennese* 22 23 21 E

Innere Stadt | Museum für Angewandte Kunst | Stubenring 5 | (43-1) 714-0121 | fax 710-0121 | www.oesterreicherimmak.at

"One of the best chefs in Austria", Helmut Österreicher (ex the highly rated Steirereck), brings *his* culinary art to The MAK (Museum for Applied Arts) at this expansive venue and the result is "well-done" "traditional and slightly modernized" Viennese food; the "wonderful location" is only exceeded by the "even greater interior design", which includes soaring ceilings and a chandelier made from 200 wine bottles.

Plachutta *Austrian* 22 14 19 E

Döbling | Heiligenstädterstr. 179 | (43-1) 370-4125 | fax 370-4125-20
Hietzing | Auhofstr. 1 | (43-1) 8777-0870 | fax 877-7087-22
Innere Stadt | Wollzeile 38 | (43-1) 512-1577 | fax 512-1477-20
www.plachutta.at

"If you like *tafelspitz,* you can't go wrong" at this "dependable", "authentic" trio of Austrians where that signature Viennese dish and other "varieties of traditional boiled beef" are "unbeatable" if a bit "expensive"; you feel "like you're in good hands" with a "charming", "helpful" staff that presides over "simple", "bourgeois" digs that are "comfortable" even when they get "noisy and crowded."

NEW Procacci ◐ *Italian* 20 19 22 E

Innere Stadt | Göttweihergasse 2 | (43-1) 512-2211 | fax 512-1111 | www.procacci.at

The prestigious wine-producing Antinori Group has opened this "delightful" new Italian showcasing their wines among others, along with dishes that feature upscale ingredients like truffles; located in Innere Stadt, near the fashionable boutiques of Graben, the "pleasant" streamlined space features "floor-to-ceiling windows", so much the better for the well-heeled crowd that comes here "to be seen."

Sky ☒ *Austrian/International* 16 20 17 E

Innere Stadt | Steffl | Kärntner Str. 19 | (43-1) 513-1712 | fax 513-1712-20 | www.skyrestaurant.at

"Excellent views" "both inside and out" are the main draw of this Austrian-International perched atop the trendy steel-and-glass Steffl mall in Innere Stadt, where "well-heeled Viennese" "come to see and be seen" in the "sophisticated" setting when they're not gazing at the city's rooftops or St. Stephan's Cathedral; service is "competent" and "friendly", and the menu, which ranges from *tafelspitz* to spring rolls, contains some "unusual variations."

Steirereck ☒ *Austrian/International* 28 | 25 | 26 | VE

Landstrasse | Im Stadtpark | Am Heumarkt 2A | (43-1) 713-3168 | fax 7133-1682 | www.steirereck.at

"By far the best" restaurant in the city and voted No. 1 for Food here, this Landstrasse landmark is a "fairy-tale" experience, featuring chef Heinz Reitbauer's "exquisite" Austrian-International cuisine, "cheese and bread carts that put others to shame", an "excellent" wine cellar and "first-class" service; the move in 2005 to its current Stadtpark address "has been a fantastic success", thanks to the "exquisite" renovation of a century-old pavilion into a "knockout" location with "no shortage of space."

Vestibül ☒ *Austrian/International* 21 | 24 | 20 | E

Innere Stadt | Dr. Karl Lueger Ring 2 | (43-1) 532-4999 | fax 532-4999-10 | www.vestibuel.at

Blessed with a "perfect location" in the Burgtheater (in what was formerly the emperor's secret entrance), this Innere Stadt Austrian-International (a sibling of Hansen) is "ideal for business meetings and impressing foreigners" thanks to its "sensational" "marble ballroom" interior and "quiet, classy" ambiance; still, surveyors are split over the cuisine - while some feel it "doesn't justify the prices", to others it's a "pleasant surprise."

Walter Bauer ☒ *Austrian/International* 24 | 18 | 26 | E

Innere Stadt | Sonnenfelsgasse 17 | (43-1) 512-9871

Regulars have "never been disappointed" by this "hidden gem" in a small medieval house (circa 1505) "on a quiet street" near Stephansplatz in one of the oldest parts of Innere Stadt; a "wide-ranging" Austrian-International menu is complemented by a "superb wine list", "attentive staff" and "intimate" setting

Wein & Co Bar *International* 17 | 14 | 15 | M

Innere Stadt | Jasomirgottstr. 3-5 | (43-1) 535-0916-12 | fax 532-1034 | www.weinco.at

Located in the flagship store of a wine shop chain, this small but "fully functional" eatery near Stephansplatz in Innere Stadt is an "excellent place for sampling Austrian wines" and "incredible cheeses" in a "cheerful", "modern" space with a long bar and a retail section; although the International fare is "secondary" to the sips, fans insist it's "really quite good", while the service is "friendly" and "fast."

Weinkellerei Artner *Austrian* 21 | 20 | 18 | E

Wieden | Floragasse 6 | (43-1) 503-5033 | fax 503-5034 | www.artner.co.at

The Artner family makes up for an "unglamorous" Wieden location with a "creative" regional menu that's a "welcome relief from typical Austrian cuisine", as well as "great goat cheese" and wines from their farm and winery in Höflein; the "brightly furnished", "modern" room is an "attractive place to eat and watch folks" in a "relaxing" atmosphere, although sometimes service is "not very attentive."

Wrenkh [S] *Vegetarian* — 21 | 14 | 19 | M

Innere Stadt | Bauernmarkt 10 | (43-1) 533-1526 | www.wrenkh.at

Chef-owner Christian Wrenkh's meatless cuisine is "as good as vegetarian can be" swear fans of this Innere Stadt spot near Stephansplatz, which offers a "wide selection" of flesh-free fare, including "salad dressings that are poetry" to the palate, as well as a "small but good wine list"; the '90s decor is "nothing out of the ordinary", but the "friendly" staff is "witty" and "patient."

Zum Schwarzen Kameel [S] *Austrian/International* — 20 | 17 | 18 | E

Innere Stadt | Bognergasse 5 | (43-1) 533-8125 | fax 533-8125-23 | www.kameel.at

Viennese come to "see and be seen" at this 'Black Camel' in Graben, the city's oldest restaurant (circa 1618) and former purveyor to the imperial palace, which offers a "wide selection of delicacies" from its sandwich shop and "reliable" Austrian-International fare in an "exquisite, small" Jugendstil-inspired dining room; though the service "could be friendlier", the staff "knows more about Austrian wines than Beckham knows about football."

Zum weißen Rauchfangkehrer [S][M] *Austrian* — 23 | 20 | 23 | E

Innere Stadt | Weihburggasse 4 | (43-1) 512-3471 | fax 512-3471-28 | www.weisser-rauchfangkehrer.at

For a "taste of Vienna", fans tout this "lovely old place" (circa 1844) near Stephansplatz in Innere Stadt offering "outstanding" organic "takes on traditional Viennese fare"; it's a bit "pricey", but "high-quality" *essen,* "personable, professional service" and a "classic setting" with lots of "country-style" "charm" make it "worth a return visit" for many; N.B. live piano music daily.

Other Noteworthy Places

Bordeaux [S] *International*
Servitengasse 2 | (43-1) 315-6363 | fax 315-6363-63 | www.bordeauxbar.at

Eckel [S][M] *Viennese/International*
Sieveringerstr. 46 | (43-1) 320-3218 | fax 320-6660 | www.restauranteckel.at

Fadinger [S] *Austrian/International*
Wipplingerstr. 29 | (43-1) 533-4341 | fax 532-4351 | www.fadinger.at

Gaumenspiel [S] *Austrian/International*
Zieglergasse 54 | (43-1) 526-1108 | fax 526-1108-30 | www.gaumenspiel.at

Graf Hunyady [M] *Austrian/International*
Trabrennbahn Krieau | Tribüne 1, Nordportalstr. 247 | (43-1) 729-3572 | fax 729-3573 | www.grafhunyady.at

Grünauer [S]≠ *Austrian*
Hermanngasse 32 | (43-1) 526-4080

Harry's Time ●[S] *Austrian/International*
Dr. Karl Lueger-Pl. 5 | (43-1) 512-4556 | www.harrys-time.at

Le Ciel [S] *French/Viennese*
Grand Hotel Wien | Kärntner Ring 9 | (43-1) 515-809-100 | fax 515-1313 | www.grandhotelwien.com

Le Salzgries [S] *French*
Marc Aurel-Str. 6 | (43-1) 533-4030 | fax 533-4030-20 | www.le-salzgries.at

VIENNA

Limes *International*
Hoher Markt 10 | (43-1) 905-800 | fax 905-800-80 | www.restaurant-limes.at

Novelli *Mediterranean*
Bräunerstr. 11 | (43-1) 513-4200 | fax 513-42001 | www.novelli.at

ON *Chinese*
Wehrgasse 8 | (43-1) 585-4900 | www.restaurant-on.at

Pan e Wien *Italian*
Salesianergasse 25 | (43-1) 710-3870 | www.panewien.at

Piccini Piccolo Gourmet *Italian*
Linke Wienzeile 4 | (43-1) 586-3323 | fax 587-2026 | www.piccini.at

Ra'mien *Pan-Asian*
Gumpendorferstr. 9 | (43-1) 585-4798 | fax 941-1863 | www.ramien.at

RieGi *French/Mediterranean*
Schauflergasse 6 | (43-1) 532-9126 | fax 532-912-620

Rote Bar *Austrian/International*
Hotel Sacher Wien | Philharmonikerstr. 4 | (43-1) 5145-6841 | fax 5145-6810 | www.sacher.com

Ruben's Brasserie *Austrian*
Fürstengasse 1 | (43-1) 319-239-611 | fax 319-239-696 | www.rubens.at

Shambala *French/International*
Le Méridien | Opernring 13 | (43-1) 588-900 | fax 588-909-090 | www.lemeridien.com

Theater Cafe *Austrian/International*
Linke Wienzeile 6 | (43-1) 585-6262 | fax 595-305-022 | www.theatercafe-wien.at

Unkai *Japanese*
Grand Hotel Wien | Kärntner Ring 9 | (43-1) 515-809-110 | fax 515-1313 | www.unkai-grandhotel.com

Vikerl's Lokal *Austrian*
Würffelgasse 4 | (43-1) 894-3430 | www.vikerls.at

Vincent *Austrian/International*
Grosse Pfarrgasse 7 | (43-1) 214-1516 | fax 212-1414 | www.restaurant-vincent.at

Weibel 3 *Austrian/International*
Riemergasse 1-3 | (43-1) 513-3110 | fax 513-3110 | www.weibel.at

Wolf *Austrian*
Burggasse 76 | (43-1) 990-6620

Yohm *Asian*
Petersplatz 3 | (43-1) 533-2900 | fax 533-2900-16 | www.yohm.com

Zum Finsteren Stern II *International*
Schulhof 8 | (43-1) 535-2100 | fax 535-2100

FOOD | DECOR | SERVICE | COST

Warsaw

TOP FOOD RANKING

	Restaurant	Cuisine
25	Rest. Polska Tradycja	Polish
	Dom Polski	Polish
23	U Kucharzy	Polish
	Parmizzano's	Italian
22	Malinowa	Polish
	Michel Moran Bistro/Paris	French
	Belvedere	Polish/International
21	Qchnia Artystyczna	International
	Boathouse	Italian/Mediterranean
	Oriental, The	Asian/Sushi
19	Chianti	Italian
	La Bohème	International
18	Santorini	Greek
	Dom Rest. Gessler	Polish
17	U Fukiera	Polish
16	Blue Cactus	Southwestern/Tex-Mex

Belvedere *Polish/International* 22 | 26 | 23 | E

Srodmiescie | ul. Agrykola 1 | (48) 22-841-2250 | fax 22-841-7135 | www.belvedere.com.pl

After "a welcome revamp" of its "stupendous location" - a "grand", "glass-facaded" 19th-century "orangery in Lazienki Park" with an "adjacent open-air terrace" overlooking "lush grounds" - this "classic" "fine-dining" venue in Srodmiescie is now not only "posh but trendy", attracting those who "enjoy people-watching" while "indulging" in "well-executed" Polish-International fare; it's an "excellent" place "for that special dinner", as long as "you have money to throw around."

Blue Cactus *Southwestern/Tex-Mex* 16 | 15 | 14 | M

Mokotów | ul. Zajaczkowska 11 | (48) 22-851-2323 | fax 22-851-2322 | www.bluecactus.pl

Amigos assess this "usually crowded" Southwestern spot in Mokotów as "a fun place to get a bite to eat and have some drinks with friends" thanks to the "Latin flair" of its "good Tex-Mex" eats and its "lively" atmosphere; enemigos, though, judge it "a bore", blaming "food that's mediocre at best", "loud decor" and a staff that makes "you feel like you are not wanted."

Boathouse *Italian/Mediterranean* 21 | 17 | 17 | E

Saska Kepa | Wal Miedzeszynski 389a | (48) 22-616-3223 | fax 22-616-3332 | www.boathouse.pl

"Ideal for larger groups" and families, this spacious ground-floor "haven" "right on the river" in Saska Kepa is "a lovely place to dine" upon "excellent" Italian-Med fare; it's especially "noteworthy" "in the summer" when you can choose the "charming outdoor seating" "with its pretty garden views" - just "beware the mosquitoes!"

FOOD | DECOR | SERVICE | COST

Chianti *Italian*

19 | 19 | 20 | M

Srodmiescie | ul. Foksal 17 | (48) 22-828-0222 | www.kregliccy.pl

"Run by well-known restaurateurs" Agnieszka Kreglicka and Marcin Kreglicki, this "reliable", "simple trattoria" "conveniently located" in Srodmiescie, in the hip bar district next to Nowy Ýöwiat, is "still providing quality Italian fare" such as "good homemade pastas" and "one of the best tiramisus in town"; still, a few sigh that it "has run out of steam", saying there are now "better" venues in Warsaw for food from The Boot.

Dom Polski *Polish*

25 | 21 | 21 | E

Saska Kepa | ul. Francuska 11 | (48) 22-616-2488 | fax 22-616-2488 | www.restauracjadompolski.pl

"If you want to taste real", "traditional Polish" fare, "look no farther" than this "fabulous restaurant" in Saska Kepa, a beautiful residential area on the Vistula River's right bank; it's "still one of the best" of its kind, and a "great place to get to know" the cuisine thanks to a kitchen that "excels at old", "tried-and-true recipes" ("particularly" the "excellent desserts") – just "be hungry when you come as the portions are big"; N.B. a recent expansion and the addition of a winter garden may outdate the above Decor score.

Dom Restauracyjny Gessler *Polish*

18 | 24 | 20 | E

Stare Miasto | Rynek Starego Miasta 21/21a | (48) 22-887-0344 | www.gessler.pl

Its "excellent location" in Stare Miasto, "at the very center" of the Old Town, and a "unique setting" of "low-beamed rooms" in a 16th-century house is what "pulls in" the crowds of "mostly wealthy" travelers at this "obviously touristy" spot; but since its "hearty Polish" fare is only "alright", foodies feel "let down by the quality."

La Bohème *International*

19 | 22 | 19 | E

Srodmiescie | Plac Teatralny 1 | (48) 22-692-0681 | fax 22-692-0684 | www.laboheme.com.pl

Blessed with a "spectacular location", a stone's throw from the National Theatre, a "sophisticated" setting and "nice terrace", this Srodmiescie "oasis" "crowded with businessmen, politicians" and artists offers "satisfying" International fare and an "extensive wine list"; supporters say it's "simply one of the finest overall dining experiences" around, but cynics snipe it's "too expensive for the quality of food."

Malinowa *Polish*

22 | 21 | 27 | VE

Srodmiescie | Le Royal Méridien Bristol | ul. Krakowskie Przedmiescie 42/44 | (48) 22-551-1000 | fax 22-625-2577 | www.starwoodhotels.com

An "intelligent staff" oversees this "very expensive", "elegant restaurant in the famous" Le Royal Méridien Bristol hotel in Srodmiescie, where the mostly "traditional" Polish menu features "some modern variations"; a few find it "a bit unexciting", saying "Warsaw has developed more interesting [venues] in recent years", but a majority reports an experience "worth repeating"; P.S. "Sunday brunch is fabulous."

Michel Moran Bistro de Paris *French*

22 | 16 | 19 | E

Srodmiescie | pl. Pilsudskiego 9 | (48) 22-826-0107 | fax 22-827-0808 | www.restaurantbistrodeparis.com

Amis assert "*mercis beaucoup*" are due to this Srodmiescie French in the rear of the National Theatre, where "talented" chef Michel Moran prepares "very good" cuisine that emphasizes seafood and relies on "excellent ingredients"; the "elegant" wood-paneled setting provides a view of Norman Foster's Metropolitan building, and in season the impressive, columned terrace makes for a prestigious perch that comes with a "charming summer menu."

Oriental, The *Asian/Sushi* 21 19 22 E

Srodmiescie | Sheraton Warsaw Hotel | ul. Prusa 2 | (48) 22-450-6705 | fax 22-450-6200 | www.sheraton.pl

The "most-attentive service" from a "staff that couldn't be more helpful" "makes meals exceptional" at this "good bet" situated in Srodmiescie's Sheraton Hotel; folks who "walk in to see what smells so delicious" usually "stay" for the "authentic", "quality" Asian fare (as well as sushi) served in a "pleasant", "atmospheric" space.

Parmizzano's *Italian* 23 18 21 E

Srodmiescie | The Marriott Warsaw | al. Jerozolimskie 65/79 | (48) 22-630-5096 | fax 22-830-0311 | www.marriott.com/wawpl

"Forget the usual hotel-type places" – this Srodmiescie spot "is a true gem of an Italian restaurant", "in spite of being located" on the second floor of The Marriott Warsaw, thanks to a staff providing "great service", a "chef who's really passionate" about turning out "heavenly" dishes and a setting that reminds some of "a nice, quiet place in Sicily"; P.S. business sorts also say "it's a safe choice" for an "excellent light lunch."

Qchnia Artystyczna *International* 21 21 17 E

Srodmiescie | al. Ujazdowskie 6 | (48) 22-625-7627 | fax 22-625-7627 | www.qchnia.pl

Supporters of this "stylish" Srodmiescie venue "set in Ujazdowskie Castle" (home to the Center for Contemporary Art) say it possesses an "artistic" kitchen that produces "imaginative" International dishes within a "vibrant" space with "a great view of the park"; it's "popular with the hip and wealthy" for a "lovely lunch" or "a romantic dinner", even though some say "the service should be more professional and less arty."

Restauracja Polska Tradycja *Polish* 25 25 25 E

Mokotów | ul. Belwederska 18a | (48) 22-840-0901 | fax 22-840-0950 | www.restauracjatradycja.pl

"Outstanding in every way", "this fabulous find on a quiet little street" in Mokotów, "an elegant residential area", is rated No. 1 for Food in Warsaw on the strength of its "authentic and oh-so-good" "traditional Polish cuisine", which is complemented by a "great wine list" and "first-class" staff; its "magical setting", "a beautiful old" renovated "villa close to Lazienki Park", is always "bustling with people enjoying themselves", making it "a wonderful place for a romantic dinner, business" gathering or any "special-occasion" "celebration."

Santorini *Greek* 18 18 19 M

Saska Kepa | ul. Egipska 7 | (48) 22-672-0525 | www.kregliccy.pl

"If you've a hankering for" Hellenic fare, "check out this" "charming", "established" spot in Saska Kepa that offers "a real taste of Greece" that includes a "good choice of meze"; visually, its "first impression is not good", but insiders say look past the facade of its "ugly communist-style building", as "inside" awaits a "nice" blue-and-white taverna that brings "a touch of the Mediterranean to Eastern Europe."

U Fukiera *Polish* 17 | 23 | 18 | E

Stare Miasto | Rynek Starego Miasta 27 | (48) 22-831-1013 | fax 22-831-5808 | www.ufukiera.pl

Given its "beautiful" "central" setting in Stare Miasto, it comes as no surprise this "upscale", "atmospheric place" "has become a touristy" "favorite" of "rich" travelers, who tout its "attentive service" and Polish menu featuring "a fabulous selection of game"; still, foes who "expected more" assert it's "too expensive" and "banks on location" too heavily.

NEW **U Kucharzy** ◐ *Polish* 23 | 20 | 21 | E

Srodmiescie | Hotel Europejski | ul. Ossolinskich 7 | (48) 22-826-7936 | www.gessler.pl

At this new Polish venue set in the vast kitchen of the Hotel Europejski, which is currently closed for renovation, the chefs not only prepare "delicious" meals out in the open (using organic ingredients from the restaurant's own farm), they serve them in a series of white-tiled rooms as well; but surveyors are split on whether they find the overall experience here "unique" or "uneven."

Other Noteworthy Places

Absynt *French*
ul. Wspólna 35 | (48) 22-621-1881 | www.kregliccy.pl

AleGloria *Polish*
pl. Trzech Krzyzy 3 | (48) 22-584-7080 | fax 22-584-7081 | www.alegloria.pl

Arsenal *Italian*
ul. Dluga 52 | (48) 22-635-8377 | fax 22-877-9236 | www.restauracjaarsenal.pl

Bacio ◐ *Italian*
ul. Wilcza 43 | (48) 22-626-8303 | fax 22-626-8303 | www.bacio.bacio.pl

Balgera *Italian*
ul. Rejtana 14 | (48) 22-849-5674 | fax 22-856-8002 | www.balgera.pl

Bazaar *International*
ul. Jasna 14/16a | (48) 22-826-8585 | fax 22-827-4353 | www.bazaar.com.pl

Canaletto *International/Italian*
Hotel Sofitel Victoria | ul. Królewska 11 | (48) 22-657-8382 | fax 22-657-8057 | www.sofitel.com

Chez Lautrec *French*
(aka U Lautreca)
Warsaw Tower | ul. Sienna 39 | (48) 22-654-2675 | fax 22-654-5825 | www.chezlautrec.com.pl

Deco Kredens *Polish/Italian*
ul. Ordynacka 13 | (48) 22-826-0660 | www.kredens.com.pl

El Popo ◐ *Mexican*
ul. Senatorska 27 | (48) 22-827-2340 | www.kregliccy.pl

Frida *Mexican*
Intercontinental Warsaw | ul. Emilii Plater 49 | (48) 22-328-8888 | fax 22-328-8889 | www.interconti.com

Fusion *Eurasian*
Westin Warsaw | al. Jana Pawla II 21 | (48) 22-450-8631 | fax 22-450-8111 | www.westin.pl

India Curry *Indian*
ul. Zurawia 22 | (48) 22-438-9350 | fax 22-438-9352 | www.indiacurry.pl

KOM *International*
ul. Zielna 37 | (48) 22-338-6353 | fax 22-338-6333 | www.komunikat.net

Kurt Scheller Restaurant & Bar *Polish/International*
Hotel Rialto | ul. Wilcza 73 | (48) 22-584-8771 | fax 22-584-8772 | www.hotelrialto.com.pl

La Rotisserie *French/Polish*
Hotel Le Régina | ul. Koscielna 12 | (48) 22-531-6070 | fax 22-531-6001 | www.leregina.com

Le Cedre *Lebanese*
Hotel Praski | al. Solidarnosci 61 | (48) 22-670-1166 | fax 22-818-5260 | www.lecedre.pl

99 *International*
al. Jana Pawla II 23 | (48) 22-620-1999 | fax 22-620-1998 | www.restaurant99.com

NU Jazz Bistro ◐ *Euro. Fusion*
ul. Zurawia 6/12 | (48) 22-621-8989 | fax 22-622-2268 | www.nu.jazzbistro.pl

Osteria *Seafood*
ul. Krucza 6/14 | (48) 22-621-1646 | fax 22-354-4666 | www.osteria.pl

Pod Gigantami *Mediterranean/Polish*
al. Ujazdowskie 24 | (48) 22-629-2312 | fax 22-621-3059 | www.podgigantami.pl

Pod Samsonem *Jewish/Polish*
ul. Freta 3/5 | (48) 22-831-1788

Podwale 25 Piwna Kompania ◐ *Polish*
ul. Podwale 25 | (48) 22-635-6314 | fax 22-635-6314 | www.podwale25.pl

Poezja *International/Italian*
ul. Ksiazeca 6 | (48) 22-622-6762 | www.poezja.waw.pl

Portucale *Portuguese*
ul. Merliniego 5 | (48) 22-898-0925 | fax 22-898-0927 | www.portucale.pl

Restauracja Polska Rózana *Polish*
ul. Chocimska 7 | (48) 22-848-1225 | fax 22-848-1590 | www.restauracjatradycja.pl

Ristorante San Lorenzo *Italian*
al. Jana Pawla II 36 | (48) 22-652-1616 | fax 22-654-3377 | www.sanlorenzo.pl

Smaki Warszawy *Polish*
ul. Zurawia 47/49 | (48) 22-621-8268 | fax 22-621-8269 | www.smakiwarszawy.pl

Tokio *Chinese/Japanese*
ul. Dobra 17 | (48) 22-827-4632

Venti Tre *Italian*
Hyatt Regency Warsaw | ul. Belwederska 23 | (48) 22-558-1234 | fax 22-558-1235 | www.warsaw.regency.hyatt.com

Zen Jazz Bistro ◐ *Asian Fusion*
ul. Jasna 24 | (48) 22-447-2500 | fax 22-447-2501 | www.jazzbistro.pl

Zurich

TOP FOOD RANKING

	Restaurant	Cuisine
27	Petermann's Kunststuben	French
26	Rest. Français/Le Pavillon	French/Mediterranean
	Lindenhofkeller	Swiss/International
24	Ginger	Japanese/Sushi
	Casa Aurelio	Spanish
	Ristorante Orsini	Italian
23	Casa Ferlin	Italian
	Sala of Tokyo*	Japanese/Sushi
	Asian Place	Asian
	Sein	International
	Accademia	Italian
	Emilio*	Spanish
	Il Giglio	Southern Italian
22	Widder	International
	Rive Gauche	Mediterranean
	Zentraleck	International
	Ristorante Bindella	Northern Italian
	Blu	Mediterranean/Italian
	Haus Hiltl	Vegetarian/Indian
	Veltliner Keller	Swiss/French
	Kronenhalle	Swiss/French
21	Sonnenberg	Swiss
	Florhof	French
	Haus zum Rüden*	French/Swiss
	Rôtisserie	International/French
20	Giersserei Oerlikon	Swiss
	Urania	Spanish/Tapas
	Alpenrose	Swiss
	Bürgli*	French/Mediterranean
	Cantinetta Antinori*	Northern Italian
	Zunfthaus/Zimmerleuten*	Swiss/French
19	Caduff's Wine Loft	Swiss/International
	Parkhuus	Swiss/International
	Carlton Restaurant & Bar	Swiss/International
18	Vorderer Sternen	Swiss
	Blaue Ente	French/International
	Brasserie Lipp	French Brasserie
	Zum Grünen Glas	French Bistro
17	Oepfelchammer	Swiss
	Quaglinos*	Asian/Mediterranean
	LaSalle	International
	Kaufleuten	International
	Zeughauskeller	Swiss
16	Blindekuh	International
15	Seerose	International

* Indicates a tie with restaurant above

	FOOD	DECOR	SERVICE	COST
Accademia Ⓢ *Italian*	23	18	23	VE

Kreis 4 | Rotwandstr. 62 | (41-44) 241-4202 | fax 241-6243
"One of Zurich's stalwarts", this "classic Italian" in Kreis 4 features "superb food" (including "extremely good pastas") made from "fresh ingredients" and offered amid "authentic decor"; expect "excellent service as well", even if a few feel "the formal staff" is "a little stuffy" and perhaps "slightly supercilious if you don't arrive dressed in an Armani suit"; just be warned that the "exceptional food comes at an exceptional price" - leading the cost conscious to exclaim "ouch!"

Alpenrose Ⓜ *Swiss* | 20 | 19 | 20 | M

Kreis 5 | Fabrikstr. 12 | (41-44) 271-3919 | fax 271-0276 | www.restaurant-alpenrose.ch
"The pleasure begins when you read the menu", which features many favorite dishes from the cantons of Ticino and Graubünden at this "cozy, old-fashioned place" in Kreis 5, "where the locals dine" on "absolutely delicious" fare that's "as Swiss as Swiss can be"; "reasonable prices" and "pleasant, attentive service" are also selling points, as are the "antique furnishings" within the "stylishly kitschy and very cozy" setting.

Asian Place Ⓢ *Asian* | 23 | 17 | 20 | E

Glattbrugg | Renaissance Zurich Hotel | Talackerstr. 1 | (41-44) 874-5721 | fax 874-5001 | www.asianplace.ch
Its descriptive "name says it all" at this "delightful surprise" "in the Renaissance Zurich Hotel, near the airport" in Glattbrugg, that makes "you feel as if you were in Asia" with its "wide selection" of "exciting", "exotic dishes" "from Japan, China and Thailand", all "graciously served" by a "friendly, efficient" staff; some call the prices "inflated", but others say they're "justified by the quality of the food" and the "tranquil" location.

Blaue Ente *French/International* | 18 | 18 | 17 | E

Kreis 8 | Mühle Tiefenbrunnen | Seefeldstr. 223 | (41-44) 388-6840 | fax 422-7741 | www.blaue-ente.ch
"Popular with the young, hip crowd", this "stylish place" "in an old industrial complex" in Kreis 8, "just outside Zurich", boasts a "renovated factory space" whose "loft atmosphere" "and modern art provide a dramatic" backdrop for an "inventive" French-International menu that, not surprisingly, given the eatery's name, includes "creative duck dishes"; sure, it's "fairly expensive", "but what's *not* expensive in Switzerland?"

Blindekuh *International* | 16 | 19 | 20 | M

Kreis 8 | Mühlebachstr. 148 | (41-44) 421-5050 | fax 421-5055 | www.blindekuh.ch
Though "not for the claustrophobic", this Kreis 8 spot definitely offers visitors a "wild experience" - namely, "eating in complete darkness", attended by a "dedicated" and "sure-footed" staff of "blind or partially sighted waiters and waitresses" who provide "loving service"; not only does it give you "something to think about", but the "modest cost" for such "creative and tasty" International fare means you also get "very good value for the money"; N.B. reservations are essential.

Blu *Mediterranean/Italian* 22 23 16 E

Kreis 2 | Seestr. 457 | (41-44) 488-6565 | fax 488-6566

With its "beautiful setting" and "modern but charming" decor featuring multi-"meter-high windows", this Kreis 2 spot boasts "wonderful views of Lake Zurich", not to mention a "lovely" menu of Med-Italian specialties; still, critics among its "trendy crowd" contend that the "young, overtaxed" staff "does its best, but service is not really at the level it should be for the cost."

Brasserie Lipp *French* 18 17 16 E

Kreis 1 | Uraniastr. 9 | (41-43) 888-6666 | fax 888-6667 | www.brasserie-lipp.ch

Like its famed Parisian namesake, this "must-see" spot in Kreis 1 is "a true French brasserie" in every respect - from its "authentic" decor, "suitable furnishings" and "high noise level" to its "nostalgic bar", "big wine list" and "dependable" (if "expected") menu sporting "specialties from *plateau de fruits de mer* to Alsatian choucroute"; most find it "enjoyable", even if the fact that it's "always crowded" means you may "have to wait and wait."

Bürgli *French/Mediterranean* 20 18 17 E

Kreis 2 | Kilchbergstr. 15 | (41-44) 482-8100 | fax 482-8125 | www.restaurantbuergli.ch

Perched "on a hill overlooking the lake", this "good, traditional restaurant" in Kreis 2 is a "lovely" spot for a "romantic" rendezvous thanks to a "perfect view" and "classic" French-Med fare (the "simply fantastic" signature "entrecôte is a must"); not only is it "satisfying" for a "candlelit dinner" "on a cold, snowy night", but it's also "especially [suited for] a summer brunch outside under the trees" "on a beautiful Sunday morning."

Caduff's Wine Loft *Swiss/International* 19 17 17 E

Kreis 4 | Kanzleistr. 126 | (41-44) 240-2255 | fax 240-2256 | www.wineloft.ch

"Wine aficionados love" to "go down into" "the outstanding cellar" at this "pleasant place" with a "trendy New York loft feel" in Kreis 4 "to look for" their favorite vintages, while neophytes avail themselves of the advice of the staff that is "quite knowledgeable about the selection" (20 choices by the glass, 3,300 by the bottle); either way, all "savor" the "extensive collection", which most maintain "makes up for" any shortcomings in the "interesting" Swiss-International fare and "not-always-consistent service."

Cantinetta Antinori *Italian* 20 16 18 E

Kreis 1 | Augustinergasse 25 | (41-44) 211-7210 | fax 221-1613 | www.antinori.it

When you're "thinking of holidays and sunshine", visit this "casual, stylish spot" (part of an international family of "upscale, pricey Northern Italians" and "a favorite" "after shopping on the Bahnhofstrasse") set on a "hard-to-find little side street" in Kreis 1; perhaps the "predictable" menu and "decor could use more imagination", but the "solid food" is "consistently", "qualitatively good", and "what a wine list!" - a fact that "shouldn't surprise" anyone considering its affiliation with the distinguished Antinori winery.

	FOOD	DECOR	SERVICE	COST

Carlton Restaurant & Bar ⊠ *Swiss/International* 19 19 20 E

Kreis 1 | Bahnhofstr. 41 | (41-44) 227-1919 | fax 227-1927 | www.carlton.ch

"Super service" from an "excellent" staff that knows how to "analyze their guests' wishes" sets the tone at this Swiss-International "conveniently located on the Bahnhofstrasse" in Kreis 1; the "fine cuisine" and "good wine cellar" make for "excellent business lunches" and dinners that are complemented by an authentic art deco interior; P.S. its "fun bar" hosts "a great after-work scene" that draws young professionals from the nearby banks.

Casa Aurelio ⊠ *Spanish* 24 17 18 E

Kreis 5 | Langstr. 209 | (41-44) 272-7744 | fax 272-7724 | www.casaaurelio.ch

"There's always something special about eating at" this "Spanish place in Zurich's" Kreis 5, which is perennially "popular" with an interesting mix of locals and celebrities for its "substantial portions" of "outstanding food" and "nice wine list" offered by an "obliging staff"; some say the environment is "somewhat noisy" and "slightly worn-out", but then sometimes "patrons are the best decor."

Casa Ferlin ⊠ *Italian* 23 16 21 E

Kreis 6 | Stampfenbachstr. 38 | (41-44) 362-3509 | fax 362-3534 | www.casaferlin.ch

"It's been around a long time but it holds up well" is the consensus on this family-owned Italian in Kreis 6, where "large portions" of "excellent traditional dishes", particularly "fresh pasta" like "the best homemade ravioli", are served by an "attentive" staff; some find the decor "dark and dated", but devotees declare "that's just part of the charm."

Emilio *Spanish* 23 9 18 E

Kreis 4 | Zweierstr. 9 | (41-44) 241-8321 | fax 241-8325 | www.restaurant-emilio.ch

A genuine "Spanish feel" pervades this Kreis 4 spot that "always delivers the same good quality" with its authentic fare, including "paella that can't be beat" and some of "the best chicken in the world" (which "is worth the nearly obscene price"); still, the "sometimes not-so-attentive service" "could be better" - and as for the "rather poor" decor, "well . . ."

Florhof *French* 21 18 19 E

Kreis 1 | Hotel Florhof | Florhofgasse 4 | (41-44) 250-2626 | fax 250-2627 | www.florhof.ch

"Like a country home right in the city", this "charming, out-of-the-way dining room" "in a romantic hotel" "in the University area" of Kreis 1 offers a "cozy atmosphere" within a "lovely setting", not to mention "excellent", "high-quality" French cuisine; P.S. the "beautiful" terrace with its large, white umbrellas is a big draw in the summer.

Giersserei Oerlikon *Swiss* 20 22 20 E

Kreis 3 | Birchstr. 108 | (41-43) 205-1010 | fax 205-1011 | www.diegiesserei.ch

The "spectacular setting" in Kreis 3 - a sprawling and soaring "former foundry" space softened by romantic touches like a hearth and candlelight - attracts a "hip" crowd that also comes for the "imaginative", albeit limited, menu of seasonal takes on Swiss cuisine; it "may not be very central" but it is "cool" and "even better in summer when you can sit outside."

Ginger [S] *Japanese* | 24 | 18 | 19 | VE

Kreis 8 | Seefeldstr. 62 | (41-44) 422-9509 | www.shinsen.ch

Some of the "very best and freshest sushi in town" can be found at this "small", "cool" Japanese venue in Kreis 8, where "creative" chefs fashion "great" "authentic" fare; sit at the H-shaped bar and choose from the fin fare that "revolves before you" on a carousel or is "obligingly served" to you in one of the few booths; remember, though, that it all comes "at a premium price", and those "little plates add up quickly."

Haus Hiltl *Vegetarian/Indian* | 22 | 12 | 16 | M

Kreis 1 | Sihlstr. 28 | (41-44) 227-7000 | fax 227-7007 | www.hiltl.ch

"Europe's first vegetarian restaurant", this "definite don't-miss" "institution" with an Indian accent in Kreis 1 "opened its doors in 1898" and has since been serving a "marvelous selection" of "healthy" dishes that "make eating without meat a pleasure"; the "approachable staffers" help novices navigate the "reasonably priced" International menu, even though they're "often stressed" by the "hectic", crowded setting; N.B. a recent renovation may outdate the above Decor score.

Haus zum Rüden [S] *French/Swiss* | 21 | 22 | 22 | E

Kreis 1 | Limmatquai 42 | (41-44) 261-9566 | fax 261-1804 | www.hauszumrueden.ch

Set "in one of the oldest buildings in Zurich", a "beautifully maintained" "historic Guild House" in Kreis 1, this French-Swiss is in an "amazing, wood-beamed" "Gothic room" with a "great view of the [Limmat] River and Old Town"; further enhancing the "superb ambiance" are "attentive" service and "modern, imaginative and excellent" dishes, leading satisfied surveyors to say they'll "surely return."

Il Giglio [S] *Italian* | 23 | 16 | 19 | E

Kreis 4 | Weberstr. 14 | (41-44) 242-8597 | fax 291-0183 | www.ilgiglio.ch

Locals "love this small, intimate [Southern] Italian place" in Kreis 4 for its "nice, clean" dishes, many of which are accented with tomatoes imported from Calabria; the decor may be "nothing special", but the "pleasant" staff always provides "polite service"; P.S. look for "excellent wines of the month at moderate prices."

Kaufleuten *International* | 17 | 20 | 14 | E

Kreis 1 | Pelikanplatz | (41-44) 225-3333 | fax 225-3315 | www.kaufleuten.com

"Still the 'sceniest' place" in town, this "in" spot in Kreis 1 is "popular" with a "young crowd" of "trendy people" that "craves seeing and being seen" in the "stylish" neo-"baroque" setting; though the "creative" International fare is "usually good", most maintain "you don't really go for the food", while others report "visits marred by" a "sometimes snobbish" staff that "could be more pleasant"; P.S. diners "have access to the [adjoining] nightclub without having to pass the bouncer outside."

Kronenhalle *Swiss/French* | 22 | 24 | 22 | VE

Kreis 1 | Rämistr. 4 | (41-44) 262-9900 | www.kronenhalle.com

"The owner's splendid collection" of "genuine" art treasures including "original works by Picasso, Chagall and Matisse" "makes for a wonderful atmosphere" at this "pricey" "perennial favorite" "centrally located" in Kreis 1, but there are "masterpieces on the plate", as well, in the form of "fabulous traditional Swiss-French fare" "elegantly served" by an "expert" staff; P.S. to watch "celebrities fight for tables", "get a seat on the main floor."

LaSalle *International* 17 | 20 | 16 | E

Kreis 5 | Schiffbaustr. 4 | (41-44) 258-7071 | fax 259-7071 | www.lasalle-restaurant.ch

Ensconced within a "concrete-and-glass" "former factory building" in Kreis 5, this "appealing" room boasts "cool decor", "high ceilings" and a "romantic chandelier" that combines "edgy" and "old" to "elegant effect"; some who "expected more" "given the dramatic setting" say the "multicultural" dishes on its "complicated" International menu "leave something to be desired", but many are "impressed" with the "imaginative" offerings.

Lindenhofkeller 🅂 *Swiss/International* 26 | 20 | 24 | E

Kreis 1 | Pfalzgasse 4 | (41-44) 211-7071 | fax 212-3337 | www.lindenhofkeller.ch

"Outstanding meals" await at this "upmarket" venue in Kreis 1, where the "very good wine list" has "depth and breadth" and the "excellent" menu "changes with the seasons", but always features "imaginative nouvelle Swiss"-International fare that's "more sophisticated than the typical" indigenous cuisine; additionally, the "pleasant, competent" staff is "amenable to customers' wishes", leading some who love "to linger" within the "cozy, comfortable" interior or in the "beautiful garden" to quip "when can I move in?"

Oepfelchammer 🅂 🄼 *Swiss* 17 | 18 | 19 | E

Kreis 1 | Rindermarkt 12 | (41-44) 251-2336 | fax 262-7533 | www.oepfelchammer.ch

Rowdy regulars "keep coming back" to this "traditional Zurich place" "in the Old Town" section of Kreis 1, and "despite the full house" they create, the "competent" staff usually manages to provide them with "good" service, along with "huge portions" of "just-right" Swiss "local dishes"; P.S. if you've an urge for immortality, "sit in the Gottfried Keller room" decorated with "lots of woodwork", where patrons wanting to "leave their hieroglyphics behind" are actually encouraged to scratch their initials into the walls and tables.

Parkhuus 🅂 *Swiss/International* 19 | 21 | 17 | VE

Kreis 2 | Park Hyatt | Beethovenstr. 21 | (41-43) 883-1075 | fax 883-1235 | www.zurich.park.hyatt.com

Quite "a scene" surrounds this "trendy, crowded" spot in Kreis 2's Park Hyatt hotel; a "modern", "elegant setting" with glass-paneled walls that slide open in warm weather is the dramatic backdrop for an open kitchen that turns out "innovative" Swiss-International fare; still, some suggest that the staff could be more "efficient", while "long waits to get in" have others planning to "try again when it calms down a bit."

Petermann's Kunststuben 🅂 🄼 *French* 27 | 24 | 26 | VE

Küsnacht | Seestr. 160 | (41-44) 910-0715 | fax 910-0495 | www.kunststuben.com

"Absolutely one of the finest restaurants in Switzerland", this "splendid" French "classic" is "first rate in every way", and ranks No. 1 for

Food in Zurich; "outstanding cook Horst Petermann" maintains the "highest standards", producing "unbelievably good culinary" creations that are "almost too beautiful to eat", while "his wife, Iris, a wonderful hostess", presides over the "special" staff and "intimate setting"; all told, it's "an unforgettable dining experience" that's "worth the short trip to Küsnacht" - just be warned that "the bill will also be unforgettable."

Quaglinos ◐ *Asian/Mediterranean* 17 | 15 | 15 | E

Kreis 8 | Hotel Europe | Dufourstr. 4 | (41-44) 261-1700 | fax 251-0367 | www.quaglinos.ch

Fans find this "trendy" dining room in Kreis 8's Hotel Europe a "fun place that's close to theater, opera and the lake" and feel the "nice variety" of "light, interesting" Asian-Med dishes offer "good value for the money"; foes, though, fault "uneven", "expensive" fare and a "cramped, noisy and hectic" setting that's overseen by an "inefficient" staff.

Restaurant Français/ Le Pavillon *French/Mediterranean* 26 | 23 | 26 | VE

Kreis 1 | Baur au Lac | Talstr. 1 | (41-44) 220-5020 | fax 220-5044 | www.bauraulac.ch

"Top class all the way", these "exceptional" Kreis 1 spaces, "in one of Europe's classiest hotels", are facets of a single "Zurich institution", offering "outstanding meals" of "grand" fare, along with an "excellent wine selection"; from October to April, an "extremely attentive staff" presides over the "relaxing, elegant" main dining room and its French cuisine, then from April to October guests order from the Med menu "in the heavenly pavilion" with "a view of the garden and canal"; yes, it's very "expensive", but "you get what you pay for and then some."

Ristorante Bindella *Italian* 22 | 17 | 21 | E

Kreis 1 | In Gassen 6 | (41-44) 221-2546 | fax 221-0292 | www.bindella.ch

"Centrally located" in Kreis 1, this "very nice" venue "is convenient after shopping", "popular with the business crowd" and "always a good place for friends or couples" thanks to a "frequently changing menu" of "delicious" Northern Italian fare that's prepared "with Swiss attention to detail"; an "extensive wine list", "friendly" staff and "smart" surroundings boasting "subdued lighting" add to the experience.

Ristorante Orsini *Italian* 24 | 19 | 25 | VE

Kreis 1 | Hotel Savoy Baur en Ville Paradeplatz | Am Münsterhof 25 | (41-44) 215-2727 | fax 215-2500 | www.savoy-baurenville.ch

"Superb service" from an "attentive" "old-school" staff "satisfies" visitors to this "reliable" "businessman-and-banker hangout" in Kreis 1's Savoy Baur en Ville hotel, while "cuisine purists" praise the kitchen for its "no-nonsense" Italian fare, calling it nothing short of "splendid"; factor in the "excellent selections" on its "good wine list" and the "bright, classic decor" of its "formal" dining room and you'll see why patrons predict "you will not be disappointed."

Rive Gauche ⊠ *Mediterranean* 22 | 22 | 22 | VE

Kreis 1 | Baur au Lac | Talstr. 1 | (41-44) 220-5020 | fax 220-5044 | www.agauche.ch

As "the informal restaurant for the very formal Baur au Lac hotel", this Mediterranean draws a mix of local professionals, affluent guests and celebrities to its "central location" in Kreis 1; with its "classic" clubby decor and an "excellent" selection of "inventive cuisine" that emphasizes light seasonal dishes and is "served with Swiss efficiency and grace", no wonder that for many It's a "favorite place to dine in Zurich."

Rôtisserie *International/French* 21 | 18 | 21 | E

Kreis 1 | Hotel zum Storchen | Am Weinplatz 2 | (41-44) 227-2113 | fax 227-2700 | www.storchen.ch

It's no surprise most are "completely satisfied" after a visit to "this fine restaurant" in Kreis 1's Hotel zum Storchen once they've "enjoyed" its "tasty, imaginative" and "justifiably expensive" International-French fare (as well as some Zurichois specialties); "obliging" "old-school" service and a "wonderful setting" "on the Limmat", "overlooking the river and the Old Town", are other reasons it's "a great find."

Sala of Tokyo S M *Japanese* 23 | 15 | 19 | VE

Kreis 5 | Limmatstr. 29 | (41-44) 271-5290 | fax 271-7807 | www.sala-of-tokyo.ch

"Quality and presentation" "make lunch or dinner always a great experience" at this "traditional" spot in Kreis 5; of course there's "excellent sushi", but the "varied" menu also features "all the Japanese specialties (such as shabu-shabu, sukiyaki, robatayaki, tempura)"; many consider the decor "nice", but even those who see it as merely "ok" concede it "could be worse" - and the "ever-so-charming presence of [chef/co-owner] Sala" Ruch-Fukuoka adds to the ambiance.

Seerose *International* 15 | 19 | 15 | E

Kreis 2 | Seestr. 493 | (41-44) 481-6383 | fax 481-6385 | www.dinning.ch

"Location, location, location" is the draw at this "busy meeting place" whose "amazing setting" "right on the lake" in Kreis 2, with its "wonderful views" "of the city beyond" and "boats mooring for dinner", just "can't be beaten"; crowds of "so-cool guests" also make it a "see-and-be-seen" scene, though some critics "don't like" the "limited [International] menu" or "average service" from staffers who were "apparently picked for their good looks, not for their skills."

Sein ◐ S *International* 23 | 20 | 21 | E

Kreis 1 | Schützengasse 5 | (41-44) 221-1065 | fax 212-6580

"Innovative" International fare, "luxurious" tapas at the bar and "real Swiss service" cater to dueling crowds at this Kreis 1 restaurant/bar: "suits and ties" at lunch vs. hip types at night; a "bold, beautiful and bright" vibe permeates this vibrant mirrored red space, luring in all who just want to be "Sein."

Sonnenberg *Swiss* 21 | 22 | 21 | VE

Kreis 7 | Hitzigweg 15 | (41-44) 266-9797 | fax 266-9798 | www.sonnenberg-zh.ch

A "favorite", this "winner" "on a hillside overlooking the city and lake" in Kreis 7 scores on all counts - from its "majestic views" (especially "magnificent" "at sunset") and "star chef Jacky Donatz's" "excellent" cuisine ("a testimony to Swiss perfectionism") to the "obliging service"; P.S. "the place belongs to FIFA", the Fédération Internationale de Football Association, so "you may see Europe's soccer heroes" at the next table.

Urania ☒ *Spanish* 20 | 17 | 17 | E

Kreis 1 | Uraniastr. 7 | (41-44) 210-2808 | fax 210-2809 | www.uraniatapasbar.ch

"Bringing Spanish flair to the center of the city" is this establishment where you can hit "the bar for a drink and some tasty tapas" or try "the restaurant for a nice un-Zurich-like meal" of Iberian entrees; the airy interior has high ceilings and mirrors and there's expansive sidewalk seating at umbrella-topped tables.

Veltliner Keller ☒ *Swiss/French* 22 | 23 | 23 | E

Kreis 1 | Schlüsselgasse 8 | (41-44) 225-4040 | fax 225-4045 | www.veltlinerkeller.ch

"Everything is just right" at this "charming" Kreis 1 venue "in a medieval townhouse" "near St. Peter's church in Old Town": the "classy ambiance" of its dark-wood setting replete with "beautiful carvings" is matched by the "formal but warm service" from its "professional" staff, and the "delicious, if heavy", "traditional Swiss-French food" (including "good regional selections") "wins you over with its simple style", leading acolytes to assert that "the price is irrelevant."

Vorderer Sternen *Swiss* 18 | 12 | 14 | M

Kreis 1 | Theaterstr. 22 | (41-44) 251-4949 | fax 252-9063 | www.vorderer-sternen.ch

If "you want to be a Zürcher", follow the locals to this "sausage institution" in Kreis 1 that's been serving up "typically Swiss food" for more than four decades; the "plain decor" is "nondescript" and the staff is "sometimes a bit slow" and "inattentive", but the "cost is reasonable"; P.S. some say that "the best thing about this place is its" "outside alley grill", where "everyone goes" to "indulge" in some of "the best bratwurst in town" while "freezing their fingers off."

Widder *International* 22 | 23 | 23 | VE

Kreis 1 | Widder Hotel | Rennweg 7 | (41-44) 224-2526 | fax 224-2424 | www.widderhotel.ch

A "classy" hotel composed of a series of historic Kreis 1 townhouses that "blend modern and old superbly" provides the "lovely setting" for this "upmarket" "fine-dining" venue; its "true professionals" "take pride in what they do, and it shows" in the "discreet service" and "great menu" of "excellent" International dishes they provide; with such "all-around quality", it's no wonder the place is "popular" – and a visit to the Widder "Bar afterwards", with its live piano music and "phenomenal jazz" concerts twice a year, is "the cherry on the cake."

Zentraleck ☒ *International* 22 | 20 | 21 | E

Kreis 3 | Zentralstr. 161 | (41-44) 461-0800 | www.zentraleck.ch

The young chef/co-owner of this small Kreis 3 International concocts "creative" dishes that are matched with "excellent wines" and served by a "flawless" staff in a simple, "cozy" setting of polished wood set against a sea of white; in sum, most proponents pronounce it a "Swiss delight!"

Zeughauskeller *Swiss* 17 | 15 | 15 | M

Kreis 1 | Bahnhofstr. 28a | (41-44) 211-2690 | fax 211-2670 | www.zeughauskeller.ch

"You're sure to find a sausage you like" among the "many varieties offered" at this Kreis 1 "classic" that's "jam-packed" with "locals" and "tourists" alike, all gorging on "generous portions" of "good" Swiss cooking; set "in an amazing medieval armory" decorated by someone with "a weapons fetish", its "cavernous" space strikes some as too "noisy", while others wish for "more-agreeable service" from the staff.

Zum Grünen Glas ⓢ *French* 18 | 16 | 17 | E

Kreis 1 | Untere Zäune 15 | (41-44) 251-6504 | fax 251-6516 | www.gruenesglas.ch

"Tasty French cuisine" is offered with "pleasant service" at this Old Town bistro in Kreis 1, where a "cozy, comfortable" setting hosts cultured patrons of the nearby theaters and art galleries; still, some critics claim the "plain decor" is "a bit unsophisticated" and report "a few disappointments" from the "inconsistent" kitchen, adding that the "sometimes excessive prices" mean it's "not for every day."

Zunfthaus zur Zimmerleuten *Swiss/French* 20 | 25 | 20 | E

Kreis 1 | Limmatquai 40 | (41-44) 250-5361 | fax 250-5364 | www.zimmerleuten.ch

A "stunning old guild hall" in Kreis 1 houses this "sumptuous", "stylish" spot where the "good team in the kitchen" produces "delicious" Swiss-French cuisine, including some "superlative local specialties" such as their "heavenly *leberspaetzle*" that's delivered by a "well-trained" staff; some note that it's "certainly not cheap, but" most insist "good value" makes it "worth the money."

Other Noteworthy Places

Bü's ⓢ *Swiss/Mediterranean*
Kuttelgasse 15 | (41-44) 211-9411

Da Angela ⓢ *Italian*
Hohlstr. 449 | (41-44) 492-2931 | fax 492-2932 | www.daangela.ch

Don Pepe *Spanish/Italian*
Birmensdorferstr. 313 | (41-44) 463-9922 | fax 463-9955 | www.don-pepe.ch

Eders Eichmühle Ⓜ *French*
Neugutstr. 933 | (41-44) 780-3444 | fax 780-4864 | www.eichmuehle.ch

Goethe-Stübli ⓢ *Swiss/International*
Glockengasse 7 | (41-44) 221-2120 | fax 221-2155 | www.kaisers-reblaube.ch

Greulich *Catalan*
Hotel Greulich | Hermann-Greulich Str. 56 | (41-43) 243-4243 | fax 243-4200 | www.greulich.ch

Josef ⓢ *International*
Gasometerstr. 24 | (41-44) 271-6595 | fax 440-5564

Lawrence ⓢ *Mediterranean/Mideastern*
Hotel Ascot | Tessinerplatz 9 | (41-44) 208-1414 | fax 208-1420 | www.ascot.ch

Mesa ⓢⓂ *Mediterranean*
Weinbergstr. 75 | (41-43) 321-7575 | fax 321-7577 | www.mesa-restaurant.ch

Rigiblick ⓢⓂ *International*
Aparthotel Rigiblick | Germaniastr. 99 | (41-43) 255-1570 | fax 255-1580 | www.restaurantrigiblick.ch

Ristorante Conti *Italian*
Dufourstr. 1 | (41-44) 251-0666 | fax 251-0686 | www.bindella.ch

Sale e Pepe ◐ⓢ *Italian*
Sieberstr. 18 | (41-44) 463-0736 | fax 463-0701

Seidenspinner ⓢⓜ *Swiss*
Ankerstr. 120 | (41-44) 241-0700 | fax 241-0710 | www.seidenspinner.ch

Sento ⓢ *Italian/Mediterranean*
Hotel Plattenhof | Zürichbergstr. 19 | (41-44) 251-1615 | fax 251-1911 | www.sento.ch

Sihlhalden ⓢⓜ *French/Mediterranean*
Sihlhaldenstr. 70 | (41-44) 720-0927 | www.smoly.ch

Tizziani ⓜ *International*
Hönggerstr. 10 | (41-44) 273-5040 | www.tizziani.ch

Tre Fratelli ⓢ *Swiss/Italian*
Nordstr. 182 | (41-44) 363-3303 | fax 363-3314 | www.trefratelli.ch

Vis-à-Vis ⓢ *French*
Talstr. 40 | (41-44) 211-7310 | fax 211-7323 | www.vis-a-vis.ch

Wirtschaft Flühgass ⓢ *Swiss*
Zollikerstr. 214 | (41-44) 381-1215 | fax 422-7532 | www.fluehgass.ch

Wirtschaft zum Wiesengrund ⓢⓜ *Mediterranean/Swiss*
Kleindorfstr. 61 | (41-44) 920-6360 | fax 921-1709 | www.wiesengrund.ch

Wolfbach ⓢ *Mediterranean/Seafood*
Wolfbachstr. 35 | (41-44) 252-5180 | fax 252-5312 | www.ristorante-wolfbach.ch

Zunfthaus zur Schmiden ⓢ *Swiss*
Marktgasse 20 | (41-44) 250-5848 | fax 250-5849 | www.zunfthausschmiden.ch

INDEXES

Names in bold have full reviews. All other listings are in the Other Noteworthy Places category.

Special Features

ADDITIONS

(Properties added since the last edition of the book)

AMSTERDAM

FLO Amsterdam 19
Gala 22
Janvier 21
Pont 13 21
Zina 21

ATHENS

Parea 23
Pasaji -
Pil Poul/Jérôme Serres 24
7 Thalasses 22
Telemachos -
Vassilenas 23

BARCELONA

Àpat -
Bilbao 24
Cardamon -
Cuines/Caterina 22
El Lobito -
Evo 21
Inòpia 21
Mondo 22
Tapaç 24 24
Tapioles 53 23

BERLIN

Grill Royal 21
Hartmanns 22
San Nicci 21

BRUSSELS

Bon-Bon 24
Café des Spores 24
Friture René 22
Jaloa -
Le Fourneau 23

BUDAPEST

Papageno 23
Segal 23
Trattoria Pomo D'oro -

COPENHAGEN

Custom House 20
Fifty Fifty 22
Geranium -
Kiin Kiin 21
Slotskælderen 23
Søllerød Kro 26

DUBLIN

Alexis B&G 21
Balzac 23
Still -
Winding Stair 21

FLORENCE

Ora d'Aria 24

FRANKFURT

Beyond
Goldman -
King Kamehameha -
La Stalla di Ugo -
Medici 20

GENEVA

Floortwo/Grill -
Sapori -
Vertig'O 23

HAMBURG

Die Bank 18
Le Canard Nouveau 23

Wa Yo	-
Zum Wattkorn	-

ISTANBUL

Banyan	19
Del Mare	23
Flamm	-
Leb-i Derya	21
Nisantasi	18

LISBON

Adega Tia Matilde	24
Ad Lib	21
BBC	20
Pragma Fausto Airoldi	-
Solar dos Presuntos	23

LONDON

Bincho Yakitori	-
ffiona's	-
Galvin Bistrot	-
Glasshouse, The	-
Haiku	-
Harry's Bar	-
Jin Kichi	26
Kiku	-
La Fromagerie	-
Lanes	-
La Petite Maison	-
L'Atelier/Robuchon	26
Latium	25
La Trompette	27
Miyama	26
Olivomare	-
Quilon	25
Rhodes W1 Rest.	-
Rist. Semplice	-
Roka	25
Skylon	-
Theo Randall	26
Wild Honey	-

Yoshino	-
Ziani	-

MADRID

Alboroque	-
Azabara	-
Lágrimas Negras	21
Lavinia	23
Pan de Lujo	19
Rubaiyat	23
Shiratori	23
Tras Os Montes	-

MILAN

Bebel's	24
Giannino	23
Gold	20
Gref	-
Innocenti Evasioni	22
L'Altra Isola	-
Livet	-

MOSCOW

Bistrot	21
Most, The	-
Nabi	-
Nedalny Vostok	-
Yoko	-
Zolotoy	-

MUNICH

Fleming's	22
Hippocampus	22
Le Stollberg	-
Le Sud	-
Retter's	23

PARIS

Aub. du Champ de Mars	-
Au Bon Accueil	-
Au Trou Gascon	-
Chen Soleil d'Est	-

Chez Michel -
Dominique Bouchet -
Goumard -
La Braisière -
La Gazzetta -
L'Angle du Faubourg -
Le Chiberta -
Le Christine -
L'Epi Dupin -
Le Rech -
Le Sensing -
L'Obélisque -
L'Os à Moëlle -
Passiflore -
Spring -

PRAGUE

Casanova -
Coda 23
Cowboys 20
Essensia 25
La Casa Argentina -
Oliva 23

ROME

Acquolina Hostaria 23
Al Vero Girarrosto 25
Ambasciata d'Abruzzo 23
Antica Pesa 21
Brunello 23
Checco/Carretiere 23
Costanza 23
Da Fortunato 22
Girarrosto Fiorentino 21
I Due Ladroni 22
Il San Lorenzo 24
I Sofa'/Via Giulia 24
La Cantina/Ninco -
La Carbonara 22
L'Acino Brillo -
Romolo 23
Taberna de' Gracchi 22

STOCKHOLM

Clas på Hörnet 21
Kungsholmen 22

VENICE

Il Ridotto 23

VIENNA

Ella's 21
Goldene Zeiten 22
Mraz & Sohn 24
ON -
Procacci 20
RieGi -

WARSAW

Bazaar -
Pod Gigantami -
Poezja -
U Kucharzy 23
Zen Jazz Bistro -

ZURICH

Casa Ferlin 23
Giersserei Oerlikon 20
Sale e Pepe -
Sein 23
Zentraleck 22

HOTEL DINING

AMSTERDAM

Dylan Hotel
Dylan, The 24
InterContinental Amstel
La Rive 27
Jolly Carlton, Hotel
Caruso -
L'Europe, Hotel de
Excelsior 25

NH Amsterdam Centre Hotel

Bice 19

NH Barbizon Palace Hotel

Vermeer 24

Okura, Hotel

Ciel Bleu 22

Yamazato 27

Pulitzer, Hotel

Pulitzers 21

ATHENS

Athenaeum InterContinental

Premiere 20

Athens Ledra Marriott Hotel

Zephyros -

Eridanus Hotel

NEW **Parea** 23

Grande Bretagne, Hotel

GB Corner 21

Hilton Athens

Milos Athens 22

Pentelikon, Hotel

Vardis -

Sofitel Athens Airport

Karavi -

St. George Lycabettus Hotel

Le Grand Balcon -

BARCELONA

Arts, Hotel

Arola 24

Barceló Hotel Sants

El Bistrot de Sants -

Condes de Barcelona

Lasarte 25

Cram Hotel

Gaig 27

Hesperia Tower

Evo 21

Majestic, Hotel

Drolma 28

Omm, Hotel

Moo 21

Palace, Hotel

Caelis 25

Rey Juan Carlos I

Garden 21

BERLIN

Adlon Kempinski, Hotel

Lorenz Adlon 24

Quarré -

Brandenburger Hof

Die Quadriga 23

Grand Hyatt

Vox 23

Hilton Berlin

Fellini 19

InterContinental, Hotel

Hugos -

Mandala Hotel

Facil -

Maritim Hotel

Grand Rest. M -

Marriott Hotel

Midtown Grill -

Palace, Hotel

First Floor -

Regent Berlin Hotel

Fischers Fritz -

Ritz-Carlton Berlin

Desbrosses -

Vitrum -

Schlosshotel

Vivaldi -

Swissôtel

44 23

BRUSSELS

Amigo, Hotel

Bocconi -

Hilton Brussels

La Maison/Boeuf 23

Le Méridien
- L'Epicerie –

Métropole, Hôtel
- L'Alban Chambon –

Radisson SAS Royal Hotel
- **Sea Grill** 27

BUDAPEST

Andrássy Hotel
- **Baraka** 28

Art'otel
- Chelsea –

Corinthia Grand Hotel Royal
- Bock Bistro –
- Brass. Royale –

Four Seasons Gresham Palace
- **Páva** 27

Hilton Budapest WestEnd
- Arrabona –

InterContinental Budapest
- Corso –

Kempinski Hotel Corvinus
- **Bistro Jardin** 23

Le Méridien Budapest
- Le Bourbon –

New York Palace
- Mélyvíz –

COPENHAGEN

Alexandra, Hotel
- Brass. Mühlhausen –

Copenhagen Admiral Hotel
- **Salt** 21

D'Angleterre, Hotel
- **D'Angleterre** 22

Fox, Hotel
- Fox Kitchen –

Hilton Copenhagen Airport
- Hamlet Nordic Grill –

Radisson SAS Royal
- **Alberto K** 25

Radisson SAS Scandinavia
- Kyoto –

Skt. Petri, Hotel
- Bleu –

DUBLIN

Bewley's Hotel
- **O'Connells** 23

Brownes Townhouse Hotel
- **Brownes** 20

Clarence, The
- **Tea Room** 24

Dylan Hotel
- Still –

Fitzwilliam Hotel
- **Thornton's** 27

Four Seasons Hotel
- **Seasons** 26

La Stampa Hotel & Spa
- NEW **Balzac** 23

Merrion Hotel
- **Patrick Guilbaud** 27

Morrison Hotel
- **Halo** 21

FLORENCE

Centanni Residence
- Centanni –

Grand Hotel
- **InCanto** 24

Grand Hotel Cavour
- Angels –

Lungarno, Hotel
- Borgo/Jacopo –

Villa La Massa
- Il Verrocchio –

Villa La Vedetta
- Onice –

Villa San Michele
- **Villa San Michele** 25

FRANKFURT

ArabellaSheraton Grand Hotel
- **Sushimoto** 23

Goldman 25hours Hotel
- Goldman –

Hessischer Hof, Hotel
- Sèvres –

Hessler, Hotel
- Hessler –

InterContinental Frankfurt
- **Signatures Veranda** 19

Maingau, Hotel
- Maingau Stuben –

Steigenberger Frankfurter Hof
- **Rest. Français** 24

GENEVA

Beau-Rivage
- **Le Chat-Botté** 23

Beau-Rivage, Hôtel
- **Patara** 25

d'Angleterre, Hôtel
- Windows –

Domaine de Châteauvieux
- **Dom./Châteauvieux** 29

Four Seasons Hôtel des Bergues
- **Il Lago** 23

Grand Hotel Kempinski Geneva
- Floortwo/Grill –

Hostellerie de la Vendée
- **La Vendée** 24

InterContinental
- **Woods** –

Lac, Hôtel du
- La Rôtisserie –

La Réserve Geneve
- Le Loti –
- Le Tsé-Fung –

L'Auberge d'Hermance
- **L'Auberge d'Hermance** 24

Les Armures
- **Les Armures** 19

Paix, Hôtel de la
- NEW **Vertig'O** 23

Parc des Eaux-Vives
- **Rest. du Parc** 24

Président Wilson
- **L'Arabesque** 19
- **Spice's** 24

Richemond, Hôtel
- Sapori –

Swissôtel Métropole Genève
- Le Grand Quai –

Tiffany, Hôtel
- Tiffany –

HAMBURG

Abtei, Hotel
- Prinz Frederik –

Fairmont Hotel
- **Doc Cheng's** 23
- **Haerlin** 25

InterContinental Hamburg
- **Windows** 18

Landhaus Flottbek
- **Landhaus Flottbek** 16

Louis C. Jacob
- **Jacobs** 23

Nippon Hotel
- Wa Yo –

Steigenberger Hotel Hamburg
- Calla –

Süllberg Hotel
- Seven Seas –

Wattkorn, Hotel
- Zum Wattkorn –

ISTANBUL

Bosphorus Palace Hotel
- Bosphorus Palace –

Çiragan Palace Kempinski
- **Laledan** 24
- **Tugra** 25

Divan Hotel
- Divan –

Four Seasons Hotel
- **Seasons** 25

InterContinental Ceylan
- Safran –

Kariye Hotel
- **Asitane** 21

La Maison Hotel
- La Maison –

Marmara Pera Hotel
- Mikla –

Mavi Ev Hotel
- Mavi Ev/Blue Hse. –

Richmond Hotel
- **Leb-i Derya** 21

Turing Ayasofya Konaklari
- **Sarniç** 14

Villa Zurich
- Doga Balik –

Yesil Ev Hotel
- **Yesil Ev** 20

LISBON

Bairro Alto Hotel
- Flores –

Dom Pedro Palace
- Il Gattopardo –

Four Seasons Hotel Ritz
- **Varanda** 27

Lapa Palace Hotel
- **Rist. Hotel Cipriani** 27

Pestana Palace Hotel
- **Valle Flôr** 22

Sofitel, Hotel
- **Ad Lib** 21

Tivoli Lisboa
- Terraço –

York House Hotel
- A Confraria –

LONDON

Berkeley Hotel
- **Pétrus** 28

Capital Hotel
- **Capital Rest.** 27

Claridge's Hotel
- **Gordon Ramsay/Claridge's** 25

Crowne Plaza St. James Hotel
- **Quilon** 25

Cumberland Hotel
- NEW **Rhodes W1 Rest.** –

Four Seasons Hotel
- Lanes –

Halkin Hotel
- **Nahm** 26

Hyatt Regency - The Churchill
- **Locanda Locatelli** 25

InterContinental Park Ln.
- NEW **Theo Randall** 26

Mandarin Oriental Hyde Park
- **Foliage** 26

Metropolitan Hotel
- **Nobu London** 27

MADRID

Aristos, Hotel
- **El Chaflán** 26

Bauzá Hotel
- Bauzá –

Casa Palacio
- Alboroque –

Hesperia, Hotel
- **Santceloni** 28

Meliá Castilla Hotel
- **L'Albufera** 22

Carlo IV

- Box Block –

Four Seasons Hotel

- **Allegro** 26

Hoffmeister, Hotel

- ADA –

InterContinental Praha

- **Zlatá Praha** 20

Le Palais, Hotel

- Le Papillon –

Mandarin Oriental Hotel

- NEW **Essensia** 25

Palace, Hotel

- Gourmet Club –

Paris, Hotel

- **Sarah Bernhardt** 20

Radisson SAS Alcron Hotel

- **Alcron** 21

U Zlaté Studne

- U Zlaté Studne –

ROME

Aldrovandi Palace Hotel

- **Baby** 25

Aleph Hotel

- Maremoto –

Atlante Star

- **Les Etoiles** 19

Cavalieri Hilton

- Giardino dell'Uliveto –
- **La Pergola** 26

Eden, Hotel

- **La Terrazza** 23

Grand Hotel Parco Dei Principi

- Pauline Borghese –

Hassler, Hotel

- **Imàgo** 24

Lord Byron, Hotel

- **Sapori/Lord Byron** 22

Radisson SAS Hotel

- Sette –

Regina Hotel Baglioni

- NEW **Brunello** 23

Russie, Hotel de

- **Le Jardin/Russie** 22

Splendide Royal

- **Mirabelle** 26

St. George Hotel

- NEW **I Sofa'/Via Giulia** 24

St. Regis Grand Hotel

- **Vivendo** 26

STOCKHOLM

Berns Hotel

- **Berns Asian** 19

Clas på Hörnet

- **Clas på Hörnet** 21

Elite Hotel Stockholm

- **Vassa Eggen** 26

Grand Hôtel

- **Grands Veranda** 21

Victory Hotel

- **Leijontornet** 24

VENICE

Cipriani, Hotel

- **Cip's Club** 24
- **Fortuny** 25

Danieli, Hotel

- **La Terrazza** 23

Gritti Palace

- **Club del Doge** 25

Il Palazzo at Hotel Bauer

- **De Pisis** 25

Londra Palace

- **Do Leoni** 24

Luna Hotel Baglioni

- Canova –

Monaco, Hotel

- **Grand Canal** 22

San Clemente Palace
Cà dei Frati -
Saturnia, Hotel
La Caravella 20

VIENNA

Ambassador
Mörwald/Ambassador 21
Bristol, Hotel
Korso bei der Oper 24
Grand Hotel Wien
Le Ciel -
Unkai -
Imperial, Hotel
Imperial 26
Le Méridien
Shambala -
Palais Coburg
Coburg 25
Sacher Wien
Rote Bar -

WARSAW

Europejski, Hotel
NEW **U Kucharzy** 23
Hyatt Regency Warsaw
Venti Tre -
Intercontinental Warsaw
Frida -
Le Régina, Hotel
La Rotisserie -
Le Royal Méridien Bristol
Malinowa 22
Marriott Warsaw
Parmizzano's 23
Praski, Hotel
Le Cedre -
Rialto, Hotel
Kurt Scheller -
Sheraton Warsaw Hotel
Oriental, The 21
Sofitel Victoria
Canaletto -
Westin Warsaw
Fusion -

ZURICH

Aparthotel Rigiblick
Rigiblick -
Ascot, Hotel
Lawrence -
Baur au Lac
Rest. Français 26
Rive Gauche 22
Europe, Hotel
Quaglinos 17
Florhof, Hotel
Florhof 21
Greulich, Hotel
Greulich -
Park Hyatt
Parkhuus 19
Plattenhof, Hotel
Sento -
Renaissance Zurich Hotel
Asian Place 23
Savoy Baur en Ville Paradeplatz
Rist. Orsini 24
Storchen, Hotel zum
Rôtisserie 21
Widder Hotel
Widder 22

ALPHABETICAL PAGE INDEX

CITY ABBREVIATIONS

AMS	Amsterdam	LON	London
ATH	Athens	MAD	Madrid
BAR	Barcelona	MIL	Milan
BER	Berlin	MOS	Moscow
BRU	Brussels	MUN	Munich
BUD	Budapest	PAR	Paris
COP	Copenhagen	PRA	Prague
DUB	Dublin	ROM	Rome
FLO	Florence	STO	Stockholm
FRA	Frankfurt	VEN	Venice
GEN	Geneva	VIE	Vienna
HAM	Hamburg	WAR	Warsaw
IST	Istanbul	ZUR	Zurich
LIS	Lisbon		

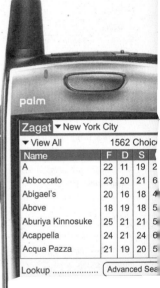

Zagat Products

RESTAURANTS & MAPS

America's Top Restaurants
Atlanta
Boston
Brooklyn (best of)
California Wine Country
Cape Cod & The Islands
Chicago (guide & map)
Connecticut
Downtown NYC
Europe's Top Restaurants
Hamptons (incl. wineries)
Las Vegas (incl. nightlife)
London
London (best of)
Long Island (incl. wineries)
Los Angeles I So. California (guide & map)
Miami Beach
Miami I So. Florida
Montréal (best of)
New Jersey
New Jersey Shore
New Orleans (best of)
New York City (guide & map)
Palm Beach
Paris
Philadelphia
San Francisco (guide & map)
Seattle
St. Louis
Texas
Tokyo
Toronto (best of)
Vancouver (best of)
Washington, DC I Baltimore
Westchester I Hudson Valley

LIFESTYLE GUIDES

America's Top Golf Courses
Movie Guide
Music Guide
NYC Gour. Shopping/Ent.
NYC Shopping

NIGHTLIFE GUIDES

Las Vegas (incl. restaurants)
London
Los Angeles
New Orleans (best of)
New York City
San Francisco

HOTEL & TRAVEL GUIDES

Top U.S. Hotels, Resorts & Spas
U.S. Family Travel
Walt Disney World Insider's Guide
World's Top Hotels, Resorts & Spas

WEB & WIRELESS SERVICES

ZAGAT TO GO℠ for handhelds
ZAGAT.com
ZAGAT.mobi